SOVIET BUT NOT RUSSIAN

UNION OF SOVIET

Homelands of some of the many peoples of the Soviet U
are indicated. Since peoples of any Soviet nationality are fre
live anywhere in the USSR, and the Soviets are very mol

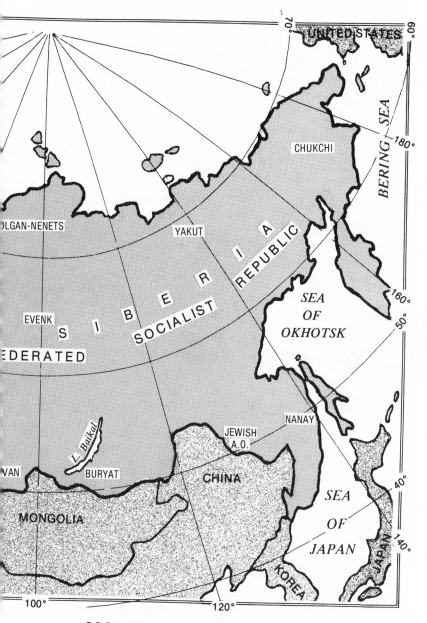

SOCIALIST REPUBLICS

e numbers of every nationality live and work far from their
ditional homelands.

Also by William Mandel:

The Soviet Far East and Central Asia

*Soviet Source Materials on USSR Relations
with East Asia, 1945-50 (documents)*

A Guide to the Soviet Union

*Russia Re-Examined: The Land,
the People and How They Live*

Soviet Women

Soviet Marxism and Social Science

To my father, Max, born in 1894, who first took me to the Soviet Union, and who at 90 continues to challenge and stimulate my thinking.

SOVIET BUT NOT RUSSIAN
The 'Other' Peoples of the Soviet Union

William M. Mandel

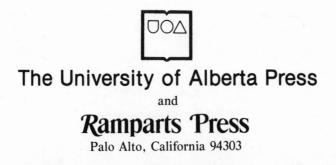

The University of Alberta Press

and

Ramparts Press

Palo Alto, California 94303

Library of Congress Cataloging in Publication Data

Mandel, William M.
   Soviet but not Russian.

   Includes bibliographies and index.
   1. Ethnology--Soviet Union.   2. Soviet Union--
Ethnic relations.   I. Title.
DK33.M26   1985   305.8'00947   84-42759
ISBN 0-87867-095-5
ISBN 0-87867-096-3 (pbk.)

Published by
The University of Alberta Press,
141 Athabasca Hall, Edmonton, Canada T6G 2E8
and
Ramparts Press, Palo Alto, California 94303

Library of Congress Catalog Card Number 84-42795
ISBN 0-87867-095-5
ISBN 0-87867-096-3 (paperback)

Printed in the United States of America

CONTENTS

MAPS

UNION (Full Ethnic) REPUBLICS

Armenia S.S.R.	3,119,000	
Azerbaijan S.S.R.	6,202,000	The nation
Belorussian S.S.R.	9,675,000	for which each
Estonian S.S.R.	1,485,000	Soviet Socialist
Georgian S.S.R.	5,071,000	Republic is named
Kazakh S.S.R.	15,053,000	is a majority
Kirgiz S.S.R.	3,653,000	within its
Latvian S.S.R.	2,539,000	borders except
Lithuanian S.S.R.	3,445,000	for the Kazakhs
Moldavian S.S.R.	3,995,000	and Kirgiz,
Russian S.F.S.R.	139,165,000	who are less
Tajik S.S.R.	4,007,000	than half
Turkmen S.S.R.	2,897,000	the populaltion
Ukrainian S.S.R.	50,135,000	in their native
Uzbek S.S.R.	16,158,000	territories.

AUTONOMOUS REPUBLICS

Abkhaz A.S.S.R. (Georgia)	509,000	
Adzhar (Ajar) A.S.S.R. (Georgia)	362,000	Many of
Bashkir A.S.S.R. (Russia)	3,865,000	these
Buryat A.S.S.R. (Russia)	929,000	peoples
Chechen-Ingush A.S.S.R. (Russia)	1,170,000	are
Chuvash A.S.S.R. (Russia)	1,311,000	minorities
Daghestan A.S.S.R. (Russia)	1,672,000	in their
Kabardin-Balkar A.S.S.R. (Russia)	688,000	own native
Kalmyk A.S.S.R. (Russia)	301,000	territories,
Karakalpak A.S.S.R. (Uzbek)	957,000	but the
Karelian A.S.S.R. (Russia)	746,000	top Party
Komi A.S.S.R. (Russia)	1,147,000	and
Mari A.S.S.R. (Russia)	711,000	government
Mordovian A.S.S.R. (Russia)	984,000	posts
Nakhichevan A.S.S.R. (Azerbaijan)	247,000	are
North Ossetian A.S.S.R. (Russia)	601,000	reserved
Tatar A.S.S.R. (Russia)	3,453,000	for
Tuva A.S.S.R. (Russia)	269,000	them.
Udmurt A.S.S.R. (Russia)	1,516,000	
Yakut A.S.S.R. (Russia)	883,000	

PREFACE

With one exception, the "other" peoples described are not minorities in the American sense. They are majorities or in two cases pluralities in the territories in which they developed over the centuries. That explains the name of the country: Union of Soviet Socialist Republics, or Soviet Union for short. It does not include the neighboring Communist-governed countries such as Poland.

In the USSR, the Russians are one-half the population. The others are native to languages other than Russian. One-quarter of the entire population does not even claim to know Russian well, their census tells us. These are chiefly among peoples whose languages do not belong to the same family as Russian.

People of any nationality may and do live all over the country. When outside their ancestral territories, they do form minorities in our sense. The Russians themselves are minorities, sometimes large, sometimes very small (as in Armenia), outside the Russian Republic of the USSR.

This book provides separate chapters on the major and some smaller but particularly distinctive geographic nations of the Soviet Union. Other chapters treat related nations grouped to make it possible to relate to them from an American frame of reference. Because of the large Jewish population in the United States, there is a very substantial chapter on the Soviet Jews, although they are less than one percent of the people of the USSR. Not being a majority or plurality anywhere in that country, they are a true minority. There are many other true minorities — Germans, who outnumber the Jews; Poles, outnumbered by the Jews — but public interest in them does not justify separate treatment in a book

9

designed to be read, hopefully studied, but not meant to be an encyclopedia on this subject.

My writing is grounded upon 10 visits to the USSR, beginning with a year of residence, 1931-32. I was United Press (UPI) Expert on Russia during World War II, have been a Hoover Institution Fellow at Stanford University, and have taught at U.C. Berkeley, San Francisco and San Jose State universities, and Golden Gate University Law School. My view of what North Americans want to know about the USSR is based largely on the questions put to me by listeners to my radio program on that country, now in its 27th year, students' queries in class, and readers' letters prompted by my earlier books about that country.

My travels, taking me to all 15 ethnic republics, most of them more than once, have included such means as a rented Soviet car in which I taped hitch-hikers of all ages.

When words have the exact flavor of the manner of a living human being, it is hard to disbelieve them even if they are contrary to everything one's education and the media have conditioned one to believe is true. But the moment they show signs of processing by an intermediary, one's prejudices take over and one can relax into the comforting thought that the intermediary is selling a bill of goods, even though he has simply cut and re-arranged for logical sequence and third-person English. Joyce and Faulkner discovered that a long time ago in the field of imaginative writing. The success of Studs Terkel's documentary books is that they present their tape transcripts as they were spoken.

As a consequence, I will make much use of that style. Today that is recognized as sound anthropology.[1] I first started using tape recorders in the Soviet Union in 1966, and have done so on six visits. Some people there are mike-shy, exactly as here. Some will object to being taped but will then say, off mike, essentially the same things others are willing to say into it. Less educated individuals are often, not always, less articulate, which is why I have fewer workers and farmers to quote, relatively. But my intellectuals and professionals are almost always people born at the bottom of the social heap, who moved up thanks to affirmative action or simply the abolition of discrimination.

Although I had both students and travelers very much in mind in the writing, this book does not follow the normal rules for academic texts and certainly not for tourist guides. While a reader's ethnic background may cause him to be most interested in some particular chapter, the book is written to be read through.

My space allocation per country is not in proportion to population, but to Western interest arising out of ethnic backgrounds, and to the richness of my own eyewitness observations or those of highly qualified and vivid authors who knew the situation before my time. I have had colorful contact with writers in the Soviet East, South, and West, but social attitudes proved to be much the same, so to reproduce what was said in each case would be boring. The most gripping material about the life of the peasantry in the early Soviet years is from Belorussia. It applies equally to the Ukraine and Russia proper, except for nuances that are purely technical to anyone who is not a specialist on one of those nationalities. The differences among the Soviet countries will appear readily enough. The life of a nomad was obviously not that of a farming peasant. A people that lived in dispersion all over the world, like the Armenians, views matters differently than one very few of whose members have ever emigrated. Peoples with long histories of organized government differ in psychology from those whose first geographic ethnic administrations arose only as a result of Soviet policy.

In this as in all my writings, I am deeply indebted to my wife, Tanya, for research, criticism, and first editing. She too knows Russian and has been virtually all over the Soviet Union, repeatedly. The most detailed criticisms by others are those of Laura X (as she is publicly known), my son David, Drs. Shura and Sidney Saul, and Dr. Stephen Dunn. Particular thanks are due to Jon "Paka" Meachum, who made meticulous comments under the difficult circumstances of a prisoner sharing a cell in a state penitentiary. My colleague at radio station KPFA, Michael Butler, and Prof. Lynn Turgeon, also read an early version of the entire manuscript, and offered comments. An American anthropology graduate of Moscow University, Paula Garb, my daughter Phyllis, and my friends George David, Daisy Goodman, Louis Laub, and Sol Zeltzer, read and offered opinions, some at great length, on individual chapters. All those listed will have to forgive me where I did not accept sound advice for reasons of space, time, or feeling that I had simply done all that I had the energy to do. All are free to offer criticism of the finished product, in print if they desire.

NOTE

1. William Mandel among others, "Comment on Ivan Polunin, 'Visual and Sound Recording Apparatus in Ethnographic Fieldwork'," *Current Anthropology*, XI, No. 1 (1970), pp. 18-21.

1

Overview

"How will I recognize you?" I asked Dr. Lily Golden-Hanga over the phone. We were arranging to meet in the lobby of my Moscow hotel.

A peal of contralto laughter accompanied her answer, in English with a heavy Russian accent. "I'm big and black and fat!"

She turned out to be regal in bearing, large, and most definitely black.* A historian, whose doctoral studies focused on the history of African music, she is now a researcher at the Africa Institute of the Soviet Academy of Sciences. She was writing a paper on Black nationalism worldwide when we met. Since then she has assisted an isolated village of a Soviet sub-Arctic ethnic minority to get the community center promised them but delayed by bureaucratic neglect.

Her name is not Russian, obviously. The Golden is from her father, who in 1931 organized a group of sixteen Black families— the men were all graduates of Tuskegee Institute in Alabama—to move to the Soviet Union and teach modern farming to, in her words, the "people of color" in Uzbekistan near Iran, in the Asian part of the country. That is where she was born and grew up. "Some Uzbeks are much blacker than I am." Her own daughter, a Moscow University graduate, is half African.

Actually, there are very few persons of African descent in the

---

*"Contrary to popular belief, the Soviets are not a 'white' monolith."[1]

Union of Soviet Socialist Republics — old Russia didn't need to import slaves, since the landowning nobility kept their own fellow-Russians in a very slavery-like condition called serfdom. However, over 30,000,000 people (nearly an eighth) don't look "white," but more like Mexicans of Indian heritage or like Orientals or a mixture of both. One such is Tolomush Okeev, Kirgiz film director born in a Soviet village on the Chinese frontier. The story of his assistant, a Kirgiz woman, contains elements of the Soviet "minorities" story in almost classical form. ("Minorities" is placed in quotes, as the Kirgiz are a plurality and, with related Asian people, a majority in the Kirgiz Republic.)

"My name is Rakhia. I was born in the family of the very first to be a Communist." — the word is used in the USSR only to describe actual members of the party. "My father was 19 when they gave him his membership card in 1927."

Like most Kirgiz, her parents were nomadic peasants, but "In 1925, they joined a collective farm. My father was the chairman of the farm, then head of the county committee of the Communist Party. Now he's retired, with a personal pension." That is a high honor, something like the result of a private bill in the U.S. Congress.

"I too am one of the 'children of wartime.' I was born in 1942. I saw my father very infrequently because he was always away at work, but my mother was always there by my side. Among us Kirgiz, all children are treasured dearly by their parents, whether there is one in the family or 15.

"And so that's how I grew up, held very dear, the only daughter in the family, and mama always said, 'Be whatever you want, but the most important thing is to respect people. If a person comes into your house, do not ask him questions. Give him water, give him bread. Then ask him, Have you come a long way? From where? If he's from far away, give him your last horse'."

Immediately after graduation from high school, she went to work at the film studio, and later graduated from the USSR Institute of Cinematography in Moscow. "So that's been my work. I'm very happy in it. My husband, Arshan, assists me a great deal. Sometimes I'm away filming for three months at a stretch. We have two little boys, and he takes care of them. In my work, there are times when one works day and night, paying no attention to time. So I'm fortunate that he gives me support, and understands me.

"I regret only that my children did not see how my parents

lived, how they were never lazy, and never begrudged anything to anybody. Somebody wanted tea, they always found time for that. They were accustomed to working all the time. I grew up that way; I don't know how to sit around not doing anything. I would like our children's generation to grow up with a love for work. That is our happiness."

At least one film on which she has worked is shown on the art and college circuit in the United States — *The Ferocious One*, sometimes titled *Wolf Kokerek*, a moving story of human relations.

Most people don't become anthropologists or movie directors. Nor does everyone have understanding parents who are eager for change. For that very reason the values that seem to have reached the younger generation in the most remote places are particularly impressive. In a park in Dushanbe, capital of Soviet Tajikistan, near the Afghan border, I talked with a young man of 23 who was born not very far away in one of the most desolate and isolated pieces of the Soviet Union, in mountainous country where a peak rises to 25,000 feet. He is a Tajik, some of whom are the dark brown color of most of the peoples of India. There are twice as many Tajiks in Afghanistan as in the USSR.[2]

In the 1960s, he had said to his father: "I'm going to school. I want to be a real person when I grow up, and not a slave in your hands." My father said: 'What do you mean, you don't want to be here and be in my hands? I want it.' But I said to him: 'Now we have Soviet laws. I want to be a person. I love my whole people, no matter what nationality. There's more. I want to be an educated person, and not a worker on a collective farm or a state farm.' Well, he cursed me and I ran away from home again. I graduated from high school. I went to a trade school. I studied there for a year and became an electrician." There could be no thought of not finding work, as guaranteed full employment is built into the system. This one fact has done more to reduce ethnic prejudice than all other measures combined. No one need protect his job by convincing himself that he has more right to it than someone of different appearance or language or religion or gender.

Soviet Turkmenia is the southernmost Soviet republic. On a collective farm there, only 25 miles north of Iran, there is a gallery of paintings commissioned by the farmers to record their lives, past and present. My guide explained that the people on the farm had started at the level of Iran today.

"You see, this one has experienced every hardship, and those people's child is dying, and yet they have to pack up and leave the area," because the landlord wanted them no longer. "Over there you see a peasant: he ploughed the land himself, sowed it himself, threshed it himself, and what's left for him? The ruling khan took his share, the mullah [clergyman] took his, others took theirs, and he's left with a few sacks. That's his share. But *this* painting is already the period of collectivization, farming getting on its feet. The next one is simply a horse-racing scene, something very popular among Turkmen."

A second large room is lined with portraits. The subjects here do not look defeated, ragged, hungry. An elderly local farmer explained, "These are the people who founded our collective farm, that solid core. This man is one of our brigade leaders—he still is." Waving his arm at the whole gallery and beyond to the farm outside, he went on: "They made all this, starting in 1943. I started working on this farm in 1943. I ploughed a lot of land side by side with them, with horses, with camels.*

"They all worked out in the fields. I worked with them every day. That one over there was an active worker, our first brigade leader. He died only three years ago, still young."

That portrait was distinctly larger than the others, a special distinction because, "He was the first to use water from the Kara-Kum Canal." That canal is the only one on earth with dimensions comparable to California's Central Valley Project: for 250 miles, it is wide and deep enough to be used for barge transportation through the desert it irrigates. But because its trace chemicals are different from those of well water, the pioneer in using it for cotton could have been taking a big risk.

One portrait is of a woman. The farmer explained, "When our collective farm was established, she was our first village mayor. She died not long ago. These paintings were done by very prominent artists," he said, pointing to one by Izzat Klychev, a Turkmenian, and "People's Painter of the USSR, an artist very well known throughout the entire Soviet Union." It depicted a local wedding "in accordance with our customs."

So a country where painting was forbidden by religion (Turkmenia is Islamic by heritage) now has painters of USSR-wide prominence, and people whose fathers were medieval sharecroppers not only enjoy art but encourage it financially. When we left the village, after dark, it was obvious that there was electricity in every

---

*His point was that today it's all with tractors.

American-Russian Institute

The Kara-Kum Canal and California's Central Valley Project canal
are the only human works astronauts can see with the naked eye.

home. (Iran, just over the nearby mountains, produces only a fraction as much power per head of population and the half-million Turkmenians [Turcomans] there, still semi-nomads, are demanding the simplest elements of self-government.)

In 1977, in Moldavia, the European Soviet republic bordering Romania, I spoke with a woman of the Gagauz people, who are about as numerous as Indians in Arizona. She said, "Now, as a people that has only recently acquired a written language," — they adopted an alphabet, based on the Russian, for the first time in 1957 — "we are developing our culture."

"There are some 125,000 Gagauz in Moldavia; about 200,000 in the Soviet Union altogether. The bulk of the Gagauz villages are ethnically pure, though there is now some mixture, due to professional people from the outside who help raise the level of our people's culture, teachers and physicians. But we already have our own people in all the professions that serve a population at a modern level of development.

"We have artists, we have composers, we have our own poets and writers: those who write on the basis of folk themes, legends and those who collect our folklore. Among scholars we have linguists, historians. The anthropology of the Gagauz is being studied by Stepan Karoglu and me. He is researching the intellectual culture of the Gagauz, and I the material culture. Each of us has already written a book — I took my PhD this year. Then in Moscow we have Comrade Guboglo."

I admit I was surprised to learn Guboglo is a Gagauz; I had translated articles of his into English for the American journal, *Soviet Anthropology and Archeology*. So one of the Soviet Union's leading anthropologists, a man who theorizes on matters far beyond the bounds of his own nationality, is a member of a people who did not even have an alphabet little more than 20 years ago.

That interview was near the Black Sea, at the southernmost end of the European Soviet republics. At the northwestern end, on the Baltic Sea across from Sweden, lies Lithuania, the only Roman Catholic country in the USSR. In the Department of Philosophy, Law and Sociology of the Lithuanian Academy of Sciences, I asked about the origins of the scholars I was taping. The department head, Jonas Macevicius, said he was of peasant birth. Another answered: "Peasant," a third: "workingclass." Dr. Macevicius said: "A majority are from the peasantry. We all started in life by taking cows to pasture. Then we gained the opportunity to study," in Soviet times, which for Lithuania began in 1940. He spoke of his own life before that:

"My family had 14 acres. Naturally it was impossible for us all to go to school. To begin with, you had to pay and then you needed what to live on. Only rare individuals broke through this barrier. True, I personally did study. First I graduated the six-year elementary school, and then from a technical high school. But those were under terrible conditions of semi-starvation, when I had to ration myself. Hanging on was terrible, terrible, awful. But the mass of the people, the mass just didn't make it through school."

Many did not make it even *to* school. Macevicius had twelve brothers and sisters. "Most of them died. The doctor wasn't called. Only folk remedies. Those who got past the illnesses survived, and those who didn't died. To call a doctor cost five leetu. That was a lot — on five leetu I lived seven days, sometimes more."

Great numbers of American Jews whose parents or grandparents emigrated from the Russian Empire before the Revolution have their roots in Lithuania. Its capital, Vilnius, was a traditional focus of European Jewish culture (they called it Vilno or Wilna). During the Nazi occupation in World War II, nearly all the Jews there were exterminated. Only two categories escaped: those who accepted the Soviet offer of priority evacuation eastward (many refused because they could not believe the Germans would really murder everybody), and those who fought as guerrillas. The latter were led by Henrikas Zimanas, today a national hero of Lithuania. This one-time teacher of Yiddish is listed four times in the history of Lithuania published by its Academy of Sciences in 1978.[3]

I sought him out for an interview largely because in an article in the best Soviet newspaper of nationwide circulation, he reminded his millions of readers that "The Hitlerites . . . sought to exterminate the Jews and the overwhelming majority of them were in fact wiped out" and explained that of 6,000,000 Jews in the United States, only 200,000 belong to Zionist organizations,[4] a distinction not known to the general public in the USSR or here.

When we met I asked him why 40 percent of the 25,000 Lithuanian Jews who had survived Hitler had emigrated to Israel or the U.S. in the 1970s, while only two percent of those living in pre-war Soviet territory had done so. (Lithuania has been Soviet only since 1944.)

He replied, "In Lithuania the Jewish population consisted of big capitalists, comprising a small percentage; middle-level business-people, and professionals — there was virtually no Jewish peasantry. I come from the Jewish peasantry." On a map he indicated that part of the country which once belonged to Prussia. "Here the *Code Napoleon* applied, and Jews had the right to own land. My grandfather, my great-grandfather, my father all worked the land. In that country there was some number of Jewish peasants, and landlords as well.

"Most of the towns were entirely Jewish. The Jews lived in a milieu of their own. Their principal occupation was trade — the Jewish proletariat was *very* small. The principal cause [of emigration] was not ethnicity but class. They know that in the capitalist world there are those on top, and those on the bottom. And they hoped to be among those on top. Simply, as between capitalism and socialism, they chose capitalism. And we did not succeed in re-educating them in the years available to us.

"During the war years, I was First Secretary [top leader] of the underground Southern Regional Committee of the Communist Party of Lithuania, which included both Vilnius and Kaunas [Kovno]. I did everything possible to get the Jews out of the ghetto into the woods, into the guerrilla struggle. The head of the Vilnius ghetto was a man named Genz, who knew me well; in Kaunas it was Elkus, a physician. He too knew me well — he couldn't help but know me; he had been in my home a couple of times. I wrote him a letter, in Yiddish, saying we would get the young people out, we would get the old people out — we would get everybody out. If there were little children and women unable to bear arms, we would place them in villages.

"They responded: maybe that would be good, but we can't take the chance. You will expose us all, and they will kill us. And they held to what is called in Hebrew *Havlaga*, restraint. We said: 'Escape. We will take every caution.' And the fact is that we got hundreds out, despite the fact that they were blocking our activity. The Zionists thus helped the Nazis in the extermination of the Jews. Objectively. It was we who organized the escapes from the Ninth Fort . . . "*

Zimanas' wartime headquarters is now a national monument; the dugouts and underground field hospital have been rebuilt. When I visited it, alone, I saw a busload of schoolchildren, brought

---

*A bastion in the old city wall.

there as part of their civics course. Nearby is the ethnically Lithuanian village of Priciupis, which the Nazis had burned down with all its inhabitants, alive, because it had sheltered Jews at Zimanas' request. There, because the Lithuanians are Catholic, the Soviet government has erected three enormous crosses in traditional local design, as a monument. There is also a memorial stained-glass window in the secular community center.

It was not only in Lithuania that peasants saved Jews. My mother came from near Lvov (Lemberg) in the western Ukraine. On a visit in the '70s a retired organizer of theater for children told me of his time in World War II.

"I was not drafted but, having been under the [Nazi] occupation for a period, I escaped and joined up, in view of what they had done to my Ukrainian people, and personally to me." He was reluctant to explain his personal circumstances, saying only "Well, I had had to hide." The woman seated next to him, black-haired and darker in complexion than most Ukrainians, joined me in urging him to explain, but he added only; "There were reasons." Pressed, he conceded, he had to hide "Mainly because I had married a Jew. I changed my residence 16 times, and wound up with a whole briefcase full of I.D.s."

The woman who had asked him to explain was his wife, and she took up the story. "It was Ukrainians who hid me during the war. They were so wonderful about it, I was never given to feel that I was benefiting from an act of kindness." She recalled the day when "A visitor from Lvov came to the village and she said: '*Oh*, that Jewess is here. Now, what will happen! *Mm*!'. Her cousin ran to me, and he said: 'They're saying you're a Jew,' and he laughed. I said: 'This is no laughing matter. I have to get out of here.' I asked him not to tell his mother, because she was very attached to me. 'She is deeply religious, and this will be a shock to her.' He said: 'I see that you don't know my mother,' and ran off. In minutes, the old woman came toward me — he had told her — and she picked up my little baby, who was in his carriage, and hugged him: 'My dear one, my little dove, you aren't going anywhere! You have to live!' I said: 'And do you know what that threatens you with? It threatens *you* with death. Better that I should go away?' She: 'No, you may live here, and this little angel too'."

Ukrainian is a very emotional language. Recalling the conversation, the Jewish woman had switched totally to Ukrainian, but she went on in Russian for my sake, "The mother said, 'You aren't going anyplace. Either we'll all die or we will all survive. Things cannot be like this!' They had been good to me before that, but after that they were even better.

"It was Ukrainians who saved me. Of course it would not be true were I to say that all were people as good as this. Those who ran away to your country, their hands were deep in blood. But the majority—we were always on friendly terms."

Questioned, she repeated "The majority." And went on, "Our family is international. Our son is a Ukrainian on his father's side. His wife is a Tartar. The children converse in more than one language, each as it wishes. And when that began to happen, no one was surprised."

I have heard Ukrainians speak with respect of Jews as much as the other way around. A journalist told me of writing articles which resulted in a street being named for a Jew—a man who fought in the International Brigade for the Spanish Republic and then returned and died fighting for his native Ukraine.

I have been at pains to describe the Lvov-centered region as the "west Ukraine." With some 10,000,000 people, it has a distinct history, having been under Polish rule between World Wars I and II. In that time, three Ukrainian-language academic high schools (*gimnazia*) were closed down in a policy of Polonization; even small village schools were converted to Polish or—where this would have prevented all understanding—to bilingual education, and churches were required to conduct services in Polish. The landlords had been Polish from time immemorial. This period is not forgotten: when I visited in 1982 I found great bitterness against the Solidarity movement in Poland because one of its demands was that the west Ukraine be restored to Polish rule.

As these brief accounts show, language, not color, is the greatest delineator in the Soviet Union. As in the U.S., most of the people are "white." Yet there are marked differences. In the capital of Lithuania, for example, parents can choose among public schools taught either in Lithuanian or Russian or Polish. Children who study in Lithuanian are taught Russian as a second language, or vice versa.

Children's schools offer similar language choices in the cities of Armenia, the Ukraine, and elsewhere, and often in the countryside as well. In Daghestan, a tumbled Soviet mountain fastness of only a million and a half people, northwest of Iran, school is presently taught in *nine* languages.[5] This recognition that each people has the right to education in its own language—USSR-wide, instruction is in 52 distinct tongues[6]—has eliminated defensiveness from the national psychology of the various groups, and made them willing, even eager, to learn Russian as the language giving them mobility in careers outside their native territory.

Five different major alphabets are in use: Latin like ours, Cyrillic like the Russians (the most widespread, naturally), Hebrew (for the Yiddish magazine, newspaper, and over 100 books published in that language since 1968 alone), Armenian, and Georgian. In addition, Korean is used for the 400,000 people of that nationality, while Islamic religious bodies publish in Arabic.

Although race does not play as important a role as it does in the United States, physical differences among European Soviet peoples in complexion, eye and hair color, size and shape of features, and mannerisms, are sufficient to enable them usually to spot each other by nationality without saying a word—or at least so they think.[7]

As in most countries, religion goes with nationality. The vast majority of Russians, Ukrainians, Belorussians and Moldavians are of Orthodox Christian background. Religious Estonians are Lutherans; Lithuanians, Catholic; Latvians (Letts), both; while 35,000,000 people are of Moslem heritage, mostly in Central Asia and the Caucasus.[8] Religious Jews practice Judaism—there were 92 synagogues in 1978.[9] There are lamaist Buddhists of Kalmyk nationality in the European part of the country, and in Soviet Asia that is the traditional religion among the Buriats and Tuvans. Religious Koreans divide among animists, Confucians and Christians. Armenians and Georgians have distinct Christian denominations—even atheistic Armenians are proud that, at Echmiadzin, they have the oldest Christian church in the world, functioning since 303 A.D.

The contribution of religion to ethnic cultures is fully recognized. The government puts enormous sums into the restoration and maintenance of architecturally significant churches and mosques. In the "USSR" volume of the official *Large Soviet Encyclopedia*, plates titled "Sculpture of the Peoples of the USSR" include a St. George from an Orthodox church and a "Madonna and Child" from a Catholic church. The level of religious belief varies tremendously, from probably 50 percent among the Moslem Central Asians and Catholic Lithuanians to 30 percent among Armenians, 10 percent among Latvians, and less than 5 percent among Jews who, world-wide, are generally the least religious ethnic element in any country. This relates to the fact that they are urban, and urban people everywhere are less religious than rural. There are probably well over 20,000,000 Orthodox Christian believers — an impressive number, though it probably represents not much more than 10 percent of those nationalities that once had this as their religious heritage.

At that dinner in Kirgizia, where I spoke with Rakhia, one man mentioned that he was a Moslem believer. I asked him to elaborate in view of the fact that there are few religious Moslems among Soviet intellectuals. He did:

"My name is Doron-bek, surname Sadyrbaiev. I was born and raised in the family of a Party official, an unshakeable Bolshevik who, in the years of the Revolution and then in the 1930s here in our Kirgizia suffered a great deal [in Stalin's purge, he explained later], but remained a Communist to the end of his days, and even died at his post, at work.

"I was educated in the Soviet schools, traveled to Leningrad [3,000 miles away], entered the Leningrad Institute of Theater and Cinematography, majored in directing. Graduated and went to work. I don't belong to any organizations, to any party, and I have neither sympathy nor hostility toward any. The motto of my life, my striving, my goal, is to be a human being, simply a human being. I love — I am terribly in love — with art. I work at the Kirgiz TV Film Studios, where I write the scripts of my own films. I also write a lot of humor: stories published both in Russian and Kirgiz, locally and USSR-wide. I cast ridicule on no one; I laugh only at myself, at my own shortcomings, of which I have more than enough."

He did not look at all introspective: square-faced and healthy, 37 years old, with a Groucho Marx moustache and a broad and open smile, he wore the medal of an Honored Worker of Culture, "the highest recognition in our structure."

Still, I was curious as to why he considered himself a Moslem.

"I don't do those prayers five times a day. I don't pray either by myself or in a mosque, but, just as I write by myself, so I believe by myself, and in the Moslem religion there are matters, concepts with which I do not agree. There are a great many of its propositions that I edit in my own way, to suit me."

A playwright broke in: "In that respect I agree with him. To a certain degree we're all Moslems because, as you understand, our fathers, mothers, were adherents of that religion. This doesn't mean that there's any fanaticism involved. Some of its provisions in the realm of ethics are necessary, necessities."

Photo by Author

Rakhia stands in the corner, Arshan next to her. Doron-bek stands far left; Bek-Sultan stands between them. His wife sits to his left. Chokmorov picks his ear, museum director far right. Okeev's actress mother sits left, Mrs. Mandel center.

Doron-bek resumed:

"There are very many Moslems — our Kirgiz, Kazakhs, and Uzbeks — who, while not understanding the Arabic language, the routine call to prayers, the Koran, nevertheless perform rites. I know all the prayers, although only in translation. I have read the fanatical things there — there's nothing worth adopting in that. But I found fragments of love poems, of writings on education, facts from history. I understand a little Arabic. [The playwright interjected: "We took Arabic in school."] So if the occasion arises, for the sake of paying respect to custom, I am capable of reciting a number of passages from the Koran without difficulty. Although I got 'A' grades in philosophy [meaning dialectical materialism] and in the history of Marxism-Leninism, that doesn't prevent me from adhering to Islam, in which, however, I select only certain progressive aspects."

At different times, I have talked to the mullah of a historic rural mosque, to the second-ranking Islamic religious figure in Soviet Central Asia, and to the head of its seminary. All disagreed totally with Doron-bek's attitude. They are fundamentalists, as are the leaders of all organized religions in the USSR. But I strongly suspect that these attitudes of first-generation Kirgiz intellectuals

—like our Unitarians, or Quakers, or the Reformed Judaism or Roman Catholic beliefs that have developed in the past 20 years — are quite widespread among people of all religious backgrounds in the Soviet Union.

Kazakh historian whose father was illiterate; the author; PhD obstetrician-gynecologist; their musician daughter.

The United States has immigrants and dissidents of most of the Soviet nationalities, religious and racial groups, and all have publications which express various complaints about the ethnic situation in the USSR. But none claim that there is anything anywhere in the Soviet Union resembling the warfare in Northern Ireland (with its terrorist extension into England), the tribal slaughter in several African countries, the holocaust in Lebanon between Christian and Moslem Arabs further complicated by Israel, the Palestinian armed struggle for independence in their native land, the murder of a provincial cabinet minister by Quebec terrorists over the English-French division, the riots in Belgium over whether universities shall teach in French or Flemish Dutch, and the Basque terrorist effort to win self-determination from Spain by assassinations that have averaged over one per week since 1977.[10]

Nor do any of these anti-Communist emigre publications claim that anything in the USSR can compare to things reported regularly in the United States. In 1980, in Oroville, California, three whites pleaded guilty to killing a Black when they "couldn't find a deer or even a cow to kill" on a hunting trip — and a Black school official, who had escaped death in a similar incident in the same town a few years earlier, said she saw no reason to leave, because things were no worse than in her native Chicago.[11] In Dayton, Ohio, a convicted killer told police in 1977 that he and two others killed 25 to 30 Blacks randomly; records showed that number of unsolved cases.[12] That same year killings of Blacks by police themselves work out to one every six hours somewhere in the country, based on data of the Police Foundation.[13] Over half the deaths at the hands of police are Black, and the most respectable of Black organizations — the Urban League, the NAACP — have long insisted that fact is a consequence of racism.

Neither is the Soviet Union alleged by anyone to have situations like Filipino waiters being given a separate menu from whites, consisting of spoiled and leftover food, and being forbidden to speak in their native tongue;[14] Latino-populated East Los Angeles having only one-tenth the ratio of physicians to residents as that in major California urban areas in general;[15] a U.S. Court of Appeals judge expressing the belief that "there is a rise in Ku Klux Klan type of activity that we didn't see much of in the '60s or '70s. Although a lot more of it has been directed toward Jews and blacks, there has been some targeting of Asians."[16] An official commission of the State of California reported late in 1984 that "students of Asian background have been ridiculed, attacked and killed by white students."[17] All items in this paragraph appeared in the single year before this book went to press.

Not even the most stridently anti-Soviet Jewish publication alleges that there are ghettoes or housing discrimination in the Soviet Union, although that was general in prerevolutionary Russia. None claims that pogroms — mass beatings and pillage of Jews, usually accompanied by murders and rape — have occurred in Soviet-controlled territory for half a century, although the old Russia was notorious for that. An American reporter in Moscow writing about a Jewish dissident there reminds us of something long forgotten: "During World War II, his family, *like many other Jews*, was sent to Central Asia *ahead of the invading Nazis.*"[18] [Emphasis added] "Many" is an extreme understatement — most Soviet Jews had lived in the part of the country Hitler overran, and a majority, nearly

2,000,000[19] were evacuated eastward. This was under Stalin. No Western government organization or individual Jewish or otherwise, rescued remotely as many.

The editor of the Jewish-language (Yiddish) magazine published in Moscow has agreed with me (on tape and for the record) that certain Soviet journalists have published anti-Semitic materials in recent years. His own office had bas-reliefs of Jewish writers killed in a purge 35 years ago. But he was editing a literary magazine in Yiddish, now in its 24th year, and spoke proudly of very young new novelists writing in Yiddish, which they learned from lessons he had printed in the magazine, and of artists on Jewish themes who had been encouraged by his publishing reproductions of their work. He was also proud that a friend of his who is one of the two Jewish cabinet members is personally steeped in Jewish culture.

This editor, his approximately 100 contributors, his artists, the author of the grammar he is serializing, are success stories specifically as Jews, not simply as Soviet citizens who happen to be of Jewish origin. The number of Soviet Jews who are success stories in the general world—in science, technology, management, medicine, in all the arts, in law—is many times higher than their ratio to the population, higher proportionately than any other ethnic group, including the Russians themselves.

The levels of ethnic tension that have expressed themselves so explosively elsewhere in the world simply do not exist any longer in the USSR. One historical fact makes that strikingly clear. When the Russian Revolution took place in 1917, much of the world belonged to empires: British, French, Portuguese, Dutch, Belgian, Austro-Hungarian, German, Spanish, Russian. Each had colonies and/or other countries incorporated in them. Today, the pressures of nationalism, often violent, have pushed every one of those empires back to a fraction of its former size, with a single exception: the Soviet Union. It is smaller than the old Russian Empire, but not by much—it lost only Finland, whose economic and governmental systems are essentially identical to those of Western Europe, and Poland (where farming is almost entirely private and the church holds a degree of power unimaginable in the USSR). Yet the Russian Empire suffered greater human losses, greater stresses, in World War I than any other participant.

The Revolution of 1917 was followed by years of civil war and foreign intervention, including U.S. troops in the north of European

Russia and also in Siberia. In World War II Soviet losses were again the largest by a very wide margin, because most of the fighting took place on that front: 20,000,000 Soviet soldiers and civilians died, by comparison to 400,000 Americans—fifty to one. Most of the fighting was in non-Russian countries of the USSR: the Ukraine, Belorussia, the Baltic states, Moldavia. All were under German occupation for three years. Hitler expected the Soviet Union to break into pieces along ethnic lines, yet the vast majority of the non-Russians remained loyal. Soviet Armenians, Lithuanians, Ukrainians, and Jews have all recited to me the names of generals of their nationality who commanded Soviet divisions, and entire armies, against the Nazis.

Such cohesion in such extreme conditions would not have been possible unless all these peoples had been treated in a way that was fundamentally different under the Soviets than in the Western-controlled world empires and, of course, in prerevolutionary Russia —where World War I brought a massive revolt of the Central Asians. The essence of the matter is that, since the Revolution, non-Russians have had *real* power, not merely recognition of their languages and cultures.

Jews played an extremely large role in the Revolution, and the early post-revolutionary government. Trotsky, organizer of the Red Army, was Jewish, as was the first chief of state, Jacob Sverdlov. After Lenin's death, a man who was not Russian or even European actually ran the country for 30 years: Joseph Stalin (Jugashvili), a Georgian from the Caucasus. His very closest associates until his death included not only Russians but an Armenian, Mikoyan, and a Jew, Kaganovich, both members of the Political Bureau of the Communist Party, which is the day-to-day seat of power. Today that small body includes members from Soviet Asia and the Caucasus as well as Europe, two from peoples of the Turkic language group and Moslem religious heritage, a Georgian, and several non-Russian Slavs: Ukrainians and Belorussians. The most impressive aspect of this is that there has never been any claim, from any source, that voting in the Politburo divides along ethnic lines.

Like the policy-making Political Bureau, the government's cabinet, which conducts actual operations, is supposed to consist of the most competent people and therefore has no formal rules of ethnic representation. But it, too, contains several nationalities, including two Jews.

Because the tsarist empire had come into being through Russian expansion into the lands of others, Russians are only one-half the population of the Soviet Union. In 14 countries—one-quarter of the immense area of the USSR—the Russians are minorities. In those places, store and street and institutional signs are bilingual (except in Armenia, where Russian is often totally omitted in unofficial billboards and the like). In prerevolutionary times, the policy, by and large, was Russification. Indeed, the very existence of some peoples was flatly denied, in an attempt at forced assimilation. This was true of *the very largest* non-Russian nations, the Ukrainians and Belorussians (peoples far more numerous than the overwhelming majority of countries in the United Nations). Since they are Eastern Slavs, like the Russians, the tsarist government sought to force them to be Russians, and treated their languages contemptuously as dialects. Imagine forcing the Irish to be English, though most speak the same language, or Danes and Norwegians to agree they are Swedes, or Spaniards and Italians to define themselves as French.

Furthermore, there was a state religion in the Empire, Orthodox Christianity. Moslems were infidels, Jews were pariahs, Catholics represented a conquered past enemy (Poland with Lithuania), but all Christian nationalities were favored over non-Christians.[20] However, minority Christian sects of Russian ethnic origin were treated as heretics, and often either exiled en masse to Siberia or the Caucasus, or hounded until many moved to other countries: Dukhobors to Canada, Molokans to San Francisco, and so forth.

In the Russian Empire, the language even of local government offices was Russian, although at least a third of the population didn't speak it. There was a crazy-quilt of ethnic policies before the Revolution. The Baltic peoples—Lithuanians, Latvians, Estonians —were permitted schools in their own languages, but only in the primary grades; beyond that instruction was in Russian. Schools in Georgia were allowed to teach the *native* tongue only as a second language. Moslems and Jews were permitted to have their traditional schools for teaching religious subjects and did create small numbers of modern schools in the years just before the Revolution.

Although old Russia was an absolute monarchy, there was a system of elective government at the local level. Asian and Caucasus peoples had no right to vote in it, but some of the other non-Russians did.[21] Divide and rule. An unsuccessful revolution in 1905 forced the tsar to grant an elected parliament, the Duma, although it had little power. Again divide and rule: the major Moslem peoples had no right to vote for it, while the Christian nationalities did, somewhat like today's differing levels of discrimination between Blacks, Coloureds, and whites in South Africa.

Elimination of blatant discrimination of these types does not of itself bring ethnic equality or peace. If a sprinter is given a ten-yard lead over an opponent of the same class, he'll win the race. The Soviets recognized this. It was they who, for all practical purposes, invented the policy we call "affirmative action," and they pursued it consistently to eradicate the historic lag in education, economic development, and knowledge of governmental affairs. (Rakhia and Doron-bek are examples of this.) Because the Central Asian nationalities were, at the time of the Revolution, recently-conquered peoples in exactly the same state as the Islamic peoples south of the border — in some cases precisely the same peoples — comparing those two groups today provides a clear picture of what has happened among the masses, not merely a small elite.

Turkey, Iran, Afghanistan, Pakistan, India, and China flank the formerly colonial areas of the Soviet Union. In 1928 they, and the Islamic Soviet areas, were essentially still in the Middle Ages in terms of industrialization, agricultural techniques and education. Even by that very early date — when guerrilla fighting by former ethnic nobility and tribal leaders was still going on — the Soviet territories had doctors and hospital beds in quantities that Turkey did not reach until *forty* years later. By 1969 the Soviet peoples of this area were totally literate (99.7 percent to be precise), the Turks only one-third. The Turkic-and-Farsi-speaking peoples of the USSR had, in that year, four-and-a-half times as many college students, fourteen times as many newspaper readers, nearly five times as many physicians, seven times as many hospital beds as Turkey, in proportion to population.

When, in 1977, a Soviet atomic-powered icebreaker became the first surface vessel in history to make it to the North Pole, its captain was a man born into a mountain tribe in the North Caucasus — the Near East. At the International Congress of Historical Sciences in 1975, the head of the Soviet delegation was an Oriental, a Korean. The recently-retired prima ballerina of the Bolshoi Ballet, Maia Plisetskaya, is Jewish — a member of an ethnic group as totally barred before the Revolution as Black prima ballerinas are from classical ballet in "white" companies in the U.S. today. Jewish names predominate among the Soviet musical performers who travel the world: pianists Lazar Berman and Emil Gilels, the immortal Oistrakh, and many more. They have not "defected."

This pattern, the idea that success is limited only by one's

Turkmen founder of a collective-farm just outside Ashkhabad.

These could be his grandchildren in Ashkhabad, right on the border with Iran.

individual talent and effort, explains why those I interviewed in all fifteen countries of the USSR for this book, spoke of their personal progress and that of their peoples, but not in terms of having overcome obstacles of an ethnic nature. They simply don't feel there are any today. There is one exception: because Jews are greatly overrepresented in posts of status in research and technology—itself a policy of Soviet door-opening—individuals have been passed over in favor of members of underrepresented peoples. Some of these individuals feel the same resentment voiced by some American whites who were denied admission to medical schools in favor of Black applicants under quota-type "affirmative action" programs that existed in the U.S. a few years ago.

The loyalty of the non-Russians to the Soviet Union is based on what they have gained, economically and in dignity, as peoples. A U.S. government survey has found that Blacks are currently discriminated against *three times out of four* when they seek to buy or even rent living quarters. Imagine a total end to that. That is what has happened to housing discrimination in the Soviet Union. Imagine an end to the three-out-of-five unemployment rate among Black youth, the even higher rate among Indians, and nearly as high among Latinos. Imagine that Third World people in the U.S. were employed in the mass media in proportion to their number in the population, one in five—eight times their present representation—which is one in forty. Imagine a Black governor of Mississippi, statues of Dr. W.E.B. DuBois, Paul Robeson, Harriet Tubman, Martin Luther King, and Malcolm X on the State House lawn in Richmond, Virginia—instead of the generals who fought for slavery—which stand there now. Imagine the children of Spanish-speaking farmworkers not being taken out of school to follow the crops. Imagine an Eskimo woman as governor of Alaska, like the Chukchi woman who governs the Soviet territory that faces Alaska across the Bering Straits. [22]

These are the realities of the changes in the USSR. Visitors who have lived with discrimination have no difficulty in seeing the difference in the Soviet Union. The first group of Latinos to visit the Soviet Union were students and staff from the University of California, Berkeley, in the early '70s. They had never been abroad. When they changed planes in London, the scene was very familiar—the British had found people of color to do the dirty work at the airport. When they got to Moscow, those jobs were being done by whites, although they saw plenty of darker people in the USSR.

NOTES

1. *The Black Scholar*, VII, No. 6 (1976), 48.
2. Solomon Brook, *The World Population Today* (Ethnodemographic Processes) (Moscow: USSR Academy of Sciences, 1977), p. 129.
3. Institut istorii Akademii nauk Litovskoi SSR, *Istoriia Litovskoi SSR* (Vilnius: Mokslas, 1978), pp. 393, 422, 458, 460.
4. *Literaturnaia gazeta* (Moscow), April 21, 1976.
5. K. Kh. Khanazarov, *Reshenie natsional 'no-iazykovoi problemy v SSSR* (Moscow: Politizdat, 1982), p. 175.
6. P. Fedoseev, "Theoretical Problems of the Development and Convergence of Nations," *Soviet Law and Government*, XIX, No. 4 (1981), 47.
7. A.K. Kozhanov, "External Appearance as a Factor in Ethnic Identification," *Soviet Sociology*, XVI, No. 4 (1978).
8. Calculated from TsSU SSSR, *Narodnoe khoziaistvo SSSR v 1980 g.* (Moscow: Finansy i Statistika, 1981), pp. 24-26.
9. Avtandil Rukhadze, *Jews in the USSR* (Moscow: Novosti, 1978), p. 38.
10. *San Francisco Chronicle*, December 28, 1983.
11. Ibid., February 6, 1980.
12. Ibid., July 5, 1977.
13. Ibid., May 16, 1977. The situation is not improving. For example, in Oakland, California, there were 25 police killings in the decade 1969 to 1979, but 20 more in only the 4½ years that followed. Berkeley *Express*, September 7, 1984, p. 8.
14. *San Francisco Chronicle*, January 7, 1984.
15. Ibid., November 17, 1983.
16. *San Francisco Examiner*, February 26, 1984.
17. *San Francisco Chronicle*, September 11, 1984.
18. Ibid., March 10, 1977.
19. Ruvim Groyer, "Statistics About Soviet Jews," *Jewish Affairs*, X, No. 4 (1980).
20. V.I. Kozlov, *Natsional'nosti SSSR* (Moscow: Statistika, 1975), pp. 43-48.
21. Ibid.
22. *Pravda* (Moscow), April 12, 1984.

2

Before the Revolution:
Realities and Ideas

This chapter will be difficult, complicated—even irritating, if the reader has ethnic roots or associations with peoples who live in, or once lived in, the Soviet Union or what was the Russian Empire. (Poland and Finland were part of the Russian Empire but do not belong to the Soviet Union.)

Virtually everyone with such associations has a tendency to defend "one's own." When outsiders criticize points of view existing in one's ethnic group, the criticisms are resented, and characterized as prejudice—anti-Semitic, white racist, etc.—even if one happens to agree with such criticism oneself. But those who aspired to lead a country like the Russian Empire—consisting of many real territorial nations, *plus* dispersed minorities, all wracked by ethnic conflict—could not take such a narrow attitude. They had to try to develop or adopt a theory that would explain the reasons for that conflict, and a program to eliminate it.

This meant, first, independently examining the real situation. Secondly, it meant considering proposals from each nationality, debating them, and arriving at conclusions. This was necessary even though an Armenian, or Estonian, Jew, or Ukrainian might greet any disagreement with anyone speaking for any element in his own group by saying: "why pick on us?"

In this chapter the reader will find Lenin, the man who set the course of the Russian Revolution, debating, as well as agreeing

with, Jewish, Ukrainian, Polish, Armenian, and Russian spokes-
persons, some representing parties far to his right, others representing
socialists, and still others even members of his own Bolshevik
(Communist) wing of the Russian Social-Democratic Labor Party.
The discussion here is focused more on the interests of American
and Canadian readers than on what concerned peoples and political
figures in the Russian Empire and the Soviet Union. There, the
question of what to do about subject peoples who had lived from
time immemorial in their own territories — Ukrainians, Lithuanians,
Armenians, the Asian peoples — was, and is, by far the more
important issue. Canada has some understanding of this, because
of French-speaking Quebec. In the U.S., only reservation Indians
and Puerto Ricans on that island itself clearly fall into that
category. Among Blacks and Latinos, there is a point of view,
presently a small minority, holding that a large string of counties
with Black majorities in several states of the deep South comprise
an embryonic Black nation and a large area in the Southwest with
Latino majorities comprise an Aztlan nation. But the great majority of
Blacks and Latinos, and virtually all whites, think of the ethnic
question in terms of minorities living dispersed among, and surrounded by, the white population. In old Russia, that situation
applied above all to the Jews, who, although white, lived under
circumstances that can only be regarded as discriminatory in the
worst sense. For example, Jews were forbidden by law to live
anywhere but in the westernmost corner of the empire. They were
simply forbidden to own land. Mass physical violence against them
was so commonplace that a special word, "pogrom," attached to
it, just as lynching almost automatically referred to a Black in the
United States.

Therefore this discussion of the prerevolutionary debate over
ethnic problems will be illustrated disproportionately by reference
to the Jewish experience, because it pertains to a dispersed minority
resembling those in North America, and also because Jews outnumber
any other single group in the English-speaking world with roots in
what is today the Soviet Union.

This chapter will be complex because it deals with the overall
ethnic history of the Russian Empire; employment patterns by
nationality, hostilities among non-Russian peoples, housing segregation, social stratification, religious differences, "native state"
versus direct-Russian-rule arrangements, tribalism, the role of
social class oppression and struggle, language rights and education,
political organization, assimilation, values in ethnic cultures, self-

determination and secession rights for subject areas, landownership as the key to equality for pre-industrial peoples, the leveling upward of formerly underdeveloped peoples, size criteria for independent territorial recognition, immigration and emigration, distortion of census figures to justify oppression.

Why so many elements in one chapter? Because all were either part of the prerevolutionary reality, or factors that had to be considered before any solution could be attempted. True, each topic could fill a chapter, but that would have resulted in a specialized textbook. Here it is simply the historical introduction to a book on the individual nationalities. And those who find the subject matter too formidable can skip this chapter, or skim it, or return to it if the rest of the book rouses interest in these subjects.

Ridicule of minorities is one of the surest and most universal signs of ethnic oppression. In 1919, Lenin reminisced about his youth along the Volga River: "We nationals of a big nation . . . commit . . . insult an infinite number of times without noticing it. . . . Poles are not called by any other name than Polyachishka, . . . the certain way to mock at a Tatar* is to call him Prince, . . . the Ukrainians are always Khokhols and the Georgians and other Caucasian nationals always Kapkasians."[1] Jews were called *Zhid*, the Russian equivalent of "kike" or, for Blacks, "nigger."

The ideology underlying this was that of Great-Russian superiority, and Russification. ("Great-Russian" is the term used to distinguish Russians as such from Ukrainians — "Little Russians" — and Belorussians; under Russification, the tsarist government sought to force these people to abandon their own Slavic languages for Russian.) In common-sense terms, this view seemed to have every support: The Russian tsars had managed to gather under their rule the largest unbroken territory on earth, so presumably their way was better.

But the colossus had feet of clay. Not long after the Russian Empire reached its greatest size, it was defeated in the Russo-Japanese War of 1904, a defeat which shook up all elements of society. This stimulated disobedience, and even emigration by oppressed minorities. My father's oldest brother, a draftee, was killed in that war, thousands of miles from his home. The family reasoned: why should Jews fight for, or remain in, a country that then would not

---

*Identical to "Tartar," which is incorrect but used occasionally in this book because "Tatar" is so unfamiliar as to be confusing.

even let them live outside a fixed line? The monarchy did not even try to enroll in its army the peoples of Central Asia and most of those of the northern Caucasus, brought into the empire in the 19th century, some as late as 1881.

The reasons for Russia's conquests were diverse. There was the desire — as with America's taking of Indian territory — to gain land for agricultural settlement, which also meant, in Russia's case, throwing a bone to some of its own dissatisfied peasantry, including Ukrainians and Belorussians, by giving them land seized from nomadic Asian peoples. A second reason was to gain raw materials, such as cotton from Central Asia. A third was simply dog-eat-dog competition with other empires: for example, to control parts of Central Asia by advancing southward before the British, moving north from India, could get them. This has left its mark. To this day, as in Africa, boundaries established by competing European empires a century ago mark the frontiers between independent states, cutting right across ethnic lines and putting people of the same language and culture under different governments. For example, there are nearly as many Azerbaijanis in the Soviet republic of that name as in the northern portion of Iran right across the border, a situation that reflects centuries of wrestling for territory between the old Russian and Persian empires.

In old Russia, as elsewhere, oppressed peoples did the menial jobs. One-third of the Tatars were janitors, porters, and rag-pickers.[2] It took time for such situations to disappear — twenty years after the Revolution, an observer could still write: "In Moscow, . . . every shoe-black at every street corner claim(s) to be an Aisor (the Aisors declare that they are the descendants of the ancient Assyrians, some of whom immigrated to the Caucasus) . . . "[3] In countries that have been socialist only since World War II, one still finds ethnically-associated "businesses" such as shining shoes — in Bulgaria that's a Gypsy occupation — but that is no longer true in the USSR.

"Divide and rule" is a natural tactic for any rulers, particularly where different minorities lived side by side. (The situation was similar to that in which Blacks, Chicanos, Puerto Ricans have to scramble for the same jobs, and the educated among them compete for the small number of status posts available.) The Caucasus Mountains, for example, are inhabited by the Azerbaijanis, of Moslem heritage and Turkic language, and by Georgians and Armenians, both Christian, each with a distinct language. There, during the unsuccessful revolution of 1905, Russian ultra-conservatives incited the Azerbaijanis against the Armenians, while these Russians themselves directly attacked Georgians and engaged in pogroms against Jews.[4]

Ghettos existed, both spontaneous and forced. Because minorities in the Russian Empire were identified by their distinct languages, which they used as much as possible, and frequently worked for employers of their own nationality, living in ethnic neighborhoods often made sense. In addition, the ghetto offered protection against hostile actions by others. A Moslem cottongrower, reminiscing years later about one Central Asian town, said: "The past was a stairway of years carpeted with pain. The Uzbeks feared to go along the street of the Arabs; the Tajiks carried sticks when they walked through the Uzbek quarter."[5] Yet all were Moslems.

Russians were half the people of the towns of Central Asia, although only one-tenth of the total population there. This is like Mississippi and southern Alabama, where the countryside is overwhelmingly Black, the cities heavily white.

College education was nearly unknown, in some areas literally unheard-of, except among the Russians, who were therefore the doctors, lawyers, teachers, and the clergy of the official church. By and large, they also had the money, although there were some very rich traditional native rulers, land and livestock barons. Even Russian workers, miserably poor and working outrageous hours under awful conditions, with practically no rights to organize, were skilled in comparison to the indigenous peoples. Consequently, the Russian laborers earned a bit more and held somewhat steadier jobs.

Religion complicated prejudices. Every church—Christian, Jewish, and particularly Moslem, frowned strongly upon marriage out of that particular faith, and virtually everyone was religious.

In a few places, the Russian Empire, like European empires in Asia and Africa, ruled through indigenous royalty so long as they were loyal, and even where the Russian structure of government existed, it was general policy to function through the local nobility and elite. The Emir of Bokhara, a principality in Central Asia, was made a general in the Russian Army, and allowed to invest in Russian industry, but, except in such "native states," police were Russian.

The nearly universal illiteracy—three-quarters of the Russians and nine out of ten non-Russians could not read or write—tended to isolate peoples even further, and to maintain ignorant prejudices. A literate person could read a story, novel, or poem by someone of another nationality, and conclude that other people, although different, had human feelings like his own. But with no ability to read, the most vile superstitions and fears about "strange" peoples could spread easily.

In very many cases, peoples were divided within themselves along tribal lines. The most famous of all Georgians, Joseph Stalin, wrote of his own people's situation 100 years ago: "split up into a number of disconnected principalities, . . . for centuries they waged war against each other and pillaged each other, each inciting the Persians and Turks against the other."[6] This was not unlike the wars between Indian tribes in America and, just as the U.S. government used such hostilities to obtain guides from one Indian tribe to make war against another, so the Russian Empire often simply exploited existing hostilities.

Some of the countries swallowed up in the empire had themselves consisted of dominant and subjected ethnic groups, again, a situation similar to that in some places in Africa, such as Nigeria. And there were oppressed nations whose strongest hostility was not toward the Russians. The Ukrainians — by far the largest "minority," numbering tens of millions — were most hostile to Poles, because their landlords were Polish before that territory came under Russian rule. They were also hostile to Jews because, centuries earlier, the Poles had brought Jews in to manage their estates.

The Marxists argued that these hostilities were rooted in competition among propertied classes, not among peoples as such: the richer Ukrainian peasants versus Polish landlords; the capitalists and prosperous market farmers of Poland, Lithuania and the Ukraine against the Russian nobility whose privileges and laws kept them from expanding. With this understanding, Jewish, Polish, and Latvian (Lettish) Marxist parties sought to affiliate with the Russian; they saw a common interest of workers and peasants of all nationalities. They also pointed to many occasions when the wealthy cooperated across ethnic lines because the poor became too restless.

Stalin was a prominent member of the party led by Lenin which sought to develop a policy that would create unity *across* ethnic lines, unity strong enough to overthrow the monarchy and open the way to socialism. Others, also regarding themselves as Marxists, wanted to organize workers *along* ethnic lines within the overall Social-Democratic Party. The major advocate of that policy was the socialist organization of Jewish craftsmen and workers called the Bund. Lenin had the deepest appreciation of the oppression of Jews in the Russian Empire, and the highest respect for their contributions —in a 1913 article, he described them as "the most oppressed and persecuted nation," and added, "the great features of Jewish culture, progressive on a world scale, have clearly made themselves felt: its internationalism, its responsiveness to the advanced movements of the epoch (the percentage of Jews in the democratic and proletarian movements is everywhere higher than the percentage of Jews in the population as a whole)."[7]

Today no government except that of South Africa adheres to the idea of inborn racial superiority as official policy. But at the beginning of this century that ideology was professed by the United States, England, Germany, and all "civilized" countries. Segregation, justifying itself by that theory, was the law in the American South, and enforced in nearly all respects in the North without benefit of law. In light of that it is remarkable to read the statement of principles adopted — on Lenin's initiative — by the Social-Democratic Party as early as 1903. Clause 7 calls for: "Complete equality of rights for all citizens, irrespective of sex, religion, race or nationality." In 1914, just before the outbreak of World War I and just after an unsuccessful attempt by the tsarist authorities to frame a Jew, Mendel Beilis, on a charge of ritual murder,* Lenin drafted a bill to be presented in the Duma (or parliament, though with very limited powers) titled "A Bill for the Abolition of All Disabilities of the Jews and of all Restrictions on the Grounds of Origin or Nationality." In his introduction, he wrote:

> This Bill aims at abolishing all ethnic restrictions against all peoples: Jews, Poles, and so forth. But it deals in particular detail with the restrictions against the Jews. The reason is obvious: no nationality in Russia is so oppressed and persecuted as the Jewish. . . . It is sufficient to recall the anti-Jewish pogroms and the Beilis case. . . . The voice of the *Russian* workers must be particularly loud in protest against ethnic oppression. . . . We hope that the Russian workers will give particularly strong support to our Bill by their declarations.

When formally submitted, the Bill was to have a list of all the regulations and laws to be rescinded, including "about a hundred such laws affecting the Jews alone." The most important passages of his proposed law read:

> 1. Citizens of all nationalities inhabiting Russia are equal before the law.
> 2. No citizen of Russia, regardless of sex and religion, may be restricted in political or in any other rights on the grounds of origin or nationality.

---

*Ritual murder is killing humans as, or as part of, religious observance. It has never been part of the Jewish religion.

3. . . . All and any restrictions of the rights of Jews as regards residence and travel, the right to education, the right to governmental and organizational employment, electoral rights, military service, the right to purchase and rent real estate in towns, villages, etc., are herewith abolished, and all restrictions of the rights of Jews to engage in the liberal professions, etc., are herewith abolished.[8]

In that stacked parliament the bill was not passed, of course. But the revolution put its principles into force only three years later.

Conservatives often attack attempts to achieve equality as being "Communist." These charges are based on historical fact: When the Russian Revolution raised these egalitarian ideas to the level of government policy they moved from the level of a dream to the status of reality. As the U.S. ambassador to the United Nations during the Carter administration, Donald F. McHenry, put it: "The Soviets are on the side of motherhood when it comes to racial equality. . . . they identify with it."[9] Since 1917 this has raised the question in numerous countries — if in Russia, why not here?

The same may be said of Clause 8 of the 1903 platform of Lenin's party: "the right of the population to receive education in their native languages, this right to be ensured by the establishment of schools for this purpose at the expense of the state and of local government bodies." This program of education in the native language was to make it easier to educate, not to isolate nationalities from each other.

The language issue was a practical matter, not simply one of theory or a hoped-for future. When the tsarist government made some concessions to quiet the people following an immense revolutionary movement in 1905-07, and allowed Marxist papers to be published legally, the Bolsheviks began to publish not only in Russian but also a paper in the Tatar (Tartar) language. This reached people of the Turkic nationalities living along the Volga River, in the Ural Mountains, in the oil-producing Caucasus range, and in Central Asia, as their languages, like Tatar, fall into the Turkic family, and are closely related. But to understand the paper they had to be able to read, which they could obviously learn to do more quickly in their own language. Not only did they not know Russian, many hated it as the language of their oppressors and exploiters.

Similarly, on at least one occasion the Bolsheviks published a major statement in translation into Yiddish, with a special introduction by Lenin as a way of paying special attention to the largest socialist organization in the Russian Empire. The Russia-wide

Social-Democratic Labor Party, including Lenin's Bolshevik and the moderate Menshevik wing, accepted people of all nationalities, and had 31,000 members; the Polish Social-Democrats had 26,000; the Latvians 14,000, but the Jewish Social-Democratic Workers Party, the Bund, had 33,000.[10] At that time, 1906, all three ethnic parties had joined the empire-wide organization. (In proportion to population, the Latvians were the most revolutionary, followed by the Jews.) The Bolsheviks feared a repeat of the kind of situation that then existed in the Austro-Hungarian Empire, where labor unions were organized along ethnic lines: a Czech union would break a strike conducted by a union of German workers, or unite in municipal elections with other Czechs however wealthy, rather than with workers of other ethnic origins.

Lenin and his followers cited such stories in their writings as horrible examples of nationalism dividing workers living within one and the same country. They were equally outraged when speakers at a Bund conference demanded Jewish hospitals on the ground that "a patient feels more at home among his own people" and "the Jewish worker will not feel at ease among Polish workers, but will feel at ease among Jewish shopkeepers." Such issues probably arose most strongly among the Bundists because theirs was the organization of a dispersed nationality.

To Marxists this was absolutely unacceptable. Their purpose was to teach class solidarity to labor regardless of ethnic lines, while such proposals would focus the workers' attention upon members of his nationality who had "made it," as examples to be emulated.

That the real cause of ethnic hostility among workers was capitalism as a system seemed proved by the effects of unemployment, which exists under no other economic system. One consequence was that Polish workers forced Jewish workers out, justifying this in their own minds by anti-Semitism, in precisely the same manner in which certain skilled trades keep Blacks out in the U.S. to this day, justifying it to themselves by racist beliefs. Employers welcome and encourage this division in the ranks of labor. Another speech at the Bund conference responded to this: "We regard the Polish workers, who are pushing us out, as pogromists, as scabs; we do not support their strikes, we break them. Secondly, we reply to being ousted by ousting in our turn: we reply to Jewish workers not being allowed into the factories by not allowing Polish workers near the [craftsmen's] benches. . . . If we do not take this matter into our own hands the workers will follow others."

Lenin's followers argued that if workers were not organized into separate ethnic unions, as in Austria-Hungary or the self-segregated Bund in Poland, such attitudes would not have existed. U.S. labor experience confirms this. Black efforts to organize lasting segregated trade unions as a means of combating all-white organizations have never worked. However, where they and anti-racist whites won them admission into white unions or organized from the outset on an inter-racial basis, as in the auto, steel, mining and rubber industries, unions have been vastly more effective.

Lenin's party learned these lessons early in this century when it won the support of workers in the oil city of Baku, by overcoming the friction between Armenian Christian and Turkic-speaking Moslem workers, friction often characterized by massacres and shoot-outs. Such experiences had a strong influence on the policies of Lenin and his followers, then as well as later, during and after the Revolution.

Lenin continued to oppose nationalist demands that sought to advance the interests of one oppressed people at the expense of others. In 1913 a bill was proposed to permit teaching in the Ukraine in the Ukrainian language, to appoint Ukrainian teachers, to teach that language and its history, and to permit Ukrainian associations. Lenin agreed with the ultra-conservative Ukrainian Orthodox bishop, Nikon who said, in support of that bill: "the rich, beautiful, talented, flourishing and poetic Ukraine is being condemned to degeneration, gradual stultification and slow extinction" and that the issue "is one of outstanding importance." But the bishop then added that Ukrainians should be given the rights proposed in the bill because they "are not people of foreign origin" — unlike "the Jews, Poles, Georgians and others, who actually are people of foreign origin." To this Lenin responded: "the Ukrainians cannot be protected from oppression unless all peoples, without exception, are protected from all oppression, unless the concept 'people of foreign origin' is completely expunged from the life of the state, unless complete equality of rights of all nationalities is upheld."[11] He wanted these rights administered by an internationalist government, not by organizations of the various ethnic communities that would inevitably fight over turf.

In hammering out the policy regarding nationalities, a policy he would have the responsibility of carrying out only five years later, Lenin also had to combat the liberals, who were also critical of tsarism but were contending for leadership of the Russia-to-be. A major difference between them was over the issue of whether or not there should be a single official language. A liberal Moscow newspaper with the standing and much of the quality of the *New York Times* wrote, in 1913: "It is doubtful whether even an opponent of Russianization will deny that in a vast state like Russia there must be one common state language and that the language . . . can be only Russian."

Lenin objected furiously to the notion of giving Russian "any privileges whatever."[12] Yet some members of his own party, themselves from oppressed peoples, rejected nationalism and adopted internationalism in a way that made them "more Russian than the Russians." One was the outstanding Armenian Bolshevik, Stepan Shahumian, whose name is perpetuated all over the Soviet Caucasus today — he was killed soon after the Revolution by the British who invaded from Iran and temporarily overthrew the government of Soviet Azerbaijan. He did not want to deprive his own people, or any other, of the right to speak their native language, but he believed there should be an official language, Russian, which "has been and will be of great progressive importance."

Lenin replied, "I disagree emphatically. . . . The Russian language has undoubtedly been of progressive importance for the numerous small and backward nations" of the empire, but, he asked: "is not an 'official' language a stick that *drives people away* from the Russian language? Why will you not understand the *psychology* that is so important in the national question and which, if the slightest coercion is applied, besmirches, soils, nullifies the undoubtedly progressive importance of centralization, large countries and a uniform language?"[13] This has been an issue of importance in American life as well — it took nearly 50 years for Puerto Ricans to win official status for their own language, Spanish, on their own island, along with English — a quarter century after Armenian had been recognized as the official language of Armenia thanks to the revolution in the "backward" tsarist empire. (Russian is also an official language, but only in the Russian Republic of the Soviet Union.)

Five years after the Revolution, Lenin bitterly criticized his fellow-Communists Stalin (a Georgian by nationality), and Dzerzhinsky (who was Polish), for what he termed their "truly Great-Russian nationalist" insensitivity to the ethnic feelings of the peoples of the Caucasus (including the Georgians) on these very matters.[14]

The complexity of the entire problem is nowhere illustrated better than in Lenin's views regarding assimilation. He favored it, despite all his stress on the *rights* of ethnic groups to their own languages. He cited two nationalities:

> The best of the Jews, those who are celebrated in world history, and who have given the world foremost leaders of democracy and socialism, have never clamored against assimilation. Only those who contemplate the "backside" of Jewry with reverential awe shout against assimilation. . . . An approximate idea of the . . . process of assimilation that is taking place under the present conditions of advanced capitalism can be obtained . . . from the immigration statistics of the United States. . . . New York State . . . is like a mill which grinds up national distinctions.
>
> . . . A well defined process of accelerated economic development has been going on in the South, i.e., the Ukraine, and this is attracting . . . peasants and workers from Great-Russia. . . . The "assimilation" —within these limits— of the Great-Russian and Ukrainian proletariat is an undoubted fact. *And this* fact is *certainly* progressive. Capitalism replaces the dull, bigoted, stick-in-the-mud muzhik [peasant] of the Great-Russian and Ukrainian backwoods with a mobile proletarian whose conditions of life break down . . . ethnic narrowmindedness, both Great-Russian and Ukrainian. Let us assume that in time there will be a state frontier between Great-Russia and the Ukraine,* In such a case, too, the historically progressive nature of "assimilation" between the Great-Russian and Ukrainian workers will be beyond doubt, just as the grinding together of nations in America is progressive.[15]

Several of the present Soviet leadership, chief among them Chernenko, are products of this process. Of Ukrainian name, his family's assimilation took place in Siberia, to which it had moved.

Assimilation is a living issue in the USSR to this day. On the one hand, urban nationalities, such as the Jews, have assimilated to a very high degree in the past 50 years, including much intermarriage, something they once rejected to protect their ethnic existence. In the Ukraine, Ukrainians who have moved to town now tend to speak Russian in the areas which have been Soviet since the Revolution, but in the countryside they retain their own language, as do city people in the West Ukraine, which has been Soviet only since World War II.

In Armenia, on the other hand, the native language remains universal, because Armenians are the overwhelming majority in the cities as well as in villages. Nationalists — Ukrainian, Jewish and other — believe these processes endanger the existence of their nationalities. To which anthropologists reply that assimilation has always occurred in world history and always will, so long as nations

---

*Under his leadership such a frontier was instituted in response to Ukrainian demands five years later.

exist. The real issue is the extent to which the assimilation may be forced. This always engenders some degree of nationalism in response. Current Soviet scholarship seeks to grapple with this problem,[16] and the political leadership is trying to formulate guidance, as indicated by a Chernenko speech on the revision of the Communist Party platform ("Program") underway in 1984.[17]

Before the Revolution, another issue was that of maintaining ethnic culture. This was argued with particular vehemence by certain Ukrainians. Lenin's reply was, in essence, *which* Ukrainian culture? "There are two nations in every modern nation. . . . There are two national cultures in every national culture," an idea advanced half a century earlier by the British Prime Minister Disraeli in a novel which spoke of the nation of the rich and that of the poor. Lenin sought to stress everything in culture that would unite workers across ethnic lines, and attacked whatever would strengthen nationalist antagonisms. Anthropologists today recognize the concept of sub-cultures, but debate on this issue has continued throughout the history of the Soviet Union. It even cost lives on the eve of World War II and again when the Cold War began, when Stalin worried whether nationalists would be loyal. In its crudest form, the argument ran: if a cultural figure had not come from the working class or the peasantry, how could his work reflect their interests?

Lenin quite often used the word "barbarism" to describe the Russians' own level of civilization before the Revolution. Afterward, he argued that the working people, to raise themselves from that level, should make themselves the heirs of all that was good in human achievement. It made no difference, he said, if the great art works of the Renaissance, for example, had been financed by religious or other wealth obtained by squeezing the poor. But the question remained: what was "good"? Folk epics, from Homer onward, describe wars with neighboring peoples. But what if those peoples live side by side, within a single multi-national state?

Suppose a figure is a hero to his own people but a monster to another? This was the case with the Ukrainian Cossack Bohdan Hmelnitsky, who led that people against the Polish landowning nobility—but also conducted pogroms against the Jews. Or consider a people that has been told it had no history or achievements, or that it is "primitive." What mix of emphasis upon its own creative culture to support its self-esteem and that of others is needed to produce diversity within unity, and not nationalism? The post-revolutionary Soviet Union has dealt with these issues in different ways at different times; Marxists hold that truth is never abstract, always specific. The USSR has also dealt differently with different nations or ethnic groups at the same time. In the U.S., what Latinos need is not precisely the same as what Blacks need, but they share a history of ethnic oppression and neglect of their needs and rights.

As cultural figures from the different nationalities of the Russian Empire are not familiar to us, it helps to consider more familiar personalities. When Leadbelly, the Black musician, sang "It's a Bourgeois Town" about Washington, D. C., that was fine by Lenin's criterion; "Yaller Gal" was acceptable because it dealt with personal life in an ethnic framework. But in film, there was Stepin Fetchit — the very name ridiculed Blacks — who was always cast as a character that shuffled and scratched his head and was afraid of the dark and snakes. Should Blacks be proud that one Black had made it in a medium otherwise closed to them, or should they be outraged because he reinforced white feelings of superiority, and Black feelings of inferiority? The same issue continues to face minority peoples, most recently in TV comedies.

Perhaps one internationally understandable example from Soviet experience will do. Shakespeare is extremely well-known and performed in theater, opera, and film in the USSR, in dozens of languages. There is one exception, however: *The Merchant of Venice* has been prohibited since the Revolution because of its stereotype of the Jewish usurer demanding a pound of flesh.

While Lenin's objective for dispersed *minorities* was equality of rights, his target for oppressed *geographic nations* was self-determination, up to and including the right to secede. Pre-revolutionary Poland was divided among Russia, Germany, and Austria-Hungary. The Polish Social-Democrats opposed the notion of self-determination because they feared that nationalist elements would use it to establish a government that would maintain capitalism. Poland later had such a regime for a quarter of a century. Lenin argued against this holding that human progress depended upon destroying imperialism and colonialism, and that self-determination as a goal would move colonial and other subject nations to action in their entirety as nations. His view was that if this were led by Marxists of such nations, it would also bring them to socialism.

The Poles, Jews, and Latvians — the nationalities among whom socialist organization was strong — together were little more than one-fifth of the *non*-Russian peoples of the empire, and only a ninth of its total population. Marxist convictions were disproportionately strong among them because Poland and Latvia were the most industrialized areas, and the Jews were almost totally urban. Most of the other peoples had hardly entered the industrial era, had no wage-earning class to speak of, and were overwhelmingly peasant. Socialism in the Marxist sense, which conceives of power passing from the hands of essentially industrial capitalists and the banks financing them to a government acting for the workers employed in industry, was an abstraction to peoples who had neither capitalists nor their workers. For them, the economic aspect of their ethnic oppression lay in deprivation of land.

The unsuccessful 1905-1907 revolution did result in the establishment of a parliament, the Duma. That Duma was powerless, but members could at least place their complaints on the record. After 1905, a representative from the Bashkirs (a Moslem people at the south end of the border between Europe and Asia) said the government had stolen 5,400,000 acres of land from that nationality alone, and demanded it back. He complained that individual Russian officials and high police officers had been granted as much as 5,000 to 15,000 acres each, and that the governor-general of the region had told a Tatar applying for land that only persons of the Christian faith could homestead.

Complaints such as this made Lenin's party recognize that, in the agricultural Russian Empire, the nationalities issue was, in its economic aspect, fundamentally a question of landownership. For American Indians, and Blacks in the rural South the relationship between ethnic oppression and land is equally clear.

The analogy is not just my own. Lenin followed the status of American Blacks very closely. In 1913 he wrote a very brief article that is worth reproducing in full:

RUSSIANS AND NEGROES

What a strange comparison, the reader may think. How can a race be compared with a nation?

It is a permissible comparison. The Negroes were the last to be freed from slavery, and they still bear, more than anyone else, the cruel marks of slavery — even in advanced countries — for capitalism has no "room" for emancipation except as a legal matter, and it curtails even the latter in every possible way.

With regard to the Russians, history records that they were freed, "almost," from the bondage of *serfdom* in 1861. It was about the same time, following the civil war against the American slave-owners, that North America's Negroes were freed from slavery.

The emancipation of the American slaves took place in a manner less like a "reform" than that of the Russian slaves.

That is why today, half a century later, the Russians still show *many more* traces of slavery than the Negroes. Indeed, it would be more accurate to speak of institutions and not merely of traces. But in this short article we shall limit ourselves to a small illustration of what we have said, namely, the question of literacy. It is known that illiteracy is one of the marks of slavery. In a country oppressed by pashas, Purishkeviches [a proto-fascist and anti-Semitic rabble-rouser] and the like, the majority of the population cannot be literate.

In Russia *73 percent are illiterate*, exclusive of children under nine years of age.

Among U.S. Negroes, *44½ percent* were illiterate in 1900.

Such a scandalously high percentage of illiterates is a disgrace to a civilized, advanced country like the North American republic. Furthermore, everyone knows that the position of the Negroes in America *in general* is one unworthy of a civilized country — capitalism *cannot* give either *complete* emancipation or even complete equality.

It is instructive that among the whites in America illiterates number no more than six percent. But if we divide America into what were formerly slave-holding areas (an American "Russia") and non-slave-holding areas (an American non-Russia), we shall find 11-12 percent illiterates *among the whites* in the former and 4-6 percent in the latter areas!

The proportion of illiterates *among the whites* is *twice as high* in the former slave-holding areas. It is not only the Negroes that show the vestiges of slavery!

Shame on America for the plight of the Negroes![18]

Returning to Lenin's opening question, "how can a race be compared to a nation?", it is interesting to look at a list of the forms of national oppression drawn up by Stalin in the same year, which clearly applies to Blacks as slaves, and, in many respects, for a hundred years after emancipation: "Restriction of freedom of movement, repression of language, restriction of franchise, closing of schools, religious restrictions, and so on."[19]

In the East, among most of the Turkic and Iranian-speaking peoples in the Russian Empire, where capitalism was not yet so widespread, class struggle between workers and employers was far less important than feelings of resentment against Russian rule. Consequently, a Pan-Islamic movement arose which took the Moslem religion of many different peoples as a binding factor, opposing them all to tsarism, and to its official Orthodox Church.

In short, because Russia was an empire, ethnic equality was much more a question of the right of self-determination and secession for *geographic* nations than equality of rights for people living intermixed among others. This question is still very much alive in Puerto Rico — independence, statehood, or the present commonwealth status. Lenin provided his answer in another part of his 1913 letter to Shahumian, whose position was "statehood.":

"We are in favor of the *right* to secession (and not *in favor* of everyone's *seceding*!). . . . In general we are opposed to secession. But we stand for the *right* to secede owing to reactionary, Great-Russian nationalism, which has so besmirched the idea of national coexistence that sometimes *closer* ties will be established *after* free secession! The right to self-determination is an *exception* to our general premise of centralization."[20]*

With a centralized union of republics, the Soviets have been able to place the common interests of geographic nations above factors that might divide them, and to influence development so as to raise more backward republics up toward the level of the more advanced. This has avoided a situation like the one which exists in Yugoslavia. That is also a federation of geographic nations, but it allows them to compete with each other economically, and also allows the workers to own an enterprise independent of the central government. As a result, the living standard in the most advanced ethnic republic is three times as high as in the most underdeveloped. The workers in the former quite literally exploit those in the latter by building branches of worker-owned industries in them and paying the very much lower local wage.

There is a tendency everywhere for numerically larger oppressed peoples to be so intensely conscious of their own problems that they look with disdain upon, or ignore, smaller ones. Rosa Luxemburg, pre-revolutionary leader of the Polish Marxists, demanded autonomy for Poland — but not for the Lithuanians. Census figures showed the Lithuanians to be a minority in each existing province, so she concluded that there was no Lithuanian nation, but only a dispersed minority — a rural equivalent of the situation of the Jews. Lenin replied that if she had studied the statistics, not for entire provinces

---

*An American Black, who supports the idea of a Republic of New Africa, which demands the Deep South as a Black homeland, read this passage and found himself in agreement with this 70-year-old idea of Lenin's. Blacks free from the dominance of U.S. racism in a territory of their own, he reasons, might very well choose closer ties with the rest of what is now the U.S. in what would then be a *voluntary* association.

but for "counties" within them, she would have found solid blocks of counties neighboring each other across "state" lines in which Lithuanians were a majority, a situation similar to that now existing in states of our Deep South.

American Indians will be interested in Lenin's rejoinder to a Bundist named Medem, who argued, before the Revolution, that peoples numbering half a million to two million were "too small" to enjoy territorial rights. "Why there cannot be autonomous national areas with populations not only of half a million, but even of 50,000 — why such areas cannot unite in the most diverse ways with neighboring areas of different dimensions in one autonomous krai (region) if this is convenient . . . remains the secret of the Bundist Medem."[21] That is precisely the way the USSR is organized today: prerevolutionary "state" lines were disregarded in order to give geographic peoples stretches of territory providing self-rule on matters of interest to them. In one case, a territory with an Azerbaijani majority which is separated from the bulk of Azerbaijan by Armenia has nonetheless been made part of the Azerbaijan Soviet Republic. This "island" has only a quarter million people; had it been made part of Armenia for the sake of geographic convenience, there would have been no end to the hostility between the Turkic-speaking Moslem Azerbaijanis and the Christian Armenians. Today one gets no sense of any such feeling in visiting either of those republics. Some "National Areas" have fewer than 50,000 inhabitants, though none are internally segregated or limited to people of any ethnic affiliation.

The Soviet example has affected other countries, even totally non-socialist ones, in many ways. Perhaps the most visible is the United Nations, which includes as members many countries smaller than the national areas of the USSR. In the pre-Soviet era of world-wide imperialism that was unthinkable, except for freak situations left over from feudal times, such as Andorra, a tiny principality between France and Spain.

Armenians will recognize Lenin's foresight to have been quite remarkable. In the same article, he wrote: "It is extremely important to create autonomous areas of even the smallest dimensions . . . towards which the members of the given nationality scattered in different parts of the country, or even of the world, could 'gravitate'." About 220,000 Armenians have *im*migrated to Soviet Armenia from foreign countries, including some from the U.S., and hundreds of thousands more have come from other parts of the Soviet Union. Yet a million more are sufficiently assimilated to life in Russia proper, in the Ukraine, etc., to prefer living there. The same factor has been operative among Jews; from most countries, including the U.S. and USSR, only a small minority have gone to Israel. The great majority want to remain where they are, though they are interested in what happens in Israel, and some, especially in the U.S., give Israel political and other support. The Soviet support for a separate Palestinian state reflects its own experience at the time of the Revolution, and the success of solutions such as that for the Azerbaijanis encircled by Armenian-populated territory.

Lenin's party was a small minority in pre-revolutionary Russia. We focus on his views because the Soviet Union of today has been shaped essentially on them. Parties that had vastly more influence than Lenin's proved unable to deal with Russia's crisis and disappeared from the scene. The most important in the pre-war years was the Constitutional Democratic Party, which advocated liberal capitalism and ruled immediately after the tsar was overthrown. On the fundamental issue of the colonies and semi-colonies that comprised half the population of the Russian Empire, its newspaper stated that members of the party "have never pledged themselves to advocate the right of 'nations to secede' from the Russian state,"[22] but only freedom of languages. Lenin did not mince words in responding:

"Herein lies one of the root causes of your chauvinism and of your ideological and political alliance with the Purishkeviches. . . . The Purishkeviches and their class inculcate in the ignorant masses the 'hard-line' belief that it is 'right' to 'grab 'em and hold 'em,'"[23] the non-Russian peoples.

Reading the records of that far-off time and place, it is amazing to see how closely the acts of governments seeking to maintain the dominance of one ethnic group parallel each other. It has now been established in response to persistent protests and research by U.S. Black and Latino organizations that census gathering techniques through 1970 deliberately under-counted those groups, for both economic reasons (to reduce the amount of federal aid) and political ones. Here is Lenin, in 1914, complaining about exactly the same thing:

"In Russia, even according to official, i.e., palpably exaggerated statistics, which are faked to suit the 'government's plans,' the Great-Russians constitute no more than 43 percent of the entire population of the country."[24] He attacked the government for seeking to rule on behalf of what was, by its own admission, a minority—but he never failed to point out that it was not the Russian people that gained by this but primarily the landlord class.

The government tried to overcome this problem by forcing the Ukrainians to regard themselves as Russian. For example it sought to ban celebrations in honor of the hundredth anniversary of the birth of Taras Shevchenko, a poet, painter, and revolutionary democrat whose picture hung in every Ukrainian home. Lenin waxed merrily sarcastic over this gross insensitivity:

> The ban on the celebrations in honor of Shevchenko was such an excellent, splendid, exceptionally happy and well-chosen measure as far as anti-government agitation is concerned that no better agitation could be conceived. I think that none of our best Social-Democratic agitators against the government could ever have achieved such sensational success in so short a time as was achieved by this measure in rousing opposition to the government.[25]

Four months after this was written, World War I broke out. Within a year, just south of Russia's border, a million and a half Armenians had been exterminated or starved to death by the Turkish Empire in the first mass genocide of the 20th century. Another year, and Russian manpower losses in the war were so great that the tsar tried to draft colonial Central Asians — for labor service, as he didn't dare put modern weapons in their hands. They revolted, spontaneously and without organization, over a huge area. And although they were put down by massacre and cruelty, this was the handwriting on the wall; one more year, and the Russian armies themselves were in revolt, joined by starving soldiers' wives and the workers of the cities. The monarchy was overthrown in March 1917. On November 7 of that same year, the Communists came to power. The time for talk was over. Now they had to prove to the non-Russian majority of the people that they meant what they said.

NOTES

1. V.I. Lenin, *Collected Works* (Moscow: Progress, 1966), XXXVI, pp. 607-608.
2. *Soviet Life*, August, 1971, p. 33.
3. F. Halle, *Women in the Soviet East* (New York: Dutton, 1938), pp. 17-18.
4. D.M. Lang, *A Modern History of Soviet Georgia* (New York: 1962), p. 131.

5. C. Lamont, *The Peoples of the Soviet Union* (New York: Harcourt, Brace, 1944), p. 149.

6. J.V. Stalin, *Works* (Moscow: Foreign Languages Publishing House, 1953), II, p. 305.

7. V.I. Lenin, *Questions of National Policy and Proletarian Internationalism* (Moscow: Foreign Languages Publishing House, 1959), p. 31.

8. Lenin, *Works*, XX, pp. 172-173.

9. *San Francisco Examiner*, April 19, 1981.

10. Lenin, *Works*, XI, p. 195.

11. Ibid., XIX, pp. 379-381.

12. Lenin, *Questions of National Policy*, p. 25.

13. Lenin, *Works*, XIX, p. 499.

14. Ibid., XXXVI, pp. 605-606˙

15. Ibid., XX, pp. 29-31 *passim*.

16. M.I. Kulichenko, ed., *Natsional'nye otnosheniia v razvitom sotsialisticheskom obshchestve* (Moscow: Mysl', 1977), pp. 147-148 and *passim*.

17. *Pravda*, April 26, 1984, "V TsK KPSS," p. 1.

18. Lenin, *Works*, SVIII, pp. 543-544.

19. Stalin, *Works*, II, p. 316.

20. Lenin, *Works*, XIX, p. 501.

21. Ibid., XX, p. 49.

22. Ibid., p. 57.

23. Ibid.

24. Ibid., p. 218.

25. Ibid., p. 219.

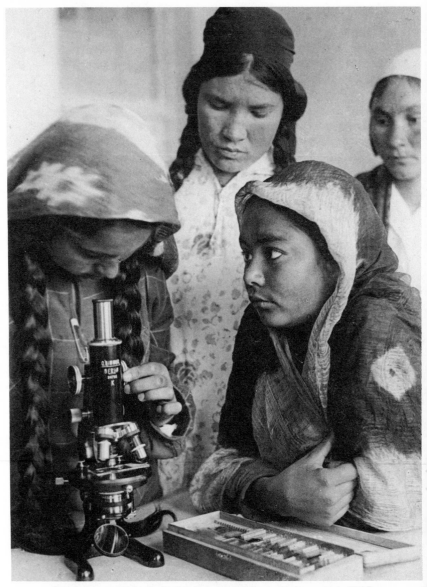

Beginnings: Medical Technical School, Turkmenia, 1937.

5

Revolution:
Time to Deliver

The Provisional Government that took over upon abdication of Tsar Nicholas II in March 1917 did not act decisively to solve the problems that had come to a head.[1] Most important of these was how to seek peace in World War I, then in its third year, a war in which the backward Russian Empire had lost more millions killed and wounded than any of its allies or its enemies. Next was the demand of the peasants, in that overwhelmingly agricultural country, that landowners' land be turned over to those who worked it. A third was simply providing bread to feed a population starving — partly because the country's meager resources had been diverted to the army, but increasingly because the absence of men and horses from the farms meant that production could not be kept up. The fourth was the demand for independence or restoration of rights by the conquered nations within the Russian Empire, and for equal rights by minorities dispersed therein.

Of the Ukrainians, Lenin wrote at this time: "Accursed tsarism made the Great-Russians executioners of the Ukrainian people, and fomented in them a hatred for those who even forbade Ukrainian children to speak and study in their native tongue."[2]

With respect to the massive stealing of Bashkir land, described in the previous chapter, he had written: "This is a tidbit of colonial policy that will stand comparison to any of the feats performed . . . in . . . Africa."[3] That indictment is borne out by the fact that in some counties the Bashkir death rate reached genocidal levels.

The Ukraine is on the western frontier. Bashkiria is in the Ural Mountains separating Europe and Asia, Kirgizia deep in Central Asia, on China's westernmost border. Just a year before the overthrow of the tsar, the Russian Army had taken hundreds of thousands of sheep from the nomadic Kirgiz, and paid in rubles. But in that subsistence economy, large sums of money were meaningless: there was nothing to buy. Sheep's wool provided clothing and shelter, sheep's milk and meat were food, sheep's intestines became bags, their sinews served as cord. With the inefficiency of that day, of that country, and of armies in general, the sheep had been slaughtered by the tens of thousands before provision for storage was made, and the Kirgiz had seen them rot uselessly, while they themselves hungered. On top of this came the decree conscripting Central Asians for unarmed labor service at the front, thousands of miles away. A rebellion broke out which "took the form of an indiscriminate slaughter of Russian peasants."[4] As a Russian geologist told Anna Louise Strong in Kirgizia, a dozen years later, perhaps 10,000 were wiped out. The Russian colonial occupation army, plus divisions moved from the front, responded ruthlessly. About a million of the nomadic Kirgiz and Kazakhs — one-out-of-ten people in the affected area — fled to Chinese Turkestan, where they were sold into slavery.

At the very opposite end of the country, north of Leningrad, bordering Finalnd, live the "white" European Karelians. Their language resembles Finnish, but "To sell a Bible written in Finnish was punishable by exile. . . . Children were punished for speaking Karelian even in the schoolgrounds."[5] (Native Americans have had that experience in Bureau of Indian Affairs schools, and Chicanos did until very recent years.) Those Karelian children were lucky simply to be in school at all: in Bashkiria, of 4,778 children in secondary schools in 1910, only *ten* had been Bashkirs.[6]

This was the reality when the tsar was overthrown. When, after eight months, the Provisional Government failed to move on these issues, and refused to withdraw from the world war, the people lost patience. Among the industrial workers in the major cities, and also among the soldiers and sailors, who were still being killed, the Communists (then the Bolshevik wing of the Social-Democratic Party) won great support. This was based on their argument that nothing had changed because continuation of the war, of landlordism, and of food hoarding were in the interests of the capitalist and landlord classes. They also pointed out that even the most Left of the governing parties thought Russia was not ripe for socialism, and was therefore committed on principle to seeking only reforms within the existing socio-economic system.

On November 7, 1917, the Communists seized power with the aid of armed workers in the capital, sailors and vessels of the Baltic Fleet, and soldiers in urban garrisons. They proceeded literally overnight to deliver the land to the peasants, bid for peace in the war, and distribute what bread was available. As a consequence, in four months time their rule spread over nearly the entire immense empire, though they had no army of their own, and there were millions of armed men who could have opposed the regime.

The Communists' easy early success also came because the Provisional Government had brought little or no significant change from tsarist oppression. The Ukraine (with nearly 30,000,000 people) and Poland were the largest non-Russian countries in the empire. When the tsar abdicated, a Ukrainian congress, the Central Rada, came into being much like the Continental Congress during the Revolutionary War. But the Provisional Government claimed the Ukraine's richest industrial area, and much else, as Russia, and appointed an official as supreme authority over the Ukraine. Lenin argued: "Force will not check the Ukrainians. It will only embitter them. Accede to the Ukrainians, and you will open the way to mutual confidence and brotherly union between the two nations on the basis of equality!"[7] A few weeks earlier he had spelled out his own program: "If there is a Ukrainian republic and a Russian republic, there will be closer contact and greater trust between the two."[8]

A similar situation arose in Finland, which asked only for restoration of the rights enjoyed before annexation to Russia. The Provisional Government rejected this. Lenin said: "We are for giving the Finns complete freedom, because then there will be greater trust in Russian democracy and the Finns will not separate."[9] They did secede in 1917, but remained separate only because after 1918, the Western allies of World War I left an enemy — German — division intact so it could help the anti-socialist element in Finland win the civil war. After its victory a rightist government under Marshal Mannerheim massacred the defeated local socialists much as Pinochet did in Chile in 1973.

In Central Asia the Provisional Government of March-November 1917 actually left in command the tsar's general who had slaughtered the indigenous rebels the previous year. In addition, that government's language policy was unacceptable. *Language is a much greater natural barrier than race.* People of different races can communicate if they speak the same language; people of the same race cannot, if their languages differ. The Provisional Government had extended recognition to non-Russian languages only in private affairs. Joseph Stalin, who was to be the Soviet Commissar for Nationalities, immediately took issue with this, in one of the earliest legal issues of *Pravda* after the overthrow of the tsar: "But what about the regions with compact majorities of non-Russian citizens whose language is not Russian (Transcaucasia, Turkestan, the Ukraine, Lithuania, etc.)? There is no doubt that they will have (must have!) their parliaments. . . . Is it the idea of the Provisional Government . . . to deprive these regions of the right to conduct 'affairs' . . . in their native languages . . . in their [own] institutions?"[10]

But the Provisional Government could not live up to its pledges of ethnic equality because the liberals in power did not actually believe that the non-Russians, in most cases, were the Russians' equals. The Provisional Government had qualitatively the same attitude of Great-Russian superiority as the tsarist monarchy it had replaced. In the words of a Soviet anthropologist; "At that time things were interpreted as follows: everything Russian is good, everything Komi bad. Masterpieces of ethnic art were held to have no value."[11] Referring to the judgment of a prerevolutionary anthropologist, Smirnov, she writes indignantly: "the Permiak (Komi), allegedly at the 'embryonic level of creativity,' was not quite the ignoramus Smirnov conceived him to be." When a certain motif was found to be shared both by Russian folk art to the west, and the Komi, it was taken for granted that the latter had learned it from the former. But the recent study finds: "there are no grounds for saying that the motif was taken from the northern Great-Russians." A similar neighboring people, the Mari, had gloves 500 years before the rest of Eastern Europe.

The Komi and Mari are perhaps more blonde and Nordic than the Russians, but the prejudice here did not need to be based on race: it was colonial and served to excuse exploitation.

While the Komi are somewhat fewer than American reservation Indians today, the millions of Turkic-speaking people along the Volga in the heart of European Russia are as numerous as Jews in the U.S. One of them, the Tatars, actually ruled over the Russians for 200 years, but the tables were turned several hundred years ago, and the general Russian belief was that this proved them superior. The achievements of the Volga peoples were put down, yet these nationalities had brick buildings with central heating about a thousand years ago. Some of the ancient churches of which the

Russians are proudest were built of stone cut by ethnic Volga craftsmen and hauled to Russian territory.[12]

The Tatars were nomads when they conquered the Volga peoples, but adopted the existing urban culture, with its thousands of towns, and it is possible that the Russians learned to build with brick from Tatars; the Russian word for brick is of Turkic origin, and Tatar is a Turkic language.* The earliest Communist historian, Pokrovsky, held this view, even though the archeological proof was not yet available when he wrote.[13]

The Tatar, Komi, and other subject peoples were not familiar with these points of scholarship in 1917. They knew perfectly well, however, that the liberal government looked down upon their cultures as essentially worthless, primitive, and savage, and were therefore in no way moved to support that regime.

When the Communists took power, they were at first in no better position to command the support of non-Russians. Although they were not all Russians, they were, with very few exceptions, what the Moslem peoples classed as Europeans. When confronted with the accomplished fact of an autonomous Bashkir nationalist government, established between the overthrow of the tsar and the founding of the Communist government, Lenin recognized that, "in these remote places the name 'Great-Russian' means to the Bashkir 'oppressor,' 'swindler.' We have to consider this and we have to struggle against it. But this is a long-term proposition. This is not the kind of thing that anybody will eliminate by decree. We have to be exceedingly cautious in this matter."[15]

On another occasion he had said: "We do not regard the Bashkir movement as a counterrevolutionary movement directed against us. . . . We believe that the national [liberation] movements of the peoples of the East are entirely natural and very necessary. The peoples of the East come to the social revolution only through the national [liberation] revolution,"[16] and "the Bashkir movement, if it is granted the autonomy it demands, will not be directed against the Soviets but will constitute a tremendous force in the struggle against Dutov," a Russian Cossack counterrevolutionary general operating in that area.[17]

The Bashkirs were the first indigenous people living in an island of territory within Russia to have their autonomy recognized. But for those not surrounded or outnumbered by Russians, within

---

*There are thousands of Turkic words in the Russian language.[14]

their own traditional territory, the issue was not autonomy but actual independence and whether or not to secede, as Lenin had predicted in the endless theoretical battles of prerevolutionary years. Poland and Finland did secede, and the Soviet government recognized those acts as it had promised in its platform. Lenin granted Poland independence even before a Polish government was organized. When one appeared, it sought to regain as much of its 18th-century empire as possible. Armed and provided military advisors by France, after Germany surrendered in 1918, Poland took Lithuania's largest city and capital, Vilnius, and held it and large territories with Ukrainian and Belorussian majority populations until 1940. Poland's rulers were blind to the contradiction between independence for their own previously subject people and Polish rule over non-Polish areas.

All this was part of an enormously complicated struggle that also involved the Ukraine, the Baltic states (Latvia, Lithuania, Estonia), and the Trans-Caucasus (Armenia, Georgia, Azerbaijan). It involved pro- and anti-Soviet parties within those nations, divided more or less along lines of economic class. There was also military intervention by 14 countries, including both Russia's former allies in World War I (the United States, Great Britain, France, etc.) and her enemies (Germany and Turkey, chiefly) — all now joined by the desire to prevent the establishment of any government that would seek to prove people could live without capitalism. Finally, it came to involve the Soviet government itself, which argued: that if world capitalism could aid anti-communist forces, Moscow could aid pro-communists.

Entire libraries have been written about those struggles. The United States was confident that the Soviet government would not last, and wanted to have the inside track with whatever non-Communist Russian government might succeed as heir to the old empire. So Washington did not favor independence of Russia's former subject peoples for fear that would antagonize such a government. This attitude, and those taken by other Western countries, plus Japan, China, and Turkey — all of which put armies on Soviet soil — strengthened Lenin's position. He argued that the intervention proved that no abstract independence for the countries once under the tsar was really possible: they had to choose between what we would now call neo-colonialism under capitalist powers or association with Russia to develop socialism. He promised that in the latter case exploitation of one nation by another would cease, and that the language, culture, and territorial boundaries of each would be respected.

The results in each case depended upon the complicated combination of forces involved, domestic and foreign. There were not, and could not be, any nice, clean, honest elections, supervised by impartial honest ballot associations. The fighting, which lasted three years in most places (and didn't totally end until 1931 on the mountainous Afghan border), was as bitter and cruel as in the U.S. Civil War. The very real memory of this struggle is the historical origin of the impenetrable guarding of Soviet and East European borders that exists today.

We have already described what happened in Poland and Finland. When the Civil-War-and-Intervention ended, essentially in 1920, Latvia and Estonia were independent, thanks to the work of that German division which the Allies allowed to operate in the region, in cooperation with the British Navy. Those countries remained greatly dependent upon England until World War II. Lithuania was in the same general situation, except that Poland occupied her capital. Bessarabia, today called Moldavia, had been taken by the Romanian monarchy which treated it as a colony. But most of the Ukraine, most of Belorussia, nearly all of the Caucasus (though the larger part of Armenia was taken by Turkey) — Georgia, Azerbaijan — and nearly all of the former Central Asian Moslem colonies of the tsar wound up Soviet.

Russia proper was quite literally starved during the Civil War. The bread ration — there was nothing else at times — went down to four ounces a day in the biggest cities. It had no friend or ally — *the West refused to permit even medical instruments and drugs to enter Soviet territory.* The Soviet government was able to organize an army only because the peasants wanted to defend the land they had been given. Industry slowed to a standstill because its raw materials bases were in enemy hands for long periods. Many workers who were not Communists fighting at the fronts drifted back to their home villages in the hope of finding something to eat.

Geographically crazy as it may seem, Siberia was for a period in the hands of a Czechoslovak anti-Communist army consisting of former war prisoners. The other anti-Communist armies were also all led by professional officers, backed by British or French military advisers, and equipped by those countries with U.S. aid. The Red Army, on the other hand, was led by a complete civilian, Leon

Trotsky and another civilian, Joseph Stalin, was in charge of
various fronts while still another, Lenin, made the final decisions.
Not one of them had ever been even an army private, although they
all listened carefully to those professional officers who were loyal.
By the time the fighting was over, a one-day railroad trip took eight
to ten days, so great had been the destruction of bridges, tunnels,
signals, locomotives, cars.

In all, 65,000,000 non-Russians, most living as compact territorial
majorities bordering the outside world, wound up Soviet in the
1920s. Under the conditions described, the only rational explanation
for this is that the great bulk of them wanted it that way. Those
decisions were not made quietly under Robert's Rules of Order or
by consensus, but with a stupendous amount of debate — family by
family, village by village, regiment by regiment, town by town —
probably to a degree without precedent in human history. The
arguments were usually not over broad concepts of political theory,
although there was a surprising leaven of that. The American
Revolution stimulated the whole people of that day to make up its
mind about Tom Paine's *Common Sense*, which sold half a million
copies in a population of no more than 3,000,000, including babies
and the illiterate. After the Communists took power, the same role
was played by the "Declaration of Rights of the Peoples of Russia,"
which was issued within one week of the formation of the Soviet
government, and later by the appeal "To all the Working Population
Among the Moslems of Russia and the East," which was adopted
at a conference in Baku.*

The Declaration proclaimed all peoples equal and sovereign. It
said that each could secede or not as it chose, that all privileges or
restrictions based on nationality or religion were abolished. For
peoples not comprising majorities in their native territories or with
no territories of their own, it guaranteed: "freedom of development
for the national minorities and ethnographic groups inhabiting the
territory of Russia . . . " The very first Soviet cabinet, established
the day after the Revolution, included a department (Commissariat) of
Nationalities. It was headed by Joseph Stalin, not Russian, but a
Georgian, who had authored the accepted Communist analysis of
this subject four years earlier.[18]

Russian oppression was only one obstacle to establishing har-

---

*Attended by the American journalist and Communist John Reed, and pictured in
the recent film, "Reds."

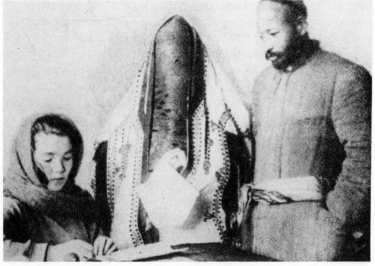

American-Russian Institute

Paranja-wearing Central Asian bride before unveiling movement of 1927.

monious relations with the other nationalities and to overcoming underdevelopment. Their own differing levels of development was another. Opium addiction was widespread in Central Asia.[19] A scholar of Kazakh nationality has described the condition of his people before the Revolution when they numbered 4,000,000: 15 percent of the people had 60 percent of the livestock, and these were nomads for whom livestock was everything. "Blood vengeance, raids to seize herds, attacks on grounds of tribal and clan hostility were frequent phenomena, and persons committing such deeds believed that they, in defending clan and personal interests were engaging in acts 'permitted by custom and tradition'."[20] Under *adat* and *shariat*, Moslem customary and religious law, the marrying of minors not even in their teens, polygamy, and compulsory marriage of a widow to her husband's nearest surviving male relative "were not only not regarded as crimes but were sanctified and legitimized. . . . Attempts to violate the norms of the *adat* and to challenge backward customs . . . were punished in the very cruelest fashion," like stoning to death for adultery, as is still the case in Saudi Arabia and Iran. This legitimized oppression of women was universal among all Moslem nationalities in the Empire, who then numbered 15,000,000. As a problem for the new government, the situation was made more difficult by the fact that these women themselves accepted it. A female Uzbek poet reminiscing about that period wrote in 1970:

"The centuries of oppression, the Koran and Shariat placed their dark imprint upon the psychology of women themselves. Being sequestered in women's quarters seemed to many of them a norm of life, submission to the will of fate. It was necessary to overcome the internal inertia of the woman herself."[21]

When a mass movement among women to take off their veils developed a decade after the Revolution, hundreds were murdered or seriously injured.[22]

The persistence of habitual beliefs and notions led to some truly ludicrous situations in the early postrevolutionary period as the desire for social change—or, in some cases, a self-serving adaptation to change—combined with habitual notions. In 1925 a young Ukrainian (later to become a distinguished historian) took a job as village librarian among the Islamic Adygei people in the Caucasus. (Libraries were one of the first means of bringing enlightenment to the countryside.) He had also been appointed to head the local Young Communist League. When he entered the room for the first meeting, a virtual brawl was going on. Through a translator, he learned that Adygei society had had castes, as in India: there was a caste of slaves, one of peasants of various status, one of nobility, and one of princely clans. Children of all of these castes belonged to the Young Communist League, and those from the nobility had tried to grab the front benches in accordance with their ancient privilege, but their ex-slaves and general peasantry resisted, and he was witnessing what amounted to class struggle inside a Communist organization![23]*

The same historian recalls another meeting, when a heated discussion was under way until the muezzin's call to prayer was heard, and the most zealous Moslems dashed out to perform their devotions. He also witnessed weddings involving mock armed clashes between squadrons of mountaineers on horseback and pre-Islamic

---

*Reading this helped me understand the problems reported in the 1960s at Moscow's Lumumba University and the Leningrad Academy of Arts with some African students with high status.

shamanist cures with witch-doctors driving out the devil by music and dances.

His work involved helping to establish membership organizations consisting of persons of their own ethnic groups and conducted in their own languages. This is why, as appointed temporary leader, this Ukrainian outsider needed an interpreter — no one would have come to a meeting in his language because they knew only their own. That is also why, in the early years, members of different castes and classes were allowed to join the Young Communist League. There was a wall of hostility against Russians, whose conquest of them was within living memory — he met a man in his eighties who personally remembered the war in which the Russians had seized the Caucasus, and had himself been in raids burning Cossack villages and taking captives. In this atmosphere, any indigenous person who saw merit in the new society was welcome to join, though none yet understood its principles well enough to head its local branch.

At this time — 1925 — "USSR" was a new term. From 1917 to 1922, the striving for independence from Russia had been manifested in the founding of four separate Soviet republics: the Russian, the Ukrainian, the Belorussian, and a Trans-Caucasian Federation consisting of Armenia, Georgia, Azerbaijan. The four republics had treaty relations with each other, but, as Lenin had predicted, the granting of the right of secession caused a majority (by no means all) of these peoples to cease focusing on independence, and to turn instead to solving their internal problems.

What happened then was very well described by a Ukrainian from the very poorest strata of the peasantry, H.M. Odinets. He had been placed in the Secretariat, the most important body in the nationalist government of the Ukraine, to convince the mass of the people that the peasantry was in power. But he was a socialist, and he was imprisoned for that:

"When we socialists sat in a Ukrainian jail, we thought over what all that meant, and why, even though the letters over the entry read not *tiur'ma* [Russian for prison], but *v'iaznitsia* [Ukrainian, ditto], serving time in it was no different whatever."[24]

But he still faced the question of what would happen to his freedom to be Ukrainian if he changed to the other side in that civil war. The Ukrainian Soviet Republic took as its principle that socialism could only really be built, under the circumstances of the day, in conjunction with Russia. He made that change, with misgivings, and was among the delegates of the Ukrainian soviets to the congress in Moscow that joined the separate republics into the Union that exists today. At that 1922 gathering he said:

"We see that we now have our own schools, that Ukrainian schooling already exists, that no one is prohibiting such schools. The peasant sees: they really aren't forbidding them. If you want to read in Ukrainian, go ahead and read; if you wish, write in Ukrainian; if you want to speak it, speak it. That one can already do freely! A rumor was spread: they say that an end has been made to Ukrainian music, that its last notes have been played, that once again we've got that old 'indivisible' (Russian Empire). . . . I can now say boldly and with a clear conscience: the idea that the Ukraine is being abolished is all a lie. . . . The Soviet government is guiding us along the right lines. Now I believe that and many besides me believe it."[25]

I happened to be traveling in Soviet ethnic republics when the current Constitution was adopted in 1977. In Azerbaijan I watched a rehearsal of that people's songs and dances to be performed at the close of the "constitutional convention" in Moscow. It seemed to me an artificial and stagey show, set up purely for a governmental event, but it turns out to be a tradition dating back to that 1922 founding convention. One of its Central Asian delegates, reminiscing 50 years later, said:

"Actors and musicians of all the constituent and autonomous republics participated in a great entertainment after the closing of the congress. They not only performed for the delegates the fiery dances of the peoples of the Caucasus and the songs of the peoples of Central Asia, but displayed their 'wealth' right on the stage, including live camels, karakul lambs, the riches of the soil and mountains."[26]

That assemblage needed no entertainers to provide ethnic flavor, another delegate recollected: "I recall one gathering of our Ukrainian delegation. Powerful choral singing got under way as we waited for the meeting to start. Delegates from other republics surrounded us on all sides. I remember the colorful national costumes of the Kazakhs, Kirgiz, Uzbeks, and the peoples of the Caucasus. They listened to us with eager attention, amazement, enraptured. A merry tune was sung, and suddenly a gray old uncle, a delegate from the Kharkov country, leaped out and danced the hopak" (the Ukrainian national dance).[27]

This totally new kind of government consisted of people with no previous experience of power. The Communist Party was the glue that held things together. To make sure it would not be diluted by people who did not understand its principles, the Party admitted new members very carefully — in some underdeveloped areas, this meant that it had no organization whatever for a period. Looser rules of membership existed in the Young Communist League. At times, this produced an odd kind of vote of confidence. A man who had been a 19-year-old delegate from the mountaineer Daghestan Republic at that founding congress recalled:

"In 1922 I was at a Daghestan Komsomol (Young Communist League) Conference . . . and saw among the delegates bearded men pretty nearly 40 years of age. They said: 'You think age interferes with being a Komsomol, a delegate? But age didn't interfere with fighting in partisan units against the white jackals, did it'?" (White was the political color of the anti-Communists just as red was of the Soviets. It had nothing to do with race.) "'And age didn't prevent organizing a unit of the mountaineer poor in the village, did it? And age didn't prevent us from fighting for the new life against rich peasants and mullahs? So don't look cross-eyed at my beard'!"[28]

Similarly practical, and totally non-theoretical, judgments governed people's behavior when it came to organizing the first collective farms. As late as 1929 in isolated near-desert country in Central Asian Turkmenia, when the Communist Party assigned a Russian urban industrial worker to convince the poor that they would be better off in a collective, he found only one man in the village who knew any Russian at all, a 21-year-old farmer. The Russian suggested the name "Socialism" for that farm. Nearly 50 years later the farmer recalled, "I asked him then what socialism meant. What I understood from his answer was: we will work jointly on our land, we will bring water to it, we will grow crops and divide our harvest equitably. And I reminded my fellow villagers that our life had always been bad. It had been bad for our fathers, and for the fathers of our fathers, and for their fathers before them. Socialism means a good life, a just life. So we called our collective farm 'Socialism'."[29]

That man went on to get a higher education under the affirmative action program, and became a school principal. His Russian organizer was one of 25,000 industrial workers assigned to this job by the Communist Party, two-thirds of them from the Steel and Metalworkers Union, the element of labor constituting the Party's single strongest source of support.[30]

This method — which involved very careful individual selection — of sending manual workers who had known a lifetime of wage exploitation to help those who had lived under landowner exploitation was quite deliberate. Lenin had made the underlying reasoning clear in a 1919 speech warning that "measures must be immediately taken to prevent Soviet institutions from being flooded with Ukrainian urban petty bourgeoisie, *who have no conception of the living conditions of the peasant masses* and who frequently masquerade as Communists."[31]

This was not at odds with the policy which allowed the offspring of both princes and slaves to join the Young Communist League in the Caucasus. Today we see the 3,000,000 recently-Stone-Age inhabitants of Papua New Guinea emerging into self-government, just as the industrialized Basques of Spain make similar demands. Soviet ethnic policy is instructive because the Russian Empire included peoples across that entire spectrum of development. While Ukrainians were overwhelmingly rural, feudalism was well behind them, tribalism a thousand years in the past, and castes had never been a factor. Ukrainian women, while not remotely equal to men, were a shade better off than among the Russians. Most important, except for what the peasants made for home use, processing in the Ukraine was in factories, relatively little by craftsmen. As a consequence, the Soviet government of the Ukraine could act from the very outset in accordance with its Marxist principles, and base itself on the urban wage-workers who were rid of private employers and the peasants who were rid of landlords.

Among the Moslem peoples, however, the only significant industry was in the oil city of Baku. Capitalism was not the dominant economic system. Lenin identified the problem there in two statements of November 1919. The first concerned Turkestan —the name given by the monarchy to those conquered areas in Central Asia it ruled directly. As we have noted, the Empire ignored geographic ethnic differences within that huge territory, and even called one people by the name of another. In a telegram to the Communists of Turkestan, almost all Europeans at that time, Lenin wrote, "Demonstrate to [the peoples of Turkestan] by your actions that we are sincere in our desire to wipe out all traces of Great-Russian imperialism."[32] And in a speech to a Congress of Communist Organizations of the Peoples of the East, he said: "you must adapt yourselves to specific conditions such as do not exist in the European countries; you must be able to apply that [Communist] theory and practice to conditions . . . in which the task is to wage a struggle against the survival of medievalism and not against capitalism."[33]

Prior to this time, Marxist political activity had addressed itself solely to the notion that socialism was the solution to the problems of industrial countries. Even in Russia, a major wing of the socialists called Mensheviks, and later the Trotskyist current among Communists, held that socialism could not be established there because it was not primarily an industrial country. Now history was forcing a Marxist party in power to grapple with practical realities. The last quotation above from Lenin marked the beginning of what has since come to be known as the "non-capitalist" path to socialism from pre-industrial societies, and represents the Soviet view of what is desirable for African countries today.[34]

The most important aspect of the early experience in Central Asia was the appearance of transitional governments that were not yet Communist. Tsarism had permitted two "native states" — the emirates of Khiva and Bokhara — to remain when it conquered Central Asia half a century before the Revolution. The Emir of Bokhara was granted the title of aide-de-camp to the tsar. He was also allowed to invest 100,000,000 rubles, a stupendous sum in those days, in Russian industry and finance. That money (and another $175,000,000 in bullion and gems with which he fled to Afghanistan in 1920), came from an age-old system of exploiting the tillers of irrigated farmland. Russia offered a tremendous market for cotton, and that had been one of the reasons for the conquest.

The emir was the biggest feudal lord, but there were also private landholdings and those of Moslem religious institutions. Sharecropping was the rule, and the peasant retained but one-fourth of the crop! The peasants also had to build and dredge canals, maintain roads and bridges, build and repair brick fortress walls. There was a very large class of artisans and tradesmen in the cities, as in the Arab countries today. Judges retained a percentage of the fines they levied; administrators received no salaries, but lived off tolls and taxes they imposed. But the system was largely stable: the croppers at least owned the land on which their homes sat, a wooden plow, a working animal. After the Russian conquest, they continued to work for a member of their own nationality, and in a way hallowed by tradition. This, their sense of property, of clan loyalty — the man who took 75 percent of the crop was usually of the same clan — plus religious loyalty, created a firm wall of resistance to social change.[35] At this writing, Saudi Arabia, Iran and Afghanistan are examples of persistence of similar traditions.

However, the cotton trade with Russia, the contact with a different world provided by the new railroad, and the building of local cotton gins led to the emergence of a non-traditional merchant class. A desire for a type of education more utilitarian than the traditional Mohammedan schooling arose, and some such schools were opened. In the most medieval areas, the very name for such schools was taken as a synonym for rebellion, and their advocates were flogged, often to death—this happened to one of the major Eastern poets of modern times, the Tajik, Sadriddin Aini.*[36] He survived.

A few people in tsarist Central Asia were sent to higher educational institutions in Russia to train as veterinarians and the like. Some secular literature appeared, and modernization became a goal among the new class. This was the situation on the eve of the Revolution.

When Lenin came to power, the Soviets offered national independence without demanding a new economic or social order. Even in the directly Soviet territory in Central Asia—not the "native states" like Bokhara—no attempt was made to interfere with feudal ownership of land and water for several years. It was clear that the idea of taking the land of the bey (nobleman) or, even worse, that of the mosque, was foreign to the mind of the *dekkan* (peasant), as immoral by his standards as the tsarist conquerors' seizure of native lands. A period of education and practical elementary training in democracy would have to come first. In the Kazakh steppes outside the irrigated Uzbek and Tajik oases, the Communists granted amnesty to those who had been active in the nationalist movement that initially opposed them, when they lay down their arms.

Witnessing all this, the liberals of merchant background in Bokhara decided the time had come to revolt against this last enclave of feudalism. They rallied the poorest sections of their society by pointing to the improved position of the peasantry in nearby areas under Soviet rule and the increasing number of indigenous people in responsible government positions. They overthrew the power of the emir except in the capital city of Bokhara, where the inhabitants, roused by the Moslem clergy, resisted strongly, until Red forces from Tashkent, Soviet Turkestan, won the day. This was in August 1920.

The new governments in Bokhara and Khorezm (successor to another emirate in Khiva) called themselves Soviet but not socialist. The position of the rank-and-file improved only in so far as they shared in the property confiscated from the emir and his highest

---

*The rebels active in Afghanistan at this writing pursue an identical policy toward educators.

officials and the abolition of the old taxes.[37] Russia was able to provide a new kind of help from without: 24 medical specialists, 136 general practitioners and 154 nurses were sent to Bokhara in 1923. Except for a single physician and perhaps four nurse practitioners (*feldshers*) serving the emir and high Russian officials, these were the only source of medical help for the entire population. Yet even these 300 people represented a sacrifice by Russia, for a very large proportion of her medical personnel had emigrated due to the hardships of life after the Civil War and Intervention. This in fact is what prompted the Soviet policy of barring free emigration. The population in 1922 was 7,000,000 less than in 1918. Millions had died of disease and starvation, 2,000,000 in the fighting, and 2,000,000 including a great many professionals, had emigrated.[38]

The structure of Soviet nationality policy was put in place in the 20 years after the Revolution, and embodied in the Constitution of 1936. A form of territorial autonomy was devised for small tribal nationalities in 1926; larger tribal peoples consolidated themselves into nations, and were given the status of full republics of the USSR. Kazakhstan and Kirgizia were at first autonomous republics within the Russian Republic, but in 1936 were separated out to become the last two full republics on a par with Russia.

Because most Blacks and Latinos, a great many Indians, and all Asian-Americans constitute dispersed minorities in the United States, the Soviet experiences most pertinent to them are those of the Jews, Tatars, and Gypsies. Like the Ku Klux Klan here, old Russia had violent racist organizations of private citizens. The Soviet government outlawed such organizations, tried, imprisoned, and in some cases executed their leaders. That took care of that, because the conditions giving one a personal interest in maintaining racism or discrimination were abolished. Therefore the mass base for even secret revival of such organizations disappeared. But some mental prejudice persists, and very small illegal dissident groups of Russian nationalists crop up at rare intervals.

The change from a pro-racist government that encouraged pogroms to an anti-racist one made an end to the acquittal or failure to prosecute persons engaging in killing, maiming, or defrauding members of ethnic minorities. The regular police force of tsarist times, recognized as hopelessly racist and anti-working class, was totally disbanded, and its former members were denied the right to vote or hold office for many years after the Revolution. The very word, "police," has disappeared from the language. Public safety functions were performed by a new force, drawn from workers and peasants known to share the interests of their own social classes and to be opposed to racism. Today, in contrast to the situation in most American inner cities, the "militia," (as the Soviet public-safety force is now called) accurately reflects the make-up of the local population everywhere in the Soviet Union, both in terms of physical characteristics and languages.

Residential ghettoes in old Russia arose both out of legal prohibitions, in the case of the Jews, and out of economic factors. Confiscating rental property eliminated discrimination by landlords, and reducing rents to a very tiny fraction of income eliminated economic bars to housing integration. No complaints on this score are heard today even from the most bitterly anti-Communist emigrants from the Soviet Union.

Discrimination in employment was also abolished. Jews had been legally barred from government service, work in the railroads or in the postal service; these laws were simply wiped off the books. Affirmative-action placed 150,000 Jews in industrial jobs in the years before unemployment was totally eliminated by socialist economic planning. With the organization of government farms the proportion of Jews earning a living from agriculture rose from 2 percent to 11 percent in the years before World War II. Only civil marriage was recognized (although anyone could also have a religious wedding) which automatically removed bars to intermarriage, such as the U.S. had with its miscegenation laws until recently.

Anti-Semitic quotas in education were abolished and education in one's native language was provided everywhere. This initially led to people flocking into schools in their own languages. When it became clear that all languages were truly regarded as equal in value, dispersed peoples in the following generation tended to send their children to Russian-language schools because that is the language of general communication where Russians are the majority.

Tatars and Gypsies, and numerous other dispersed minorities, had similar experiences, although discrimination against them had not been as firmly fixed in law in the old days. The Tatars overcame the heritage of their former depressed status in a single generation or at most two; with the Gypsies it took two generations for most, for some, three.

Overall, anti-minority prejudices have declined so sharply that violence on those grounds has disappeared. Some minority individuals believe they suffer from difficulties with promotion due to prejudice, and in certain cases this is undoubtedly true, but overall statistics in all cases — Jews, Tatars, Gypsies — reveal exactly the opposite as the general rule. All moved upward far more rapidly than the Russians. The Jews are far ahead of the Russians in proportion to population. Peoples without the Jews' traditional striving for education are either about even with or still somewhat behind the Russians, but now their progress is entirely up to themselves.

World War II disrupted everything in the Soviet Union, including the patterns just described. Post-war developments affecting particular nationalities are discussed in detail in the chapters which follow.

On December 21, 1982, the sixtieth anniversary of the joining of the six Soviet republics then existing into the Union of Soviet Socialist Republics, then Soviet President Yuri Andropov delivered a speech setting forth the present view of the Communist Party and the government on the ethnic situation:

> Marxism was the first doctrine to show that the nationalities question is linked organically to society's social class structure, to the predominating type of property. . . . For the first time in history the multinational character of a country has turned from a source of weakness into a source of strength. . . . The successes in settling the nationalities question by no means signify that all the problems generated by the very fact of the life and work of numerous nations and nationalities in a single state have vanished. *This is hardly possible as long as nations exist,* as long as there are national distinctions. And these will exist for a long time to come, *much longer than class distinctions.* That is why the further improvement of advanced socialism . . . must include a carefully considered, scientific policy with respect to the nationalities question. . . . We must remember that there are both good and bad, outdated elements in the cultural heritage, traditions and customs of *each* nation. . . . It is important, however, that the natural pride one takes in the gains achieved should not degenerate into ethnic arrogance or conceit, that it should not tend toward exclusiveness and disrespect for other nations and nationalities. Yet such negative phenomena still occur, and *it would be wrong to attribute them solely to the traces of the past.* Among other things, they are sometimes fostered by the mistakes we make in our work. Here, comrades, nothing can be dismissed as insignificant. Everything counts — the attitude to the language, to artifacts of the past, the interpretation of historical events and the way we transform rural and urban areas and influence living and working conditions.
>
> The natural migration of the population is making each of our republics — and, to varying degrees, each region and each city — increasingly multinational. . . .
>
> In some of them, however, the indigenous nationality should be represented in the working class more fully. Hence the task set by the

26th Congress of the Communist Party—to expand and improve the training of skilled workers from among all the nations and nationalities residing in the republics. The need for this is both economic and political. Multi-ethnic work forces, above all those in industry, are that very milieu in which the internationalist spirit is fostered best . . .

Representation in Party and government bodies . . . is also a highly important question. . . . There should be a consistent effort to ensure proper representation of *all* nationalities in any republic at *all* levels of the various Party and government bodies. . . . Great tact in selecting and assigning personnel are especially necessary in view of the multi-national composition of the union and autonomous republics. . . .

To continue instilling in Soviet people a spirit of mutual respect and friendship for all the nations and nationalities of the country . . . should also be an everyday concern of all educational establishments in our country. . . .

All this means that problems of relations among nations are still on the agenda in the society of mature socialism."[39] (my emphasis-W.M.)

Early in 1983, Mr. Andropov brought this same matter before the Presidium of the Supreme Soviet. *Izvestia*, the government's official daily, reported him as saying that there was need for "more concrete and deeper consideration of ethnic characteristics, for more concern for all-round development of *all* the nations and peoples, particularly the small ones. He emphasized the need for persistent efforts to eliminate from existing practices any deviations from Lenin's nationalities policy and for consistently providing for *total* equality of Soviet people of all nationalities."

The resolution adopted by the Presidium on that occasion charged educational institutions with "socializing the people in the spirit of mutual respect and friendship among all the nations and peoples of the country . . . [and] persistently to develop forms and methods of work, meeting contemporary requirements, to enrich the ethnic cultures and to make use of the best that is provided by the intellectual heritage and traditions of each of the peoples of our country, to resist actively attempts to idealize obsolete manners and morals . . . and to struggle against such negative phenomena as ethnic conceit, bragging and a disrespectful attitude toward other nations and nationalities.[40]

Mr. Andropov died only a year after this program was adopted. The Chernenko administration is still too new for us to judge its implementation of these principles. However, a mid-1984 article in *Pravda*, the Communist Party's national daily, pointed the finger at non-Marxist trends of thought in the USSR that could bring problems in the ethnic sphere: It charged that, "Some scholars are showing a conciliatory attitude toward the ideology of Pan-Slavism," a prerevolutionary theory that justified Russian dominance on the grounds that Russia was the protector of other Slavic peoples. The article called some conciliatory even toward "forthright apologists for the monarchy," most likely a reference to writer Alexander Solzhenitsyn, now living in exile in the United States, and went on, "Rationalizations are still current about religious figures who supposedly express the spirit of a nation, and of religion as the fount of high morality." This was directed both at Great-Russian chauvinists and at anti-Russian nationalists. Certain religions are directly associated with particular nations or nationalities in the Soviet Union, so the feeling that possessing a particular religion gives one a better morality leads to a sense of superiority over peoples who do not profess it. All religious wars have been justified thus — "God is on our side."

Lastly, the article contended that "certain published works 'derive' national character from a classless, absolute ethic, a 'national spirit,' and peasant patriarchalism is looked upon as the source of everything distinct to a people."[41] That last is unmistakeably directed against Valentin Rasputin, one of the most popular Soviet Russian writers of our day, and other literary figures of the "ruralist group," including some non-Russians, who take the same stand with respect to their own peoples. Clearly, Andropov's point that the "national question" will remain so long as nations and nationalities exist has not been forgotten.

NOTES

1. E.N. Burdzhalov, *The Second Russian Revolution: The Uprising in Petrograd*, translated as Vol. XVIII, No. 1, of *Soviet Studies in History*, 1979.

2. V.I. Lenin, *Collected Works* (Moscow: Progress, 1966), XXV, pp. 91-2.

3. Quoted in M.S. Djunusov, "Soviet Autonomy and the Vestiges of Nationalism," *Soviet Sociology*, II, No. 1 (1963), p. 12.

4. Anna Louise Strong, *The Road to the Grey Pamir*, (Boston: Little, Brown, 1931), pp. 123-125.

5. Anna Louise Strong, *Peoples of the USSR*, (New York: Macmillan, 1944), p. 102.

6. Djunusov, *Soviet Sociology*, II, No. 1, p. 20.

7. Lenin, *Collected Works*, XXV, p. 101.

8. Ibid., XXIV, p. 301.

9. Ibid., p. 300.

10. J.V. Stalin, *Works* (Moscow: Foreign Languages Publishing House, 1953), III, p. 20.

11. L.S. Gribova, "Traditional Carving on Rural Buildings of the Perm Komi," *Soviet Anthropology and Archeology*, XIII, No. 4 (1975), p. 55.

12. A.Kh. Khalikov, "The Culture of the Peoples of the Middle Volga in the Tenth Through the Thirteenth Centuries," *Soviet Anthropology and Archeology*, XVI, No. 1, (1977), pp. 60, 74-76.

13. Cited in A.M. Sakharov, "The Study in Soviet Historical Literature of the Socioeconomic Basis for the Unification of the Russian Lands," *Soviet Studies in History*, XVI, No. 2 (1977), p. 36.

14. Z.S. Chertina, "The Bourgeois Theory of 'Modernization' and the Real Development of the Peoples of Soviet Central Asia," *Soviet Law and Government*, XIX, No. 3 (1980-81), p. 14.

15. Djunusov, p. 13.

16. Ibid.,

17. Ibid.

18. "Marxism and the National Question," in J. Stalin, *Marxism and the National and Colonial Question* (New York: International Publishers, 1934).

19. Dr. E. Babayan, "Drug Addiction Can Be Eliminated," *Soviet Life*, Washington, April, 1978, p. 38.

20. U.S. Djekebaev, "The Overcoming of Social Alienation and Problems of Rooting Out Criminal Behavior Under the Conditions of the Transition of Formerly Backward Peoples to Socialism Skipping the Capitalist Stage," *Soviet Sociology*, XIII, No. 4 (1975), p. 67.

21. *Izvestia*, January 16, 1970.

22. S.M. Mirkhasilov, "Sociocultural Changes as Reflected in the Contemporary Rural Family in Uzbekistan," *Soviet Sociology*, XVIII, No. 4 (1980), p. 59.

23. V.A. Holobutskii, "Pages From My Recollections," *Soviet Studies in History*, V. No. 4, (1967), p. 17.

24. "Recollections of Delegates to the First All-Union Congress of Soviets," *Soviet Studies in History*, XIII, No. 2, (1974), p. 81.

25. Ibid., p. 82.

26. Ibid., p. 91.

27. Ibid., p. 83.

28. Ibid., p. 86.

29. *Soviet Life*, Washington, April, 1978, p. 35.

30. "Dvadtsatipiatitysiachniki," *Bol'shaia Sovetskaia Entsiklopediia*, 3rd ed. (Moscow: Sovetskaia Entsiklopediia, 1972), Vol. VII, p. 565, col. 1682.

31. Lenin, *Collected Works*, XXX, pp. 163-165.

32. Ibid., p. 138.

33. Ibid., p. 161.

34. William Mandel, *Soviet Marxism and Social Science* (Palo Alto, Ramparts, 1984), pp. 36-38.

35. William Mandel, *The Soviet Far East and Central Asia* (New York: Institute of Pacific Relations, 1944), p. 102.

36. R. Fish and R. Khashim, *Glazami Sovesti* (Dushanbe: Irforn, 1978).

37. Mandel, *Soviet Far East and Central Asia*, p. 110.

38. V.I. Kozlov, *Natsional'nosti SSSR* (Moscow: Statistika, 1975), p. 59.

39. *News and Views From the USSR*, Soviet Embassy, Washington, Dec. 21, 1982, pp. 1-6 passim.

40. *Izvestia*, Jan. 14, 1983.

41. V. Oskotskii, "V bor'be s antiistorizmom," *Pravda*, May 21, 1984.

American-Russian Institute

Thousands of students from Africa and other third-world regions now attend schools in the USSR.

4

Blacks, Russians, and Black Russians

*The Soviet Union seems to me the only European country where
people are not more or less taught and encouraged to despise and
look down on some class, group or race. I know countries where
race and color prejudice show only slight manifestations, but no
white country where race and color prejudice seems so absolutely
absent. In Paris I attract some attention; in London I meet
elaborate blankness; anywhere in America I get anything from
complete ignoring to curiosity, and often insult. In Moscow, I pass
unheeded. Russians quite naturally ask me information; women sit
beside me quite confidently and unconsciously. Children are uniformly
courteous.*

— W.E.B. DuBois* in his *Autobiography.*

Charlie Lee, also Black, was not yet born when Dr. DuBois died in
1963. At 16, in 1982, he attended a Soviet children's summer
camp. Upon his return, he told me: "It turned my life around.
Before I went, I saw people in terms of color and religion, but after
we came back we all saw people as human beings. You can't even
explain it — our society makes our youth look at people, when our
youth get together, 'hey, you're Black;' 'hey, you're white.' While

---

*Dr. W.E.B. DuBois, 1868-1963, a Harvard PhD in 1895, sociologist, novelist, a
founder of the National Association for the Advancement of Colored People, is
universally regarded as the greatest of Black intellectuals. He was kind enough to
make a positive reference to me in one of his books, *In Battle For Peace* (New York:
Masses & Mainstream, 1952), p. 73.

you were at Camp Artek, you didn't notice. People were people. They would like us. By the time we got back, we saw people as human beings."

After they came back, "A lot of people told me I was changed in many ways. People said I was calmed down. My closest friend said: 'Well, the Soviet Union did that for you.' He thought it was for the best."

Mrs. Hilda Campbell of Chester, Pa., is a Black union carpenter, a regular church-goer, and the mother of boys aged 16 and eight. In 1984, she spent three weeks with the first-ever delegation of female skilled workers to visit the USSR, a by-product of the first convention of such women. Of the 20 who went, only two had been predisposed favorably toward that country. Mrs. Campbell remembers:

"Initially I was quite hesitant. I had been given so many negative pieces of information about the Soviet Union, even to the point of being terrified because on the job there were different guys saying: 'when you look at the correspondents talking to people on television: have you ever seen any Black women or men over there?' I had in fact never seen any."

She says this made her fear "they are doing something to keep them out of there and wonder what had happened to the Black people that would have been there." She simply never thought, she admits, that because of the geography of the country "there were none located there because they didn't originate there."

She also had the idea that people "were hard, very strict, unfeeling, just no concern for anybody else's feelings."

But when she arrived — one of two Blacks in the delegation — it was "Like a totally different world. I never expected the people to accept, not only the group, but me personally. The love, the caring, inviting me into their homes. They'd see me on the subway, or on the street trying to find a place to eat — on two occasions, people stopped and took me, hand in hand, and walked me to the restaurant, and made sure I got inside and sat down and ate. I know that in the United States, most people wouldn't even stop and act concerned. But these people stopped and gave of their time and energy, and that's just the most overwhelming gift that you can ever give a person who's lost."

While in Alma-Ata — in Kazakhstan, Soviet Central Asia — a few in the group went to visit an English-speaking Kazakh woman whose address they had been given. She had moved. This was made clear by an elderly Russian woman, via sign language, who then invited them to her home. Her husband and daughter knew a very little English.

"She made me feel truly wanted, not just somebody who came along in the crowd. After I'd eaten so much, she took my plate and gave me a new plate and filled it up again. When I left, I thanked her for it, and she hugged me and kissed me."

Boxer Muhammad Ali visited the Soviet Union in 1978 while in training for the fight in which he regained the heavyweight championship from Leon Spinks.

"I saw a hundred nationalities. No such thing as a Black man, or a white man, or 'you nigger,' or get back. People say, 'Oh, well, they just showed you the best.' You mean all of those white folks rehearsed, said: 'Muhammad Ali's coming! All the whores, get off the streets — all the whores, all the whores! Muhammad Ali's coming! Everybody walk quietly and peacefully. All hundred nationalities, pretend you get along. Muhammad Ali's coming! All the policemen take your guns off — I don't want more than two of you in the whole city. Muhammad Ali's coming!' 'They just took you where they wanted to go.' I know that's a lie. I got in my car and told my driver where to go. Lying about the Russians."

"I jogged in the mornings in strange places where they hardly ever saw a Black man. I ran past two little white Russian ladies who were walking to work. They didn't look around and ask what I was doing. I can't go jogging in some streets in America in the morning in a white neighborhood. If they see a Black man coming down the street, they wonder who I'm going to jump. I love things like this that I notice. Late at night, I was running down the street, and I looked back. Again, there were two Russian ladies. They didn't even look back to see why a Black man was out here running."[1]

A friend in Moscow who spent his childhood in the United States became a journalist specializing in American affairs. He once showed me a letter to him from a cop in a small town in the Soviet Ukraine where the people are white, and speak a language related to Russian. The man wrote: "I am a militiaman [the Soviets hate the word "police" because of what it meant to the poor before the Revolution], my wife is a cook. We just had a new baby, a girl. She is our second child. Our boy, who is eleven, suggested that we name her for the brave American Communist, Angela Davis. We did so. Please send our best wishes to Comrade Angela. We hope she will soon be free." [That was during her trial.]

Dr. Lily Golden-Hanga is a Black Russian, a PhD historian specializing in Black nationalism in her research position at Moscow's Africa Institute. Her father, John Oliver Golden, was one of a group of 16 Negroes, all Tuskegee* graduates, who moved to the USSR in 1931 to teach modern agriculture to the "people of color" in Soviet Central Asia.

I introduced Dr. Golden-Hanga, a Black Russian, in opening Chapter I. Knowing that Golden was her father's name, I asked: "Who is, or was, Hanga?" "Hanga was my husband. He was the first prime minister of Zanzibar [now part of Tanzania]. Several years ago he was killed during the coup." They met in the Soviet Union. "He came especially to meet me. He had heard about me. He found me in Moscow and he waited for two years to marry me. He was a student at Oxford, but when he came here he transferred to Lumumba University, where he got Diploma No. 1."

This university is named for Patrice Lumumba, who won national liberation for the Republic of the Congo (now called Zaire), and was murdered in 1961. "Dr. DuBois, Shirley Graham (DuBois), and Paul Robeson† with Eslanda Robeson," who was an anthropologist, "participated in founding Lumumba University. I wrote an article about this, published in *Freedomways*."

The Soviet bodies founding that university were its Central Council of Trade Unions and its Committee for Solidarity with the Countries of Asia and Africa. Its purpose is to develop highly-educated indigenous personnel for the developing countries of Asia, Africa, and Latin America, with preference to applicants who could not otherwise afford college. There are always a large number of Soviet students as well. All told, there are 30,000 students from the developing countries in 300[2] Soviet higher and secondary educational institutions. I know of at least one American Black who received a medical education there and is now practicing in Oakland, California. The *Large Soviet Encyclopedia* says of it: "Students at [Lumumba] are socialized in the spirit of internationalism and friendship among peoples. Tuition, medical services and dormitories are free.

---

*Founded by the Black educator, Booker T. Washington, Tuskegee Institute in Alabama stressed the professions related to the fields in which Blacks were then overwhelmingly engaged, like farming. Members included George Tynes, Charles Noel Young, A.M. Overton, B. Conrad Powers, Hopkins Faison and John Sutton.

†Paul Robeson, 1898-1976, world-famous baritone and actor, first Black football All-American, graduate lawyer. He did me the honor of singing in support of my campaign for Congress as a peace candidate during the Korean War.

Students are given living grants," very generous ones by Soviet standards.

"The university comprises a preparatory department and six major departments: physics, math, and natural sciences; history and languages; economics and law; engineering; agriculture; medicine." The university "organizes practical work experience in their fields and graduate internships at 240 industrial enterprises, farms, clinics, and scientific institutions in 35 cities and 10 [ethnic] republics of the USSR."[3]

I asked Dr. Golden-Hanga if there were other people of African descent in the Soviet Union aside from the group which came with her father.

"Yes. In the Caucasus, in such republics as Adjaria, Abkhazia, and in Georgia — Georgia, USSR, not Georgia, U.S.A.: there's a big difference — we have many people of African descent. They are the third or fourth generation in this country, or even more. Some of their ancestors were brought here by Turkish slave traders in the 17th and 18th centuries. A lot came in the 19th century."

Some Blacks participated actively in the Revolution. One family treasures a certificate of honor issued in 1920 to Shaaban Abash, a Red soldier of the Abkhazian Mounted Regiment. Abkhazia is in the Caucasus Mountains near the Black Sea. He was later elected a member of its parliament. His brother, a shepherd, was one of the initial organizers of collective farming there. He was the first head of the collective farm in his village. His daugher, "typically African in appearance," is a gynecologist in the city of Sukhumi. Her brother is a bus driver, who told a Soviet reporter, also Black: "I am Black and I am proud of it. I am respected by all."

Dr. Golden-Hanga continued: "They're not only in the South. This year I met, in Latvia, a very beautiful girl of Ethiopian descent, whose surname, incidentally, is Hannibal, like Pushkin's great-grandfather."

I said that American Blacks regard Alexander Pushkin as a black man. She replied: "I have never thought of him as black or yellow or blue or green or any other color, but only that he is a great Russian poet. It was he who made Russian Russian. Of course we know that his great-grandfather was Ethiopian. To me that is cause for pride, but nobody thinks of him in those terms.

"He also always regarded himself as Russian. In his writings there are references to his African ancestry — you will find phrases like 'my far native land' — but he thought of himself as Russian. How else can you think of a person who never heard an African language, who had no African culture, who was born in Russia? I also consider myself Russian. Russian is my native language. My life is part of the life of the Soviet Union, not something distinctive. Of course, sometimes when people first see me, it is something strange for them.*

"But within a few minutes, when they hear my pure Russian, and sense my psychology, and realize that I think like they think and speak like they speak and have had the same life experience they have had, they forget that I am of another color."

I asked her about a book by a former Lumumba University student dealing with alleged racist attitudes. She replied,

"I've heard about that book. The problem is that so many Africans come from diverse class origins. Some had been in Europe before coming here, and were influenced by bourgeois propaganda. Moscow has three million people entering and leaving it daily. Some come from very remote villages, and sometimes they look at you as very strange. Certain Africans don't understand that this is not because anyone has anything against Black people, but simply because they've never seen such people, and they are surprised at what they see.

"But if you think that socialism can quickly solve all problems. . . . As Lenin and Karl Marx wrote, you can change a country's economic system, but it's very difficult to change psychology. So sometimes one can find people who are not politically developed or well educated who might be prejudiced. But I myself never had any experience of discrimination."

She admitted she had trouble understanding the word. "What does it mean? You are not allowed to go somewhere? Or you are not allowed to do something?" I mentioned subtler forms: someone looking at you in a manner that makes you feel he thinks you are not his equal, or people leaning over backward to be nice in a condescension that is discrimination in reverse. Any Black American, I added, could make the whole thing clear to her in ten minutes. She replied:

"You cannot find this in the Soviet Union. No segregation. Everybody can live wherever he wants, and sit and be and go where he wants, and can do everything he wants. Years ago, I was tennis

---

*African or Afro-American physical appearance is quite rare in the USSR. In a country of a quarter-billion, the few tens of thousands of African college and trade school students, and even smaller number of people of African descent, form a sharp contrast to the great number of indigenous non-white peoples, whose features are Oriental or resemble those one finds in India.

champion of Uzbekistan, and traveled a lot around the Soviet Union playing in tournaments. I have been in nearly all the 15 republics, including some that *you* would consider quite white— Estonia on the Baltic: people with straw blonde hair, blue eyes, and so on. And Uzbekistan, where people are black, and other republics. All I experienced was admiration."

We talked of others in the group that had come from America with her father in 1931. One, George Tynes, was living in Moscow. "He visits the U.S. every other year or so," she told me, and had married a Ukrainian woman." Tynes dropped in to say hello to Muhammad Ali while the latter was being interviewed by the *N.Y. Times*. The champ asked him: "What do you like about this system?" The reply, "No racism."[4] Tynes himself spelled it out more fully in an interview with the *Los Angeles Times* in 1974. He talked of his work in Uzbekistan with Golden, "Down there they thought I was a 'Uzbek'," he chuckled. "A little bigger and a little darker than most, but they tried to talk Uzbek to me. . . . I liked the work and the people and the way they treated me. I like the system very much. I feel I've been free, that there are no bars because of color on me or my children." In the U.S. he recalled, he had been made offers in professional football "but the money was not good," and in the U.S. his degree in vocational agriculture education allowed him "to teach in colored schools" but there was no work.[5] In a later interview with the San Francisco *Chronicle*, "he said that in the 47 years he's lived in Russia he's never been insulted once because of his color, or been 'made to feel inferior'."[6]

Tynes and his wife had three children, Dr. Golden-Hanga continued, "The eldest, Slava, graduated in journalism from Moscow University, and now writes for Novosti Press Service. He has traveled to Nigeria, Senegal, Tanzania and Zambia in the course of his work. Previously, while doing his military service, he became a pilot and an officer. Another son also works in Moscow; and his daughter, Emilia, married an African and is now teaching chemistry in Liberia." I wondered out loud how many Black women teach chemistry in the United States, and she replied: "*Every* Soviet Black person I know has a higher education. Ella Ross, a graduate of Moscow University, a famous singer here of blues and spirituals, tours the Soviet Union. Another, Eula-Mae Scott, was one of the best dancers in the Bolshoi Ballet, toured the U.S. and Europe several times with it. They are pensioned at 37, very early, because that's hard work. Now she is writing a dissertation, on African dance."

Ms. Scott also won a choreographers' competition, with a ballet based on the story of Angela Davis.

Dr. Golden-Hanga herself has written a short history of Africans in Russia from the 16th century on, of which she gave me a copy.[7] "I traveled to find such people. It was difficult, because they also don't consider themselves African or Black or whatever, and the descendants are products of mixed marriages with Russians, Armenians, Georgians, Adjarians. But I think I know almost all of them now."

For these reasons, she went on, it is hard to say how many there are, "Maybe about 500, maybe more, because there are thousands of Africans now studying all over the Soviet Union, and they marry Soviets, and they have children, so now there are many more than before." No one has reported incidents of any kind involving such children in Soviet schools or elsewhere, in the USSR.

Her views on questions that agitate American Blacks emerged from a personal question when I asked, "Your mother is white, and Jewish?" She replied in the affirmative, but laughed: "That sounds very funny — to say that a person is white, and Jewish." (Mother, daughter, and granddaughter live together. Mr. Golden is dead.) It was here that her distinct Russianness began to appear: "I don't understand American Blacks when they say about themselves that they are Black, because if you say you are Black it means there must be a black color! But Blacks are such different colors!" I explained the historical origin, that American whites, in justifying slavery, regarded as Black anyone with *any* African heritage at all, and that both Black and white Americans find it hard to understand that the rest of the world doesn't accept that definition.

Reminding me that she was born in Uzbekistan, "where all people are very black," (she would immediately be taken as Black in the U.S.) she explained, "Ours is a different understanding of the problem, because there are many people who are very black, and they are not Africans. People are of so many different colors that I think it is not right to identify a person by his color. I can't imagine looking at an Uzbek and saying: 'Are you black?' He would laugh at me." When I told her how the term "Negro" had been replaced by "Black" as a self-designation in the United States, she replied: "Can't you simply be American?"

There are Blacks in the United States who think that impossible, because they regard the country as hopelessly racist. But to Africans, former Ambassador Andrew Young is unquestionably American, as is Jesse Jackson. So her question reflects a view widely held abroad, and which is certainly present among Blacks in the United States. Her present work touches on this question.

"I am trying to write a paper now on the problem of Black nationalism in the world, not merely some small group or single country but the entire world — in Africa and in the United States too. I think nationalism has gone through several stages in its development. There are times when nationalism plays a positive role in the history of a nationality, a country, and so on, especially when a nation is fighting for its independence. But when national sovereignty already exists, nationalism can sometimes become very reactionary. This is very important at the present time. We know of many occasions when a country's or people's nationalism has brought it to catastrophe.

"There are also many kinds of nationalism; political, cultural, ethnic, and so on. For example, I hear of American Blacks considering themselves Muslims only because they think that Africans are Muslims, and that that is their national religion. But if one examines the history of Africa, one sees that Islam came very late in the history of the African peoples, only in the 9th century. This means that Islam is not an indigenous African religion. It was brought from Asia. So when Americans fight for the right to be Muslim, it indicates that they don't know African history. I use this to illustrate *religious* nationalism to you."

Not only Black Muslims, but others in the U.S. Black community, would differ sharply with her.

I don't think Dr. Golden-Hanga and Muhammad Ali would have too much of an argument with each other. In his *N.Y. Times* interview at the end of his visit to the USSR, he said: "So what they doin' is, they live religion — they give a man free medical and hospital care, low rent, a job . . . " He had spent most of a week visiting Moslem mosques and monuments in Tashkent and Samarkand. *New World Review* asked him: "Did you see any evidence of Russians trying to dominate the Uzbeks or other Central Asian peoples?" "No. No. Might be, but I didn't see it. Those people are free to worship, dress and do as they want. I didn't see any Russian people doing anything. The Uzbeks had their own houses, their places of business, their own little streets, their own mosques, their own clothes. They prayed by Islamic traditions."

Not all Black visitors to the Soviet Union agree, of course. On the one hand, there is the testimony of poet Langston Hughes, whom I met in Moscow in 1932: "the one country in the world that has equality for all races"[8]; of Paul Robeson: "I feel like a human being for the first time since I grew up"; [9] of Dr. DuBois and of his co-founder of the Africa nationalist movement, George Padmore; [10] of playwright and actress Alice Childress; of the American Blacks who have chosen to live in the USSR and of their children; of Black labor union officials like Bill Chester of the West Coast longshoremen; of prominent Baptist clergymen like Dr. Charles L. Evans; of newspaper publishers (more than one) like Dr. Carlton Goodlett; of William B. Davis, one of the rare Blacks included in the staffs of U.S. exhibitions in Moscow: "a dark face in Moscow has as much advantage as it would have disadvantage in Mississippi. . . . I found no public display of racial prejudice in Moscow. Such would be a criminal offense." [11] Most recently, there have been Angela Davis, Muhammad Ali, Charlie Lee, Mrs. Hilda Campbell.

On the other hand, there is Homer Smith, who from 1932 to 1935 wrote very favorably as a correspondent in Moscow for the *Afro-American* newspaper chain, but had second thoughts thirty years later in his book, *Black Man in Red Russia*, 1964. Most prominently, there is former U.N. Ambassador Andrew Young, subsequently mayor of Atlanta, who has spoken of "racism" in the USSR.

Why this disparity? Perhaps my own experiences help explain it. I have met a "closet" dissident, protected by his status high in a Soviet cultural institution, a status he enjoys because of his real skill in a specialized profession. He expressed himself to me about Angela Davis in the most vicious racist and male chauvinist way, because of his bitterness that she chooses to be a Communist. I have heard the chairman of a collective farm in the Caucasus Mts., himself of a minority nationality, say that he would never let his daughter marry a Black. I have heard a famous and talented Soviet Oriental actor actually express himself in favor of U.S. discrimination against Blacks because of the haughty and arrogant son of an African chief who had been a fellow student at a Soviet higher educational institution.

And a Leningrad teen-ager, just out of high school, said to me in the 1960s that he knew a boy of his age who believed all Blacks and Jews should be exterminated. Utterly taken aback, I said, "I have been reading the Soviet press, school textbooks, seeing Soviet films for thirty years, and have never seen anything that could possibly put such an idea into anyone's head. Where did he get that from?" The boy shrugged and said: "Where does any kid get his ideas from first of all? His parents."

Of course there are some such parents. I can only ask — as I do

to people who ask me about racism in the USSR after a lecture—
"If tomorrow morning we wake up to find that every possible law
U.S. minorities want is on the books and being enforced, do you
think there will still be racists in this country 70 years from now?"
—about the time that has elapsed since the Russian Revolution.
Whites in my audiences invariably show no visible response; Blacks
almost uniformly nod their heads in the affirmative.

Once at the Leningrad airport, I heard a Russian say to two
African students: "How does it feel to wear clothes? At home you
go around in grass skirts, don't you?" The Africans snapped an
outraged response and stalked away. I went up to the Russian and
asked: "What did you insult them for?" He was perplexed and
defensive, and said he thought what he said was true, and how
could he know? I took him by the arm, walked him to the nearest
newsstand, showed him the well-illustrated popular geography
magazine, *Vokrug sveta* (Around the World), and said: "Read
that, and you won't go around offending people." (In the other
incidents recounted here also I tried to make appropriate responses.)

The late Jessica Smith, who worked longer and harder for
mutual understanding between our countries than any other American,
put this matter frankly in 1970 to the Russian who is assistant head of
their Association for Friendship with the Peoples of Africa. She
quotes his reply: "In 1950, when Black people, many of them
students, began to appear in large numbers in Moscow, our people
had seen rather few of them and had little understanding of what
they had suffered from white supremacy attitudes. . . . They simply
had not seen people as dark-skinned as those from Africa. They
created a sensation. Our people were ready at once to make friends
with them, but were not always sensitive enough to the special
problems they faced, because they were so different from anything
the Soviet people have known in their own experience. . . . We use
many different methods in making African problems known to the
Soviet people. We use press, radio, TV, all avenues of communication, and distribute books about Africa, to make our people
cognizant of the racist propaganda and persecution to which the
Black people of the world have been subjected. This has resulted in
increasing respect and friendship for the colored peoples of the
world among the Soviet people."[12]

In my experience, that is an honest answer on all counts. But
because two of the negative experiences I have described occurred
six years later, it is clear that not enough has yet been done. I
remember as early as 1931, an electric sign—in Russian, not

English — dominating one of the busiest squares in Moscow: "Tear the Scottsboro Boys Out of the Hands of the Executioners!" (The Scottsboro Case was a rape frame up — now universally admitted to having been that — that brought the first world-wide outcry against American judicial racism.)

An earlier book of mine is dedicated to: "Neal Burroughs (1922-1963): friend, translator, and unique product of two societies." Neal was the son of Mrs. William Burroughs, a New York City schoolteacher who was fired in 1928 for trying to organize a teachers' union. She took two of her children, Neal, then seven, and Charles, ten, to the Soviet Union. There she worked as English-language editor and voice of Radio Moscow. The boys were placed in a 24-hour-a-day childcare center; Neal forgot English and grew up a Black Russian, the older Charles became bilingual.

In later years, Charles was a circus performer, and early in World War II a truck driver for the Red Army. As an American citizen — the U.S. and the USSR were allies in that war — he was drafted out of Moscow and found himself in a training camp in Georgia, U.S.A., when the army was totally segregated and apartheid was the law off-base. Talk of culture shock! Today, Charles lives in Chicago, where he and his wife continue to direct the Black History Museum they founded thirty years ago. He still thinks very highly of the Soviet Union.

Brother Neal entered Moscow University, the country's finest, where he specialized in English literature and re-learned his native tongue. The country treasured those who it expected would rebuild its cultural life after the war, so the university's student body was evacuated to Central Asia when the Nazis reached the outskirts of Moscow. Their journey eastward itself was one of the horrors of war, and vastly increased Neal's respect for the staunchness of the Soviet people. The students nearly froze and starved to death as their train was side-tracked again and again, so troop and munitions trains could move westward for the battles that saved the world from Hitler. (Most Soviet railroads were then single track. Few paved roads existed.)

In the East, for the first time, he found himself in an area where people looked more like him than his fellow students at the university. He found they still had some suspicions left over from the colonial period. Once he was addressed in the local language and responded in Russian: "I don't understand." The man who had spoken to him said: "What are you doing, passing for white?" There had been distinct advantages in being white before the

Revolution. An Uzbek friend explained to Langston Highes in 1932 why there were partitions in the middle of the old street cars then still in service: "Before the Revolution, we would have to sit in the back. But now everybody sits everywhere."[13] That was over twenty years before Blacks won that right in the U.S. South. In Ashkhabad, the city to which Neal was evacuated a decade later, Hughes saw a museum display designed to help children learn about their history: It included a sign, "Sarts Keep Out" (Sart had been the Russian equivalent of "nigger"; the people called themselves Turkmen). The sign had been taken from a beautiful public park in the heart of town built by the colonial rulers for themselves. My wife and I were in that park half a century later: the majority of people were now Turkmen, and Turkmen and Russians mixed in a natural and tension-free manner (girls of both nationalities were walking with arms linked, a very common habit in the USSR). Members of both groups were eating at the same tables in its restaurant.

Neal Burroughs returned to New York with his mother when she learned she was dying of cancer and wished to be reunited with her children. Neal's education was equivalent to that of a Harvard senior, but here he was simply a poor Black man. The first employment he found was cleaning work. By the time I met him friends in the progressive United Electrical Workers Union had found him a job assembling radios. His bitterness at the racism he found among his fellow workers — never mind the foremen and boss — was deep. Finally, he got a job which allowed him to use his knowledge of Russian at a book store on Fifth Avenue. But the management wouldn't permit a Black face among the sales staff, in the 1940s, so this extremely personable, handsome, cultivated man was kept down in the basement filling mail orders. He did manage to have published an introduction he wrote to a translation (which he edited) of Ivan Turgenev's novel *Fathers and Sons*). It is still in print in a Pocket Books edition. In the Soviet Union he would undoubtedly have had an academic career, most probably at a leading university. Here that was simply not possible. To this day, I know of only a tiny handful of Blacks among the several thousand members of American Association for the Advancement of Slavic Studies, although Black interest in Pushkin and in the darker peoples of the USSR is high. The racism of most of these white professors has to be encountered to be believed: basically, their attitude is, what can a Black know about Russian literature?

My experiences lead me to agree with Hughes, Robeson, DuBois, Davis, Ali. They are Blacks. I am not. They have had a lifetime of experiencing and sensing racism, each suffered individually from it. All have traveled widely, and each one has said, in one form or another, what Muhammad Ali expressed most succinctly when asked his impressions and feelings about the USSR: "my surprise that I saw no hate, no racism, no prejudice, no envy or jealousy in anybody's eyes."

Ali and other prominent visitors may be suspected of having been shielded from racism or as having been there too short a time to experience it. That cannot be said of rank-and-file long-term residents like the Burroughs family, Mr. Golden and his party, and their children, Mr. Tynes, George Padmore, and many others who came to the same conclusion as Ali, after long acquaintance with the USSR. Frankly, I feel more secure in my own judgments when someone like Mr. Padmore chose to quote me with approval in a book of his.[14]

NOTES

1. Marilyn Bechtel, "Mohammad Ali Speaks His Mind," *New World Review*, XXXXVI, No. 5 (1978), pp. 4-15, *passim*.

2. Dr. Vladimir Stanis, "Patrice Lumumba University," *New World Review*, XXXXVII, No. 6 (1979), pp. 18-21, *passim*.

3. "Universitet Druzhby Narodov," *Bol'shaia Sovetskaia Entsiklopediia*, 3rd ed. (Moscow: Sovetskaia Entsiklopediia, 1977), p. 17, cols. 38-39.

4. *New York Times*, June 20, 1978.

5. *Los Angeles Times*, December 16, 1974.

6. *San Francisco Chronicle*, August 20, 1978.

7. Lily Golden-Hanga, *Africans in Russia* (Moscow: Novosti, 1966).

8. Langston Hughes, *Good Morning Revolution*, (New York: Hill & Wang, 1973), p. 81.

9. cited in D.B. Gilliam, *Paul Robeson: All-American* (New York: New Republic Books, 1978).

10. "Russia's contribution in the field of mass education and cultural reconstruction among backward peoples constitutes one of the finest monuments to Communist initiative and enterprise. It is a serious challenge to the Western European Imperialist Powers in Africa and elsewhere." George Padmore, *Africa: Britain's Third Empire* (London: Dobson, 1948), p. 106.

11. William B. Davis, "How Negroes Live in Russia," *Ebony*, January, 1960.

12. Jessica Smith, "African-Soviet Friendship," *New World Review*, XXXIX, No. 1 (1971), p. 91.

13. Langston Hughes, op. cit., p. 85.

14. George Padmore, *Africa* . . . p. 106, quoting my *Soviet Far East and Central Asia* as documentation in support of his conclusion in note 10 above, based on his own three years' residence in the USSR.

Typical housing in European USSR. Asian republics decorate buildings with ethnic tile patterns, as on mosques, and provide balconies.

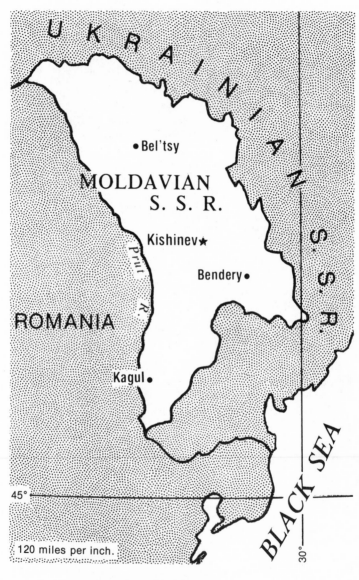

Moldavia

5

★Moscow

MOLDAVIA

The Soviet "Latins": Moldavia

A Spanish, Italian or French-speaking person would find something recognizable in 70 percent of the words in the Moldavian language — if he could read the alphabet. Because the traditional religion of the majority is Orthodox Christianity, the alphabet is like that of Russian, but the language is almost identical to that of Romania, the maverick Communist-governed country which borders Moldavia on the west. Romania, however, switched to the Latin alphabet over a hundred years ago for political reasons.[1]

The fact that Moldavia and Romania speak essentially the same language does not make them the same nation any more than English-speaking Canada and the United States, or Mexico and neighboring Guatemala, are the same. Moldavia (then called Bessarabia) was under the rule of the Romanian monarchy from 1920 to 1940, and treated as a colony. An Englishman, Julian Hale, who knows Romania and its language, has written that before World War II, "even those Romanians who owned Bessarabian estates refused to exile themselves from Bucharest [Romania's capital]. Inhabited by the poorest of the poor, remembered only by tax collectors and recruitment officers, deprived of roads . . . Bessarabia

had for centuries been *the most neglected area in Europe.*"[2]
[my emphasis-W.M.]

Today, the Romanians would find things to envy in Moldavia,
according even to a candidly anti-Soviet professor who reports that
in 1971 the number of doctors was fifty percent higher than in
Romania in proportion to the population.[3] The figure for doctors
was actually higher than in the U.S., Britain, France or Japan,[4]
yet the Moldavian figure has risen tremendously since then from
one physician to nearly 500 inhabitants to one per 340 only four
years later.[5] In 1971, Moldavia also had nearly twice as many TV
sets in proportion to population as Romania.

Moldavia is a small country, midway between Salvador and Costa
Rica in size, and densely populated, with four million people.*
From the air, flying at low altitude to and from the capital of
Kishinev, it reminds one of William Blake's England, "this green
and pleasant land." Like England, it is not spectacular, but very
thoroughly cultivated, today heavily in vines and fruits. Roads wind
in broad sweeps through gentle hills; oak and other trees provide
lovely color in the fall. Roadside wells are framed in traditional
stained wood, and bus shelters, as everywhere in the Soviet Union,
are decorated with tiles in local ethnic designs.

Farm homes don't differ fundamentally from those in the
nearby Ukraine, or even Russia, although large porches are more
frequent as this is warmer country and one thinks of sitting outside
in the shade in summer. There is also a warmth of color: Ukrainian
homes are generally whitewashed, Russian may be elaborately
carved, but Moldavians often use pastel colors and nailed-on wood
designs, often painting each strip differently.

The collective farm we visited, called "New Life," was described
to us as one of the best in Moldavia, but its homes, high school and
community center ("Casa de Culture") were not noticeably different
from those we had passed in the forty-mile drive from Kishinev.
We met with the chairman, the Communist Party leader, and the
director of an agricultural experiment station situated in the very
well-kept library occupying one wing of the community center. The
other wing held offices and a museum of the farm's history. The
central section, with its lofty colonnaded veranda, housed a combined auditorium and 850-seat movie theater, and a large dance
hall decorated with attractive frescos. Out front was a substantial
flagstoned area, and a large decorative pool.

---

*About the same as Honduras.

Photo by Author

Mexican dance by Moldavian factory workers' troupe. Director, who had visited Mexico, had been struck by cultural affinity in more than language.

Flanking this square was the high school. Like many others in the USSR it was quite plain externally and simply stunning within: gleaming parquet floors, the main corridor lined with busts of Moldavia's writers, their words displayed on stands. Before World War II, 65 percent of Moldavia's men and 85 percent of its women had been illiterate. In those times, this village had a two-year school with four teachers, themselves having only high school education. When we visited, it was a consolidated school running from first grade through high school with 58 teachers—20 with secondary education, 38 with higher education.

We asked our hosts whether the young people stay on the collective farm or go off to town once they graduate.

"We try to create all the conditions that will keep them here," came the reply, "so they'll work in the kolkhoz (collective farm). We're beautifying our streets, laying out a park." Several hundred, mostly young people, participate in the community center's performing arts groups, and its folk song and dance ensemble has been honored by the Moldavian government.

We knew that fifty nationalities live in Moldavia, and learned that on the collective farm the majority were Moldavians, but there were also Russians and Ukrainians, including the chairman. He had lived there twenty-one years, since "right after I graduated from junior college."

There were also, we were surprised to learn, Gypsies on the farm. "A dozen would settle down one year, fifteen the next, take jobs, work. They used to be wanderers. Now there are sixty families. They've built themselves good homes, designed for their extended families, and they don't drift off any more. They're doing skilled work: running tractors, operating other farm machinery, truck drivers. Two of them have graduated from the Conservatory, and one of those has become principal of the music school in Soroki."

These are free schools, with a seven-year course of instruction that children attend after regular school hours. There are about 7,000 such music schools all over the Soviet Union. The Gypsies, our host told us, "make very fine musicians." And "they all stay in high school right through graduation now."

(Two years later, I visited Kazakh friends on a street with settled Gypsy families in the large Asian city of Alma-Ata. One Gypsy woman had graduated from the Institute of Foreign Languages, majoring in French; another was a salesperson. Their homes, in this block of owner-built houses, were not ethnic in interior layout, and they were better than my friends' house — he a scholar, she a gynecologist — "because the Gypsies help each other out a great deal." In Moscow I interviewed two Gypsy sisters, one a concert singer, the other an anthropologist who had been recruited into that so that Gypsies could be studied by someone born to familiarity with their culture. Their father was a college professor and their uncle directed the professional Gypsy Theater. Their grandfather had been a tinsmith who insisted that his children take advantage of affirmative-action educational opportunities.)

At this point we were introduced to another man, considerably older and quite different in appearance, who had been seated quietly at the table. He had an intellectual air, combined with the sturdiness, and the hands of a farmer. He was head of the local agricultural experiment station of the Moldavian Academy of Sciences. He explained his tasks:

Photo by Author

Gypsy dance by Moldavian factory workers' troupe.

We worked out such things as optimal depth for plowing, because here there were absolutely no scientific research institutions in what is now our republic, much less in agriculture. Only when Soviet government was established in the 1940s was organization of such things begun. As a consequence, there were a great many matters that had to be investigated under the real conditions of the locality.

We found thirty identifiable kinds of soil on this farm, because it has everything from swamps to hilltops. With their work on seed varieties and the like, wheat yields are now two to two-and-a-half times better than ten years ago, and nearly four times better on experimental plots.

We use the best of worldwide experience, plus the things we've learned here. The outcome is that we do several things simultaneously: research, development on an experimental farming scale, and actual introduction into normal operations. Since we do our experimenting right here on the spot, the competent decision-makers on the farm see what works, and it goes into use without loss of time. So we wind up with an intimate tie between science and practice.

Before World War II a Rockefeller-funded study of a typical Moldavian village, conducted by the Romanian Department of Social Services, found that the diet for the majority "included practically no bread, fish, milk or tea."[6] A family of four averaged two pounds of meat per month. A follow-up study in the same village in 1960 brought out personal stories illustrating these figures.

One woman asked "How could we make ends meet on a half hectare [1¼ acre] of land? My husband and I worked as farm hands." They each earned five lei — a nickel — a day. "Try and live on that. Our food was hominy and pumpkin, which are now used as cattle fodder on the collective farm. Clothes and footwear were a special problem. Anyone who had a pair of high boots would hang them up in his room for all to see as if to say: 'I am not so poorly off — see, I even have a pair of high boots.' But he himself went barefooted. Just think, I had seven children, and five died." She didn't say how they died, but the pre-war study spelled it out: "Malaria, syphilis, and tuberculosis were rife in the village."[7]

Human relations were no better. In the follow-up study, another widow told how her husband, Georgi, worked for many years as a farm hand for Kiryak, a kulak [a Russian word meaning "fist," describing the skinflint peasant who managed to work himself up to employing others]:

Childless, he decided to adopt Georgi and get him to work on the farm. From hired laborers we became domestic servants. . . . I had to get up at two or three in the morning, bake the bread, cook, and feed the cattle. Just before the war Kiryak fell sick and his wife Akulina feared that the land, after his death, would pass to us [because of the adoption]. . . . In 1938 she poisoned me and my husband. . . . He died, but I recovered. . . . Akulina had already managed to bribe (the chief of police). . . . And so the murderess got away scotfree. In 1939 Kiryak died, and in 1940, when we were freed, Akulina fled to the West.

The founder of the collective farm we visited, Dr. B. Glushko, now retired, has written a memoir in which he describes how the attitudes bred by such relationships were changed. The son of one of the village teachers, he had managed to get a higher education in agricultural science in Romania, and a government research job. He records that half the village land belonged to large landowners and monasteries, about a fifth belonged to fifty kulaks like Kiryak — while the remaining 645 families had less than two acres each, on the average. He remember's his father's despair when, after explaining to a peasant the importance of clearing fallow, rotating crops, ploughing deeply, and fertilizing, the peasant would wave him off with a gesture of hopelessness and head for a saloon. What could he do with two acres? How could he spare land to lie fallow? How could he rotate crops when he needed every penny he could get from whatever crop promised to bring the highest price?

This overgrown village had five saloons. Its "society" consisted of the saloon-keepers, eight cops, two tax-collectors, two judges, four lawyers, two parish priests, the landlords and kulaks. Four teachers. No doctor. In 1940, when it became clear that the Soviets were going to — in the future chairman's view — liberate Moldavia, he got himself transferred back there, and when the Soviets did take over he became what we would call county agricultural agent. He described the problem:

> Our task did not consist solely of teaching people how to cultivate the soil properly. For centuries the sense of petty proprietorship had divided people, developed the lone-wolf aspect in their character, envy, enmity toward each other. It was necessary to persuade this kind of peasant, by visible and convincing proofs, that his strength lay in mutual assistance and friendship with those like him, and with the working class. . . . The Soviet system eliminated the very causes that gave birth to and nourished the negative aspects of the peasant's psychology. . . . Social and property inequality in the village was abolished. The peasant was given land, implements, grain . . . "[8]

One of the women in the follow-up survey talked of how this pertained to her: "For four months Kopanka was a front-line village [in World War II]. We were evacuated. When I got back with the children (my husband died in 1944) there was no trace of my hut; in its place there was nothing but weeds. Then the village Soviet helped me. It gave me a loan of ten thousand rubles and I was able to buy a cottage. I was also given an orchard spreading over two-and-a-half hectares [five acres]."[9] Where did the five acres come from? In Moldavia as a whole, 975,000 acres were confiscated from the wealthy and given to the poor.[10]

The collective farm we visited was founded August 3, 1947,

with 7 pair of horses, 12 yoke of oxen, some ploughs and harrows — and 400 pairs of hands.* The founder recalls their first lesson in cooperation 30 years before our visit:

> A plain, ordinary barn, long, low, not noteworthy in any way. Today you can't find a barn like that on the most backward farm. But in that long-ago 1948, it was a symbol, a good foretaste of the big building jobs of the future. We built it together, with our own hands, not each for himself, but for our common collective farm. . . . The then First Secretary of the county committee of the Communist Party arranged to bring people there from the whole county: let people see what 'miracles' were being performed in Chokyltiany.
>
> It wasn't the barn that was the miracle. What gave joy was to see how people gained faith in their own powers, how former farm laborers . . . became masters of their lives, skilled craftsmen, talented organizers.

These were the people who, before the war, used to emigrate from Bessarabia to western Europe, and some to the United States, as many as 50,000 in a single year. One-third of the rural population had been unemployed.[11] A situation not unlike that of Cuba at the time of its revolution.

A dozen years after founding, this farm was not only well equipped with tractors, combines, and trucks, but was able to buy an excavator to drain the swamps. Recovery from the war was now complete (the front had run through Chokyltiany for six months, and the land was crisscrossed with trenches, studded with pillboxes, deadly with mines), and the government had accumulated enough reserves to take up the work of drainage. We were told with pride that it put 16 excavators and 14 bulldozers to work, and reclaimed 2,400 acres for the farm. "As of today, the collective farm has put 60,000 rubles, and the government 900,000, into draining the valley of the Reut."

The founder remembers the more human things, like "the first person we put through college." Although Soviet higher education is free, its living-expense grants are sufficient only to maintain the student. If a farm or factory wishes to send a mature person with family responsibilities to receive a higher education, it provides that person's average earnings, on the condition that he or she returns after graduation to apply the acquired skill locally.

There were other pertinent human achievements. Moldavia's wealthy had been virulently anti-Semitic — a pogrom in Kishinev

---

*This terrible lack even of draft animals is directly comparable to some Central American situations.

early in this century is part of Jewish history, but during our visit, it was actually called to our attention as the kind of thing that today is out of the question. In his memoir Dr. Glushko pays his respect to others who helped build the farm: among them Mikhail Isakovich (son of Isaac) Chomsky, an unmistakeably Jewish name, who was assigned to the farm in 1954 as its Communist Party organizer. "He worked with us for nearly seven years. As the saying goes, his soul took root in the collective farm. He was incessantly looking for better ways, and organized people skilfully. Today . . . M.I. Chomsky is already in his fourteenth year as chairman of the Dimitrov Collective Farm."[12]

Glushko expresses satisfaction that thereafter the farm's Communists had always found a satisfactory leader from among themselves, although these individuals may have come to the farm earlier to give technical assistance. "It was in this way that our chief animal husbandry expert, Naum Evseevich Fishov," — another unquestionably Jewish name — "was elected secretary of the Party organization." Despite Hitler's gas chambers and a pogrom by his Romanian allies, who re-occupied Moldavia during World War II, it still has 80,000 Jews, or 2 percent of the population.

Among those mentioned in the memoir as contributing to the farm's progress, about thirty have unmistakeably Moldavian names, including one who was awarded the highest of all Soviet honors, the title "Hero of Socialist Labor," and another who is the local member of the republic's Supreme Soviet.

No country that lacks industry can be part of the modern world. Even if its needs for manufactures are adequately supplied from without, its own people will be handicapped so long as it lacks an urban life based on production, not just trade. When it was re-incorporated into the USSR after World War II, Moldavia was the country's most rural ethnic component, more so even than the Central Asian regions which had 15 years of Soviet modernization before the war plus the influx of industries evacuated there to escape Hitler.

As a consequence of this background and also because it is blessed with extraordinary soil and mild climate, Moldavia is still the second most rural of the republics, (after Asian Tajikistan) but the picture has changed sharply. Only one person in eight lived in town in 1940; today two in five do. Towns that were purely commercial — there was not one college in Romanian-controlled Bessarabia — have become industrial and cultural. Moldavia manufactures washing machines, refrigerators, heavy electrical machinery, over a billion cans of food per year, substantial quantities of cement, shoes and clothing for its own needs, and cognac that is sold world-wide, including the United States. The generation of electricity has multiplied 600 times! Bessarabia's only industries were primitive foundries and the manufacture of metal hoes. Today it produces ultrafine microwire, analogue computers and oscillographs.

Where there was one Ph.D. in Bessarabia before World War II, there are now 2,200. Moldavians still benefit from an affirmative-action program in the USSR: "the country's leading centers of science . . . provide places in their graduate study programs for Moldavians. . . . Today more than 100 scientific and higher educational institutions throughout the USSR are training researchers and scholars for Moldavia."[13] Moldavian institutions already graduate people in seventy-four majors. Most important, in terms of ethnic self-respect and cultural independence, by 1975 the number of ethnic Moldavian professionals and diplomaed paraprofessionals almost exactly equalled the number of those of all other nationalities in that republic combined: 133,700 to 137,600. The others had to be brought in, or came from among non-Moldavian local residents, because at the time of the Revolution there was not one single native-born doctor, engineer, or agricultural expert. Today ethnic Moldavians probably outnumber the others combined, because they increased 110 percent in professional and para-professional occupations from 1959 to 1973, more rapidly than the Russians (80 percent) or the Ukrainians (70 percent — Moldavia has half a million Ukranians), and that trend was continuing. As those figures make clear, members of the other nationalities in Moldavia are also free to advance themselves. The modern buildings in Moldavia chosen for illustrations of current architecture in Soviet Encyclopedia articles are largely designed by Jews: Gothelf, Weissbein, Shoikhet, Kaliuzhner.[14]

Perhaps most striking is the fact that other Soviet republics now send graduate students to Moldavia for training in fields in which its higher educational institutions have already won prominence: branches of theoretical mathematics, helminthology, plant physiology, computer engineering.

In view of the foregoing it is particularly shameful to read the following, in recent writing on Moldavia coming from American universities: "discrimination against Moldavian students"[15] or "Russians, Ukrainians, and Jews . . . gradually supplanting the

Moldavians"[16] or such sheer irrational trash as "perhaps it is the nature of the region which has discouraged a flourishing of culture."[17] Or, from another standard (!) source: "Leaders of the USSR and the Moldavian SSR . . . are pursuing a conscious policy of isolating the predominantly rural population from the political and urban technological order . . ."[18]

In the early 1970s Iu. V. Arutiunian, a Soviet anthropologist of Armenian nationality who enjoys international respect, found that the percentage of Russians employed in mental occupations in Kishinev barely exceeded the percentage of Moldavians, while a generation before the percentage among the Russians had been twice as high. *In a word, the Moldavians had closed a 50 percent gap in a single generation.** He found, further: "the influx of Russians from villages to the towns of Moldavia is declining, while that of Moldavians is increasing. . . . The Russian language is not displacing the Moldavian among Moldavians." and, most important: "the social structure of the [various] nationalities in Kishinev has become essentially the same."[19] The worst of it is that this information was available to the Americans quoted above at the time they wrote. It was published in a standard source carried nationally in university libraries.

In a paper delivered in the United States in 1984, reporting his subsequent studies, Arutiunian noted that Moldavians ranked among the top two Soviet nationalities in level of job satisfaction, among professionals and paraprofessionals, and that, with unobstructed opportunity for advancement, the overwhelming majority enroll for postgraduate training.[20]

I myself owe the Moldavians an apology. In a previous book, I gave their country only a cursory mention. True, in that volume I had to survey all the nationalities of the USSR in a single chapter,[21] but the fact is that I dealt with Moldavia in a cavalier fashion because I was not sure the republic was anything but a legal fiction to cover Soviet occupation of a territory that had changed hands innumerable times, like Alsace and Lorraine between Germany and France.

Now that I've been there, I know better. Even five minutes at the art museum in Kishinev made clear that the culture was distinct from that of the other republics. There is a vividness of color that probably has something to do with the sunny skies and fine light of the region. There was a southern liveliness in the work,

---

*Would that the opportunity existed for the same to happen with American Latinos or Blacks!

a broader range of experimentation in forms than one sees in most Soviet republics. And while there was no discrimination against non-Moldavians, there was a plurality of Moldavian ethnic names, and paintings with a theme often concerned ethnic subjects; village musicians and singers in native dress, or a peasant carving decorations on his house.*[22]

Opera is hardly an art one associates with underdeveloped people, and Kishinev has had a professional company with its own theater, since 1957. Maria Beishu, sent to Italy for training with Milan's La Scala, won a world-wide competition in Japan for best performance of Chio-Chio-San in "Madame Butterfly." Moldavian composers have created in the most complex musical forms, including operas on ethnic historical themes.

As everywhere in the USSR, there has been tremendous emphasis on raising folk dance to the level of professional performing art. One of the most successful companies is Moldavia's "Zhok," with its sensational ring dance in which the men, their arms around each other, fly horizontally off the floor as though being whirled by an invisible pinwheel. It has been performed on every continent, and this, too, adds to the ethnic self-confidence and pride of this small nation.

It is Soviet policy that each republic shall be assisted to develop in each of the major arts, so each has its own film studio. Moldavian films have not won the international fame of Soviet Georgian, but at least one movie has gained USSR-wide attention: *An Accusation of Murder.* It dealt with how perfectly normal young workingmen in a factory kill someone when they are on a drunken spree, and how various prestigious types pass the buck when confronted with their direct or indirect responsibility for the fact that such a social situation can arise. Except for the familiar film stereotype of the good-guy fatherly cop, it is an above average film.

At the Writers Union, I spoke with a script-writer, a graduate of the Film Institute in Moscow who explained that film-making began less than 25 years ago in Moldavia. "We've put out a respectable number of films, more documentaries than otherwise. *The Last Month of Autumn,* based on a novel by our Ion Drutse,

---

*Incidentally, the leading Moldavian sculptor, Dubinovsky, switched back and forth in conversation from Russian to Yiddish to Hebrew. None of those present showed the slightest surprise or annoyance at his using languages of the Jews.

won the Grand Prix at the Cannes Festival of Films for Youth in 1967." The studio produces five feature films a year, three for theater showing and two for television, ranging from historical themes to comedies.

Drutse is one of many writers in minority languages who are known across the country. Four of his plays have been produced all over the Soviet Union, in translations, and in 1978 one of its most demanding repertory companies, Moscow's Maly Theater, presented his work, with one of the greatest Russian actors playing Leo Tolstoy. One has to understand the extraordinary Russian reverence for literature, and the virtual worship of classics like Tolstoy, to appreciate Drutse's daring in doing a play on him, — the more so as Drutse broke with the accepted picture of Tolstoy's wife, Sophia Andreyevna, as a "harassed and hysterical woman," and made her the hero of the play.

Americans often assume there must be something of colonialism in the relationship between Russia and the ethnic republics, simply because of the great disparity in size and population. In fact, the colonial mentality is not to be found, as Drutse's iconoclastic attitude shows. Another example is offered by a Moldavian poet, Aureliu Busuiok. In 1978, the prestigious USSR-wide *Literary Gazette* surveyed writers all over the country to find out whether critics had responded to Communist party demands that they change certain practices so critics could be more useful to writers and the public. Busuiok answered bluntly, "In thinking about what help critics are to me in my work, I come to the conclusion, not much." And as one whose national reputation depends upon the quality of translation, he volunteered, "It is quite common for a poet to be cussed out for the sins of the translator or praised for merits that are not his."[23] As two volumes of his verse and two of his novels have been published in Russian, he need not fear that his talent will be known only to the very few million who read his own language.

However, a full quarter of the Soviet people—half of the non-Russians—do not know Russian very well, and hardly any non-Moldavians know Moldavian. How do they get access to his work? A member of the Writers' Union told of a "young and very able" poet who came from Latvia to study Moldavian. He now translates verse from Moldavian to Latvian—languages of very different families. And many Moldavian books appear in Kiev, the capital of the Slavic-language Ukraine that nearly surrounds Moldavia. "They recently published *An Anthology of Moldavian Poetry* in two

ШТЕФАН
ЧЕЛ МАРЕ

Photo by Author

Moldavian national hero. Religious symbolism is accepted as natural for his time.

volumes, an enormous undertaking, a literary event of outstanding importance. We will be publishing an anthology of Ukrainian poetry."

He told me of a "literary event," called Days of Soviet Literature in Moldavia. "Representatives of the literatures of all the other fourteen republics came here: large delegations from Moscow and Leningrad and even guests from abroad." Imagine the biggest names in American writing from New York and Hollywood going, say, to Texas at the invitation of this country's Latino writers in Spanish or the mixture "Spanglish" often used colloquially. Imagine, too, that a Latino writers' organization could pay their costs. "Many of them have written about Moldavia, for example, Gevorg Emin, the prominent Armenian poet. Or the prominent poet of the Caucasus, Kaisin Kuliev, who has been here many times and whose poems have been translated into our language." Kuliev is a Balkarian, a mountaineer people numbering only 42,000 within the Russian Republic. He writes in his own language, which was never put in written form until after the Russian Revolution. He enjoys USSR-wide prominence. This is as though a Cherokee or Cree (whose languages were put in written form) wrote poetry in his own language, and English-speaking North Americans were interested enough to discover that it had universal merit and went to the trouble of translating it and publishing it for the general public.[24]

"Moscow writers are very dear to us because they translate our work into the Russian language, and it is through Russian that we emerge into the larger world. Such famous poets as Anna Akhmatova and Boris Pasternak translated poetry from Moldavian and thus promoted its popularity."

Despite Busuiok's criticism, the work is done in a fashion far more painstaking and costly than any American publisher is willing to finance, as I know from my own experience. "Usually the translator familiarizes himself with Moldavia, with the republic, with our literary and cultural context. David Samoilov, for example, translated our classics, he translated our folklore, and thus worked his way to contemporary poetry, a process extending over many years. There are also meetings with the original author, and familiarization with his native places."

He gave as an example a Moldavian writer visiting Latvia, from which it is separated by three other Soviet republics of distinct ethnic cultures and languages. "One of our writers went there and wrote about all three of the Baltic republics — essays, essentially, and they turned out very interesting. They were then translated into their languages, so they got to see how they look through ouur eyes."

In different countries of the Soviet Union, I spoke with different sorts of people—in Kirgizia I came closest to film and TV people, in other places to anthropologists. But Moldavia gave me a picture of the way in which writers, as an organized body, see their relationship to society. Because that relationship is the same everywhere in the USSR, and is much discussed in the west, let us listen to the Moldavians a bit more.

I had needled them about their building—new, five stories high and half a block long, with a lobby big enough for a grand ball. I asked, "How many members in the Writers' Union?" "About 150," was the reply. I asked, what the hell do they *do* in such a building?

"You mean, isn't it too big for our hat size?"

"How do you justify it? You don't live here. You don't do your writing here. Of course, the building is merely the physical manifestation—How do you explain the extraordinary place occupied by the writer?"

One man offered a concrete example:

This year has seen the seventh edition of our school primer. This primer was written by *writers*, by two of our creative writers, in collaboration with professional educators. These are excellent writers, who for *nearly five years* gave up their own personal literary undertakings, and *created* a primer. They made the rounds of schools. They consulted with the very best teachers, with publishing-house personnel. They worked on that primer as though it were a book-length poem. Now other republics are translating and publishing that primer because it has the quality of a work of art.

This was for the first grade. And they didn't do this out of monetary considerations. The honorarium was ordinary, modest.

Soviet writers earn no royalties, but the honoraria allow the rank-and-file professional writer to earn a living—rarely the case in the West.

There are schools taught in Russian in Moldavia, but this was a primer of the Moldavian language. The speaker did go on to explain the building: on one floor, writers put out two literary magazines which have large circulations, one of them USSR-wide; another floor has a literary museum, another a large auditorium for public readings of new books—and they had recently established a publishing house of their own, for creative literature.

Writers, he explained, "feel an organic need to work for

Library in village "Casa de Culture."

society. After the war, for example, when the people of Moldavia simply did not know how to read, how did our literature get under way? The very first thing we did was to write the kind of books from which peasants could learn to read." He pointed with pride and respect to an older man at the table: "our old-timer here, Dregupanu; also Corliupanu." The older man added: "Gusev. Gusev, Evgenii Mikhailovich," — a Russian name — he was paying respects to a Russian colleague who assisted in getting their ethnic efforts off the ground.

"We did our share in everything, on the very highest and most serious level; from that first textbook on, our creative writers were *involved*. Without false modesty, we can say that writers did work of enormous importance. This includes, for example, the development of the theater. It isn't only a matter of writing: they participate. Someone will work somewhere as literary secretary, another as a director. In the development of our movie industry, Georgii Vodu here, a poet, is also a director."

This speaker wrote lyrics for topical songs for a youth newspaper. "I felt that it is not for a writer of poetry to do *articles* on social problems, but that he has to express himself on such matters through his own medium of verse." In short, he felt a duty to

Gagauz and Moldavian anthropologists.

participate in civic matters, but that he could best contribute through his art — I was reminded very much of Woody Guthrie, Pete Seeger, Paul Robeson.

Another writer explained some of the more material aspects of their work. "The Writers' Union is a professional organization, and rather a wealthy one, which had enough money to build this large building for itself. It also has enough to send its members on trips for months to gather material for their work and provide vacations for its members.

"We're not the only organization of people in a creative field. For example, people associated with theater also have a building, 'The House of the Actor.' A member of an association of creative people can arrange for foreign travel. Moldavia is no exception — you'll find the same thing in every other republic."

The overall situation in Moldavia was best summed up, quite unintentionally, by an American Sovietologist I quoted earlier. In closing a presentation to a symposium he said, and had the incredible lack of tact to publish, the following: "I apologize for my inability to produce evidence of [anti-Soviet nationalist] . . . activities in Moldavia."[25]

Perhaps he would understand why he could find no such evidence had he heard the life story of a calm and handsome woman I recorded in the Moldavian capital. She was born in 1937, seven years before the Soviet system began in Moldavia, when it was part of the Kingdom of Romania. Now an anthropologist, she told of her experiences:

I am from a peasant family, from the very depths of the people, as they say. The anthropology I write is inside me. I lived that life; there was no need for me to familiarize myself with it. I know the customs, the rituals, the milieu. I am the youngest of nine children. Two died in childhood. That's because those were hard years. Even right after liberation, 1945 was a very hard year. Another sister, my older brother and sister are now collective farmers. They didn't have the chance to become educated. They were too old for that. But they're not suffering because of that, they are honored workers, have good houses. My brother has raised five children, my sister four. All of them have made it in life, and bring joy to us and to their parents.

Of the other four of us, one beside me has higher education. She works as a county environmental protection inspector. A brother works as a collective farm bookkeeper. He's a member of the Communist Party, as is another of my sisters who is a nurse. And finally there's me.

As the last one, I went farther than any of the others. But that was a consequence of many circumstances. I entered grade school right after the war, in 1946. It was a terribly difficult year, but I had a very good teacher. He was one of the very few Gagauz teachers who had managed to get an education even under Romanian rule.*

He apparently saw ability in me. I was out working in the fields with my father. I guided the horse, and he tried to plant somehow. Everything had been destroyed. War! I wasn't going to school. But the teacher would come by the house every day and chalk on the doors in a big calligraphic hand: "Comrade Vasilioglu! Let your daughter go to school!" Every evening my father would wipe this inscription off, and the next day it would appear again. And so the teacher suffered through till he got me.

Well, I took very quickly to reading, to studying. For me going to the library was a celebration. I also had a lot of curiosity, loved to go to the movies. I read a great deal in Russian. I knew all of Balzac. Perhaps I was also lucky because the librarian was Russian. She was

---

*The Gagauz, as she explains in my introductory "Overview" chapter, are a Turkic speaking minority inhabiting twenty-six villages. Her family name had a Turkish ending.

from the intelligentsia. A very friendly atmosphere was created.

When I finished the seventh grade, [in those years as far as education went in her village] I began to think—what am I going to be? I very much wanted to find out some day from where, who, the Gagauz were. How could I find the science that would answer that question for me? The people with whom I had contact at that time were entirely unable to tell me where to turn. So I decided I'd become a schoolteacher, because a teacher could find her way later into the sciences. So I entered a normal school, I graduated, and worked there for one year in Komrat—today it is a small town, then it was simply a large village. I worked with my groups there, my children, and then I decided after all that I would go further my education. So I went to the university [founded after the war] and took the entrance exams in Kishinev, and entered in the 1957-58 year.

Her living expenses were paid, and she was provided with dormitory housing—an important benefit, as housing was still in short supply in the former battle zones. She emphasized that if she had trouble in some subject, "I knew that it had nothing to do with anything but me myself. *Never in my entire life* did I experience or hear a single denigrating word about the fact that I was a member of an ethnic minority."

You know, during the period of the Romanian occupation, 1920-1940, the Gagauz were regarded as particularly ignorant peasantry, hayseeds, and such people were not to be accepted. But the Moldavians were in the same situation, and other nationalities. The Romanian government looked upon this territory as its fief. The people who lived here—the Moldavians and the Gagauz—were to be their servitors. And my parents, before the liberation, were workers for a Romanian capitalist.

My father had very little land—he had two strips. One was a *very* long distance away, the other nearby. And we just didn't have enough to feed us from one harvest-time to the next. And when, in 1940, they liberated us [a reference to the one-year period of Soviet rule before the area was again overrun by Romania] they came, the Russians, they gave our family a lump sum of money, and a cow. I was very little then, but I remember how it was led in by a man in a military uniform, how kind he was, and he brought us the document for the gift. At that time there were seven of us children alive, so they gave us a cow. I still remember how the rich man's house servants used to call me "the Red."

I knew she had recently been appointed assistant director of the Anthropology Sector of the Moldavian Academy of Sciences, and asked whether her new administrative duties were not a burden. "Oh, I continue my research," and she handed me reprints of papers she had published, and the abstract of her thesis. "I'm so happy when I come to work each day!"

Notes

1. Julian Hale, *Ceausescu's Romania* (London: Harrap, 1971), p. 184.

2. Ibid., p. 25.

2. Stephen Fischer-Galati, "Moldavia and the Moldavians," in Zev Katz (ed.), *Handbook of Major Soviet Nationalities* (New York: Free Press, 1975), p. 417.

4. S.D. Spector, "The Moldavian S.S.R., 1964-1974," in G.W. Simmonds (ed.), *Nationalism in the USSR and Eastern Europe* (Detroit: Univ. of Detroit, 1977), p. 261.

5. *Bol'shaia Sovetskaia Entsiklopediia* (3rd ed.; Moscow, Sovetskaia Entsiklopediia, 1977), XXIV, Part II, p. 531.

6. V.N. Shubkin, "A Comparative Sociological Survey of a Moldavian Village," in G.V. Osipov (ed.), *Town, Country and People* (London: Tavistock, 1969), p. 155.

7. Ibid., p. 156.

8. B. Glushko, *Put' Novoi Zhizni'* (Kishinev: Kartia Moldoveniaske, 1976), p. 7.

9. Shubkin, "A Comparative Survey," p. 161.

10. *The Moldavian Soviet Socialist Republic* (Moscow: Novosti, 1974), p. 14.

11. Shubkin, p. 151.

12. Glushko, *Put' Novoi Zhizni'*, p. 42.

13. I.S. Puchkov and G.A. Popov, "Sociodemographic Characteristics of Science Personnel [Part 2]," *Soviet Sociology*, XVI, No. 4 (1978), p. 71.

14. *Bol'shaia Sovetskaia Entsiklopediia*, XVI, Plates 29, 31.

15. Spector, "The Moldavian S.S.R.," p. 265.

16. Ibid., p. 264.

17. Ibid., p. 263.

18. Fischer-Galati, "Moldavia and the Moldavians," p. 431.

19. Iu. V. Arutiunian, "Sociocultural Aspects of the Development and Convergence of Nations in the USSR," *Soviet Sociology*, XIII, No. 1-2 (1974), p. 180.

20. Iu. V. Arutiunian, "Sotsial'naia struktura sovetskikh natsii," unpublished paper delivered at meeting of U.S. and Soviet anthropologists and ethnographers, Tulane University, April, 1984.

21. William Mandel, *Russia Re-examined*, revised ed. (New York: Hill and Wang, 1967), pp. 46-70.

22. *The Art of Soviet Moldavia*, with introductory article and catalogue by M. Livshits (in Moldavian, Russian, and English), (Leningrad: Aurora, 1972), 54 plates.

23. "Writers About Critics," *Soviet Studies in Literature*, XV, No. 2 (1979), p. 62.

24. W.L. Morton, *The Historical Phenomenon of Minorities: The Canadian Experience*, XIV International Congress of Historical Sciences, San Francisco, 1975, 50 pp.

25. Spector, p. 267.

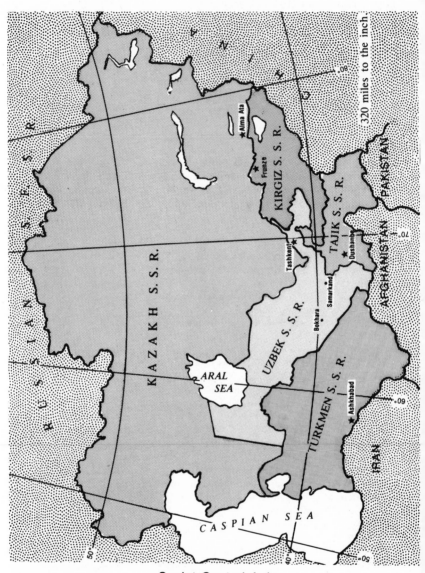

Soviet Central Asia
Uzbekistan, Tajikistan, Kazakhstan, Turkemnia, Kirgizia

Central Asia: History; Settled Peoples

A friend once left for the African state of Burkina Faso (formerly Upper Volta) to take a public health position. Curious, I looked in the *Encyclopedia Britannica* for basic information, and updated it from almanacs, It has a population of seven million; there is one doctor for 30,000 people; one child in ten is in school, which is taught in French, although Moray is the language of the great majority. One person in 14 can read and write; life expectancy at birth is 32 years; one child in four dies before it is a year old. Ninety percent of the people are in agriculture—raising livestock, cotton, rice, peanuts—and famine, due to drought, has occurred in recent years. These figures are for 22 years after independence, following 64 years of French rule.

　　Of themselves, independence and the passage of time do not change these things. Liberia, the oldest republic in Africa, has had a century and a half of contact with the United States, from which its ruling caste of Black freedmen emigrated. It has deep-water seaports, unlike landlocked Burkina Faso. Major U.S. corporations —Firestone, Goodrich—have been operating rubber plantations there for half a century, and it is one of the world's great exporters of iron ore. It earns additional money by allowing 2,600 ships to sail under its "flag of convenience," more than sail under the U.S. or Soviet flags. Effects upon the people? Infant mortality is still 148 per 1,000, virtually every single citizen has malaria, one man in three can read and write, one woman in seven; average food intake is below the hunger line and there is one doctor per 8,000 persons.

The *worst* of these statistics are *better* than those for the countries of Central Asia before the Russian Revolution of 1917 when they were colonies and protectorates of the Russian Empire. In Kirgizia there was only one doctor per 100,000 people.[1] Throughout Central Asia, infant mortality was twice as high as it is in Burkina Faso today, illiteracy *twice* as bad.

Enough of statistics. Here's a description by Arthur Koestler, who visited Turkmenia, which borders Iran, not immediately after the Russian Revolution, but in 1932. "We are all squatting on the edge of an irrigation canal which is now dry, sharing the women's midday meal. It consists of melons, soup and tea. . . . During the three or four days that we spent on the cotton plantations . . . we never had any solid food, not even bread. . . . The melons gave all of us more or less chronic diarrhea."

[A Russian Communist, Kikiloff, native to the area] "told us about the annual bloody feuds over water in the village where he had lived before the Revolution. The various strips of land were to be irrigated in an agreed order, but there was never enough water, and somebody always stole up at night to a sluice-gate to get more for his plot. In one of the brawls that grew out of such incidents Kikiloff's brother was killed — a neighbor bashed in his skull with a wooden plough. That was perhaps the incident which had turned him into a revolutionary. . . . He had travelled among the Tadzhiks [Tajiks] in the Pamirs. . . . One day a Red Army patrol on bicycles had arrived in a Tadzhik village. The villagers fled in panic. . . . A human being riding on a thing which had only two wheels and no support — surely that must be a miracle worked by the Devil."

Yet, as Koestler points out, before the Revolution, "The towns of Turkmenistan . . . were not inhabited by Turkomans but by Russians. . . . The natives were left to their semi-nomadic existence."

He writes of farm women "carrying infants on their backs, in a fold of their garments. ' There were five or six of them carrying their babies in this fashion, on backs bent nearly horizontal to the ground, for seven hours a day."

Farther east he found, "The most out-of-world place to which I have ever been in a village near the Soviet-Afghan frontier, called

Permetyab. Most of the men had sores and eye diseases; it seemed as if nearly half of them were one-eyed."

From these frontier areas he went a little north, to ancient centers of civilization, like Samarkand. "Yet all that remains in my memory are some fragments of beauty inextricably mixed with squalor and decay. . . . One wanted just to sit down in the shade of the decaying turquoise columns and cry. For the arches were crumbling, the tiles peeling off, and broken fragments were strewn among the rubble smelling of dogs' urine.

"The desolation of Samarkand had been heartbreaking. . . . For the past three centuries Bokhara had been a nightmare town where the fanatic side of Islam had degenerated into a kind of collective insanity. In Bokhara, offenders were thrown into dried-up wells . . . or hurled down from the top of a mosque, or executed by having their throats cut with a knife on the public square." Under the tsars, this region had been a "protectorate" with the ruling emir given a general's rank, the opportunity to invest in Russian business — and permission to rule undisturbed.

In Bokhara, Koestler visited the Revolutionary Museum. He describes a photograph: "It was, however, not so much a torso as a kind of anatomical study of torn flesh, with strips of skin hanging

Ancient moslem seminary painstakingly restored to its blue-tiled splendor.

loosely down, showing the bared sinews. The inscription said that these were photographs of Hadji Mir Baba, one of the leaders of the Bokharian Revolution, taken in 1920 by one of the Emir's officers, after Hadji Mir Baba's arrest and torture.

"As I was looking at the photograph, a tall old man with a stoop walked up to me and said in Russian: 'That is I.' And so he was. The old man was the custodian of the museum. In spite of his stoop, his bony frame and hawk's face still gave an impression of unbreakable physical strength and will-power."

The Hadji told Koestler his story. A widely-traveled karakul merchant, he had wanted the modernization and liberalization of Bokhara. "He joined the [Communist] Party and visited Lenin in Petersburg. Admitted to Lenin's presence, Hadji Mir Baba bared his back and said: 'This is my letter of recommendation.' He returned to Bokhara after the flight of the Emir in 1920, fought with the Red army . . . and was elected to the Central Committee. At the time of my visit to Bokhara he drew a Party pension . . . "[2]

This describes what the soviets had started from in Central Asia, and how far — in Koestler's view — they had come in twelve years. Others saw it differently. Black American poet Langston Hughes, who traveled with Koestler, was one. "As a foreign writer visiting in a nearby city, I was the especially invited guest to what might seem to many a very humble celebration in a remote rural region. The celebration was the opening of the first workers' barracks at the site where the new dam, Chirchikstroy, was to be constructed.

"The fellow who wrapped it all up into five words was an unprepossessing looking little guy of unknown ancestry, maybe Tartar, maybe Tajik. He was short and stocky and homely. His skin was a kind of dirty yellow and his short wiry hair was the same color. American Negroes would call him 'meriney.' He looked like he might be 16 or 17 years old. He was a member of the Reception Committee that greeted me at the door of a long wooden hut on a barren stretch of ground as our car drove up in the pitch black of a country night. . . .

"He said, 'Then there will be light.' He told me how there were only candles and lanterns and tallow flares now, and most of the villagers in the mud huts scarcely had those. 'But,' he said, 'when the dam is built, there will be light! And not just for us,' he said, 'but for all the world, too, because this dam will be so powerful that we can send light over the borders into India and into China! That is why we do not mind giving our labor after hours to build this first building here — this workers' barracks — and we will give many extra hours to that dam, too — because when it is done — tell your people in your America — when it is done, there will be light. Light to study by and to see — and it won't be dark any more'!"[3]

Four years before Hughes' visit, in 1928, Anna Louise Strong, a white journalist from Seattle, traveled in Soviet Central Asia. She had first come to Russia in a Quaker famine relief team in 1921. In Samarkand, where Koestler saw only the crumbling structures of an earlier civilization, Strong attended a meeting of what we would call the congress of the Uzbek Soviet Socialist Republic.

"Uzbeks in many-colored robes, padded against the sharp autumn weather, were the chief figures. The proceedings went on in the Uzbek language, but the more important parts were translated into Russian, 'for the benefit of the Europeans'." The Europeans — Russians, Jews, and one Latvian — were one-quarter of the assembly, although "A clear majority were Uzbeks." The remainder were people of other Asian nationalities who lived in Uzbekistan. Some of the top executives were of:

Asiatic nationalities of the Caucasus, which have had more education than the Uzbeks and are now supplying many organizers . . . in Central Asia. I inquired of one of these to what extent the government in Samarkand was run by the natives. In the chief assembly their predominance was obvious, but how about the civil departments of the government? He told me that the departments of Education and of Social Welfare are almost entirely manned by Uzbeks, since teaching is chiefly done in the Uzbek language. The Finance Department is seventy percent Uzbek. The Department of Agriculture is Uzbek except for its farm experts; the Water Department except for its engineers. The local courts are all Uzbek, but in the higher courts some fifteen to twenty percent are Russians. Russians persist throughout the Health Department, since practically no Uzbeks have as yet had time to learn medicine. In the higher economic departments, such as the State Planning Board or the Department of State Industries, about half the staff is Russian.[4]

One of the members of the presiding committee Strong met was a 22-year-old miner's daughter. She had been married off at ten to a middle-aged man, and had been one of the first to join the women's movement, organized by Russian women starting in 1924. "They taught her to read; they discovered and trained her capacity for eloquence; they got a divorce for her. . . . She holds great audiences spellbound with her oratory."

The president of Uzbekistan, Akbunbabay(ev), was the son of a poor peasant, and had himself been a farm laborer. For the first six years of Soviet rule, he had been a local leader of the class organization of rural poor—laborers and peasants with minimal landholdings. One of the very first non-intellectual Uzbeks to join the Communist Party, Akhunbabay had fought personally against the *basmachi** trying to restore the old regime by raids from across the border in Afghanistan where they had taken refuge. When Strong visited, his work was focused on confiscating landlords' lands and dividing them among the peasants.

They had "uncovered many landlords not on the lists of the government," he told Strong, who noted "It was clear that the participation of the farm hands in governmental activities was the most important fact in the whole land confiscation" to him.

The entire Central Asian region was a beehive of activities designed to rouse people's participation in shaping their own destinies. Koestler saw women cotton-pickers being taught to read —by an adolescent girl—during their midday meal.[5]

Today, the Central Asia these observers described can only be recognized by the ethnic features which remain: the people's physical appearance and, in some places, their dress; the colored tiles or carved plasterwork which covers the exterior walls of tall, modern apartment buildings, the music on the radio, are unmistakeably Middle Eastern. And, perhaps most impressive, there are statues everywhere of cultural, historical and labor heroes with obviously Asian features.

Ethnic character also remains apparent in the countryside and in urban "do-it-yourself" housing. Dwellings are of adobe or plastered, rather than the log or frame of the Russians, the brick of the Baltic or the masonry of the Caucasus. Droves of camels may still be seen outside Ashkhabad, the capital of Turkmenia, where the desert begins.

But the physical evidences of underdevelopment and colonialism are utterly absent. Bazaars today are more like farmers' markets— spacious, orderly, clean, with voices at the level of normal conversation. No beggars whatever (although one can still find a couple in Moscow). No stench anywhere but in public toilets—no one ragged. No sign of the gaunt, hollow-eyed look of underfeeding and overwork, never mind the pot bellies of starvation. No one living in the

---

*Counter-revolutionaries led by large landowners and clan chiefs, who were often one and the same. During my 1982 visit, Central Asians simply took it for granted, that the Afghans then raiding into Afghanistan from Pakistan were identical in social origins and purpose to the *basmachi* of the 1920s.

Tom Weber

Camels may still be seen right outside the capital of Turkmenia.

streets, no shantytowns of metal scraps, crates, mud or whatever. No open sewers or use of gutter water. There are plenty of people in the streets, but all seem to be going somewhere: no one looks to be hanging around. There are no children trying to peddle smuggled cigarettes or whatever, as in Naples in the heart of Europe.

Nor are there any sharp social contrasts. Some people are dressed better than others, but the only luxurious clothing is indigenous dress for festive events in Tajikistan. Restaurants are much nicer-looking than the stand-up snack counters, though shirt-sleeved, open-collared working men will be found in both. A Kazakh physician and her researcher husband live in a two-story private home with fruit and vegetable garden — of the size and quality an American factory worker might possess. A Tajik collective farmer has a similar home, perhaps a little poorer. I visited a Russian university vice-president and his seismologist wife in Tajikistan. Their apartment has two rooms, vestibule, kitchen, and bath, with but one advantage: it is directly across the street from the university.

Each city reflects its ethnic tradition in its architecture in a distinctive way, but apartment building developments all have very high ratios of open space, mostly planted with grass, trees, and flowers, with some playgrounds and gazebos. Only in the few oldest downtown blocks does one find buildings constructed to the sidewalk line, with no greenery in between. In a few of the ancient cities, such as Bokhara, there are still some rabbit-warren streets, though the houses have interior courtyards. Even in Bokhara, two-thirds of the population live in the planned, new neighborhoods. Indeed, Soviet urban authorities seem to be in a permanent competition over which city will have the largest plantings. One learns to listen politely as a fellow traveler insists that his town is certainly the greenest.

Approaching Dushanbe, capital of Tajikistan, from the air, one passes over or even between the tumbled masses of some of the world's highest mountains. Beneath them are narrow brown valleys with clear signs of immense seasonal mud flows and flood-carried rocks. It is forbidding country, but in the city, driving off the main avenues, we passed block after block of cozy private homes surrounded by greenery, with trees arched to form a canopy protecting the streets from the southern sun.

The city, now approaching half a million in size, used to be a semi-medieval, semi-colonial outpost of empire. In 1926, the year after its Soviet development began, it had 6,000 people. The city-to-be was treeless, and the surrounding mountains had no trees usable in construction, so each log had to be hauled by camel from the railhead, then 180 miles away. An American, Joshua Kunitz, reported that workers had to travel 12 days by cart after five by rail from central Russia, as at that time there were virtually no Tajiks skilled in 20th-century construction.[6]

Today hillmen and women still come to Dushanbe's farmers' market in their marvelous candy-striped turbans and robes, some as dark-skinned as anyone in Africa, but with high-bridged noses and narrow lips. When they have sold their wares, they walk a

Uzbek women.

block to shop in the large department store. On that same main avenue is the university. (The city's student population — there are also four other colleges — is 34,000.) There is the Tajik Theater of Drama, founded in 1929 by Tajiks trained in Moscow. In those years, it was quite literally worth a Moslem woman's life to be seen on stage, and nearly as risky for a man, because of Islamic prohibition of theater. Religious fanatics actually murdered Hamza, the founder of theater in neighboring Uzbekistan. We saw a splendidly staged performance of a Tajik play at this theater, listening to a translation in Russian through headsets. The Tajik language is a variety of Farsi, the language of Iran (they are mutually intelligible). The play showed the stoning, a century ago, of someone who violated Islamic dogma, as has recently happened in Iran. In Tajikistan that has not happened in fifty years.

On the same avenue is a soaring, airy, stunning tea-house, built in 1958, architecturally worthy of the tradition of Iranian mosques. Down the street is the main library of the republic, with 2,000,000 volumes; also the theater of opera and ballet, with a permanent company. (The city has 88 other libraries: one for every 5,000 people!) One walks past the dramatically ultra-modern, block-long, House of Political Education, and recently-constructed hotels. Monuments honor a classical poet and a writer; this would not have been permissible at the time of their deaths because of the prohibition against images.

One evening my wife and I happened upon an outdoor theater in Dushanbe's downtown park, opposite the Intourist Hotel. As we took a seat, we heard two young men on stage, being addressed by a Russian woman, who was saying:

"This is the baby's undershirt. This is the diaper. This is its cap. Here's an apron for you. Now look around very carefully. Those dolls in front of you are your babies. Here's the crib, a shirtie, booties. Now, you've got to put on your apron, put the clothes on the baby, and put it into the crib. Now, comrades, you understood? I'll count to three, and you start. The one who finishes first wins. One, two, three, go!

"The apron, the apron, the apron. Comrades, now look carefully. Think what you're doing." One of the men was refusing to don an apron, clearly because it represented being a woman. But he was willing to care for an "infant," which in the past had been solely a female function. The audience was roaring with laughter, and yelling comments and encouragement in Farsi.

One of the men put the baby clothes on all wrong and the Russian woman exhorted him: "Take it off. Pay attention. Take them all off." Both men were thoroughly into the spirit of theater — as the woman continued her instructions: "Lay it down, lay it down. Please, please, now put the sleeves on right. Okay, now put the cover over the baby. Don't rush it, comrades. Now the cap, the cap — look at how you're handling that baby!" She turned to the crowd: "If you're handling a real baby, you'll flip it around that way too, huh?" Of one of them: "He's got that baby wrapped up like a mummy!" of the other: "He's got it done!"

Finally, she announced, "Your children are going to grow up and be good people. Here's your prize!" She gave them the aprons, and the crowd roared. "Now you can go home and sleep well." But she realized she had a good thing going, and turned to the crowd again: "What should he name the baby?"

"Allah! Allah!" Hardly a religiously neutral name, and obviously not Russian. Unsurprised, she turned to the "father" and said "Now sing the baby a lullaby!" He went into an Oriental melody, but he sang loudly enough to wake the dead and the audience guffawed once more. Then she thanked them and said, "We hope that when you are fathers, you will conduct yourselves the way you did here." Another Russian woman invited the audience to a big celebration in the park's dance pavilion, an Autumn Ball.

We walked up to the stage to talk with the two women. We learned that the two young men were not actors, as we had first suspected, but had been invited up out of the audience. One of them, seeing my microphone, volunteered that he was 23, and went on, a little irrelevantly, "Me, for example, I know several languages, Azerbaijani, Ukrainian, and I can speak just the tiniest bit of English. So, you see what a big thing socialism has done for us."

Mrs. Mandel asked one of the women just what they were trying to get across. Her response reveals a great deal about the ethnic attitudes to which she had been educated and trained, as she laid a groundwork:

"The Tajik people, our community here, is very musical. Way back when Europeans hadn't the vaguest notion of music, and people there were half-apes, half human, people in Tajikistan had a high culture. They erected works of architecture — mosques — organized large-scale trade with Byzantium, and from that time left works of painting. There was mathematics, great mathematicians, a written language, books. There were schools even before the Christian era. In the context of Central Asia, the Tajiks were the most cultured, very highly cultured people.

"But because of the development of trade the Turks unfortunately came in and conquered them. As a consequence, culture in Central Asia died down — but folk culture, handed down from generation to generation, that was something no conquerors could throttle. They have lovely painting, architecture, marvelous carvings, a fundamentally musical people."

She herself is neither Tajik nor an Uzbek, but a Russian. I started to express my own pleasure in hearing her interest in the culture of the local peoples, but she cut me off: "I live here. I know

American-Russian Institute

Alma-Ata civic auditorium.

it. I work in the theater and the Philharmonic Society [which combines all the musical arts] and so I know the Tajik people. I know what things are like in Central Asia in general. And therefore it gives me satisfaction to talk to you about what I have learned of the psychology of these people and about them in general."

When we asked specifically about the scene we had witnessed, Marina, who conducted it, replied, "I decided to put the men to a test. A lot of young men come here, alone or with their girl friends or wives. So we decided to run a contest about what they know of a matter in which they will be able to help their wives when tiny new little beings appear in their families. And I simply picked two unsuspecting men out of the audience and invited them up onto the stage."

Except for a Russian university dean — under a Tajik president — these two women were the only Russians I personally encountered in positions of authority over Central Asians, even at so modest a level. The social science institutes I visited in Turkmenia, Kirgizia, and Tajikistan were all headed by members of those respective nationalities, and the staffs were totally indigenous but for two very aged Russians in Dushanbe. The heads of the tourist agencies in Alma-

Ata and Frunze were indigenous, as were all guides. The Kirgiz and Kazakh movie industries are indigenous from top to bottom, though one of the lesser directors in Kirgizia is Lithuanian. Director and docent at the art museum in Frunze were Kirgiz. So were TV producers. The city architect of Alma-Ata was Kazakh, with two (very respectful) Russian architects under him. The head of the Kirgiz Conservatory, encountered by chance at the airport, was Kirgiz.

Some population-wide statistics are enviable by any standard. They have outstripped all African, Asian, or Latin American countries but Japan in many respects. Medical care is free and there are more physicians per population than in any non-Communist country on earth but Israel. Japan's modernization began in the 1870s and by 1904 it was able to defeat tsarist Russia in modern naval warfare. Soviet Central Asia's modernization began in the 1920s some 50 years later. It has as many college students in proportion to population as Japan, and a higher percentage of women among students despite a heritage of head-to-toe veiling and segregation from men, even in the home. I know six college-educated Soviet Central Asian men personally. Each is married to a college graduate who works outside the home: assistant director of an art museum (her boss also a Central Asian woman), assistant movie director, two economists, an obstetrician-gynecologist, who teaches her speciality, and a curriculum specialist.

The Japanese undoubtedly have more electronic and mechanical appliances, and incomparably more cars. However, the quality of urban life in Central Asia is far, far better. Japanese cities are notoriously smoggy and extremely crowded due to the high price of land and absence of zoning, while even the most populous Soviet cities provide ample green space.

How did the Central Asian republics get from the state described by visitors in the late 1920s and early 1930s to what I saw and heard in five visits between 1959 and 1982? How have they been able to maintain such a rapid rate of progress for half a century—a record that has caused numerous Third World nations to turn to some form of socialism?

Over forty years ago, in my first book on this region, I wrote: "trade, and an extension of the cultural intercourse that has already begun, cannot but cause deep thought among the peoples of the Near East as to the methods whereby the kindred nations of Soviet Central Asia have risen to a position not only of political and social, but of economic equality with the Russians for whom they were formerly a colony."[7] (The "economic equality" at that time was in the character of the economy, not yet the statistics.)

Lenin ceased treating Central Asia as a colony from the moment he came to power. Not all imperialist powers had used racism in the same way. Russia, like Portugal and France, did not employ it as much as the English-speaking countries. Members of the indigenous nobility in the Russian Empire were treated as social equals, if they had the wealth to back that up. Later, noble rank became less important, riches more so. Monied Moslems, for example, were permitted to build a soaring and magnificently tiled mosque in St. Petersburg. Skin color alone was not a disqualifier: Pushkin's Ethiopian great-grandfather had been made a high nobleman by Peter the Great and Pushkin himself was accepted in the 19th century as Russia's leading poet with no question of race.

For the overwhelming bulk of Russia's Asian colonial peoples, skin color was only part of an ensemble of characteristics, including poverty (relative to most of the Russians they dealt with), "paganism," "outlandish" dress and customs — all of which made the Russians feel superior. (Even today, one finds educated Russians who joke about Central Asians mispronouncing Russian without realizing such remarks are racist.) Nepotism existed among the Russians, but it was a way of life among the colonials who placed the highest value on family and clan loyalty. And for the Russians, bribery simply helped things along; among Asian peoples, it had always been the normal manner in which government functioned. Officials had been expected to live directly off those they ruled from time immemorial.*

The Russians responded to all these differences with contempt, a contempt governed by two overriding psychological factors: first, the "rights" of conquest, resembling white Americans' attitudes toward Indians; second, religion. The idea that all peoples have an equal right to the earth is very recent. That countries should grow by conquest was regarded as quite normal — we in the United States had "Manifest Destiny."

In Russia, adherence to Russian Orthodox Christianity was the road to equal rights. Anyone was quite free to join but rejecting it meant opening oneself to approximately equal subjection to the tsar and the ethnic nobility. Virtually all Moslems rejected this cultural imperialism. But for the bulk of the colonials, their status as illiterate peasants left them essentially where they were. This was

---

*A recent novel by a Soviet Azerbaijani makes it clear that nepotism and bribery remain culturally-associated problems.[8]

even true of semi-colonials like the Slavic Ukrainians, who were already Russian Orthodox.

In Asia, the outcome of all the foregoing was a clearly colonial situation. The non-Russians existed principally to enrich the Russian royal family personally and the nobility in general. Tax rates were vastly higher in Central Asia, and merchants and exploiters of natural resources made super-profits from colonial low wages. When Russian peasant discontent threatened the tsar, brutal oppression was readily used. Then the tsar would give peasants land taken from the colonials, usually the grazing land of nomadic peoples.

The Soviets, by nationalizing the land and confiscating industry and big business, destroyed the very purpose of colonialism—propertied classes that had grown rich from it no longer existed. But these changes alone could have no effect upon the nearly universal illiteracy, the prevalence of disease—or on the long standing resentment toward Russians of all classes. Nor did they alter the typically colonial economy, based on producing a single crop: cotton for the mills near Moscow. "Industry," limited almost exclusively to primary processing of that crop, involved less than one percent of the labor force, and provided only unskilled work for indigenous people.

A majority of the Asian peoples had been nomadic cattle raisers. They were organized as clans which, particularly among the Turkmen, raided each other regularly. Some Turkmen clans were also slavers, raiding into Persia and selling the captives in Central Asian markets. There were rivalries between communities based on trade, water, and pasture rights, as well as hostilities between Shi'a and Sunni Moslems. Nor were traditional forms of authority any more democratic than those imposed from St. Petersburg, as they were based on the authority of the mullahs, in terms of Islamic law, and of clan heredity in other matters.

The Communists in the region initially were chiefly Russians exiled by the tsar or Russian railroad workers. When they took power and set up elected soviets, nominations coming from the local peoples were at first based on clan affiliation, and soviets controlled by members of one ethnic group would treat others unfavorably. There is a similar situation in Africa today, where territorial divisions do not accord with ethnic divisions. In Africa, a single people may be divided among six to eight countries (like the Malinke), and great numbers have been killed in wars and civil wars because boundaries do not correspond to ethnic territories.

American-Russian Institute

Hunting with a golden eagle is still practiced by the old and respected by young Kazakhs.

In Central Asia 50 years ago, these ethnic differences were as real as they are in Africa today. They reflected not just tribal loyalty, but differences in way of life and levels of cultural and linguistic development. The nomad Kazakhs, Turkmen, and Kirgiz regarded their lives as free, and had contempt for the farming Uzbeks and Tadjiks—who in turn hated the nomads whose wandering herds would graze on or trample their crops.

At the time of the Revolution, there were two protectorates, Khiva and Bokhara, ruled in traditional fashion by indigenous emirs under Russian guns. The rest of Central Asia was under direct Russian administration. The protectorates were the end products of conquest of certain indigenous peoples by others.

The Communists came to power in European Russia and in the largest Central Asian city, Tashkent, in 1917. In 1918, when tsarist Russian forces were withdrawn from the Khiva protectorate, Turkmen tribesmen attacked, killed the ruler, and plundered the towns and villages, which were chiefly Uzbek. In turn, Uzbeks massacred over a thousand Turkmen in a single night in 1920. The Turkmen retaliated by attacking villages, pledging to kill ten Uzbeks for every Turkmen, a promise they apparently kept. As late as 1923, about 2,000 Kazakh nomads raided the territory of the Turkmen, also nomads, and seized four desert wells. The Turkmen retreated to Iran, then came back and drove out the Kazakhs.

The Soviets moved to end this local warfare in three ways. First, they tried to demonstrate to the poor that their real enemies were not other nationalities and tribes, but the wealthy, regardless of ethnic affiliation. Second, they attempted to redraw boundaries along ethnic lines, with self-determination the governing principle. Third, they used military force when unavoidable — and when they had it.

To win the poor, they organized a union of peasants in 1919, open to those who did not employ hired labor, and the landless who worked for hire. In 1921-22 the government sought to provide them with water, land, livestock, and implements confiscated from both Russian pioneer peasants and from the indigenous wealthy, called *bais*. The Russians had to give up everything over and above what could be worked by their own immediate families. The *bais* were affected only if they did no work, and depended wholly upon sharecroppers (who received only one-fourth of what they raised). But the croppers were not yet ready for the notion that everything their labor produced should be their's, so purchase-and-sale cooperatives were established. In addition, trade unions for workers in cotton gins and the like were founded, and a Communist Youth League organized.

The first attempt to dismantle the colonial structure was organization of a Turkestan Autonomous Soviet Republic, designed to include the entire area inhabited by Turkic-speaking majorities. But this ignored the fact that these were widely-differing peoples. "The smaller and more backward nationalities did not comprehend the laws, decrees and directives which were issued either in Russian or in the languages of the other dominant [local] nationalities," writes an Indian scholar.[9]

At this early stage, this republic was headed by Russians who had made the revolution in Tashkent. Soon the royal government of Khiva was overthrown and replaced by a government of indigenous Communists, who re-named the area Khorezm. Even their leader complained that it was almost impossible to apply the same set of laws to both the Uzbeks and Turkmen there: the former valued land, the latter livestock. "The government of Khorezm was confronted with yet another problem. The Turkmen, as a rule, paid their taxes to their clan leaders which seldom reached the treasury and the burden of taxes fell almost exclusively on the Uzbek population. When the government started incurring expenditure on welfare measures for Turkmen, it encountered opposition from the Uzbeks."[10]

The first attempt to re-draw boundaries so that each ethnic group would rule in its own traditional territory was made between 1920 and 1923. Kazakhs, Turkmen, Kirgiz, Kara-Kalpaks* and each gained recognition as a country, but this could not work so long as the richest farmlands, with the best irrigation and the densest population (consisting of all these nationalities) continued to belong to the former protectorates of Bokhara and Khorezm. The royal rulers had been overthrown there, and indigenous Communists were in power. But they did not yet have the local support for moving beyond abolishing the medieval cruelties and plunderous taxation of the former regime. The Constitution of Bokhara specified that "no published laws of the republic may contradict the foundations of Islam." (Words with a particularly contemporary ring in light of recent events in Iran and Afghanistan). That constitution recognized private ownership of land, which in Russia had been nationalized. In the Khorezm People's Republic, which was even more medieval, courts based on Islamic law were recognized, as were religious schools which taught rote memorizing of the Koran to boys, beating them on the soles of their bare feet to help their recollection. *Wakuf*, mosque-owned landed estates, remained legal, as did clan leadership by tribal elders.

But the organizations — of the rural poor, of urban wage workers, of cooperatives and of Communist Youth — rapidly brought changes in social attitudes, and provided a base of support for major social change. Large-scale landownership, serfdom, and castes were abolished. The resemblance to the changes in Ethiopia, 1978-84, is striking. By 1924 the type of society in the Khorezm and Bokhara republics was the same as in the surrounding Central Asian autonomous republics that had been founded in the areas where tsarist Russia had ruled without indigenous royalty.

Meanwhile steps had been taken to give the people the basic skills needed to conduct their own affairs and to train personnel so they would be equipped to administer government and to modernize life. The first higher educational institution in Central Asia was established in 1920, with faculty and equipment sent from Central Russia. The professors, in wing collars and pince-nez, quite literally had to shoot their way through against counterrevolutionary horsemen

---

*Today they comprise an autonomous republic within the Uzbek Soviet Socialist Republic of the USSR.

trying to stop their train. One of those Russian volunteers, a woman, was still teaching, in her eighties, when I was there in 1979.

All these changes made the time ripe to end the ethnic jockeying for preference and power. The solution adopted was proposed by Faizulla Hojayev (also spelled Khodzhaev), the head of the Bokhara Republic, although some of its underlying ideas had come from Lenin and others.[11] Hojayev was a leader of the movement that had overthrown the emir. He subsequently became a Communist. In a very real sense, he was the forerunner of Fidel Castro. That is, he was leader of a revolution in a semi-colony who came to regard socialism as the solution for his people's problems. At the same time, he was an individual with the vision to understand the problems of other peoples.

Hojayev said that the multi-national Central Asian republics must be scrapped and replaced by republics as ethnically homogeneous *as possible* — homogeneous, but not segregated: minorities were free to remain, and were guaranteed equal rights, but the new borders were to correspond to ethnic limits as far as demographics permitted. This left a very difficult problem of sharing the few concentrated centers of productive wealth that existed — coal and other mines, oil wells and refineries. So borders were drawn in a way that left each of them under the jurisdiction of the government that had them before the new delimitation of territory. Thus, no one was worse or better off than before. A similar issue, disposition of the high mountain pastures needed by both the Kazakhs and Kirgiz, was solved by an agreement for joint use. A few entities needed by all the Central Asian republics — such as the then-sole university — were made common property of all.

Within three years of the delimitation, Hojayev was able to say to those who had opposed it: "look at the complete national [ethnic] peace which now prevails."[12]

With the nationalities issue resolved, it became possible to focus on social problems. Not the least of these involved the status of women, as the passage by Anna Louise Strong showed. Half a century later I heard a personal echo of those events while talking with Ikbalkhon Tokhtokhodjayeva, a female Doctor of Jurisprudence who had been Uzbekistan's vice-minister of education for a decade.

"My mother is 84. She was born in the old days, when these areas comprised the backward colony of Turkestan. She also experienced the times when our enemies held this territory, the Allies [the British, after the Revolution] and the Basmachi." These were patriarchal chieftains similar to those now operating against the government of Afghanistan. Indeed, one of those now raiding from Pakistan into Afghanistan is actually a man nearly her mother's age, who fled the USSR when defeated in his 20s.

I asked whether her mother had participated in the movement to discard the parandja, the blinding and choking horsehair overveil, without any opening for mouth or eyes, that women had been required to wear whenever they left the house in that stiflingly hot country. She answered:

"She gave birth to me in 1928, and, with me in her arms, marched to the great square, side by side with my father, and discarded that parandja." Her father's support took both enlightenment and great courage—there are stenographic records of top-level Communist Party discussions from that time in which leaders berated each other because their wives were still veiled. "An elderly Uzbek man came up to her—he was an activist in the movement for Uzbek women to discard the veil, and asked her: 'What would you like to name your daughter?' She said: 'I would like to name her "Happy Fate," so her future will be happy,' and so that's the name they gave me: 'Iqbal'.

"My mother is a living witness to the building of our country. She saw everything, and she always says to everyone, to the whole family, that one must be devoted to our country, must value it because it took us out of those difficult times when women were sequestered, wore the veil, were confined to the home, that is, had no rights at all, were totally illiterate.

"My mother got two years of schooling, my father four. But all of us, their children, have higher education. There were 10 children, but brothers of mine died in the war. My father also died during the war, because the whole country helped the front, in whatever way they could. A sister heads the chair of the Russian language at Tashkent Teachers College. She has written many textbooks. Another sister has many children and stays home. One brother is an engineer in transportation, another brother a physician in the military. The others are dead.* I have two children: my daughter is a cardiologist and my son a psychiatrist.

"Today women are cabinet members, members of parliament, scientists. I'll give you just one figure. Speaking in connection with the 60th anniversary of the October Revolution, the president of the Uzbek Republic said there are 30,000 scientists and professional scholars in our republic, of which 12,500 are women. And the

_____
*Perhaps five were killed in World War II. That would not be unique.

whole auditorium rose and applauded that. That's what has happened in the 54 years of our Uzbek Soviet Socialist Republic. I guess I'm among the women he was talking about, and I'm proud of that."

Obviously, most families consist of people who do much more modest jobs. In ancient Samarkand, I visited a huge silk mill. Some departments were intolerably noisy and workers wore special ear plugs to protect their hearing, but there were planters full of greenery within the immense rooms of machinery, the aisles were clear and the floors clean. This represented a tremendous improvement over what I had seen 20 years earlier in a textile mill in Tashkent, where conditions resembled those in the American mill depicted in the film, *Norma Rae.*

Later, at the Samarkand factory, I talked to the head of the union, an immense light-coffee-colored woman of boundless energy. She had high cheek-bones, Mongolian eyes, but an elongated rectangular face creating the distinctive Uzbek appearance. Her father and mother were both workers, she told me. She herself "worked for 16 years at a silk-winding mill in another city, then for five years in this mill. Then one year as head of its Communist Party organization and now as head of the trade union committee for this group of mills and associated enterprises."

She has three children, a girl of 13, and two boys, 12 and nine. On the day we spoke, her daughter was looking after her little brothers, but she pointed out that women working in the plant can "place their little kids in the nursery, which cares for them from 6 AM to 5 PM. So after work they can go to the bazaar to get the things for dinner, and clean the house a bit, and then they come to get the kids."

I needled her a bit, "And the husbands sit around drinking tea?" She snapped a definite "No, the husbands help. If the wife cooks, the husband washes the dishes. If the husband cooks, the wife cleans up." A Russian woman present added, "Among the Asians the men cook better than the women." And the union leader said, "If I had known of this in advance, I'd invite you home for dinner. You and I would sit and talk, and my husband would do the cooking. Among Uzbeks, it's the men who make the *plov* [pilaf]."

When I visited the Samarkand home of a former classmate of a Russian friend, I sat in the living room with his wife and 16-year old daughter for quite a while as the husband cooked. This family's own experience had given them a clear view of the status of Soviet Asians relative to their neighbors outside the USSR. The man, a

Textile mills today are dust-free.

professional linguist who knows Arabic and Persian, had been in government service in the Near and Middle East for ten years. His wife and daughter had been with him. The daughter told me she had lived in Syria, Egypt and Iraq, had become friends with many Arab children because she spoke their language. When I asked what differences she found between children her age in those countries and in Uzbekistan, she replied "Children here live better, everything is provided for them and all have equal rights. Such concern isn't extended in the Eastern countries — they live considerably worse. They don't provide things through public channels."

Both with this family and at the silk mill an interesting sidelight came up. At the factory, when I asked about the ethnic situation, the union leader replied: "There are no differences here by nationality. Here there's an Uzbek working, next to her a Russian, next to her a Korean, next to her a Jew." These, she explained, were Bokhara Jews, a Middle Eastern group whose languages are Farsi and Hebrew, not Russian and Yiddish. Later I passed their synagogue and visited their rabbi in his home.

At the linguist's home I specifically asked this couple of Moslem heritage about the status of Jews in the Soviet Union. The wife replied: "My neighbor across the hall is Jewish, and we are personal friends. I work in the Curriculum Department at the College of Agriculture. There are Jewish personnel there, and we work together in one and the same group, and I respect them very much. My younger uncle is married to a Polish Jew, who teaches French at Samarkand University. Although our grandmother, his mother, is very advanced in years, she feels such love for her that she says 'She's the best of all. My daughter-in-law Maya is the best of all.' We ourselves love her very much."

The rabbi proved to be an attractive 28-year-old who lived quite comfortably. He told me that there were 12,000 Jews in Samarkand. (Circumcision of boys was universal.) Most Jews were salespeople, others were physicians, dentists, psychiatrists, shoemakers, barbers, factory workers. He conducted three services each Saturday, with 70 or 80 attending each; a thousand come once a year at the High Holiday of Yom Kippur. "Few" youth regard themselves as religious, he said. He asked me whether I intended to emigrate to Israel, and was quite surprised when I said no. Yet I would not define him as a Zionist; he was simply an Orthodox rabbi who takes quite literally the words of the annual Passover prayer: "Next year in Jerusalem." And now that Israel exists, that is where Jews should go, in his view.

The major religion in Soviet Central Asia is, of course, Islam (although I once attended a Baptist service of ethnic Germans). Tashkent, with 1,500,000 people, has 16 functioning mosques. I attended a service with perhaps 1,000 men at worship in the courtyard of the principal mosque; women were also present, but as they were segregated behind an opaque curtain, I don't know how many. Although the men were chiefly elderly, the number in the prime of life was not small. A visiting clerical dignitary from Turkey was preaching that day. Because of the similarity of the languages and the familiarity of the subject-matter, the worshippers needed no translator.

On attendance in general, the assistant mufti said: "The number of young people in attendance is not as large as our mufti would like. But on holidays the mosques are full to bursting with young people." He was clearly a sincere believer in separation of church and state, "I have been in countries where people are beaten or otherwise punished for not performing their prayers. But there, too, there are people who do not pray. They beat them, and they still won't go. You understand, that has to be a matter of conscience for each person. So from our point of view, that is not freedom: a person has to be left alone with his own conscience, whether he goes or doesn't go. That way it's better."

He and his associates laughed when I told them how surprised I had been to see the obviously good relations between the imam at a historic shrine and the executives of a state farm which surrounds it. The assistant mufti commented: "Our imams are holy men. Why should the manager of the state farm be at odds with him? Even the manager of a state farm — for that matter, even the head of the Communist Party Committee of a state farm, if he is a Moslem — will feel in his soul that some day he will have need of that imam. The day will come when he will be in the hands of the imam." The Islamic clergy take it for granted that all ethnic Central Asians are Moslems. The imam at the shrine had told me that absolutely all funerals in the countryside are religious. Anthropologists have found this is often so to avoid offending the feelings of religious members of the deceased's family.

The shrine I visited is the tomb of al-Bukhāri, the most revered interpreter of Islam throughout the Moslem world. While we were discussing Islam in America, the imam recalled an incident that did not shed the most pleasant light upon the Voice of America. A few months earlier he had been visited by an Uzbek who had emigrated to the U.S. about 40 years ago (I would guess that

Tom Weber

Mufti Babakhan, chief Moslem dignitary of Central Asia.

meant he had been a war prisoner in Germany). He had been born nearby, and wanted to visit family. The imam quoted him: "When I received my visa, I didn't know whether to come or not. Maybe they'd kill me here. But then my eldest son said to me: 'Father, you are already an old man. You have already seen life, so it doesn't make a difference whether you live till you die here, or whether they kill you there. Better you go. If they kill you, your body will lie in your native land as a martyr.' The Intourist people met me in Moscow, and then they saw me off to Samarkand. I still didn't believe that I'd leave here alive. Maybe in Moscow they were planning to have me killed here. In Samarkand I was met by young people. One young fellow said: 'I am your kin.'

"I didn't believe him. Finally, I met my sister. She is 78. When I laid eyes on her, I burst into tears. I said: 'Now, they can hang me.' But nobody hung me. I have been here a month, and nobody yet has said anything bad to me. I think nobody is going to kill me. And in about a week I will return home to my children."

The imam commented: "I myself listen to the Uzbek radio broadcasts from America. They say there's no religion here, no Moslems here, no such thing as wife and husband. Everybody is all mixed up together as far as bearing children is concerned. The children are taken away from their fathers and mothers, and eat separately and sleep separately, and such stuff. So of course people were afraid."*

I have flown over Uzbekistan repeatedly at low altitudes. From the air, it resembles California's huge irrigated "factories-in-the-field," with straight furrows and modern machinery. But on the ground, the villages are quite different. Chicanos from New Mexico who visited there say it seems like home — adobe houses, adobe fences, unpaved streets. But there is a hospital in every large village or a short ambulance drive from every small one; schools and community recreation centers have long been taken for granted. In the state farm adjacent to the al-Bukhāri shrine, I was impressed by the computer room. Young Uzbek women clad in gorgeous traditional striped silks, were working there. On the farms themselves, women were not really allowed to operate the most important and massive field machine, the cotton-picker, until the 1970s, but now there are thousands who do this very well-paid work.

Central Asia still has two teachers' colleges for women only as some parents will not let their daughters go to school with young men. But all the other dozens of colleges and universities are co-ed, about equally divided among men and women. This in an area where, as recently as when that unveiling of 1928 took place, numbers of women were simply murdered by men in their own families for the shame this act supposedly brought upon them.

Without industry, Central Asia would have remained forever dependent on Russia: its cotton was spun and woven in Russia, and shipped back for sale; steel and railroad equipment, telegraph, and in later years, telephone and radio equipment, trucks, and

---

*I do not know Uzbek, and did not hear those broadcasts. But in 27 years of weekly broadcasts on the Soviet Union, and in hundreds of lectures, I have spoken with or received mail from probably thousands of Americans who are physically afraid to visit the Soviet Union. "Will I be able to get out again?" is the usual question. Yet there is absolutely nothing that the USSR has ever done or said that provides the slightest justification for that attitude.

tractors all came from Russia. Beyond this, in any case a formerly colonial agricultural region would have remained permanently at a much lower living standard without industry, as experience world-wide demonstrates.

Industrialization was financed chiefly by the more developed regions of the Soviet Union. During the early years 60 percent of the budgets of the Central Asian republics came from outisde. Until collectivization, progressive taxation was used to obtain the other 40 percent: in 1929-30, for example, the wealthiest 5 percent of the farmers provided over half the tax income, while the 59 percent who were subsistence farmers paid only 7 percent.

The first industries built in Central Asia were textile factories, and paper mills to meet the needs of the literacy campaign. Next, because collective farms are really more productive only if they can practice extensive farming, and this required machinery, came farm implement factories, plants to process raw materials and facilities to mine natural resources. Tremendous emphasis was placed on discovering mineral resources, and the first scientists of Central Asian nationality to attain prominence were geologists.

When tractors, all-metal plows and seeders were first provided, the peasants knew nothing about machinery, so the Communist Party organized urban workers to go out to the villages to repair the equipment. They also helped with the harvest. This served political purposes as well: about half the Central Asian working class was Russian, and their work in the countryside helped break down ethnic mistrust. (The idea of an alliance between workers and peasants has been a guiding principle of Soviet society since its founding.) In addition, Leningrad's factory workers took respon-sibility for supplying and maintaining equipment in Khorezm, Moscow's workers for Tashkent. Both cities sent teams out and this, too, transformed the local peoples' attitude toward Russia. Furthermore, the workers of Central Asian origins themselves became ethnically intermixed, as the sharing of work helped eliminate old clan and tribal divisions as well. Marriages across local *ethnic* lines followed, though inter-*racial* marriage did not become a significant phenomenon until the past decade.

The only ideology and institutions to perpetuate segregation are religious, because the Moslems are Asian and the Christians, European. The decline in religious belief, the very great decline in its intensity, as reflected by the generally low attendance at services, has contributed greatly to reducing ethnic alienation. Churches and mosques are full only because the number in use is very much smaller than it was. Only Baptists seem to be building new houses of worship.

The economy of Central Asia today is totally modern. Horse-drawn vehicles are rare, and hauling by human power — used for short carries within building sites when I was there in 1959 — did not exist in the cities I visited in 1979 and 1982. Improved seed, ample irrigation, and manufactured fertilizers have increased production — cotton yields per acre are two-and-a-half times what they were, and 80 percent of the cotton is harvested by machine. Soviet Uzbekistan and the United States are the world's only exporters of cotton-picking machines. The Central Asian machines are bought by Greece and Egypt. Tens of thousands of wells with wind-driven motors spot the pasturelands. Today, Uzbekistan even manufactures the high-technology cable used for ultra-deep geophysical drilling to probe through the earth's mantle.

This truly great leap forward has produced people who have been able to keep pace with it. Late one warm evening we sat in the central park of Dushanbe, capital of Tajikistan, and taped the life of a young Tajik. He volunteered to tell it to us. His Russian was accented, ungrammatical, but fluent. He was born in 1954 on a collective farm in mountaineer country containing a 25,000-foot peak.

When I was two, my father married another woman, not my real mother. At first she took good care of me, treated me decently. But then she gave birth to a son, and said: "Look after your little brother." I always helped him, but she didn't believe me, and she hit me a lot. One day I was told to bring in our family cow. While I was trying to, my baby brother fell into the campfire. I had set him next to it for warmth — in winter there's such snow up there in Garm.

My brother burned his right arm. She hit me and said: "You threw him down there yourself." But it wasn't my fault. She hit me many times. Anyhow, we rode off to the doctor's. There was a doctor there, a Russian woman. Other physicians came in the evening. They amputated his hand, bound it all up.

One day my stepmother said I was to haul in firewood every day on my back, and grass for feed. If I wouldn't do it, she said, she would hit me with her fist and make me work, and give me only a little flat bread and black bread to eat. One day I was carrying that firewood on my back, and a sack of dry feed for her cow. I was hungry — it was hot, May — so I took one cake of flat bread and ate it. My stepmother came home and counted those flat breads. When she found one was missing she picked up a knife and tried to cleave me right in half, murder me. Look at that finger of mine. I ran out of the house, but she kept chopping at me. I pulled my arm away, bound it up, and ran away. I spent three months in the hospital.

Then the hospital sent me — this was 1964 — to a children's home, in Kuliab. There were little children there, Russian kids too. I didn't know any Russian at all. What I knew was Tajik. My name is Bek-Makhmat [Mohammed] Ali-Makhmat Amonovich [son of Amon]. In Russian I'm called Alec. The children's home was merry. We would all play. And I studied Russian.

I graduated from school. Then one day my father came. He looked at me, and he started to cry. Well, I cried too. He was my father, but he had done whatever my stepmother wanted him to. And so he also had struck me, right here. My own real father, too.

Then came vacation time, and I went home. For three days he treated me as a guest, and then he came in with a scythe, and said: "Let's go and reap the wheat." I went, but I was no good at it, and he wanted to murder me. He said: "Why did you leave me?" He cursed me. "Why did you go to the children's home and abandon me?"

I ran away from home again. I had finished junior high school. So I went to a trade school* for a year and became an electrician. Then I went back home again, and I worked.

One hot day my father said: "Come on, son, let's go earn some money in Leninabad State." Three of us went: my father, me, and another countryman from Garm State. My father said: "There are four houses that need building for this collective farm." We worked and worked — boy, there's some stones there! Those four houses were built, so we got paid. My father took the money.

When we had started out for there, he made me a promise: "Okay, we'll get you married. We'll find you a bride." But when we got back home, he said: "No. Let's get back to work." I said: "What's that? I gave you the 1,700 rubles I earned [$2,500]! That ain't hay!" He said: "Come on, let's work." So I worked, and sent more money home.

In 1974, in November, I got my call to serve in the army, so I showed up at the induction center here in Dushanbe. But they didn't take me. I went to the military commissariat. I said: "Comrade Captain Zagarov, I want to serve in the Soviet Army. I want to serve like everybody else." So he said: "Well, let's write a request and submit it to the village soviet." I went to the chairman of the soviet, and I said: "I need your help. I need a reference from you, so I can get into the Soviet Army."

He said okay. So then in 1975, the 18th of May, they took me to the induction center. We traveled, traveled, to the city of Kuibyshev in European Russia, on the Volga. En route we were in Moscow for four hours, on May 27th, and at the railroad station there was a great crowd of Moscow people, and visiting people from all over the country,

---

*These are free, open to all, and provide bed and board.

tourists. And they welcomed us Tajiks. There was a nice guy who gave me a gift. He was from—what's that place—from Riga, Latvia. Very blonde. And I gave him something to remember me by.

My father had said: "When you come home from the army, I'll arrange a marriage." I felt, that's okay. But then I got a letter saying all the guys were saying: "your father found a bride for your brother." When I got home I said to him, "Why did you trick me? You arranged a marriage for my brother instead." "Well, Alec," he said: "I want you to stay here and work for me. Bring me money, and then I'll arrange it." I said: "If that's the case, I'm not going to live here any more. I'll go to Dushanbe and get a job."

And I began to take part in these things. [He pointed to the outdoor theater across from our park bench.] The young people get up on the stage here, and I do too. We have a very good time. I have a job as an electrician. I respect human beings. Somebody comes to me and says: "Alec, would you do some wiring in my house?" I go. I do it. I don't take any money for it. I do it as a human being.

I want to say something more. I respect people regardless of nationality. I served my two years in the army properly. I really liked my commanding officers. I want you as a guest to see to it that all this is written down, in your country, that it be published there, and here.

Obviously, a great deal has been changed in two generations, and a great deal remains as it was. But there is absolutely nothing resembling colonialism, or semi-colonialism, remaining. There are no country clubs of Russians, no slums of Asians. Police are overwhelmingly indigenous. The people do not flee from rural poverty to jobs in Russia proper the way U.S. Blacks migrated from the South seeking jobs in northern cities. One reason is, according to the most anti-Soviet source possible, NATO, that there is no relative disadvantage. The average daily wage of collective farm members in each of the five Central Asian Soviet republics is *higher* than in Russia proper, and also higher than the USSR average.[13] The farmers are overwhelmingly indigenous peoples. NATO figures also show that industrial wages are higher than the USSR average in two Central Asian republics, and slightly lower in three where skill levels have not yet fully reached those of places where industry has a much longer history.

NOTES

1. Ia. A. Ioffe, *My i planeta* (Moscow: Politizdat, 1972), 3rd ed., p. 117.

2. Arthur Koestler, *The Invisible Writing* (Boston: Beacon, 1954), pp. 108-148, *passim*.

3. Langston Hughes, *Good Morning Revolution* (Westport, Conn.: Lawrence Hill, 1973), pp. 92-94.

4. Anna Louise Strong, *Red Star in Samarkand* (New York: Coward-McCann, 1929), pp. 91-93, *passim*.

5. Ibid., p. 123.

6. Joshua Kunitz, *Dawn Over Samarkand* (New York: Covici-Friede, 1935), pp. 241-2.

7. William Mandel, *The Soviet Far East and Central Asia* (New York: Institute of Pacific Relations, 1944), p. xv.

8. Chinghiz Gusseinov, *Mahomet, Mahmed, Mamish* (New York: Macmillan, 1978).

9. R. Vaidyanath, *The Formation of the Soviet Central Asian Republics* (New Delhi: People's Publishing, 1967), p. 162.

10. Ibid., p. 163.

11. R. Tuzhmuhamedov, *How the National Question Was Solved in Soviet Central Asia* (Moscow: Progress, 1973), pp. 92-95.

12. Vaidyanath, *Formation*, p. 233.

13. NATO data cited in Michael Rywkin, *Moscow's Muslim Challenge* (Armonk, N.Y.: Sharpe, 1982), Table 5, on p. 50.

Other sources used in this chapter include:
Eliz. E. Bacon, *Central Asians under Russian Rule: A Study in Culture Change* (Ithaca: Cornell U., 1966); Devendra Kaushik, *Socialism in Central Asia* (Bombay: Allied, 1976); Bejoy Kumar Sinha, *The New Man in Soviet Union* (New Delhi: People's, 1971); A.L. Strong, *The Road to the Grey Pamir* (Boston: Little, Brown, 1931); I. Blinder and A. Ul'masov, "A Critique of Bourgeois Conceptions of Economic Development in Soviet Central Asia," *Problems of Economics*, XIV, No. 5, 1971, pp. 74-93; E.M. Primakov, "Islam and Processes of Social Development of Foreign Countries in the East," *Soviet Law and Government*, XIX, No. 4, 1981, pp. 3-23; Iu. V. Bromlei, ed., *Sovremennye etnicheskie protsessy v SSSR*, 2nd ed. (Moscow: Nauka, 1977); N.S. Kisliakov, *Ocherki po istorii sem'i i braka u narodov Srednei Azii i Kazakhstana* (Leningrad: Nauka, 1969); L.I. Klimovich, *Pisateli vostoka ob Islame* (Moscow: Znanie, 1978); G.A. Khidoiatov, *Stroitel'stvo sotsializma V Srednei Azii i sovremennyi antikommunizm* (Tashkent: Uzbekistan, 1978); TsSU Uzbekskoi SSR, *Narodnoe khoziaistvo Uzbekstoi SSR v 1971 g.*, Statisticheskii ezhegodnik (Tashkent: Uzbekistan, 1972).

Collective farmer in open-air market.

7

"Indians," Eskimos, and
Islamic Nomads

There are Eskimos in the Soviet Union. No American Indian tribe
as such exists there, but there are millions of people whose cultures
will be recognizable to American Indians of some tribe. The
Kazakhs,* Turkmen, and Kirgiz were grazers of sheep and other
livestock like the Navajo. Before the 1917 Revolution they lived in
portable homes, *yurtas*, as the Plains Indians lived in tepees; their
languages had not been written down — their cultural heritage was
preserved orally. Organized in bands, clans, and tribes, they had
no armies, though in time of conflict every man was a warrior.
There were differences in wealth among them, as among the so-called
(by whites) "Five Civilized Tribes" of the U.S. Southeast, or
the Tlingits of the Pacific Northwest, but the sense of fraternity
within each of these peoples outweighed differences due to property.
Their lives under the Soviets will be described later in this chapter.

One group of 160,000 people compares quite directly to the
Indians and Eskimos of Alaska, and to Indians of the U.S. and
Canadian Pacific. The traditional livelihood of these Siberian
peoples depended upon geography. Those who lived in the heart of

*Not to be confused with Cossacks, who are Russians or closely related to them.

this area relied upon wild reindeer or reindeer-herding, upon hunting and fishing; those near the North Pacific hunted whales, walrus and seals, and also fished; those living along the tremendous Amur River had a culture based on salmon, as did their North American counterparts. The implements of the Northeast Asian peoples were essentially the same as those of North America; so were their religious beliefs. Many anthropologists believe the ancestors of American Indians crossed from Asia when a land bridge once connected Alaska and Siberia.

Before the Revolution, Russian rulers and American whalers and fur traders treated those who lived in these regions in a manner familiar to American Indians: alcohol was used to cheat the hunter out of his ermine, sable, silver fox, or squirrel skins. Christianity served in practice as a means of reconciling him to his lot — it was God's will. New diseases decimated the people though murder was the final sanction.

The Revolution undertook to bring about complete equality among all peoples. Equality before the law is not enough: For instance, assume the law deals even-handedly with Indians and the white traders who have been granted a district monopoly on the Navajo reservation by the Bureau of Indian Affairs. What equality can there be between a trader and a rug-weaver who can't read interest charges or grocery bills? If dissatisfied, the rug-weaver would have to travel 30 miles to try another store, only to find the same situation.[1] The situation in old Siberia was like that.

When the Revolution reached these parts of Northeast Asia in 1920, the new government's first act was to fix the price of salt and grain and establish a fixed mark-up for all other store goods. The new government also organized a force to hunt down remnants of the anti-Communist army, which had treated the indigenous population even worse during the 1918-20 Civil War than the old monarchy had. Thanks to these reforms, Tungus, Ostiak, Dolgan and Samoed tribesmen fought alongside the Russian Communists, gave them reindeer harness and warm clothing, and fed them. A few of these tribesmen were still alive in the 1970s and greatly honored.[2]

A cabinet department for Nationalities was established by the Soviet government, and in 1922 it organized a conference of representatives of the indigenous peoples in Northwestern Siberia. Members of five different tribes attended this first intertribal governmental meeting. In 1923 the government forbade bringing alcohol into native areas and required all traders to register. The immense spaces and weakness of the government made those measures a dead letter, but Moscow was able to save the people from starvation by shipping in several thousand tons of flour when in one large area at one time an epidemic carried off a third of the reindeer. In those years, food and trade goods were sold on "credit," a debt that was later simply written off the books.

The first delegate sent by indigenes to a legislature turned out to be a nobleman in their structure. This faced Moscow with a problem of conscience because of its policies of giving leadership roles to those from worker or peasant background. The government accepted the man as the people's choice, and named him to the executive body. The Communists knew they faced tremendous mistrust and suspicion of Russians because of past history. Yet the indigenous peoples had no persons trained to lead them in dealing with the modern world. (The very first were sent to a government training course in 1921.)

The government established a formal body to develop and implement policy toward the Indian-type peoples in 1924. It exempted them from all direct national and local taxation, to enable them to build up their possessions, and encouraged them to form cooperatives, to which it extended considerable credit. Most important, it believed that each people was entitled to its own culture. It was convinced that education could be conducted most successfully and quickly in the native language. Therefore, alphabets were devised for the nine largest peoples, even though not one numbered as many as 20,000. There was much opposition among the Russian Communists to this alleged waste of money and "pampering," but that opposition lost. Schools in tepees followed those tribes that traveled with their reindeer. Elsewhere stationary schools were built. The government set up publicly-owned trading posts, each surrounded by a free boarding school, a hospital, a community center and a hostel — and a veterinarian. Health service, human and animal, was free.

In 1934, the first graduating class of nine completed the four years of primary school at such a post. One of them was V.N. Uvachan, an Evenk, son of a hunter from one of the world's most northerly inhabited places. He was then sent to the high school of the Institute of the Peoples of the North in Leningrad, and from there to college-level education in economics. After working among his own people for a period, he was sent back for graduate study. In 1961 he became the first PhD among his people, as a historian. He has served five terms in the Supreme Soviet (Congress) of the USSR, and is a full professor. The Soviets have an academic degree higher than PhD: *Doktor* (recipients are usually about age

50) and in 1970, he was the first of the Northern tribespeople
to attain that level, though there are now hundreds of PhDs among
them. He is a member of the Committee on Ethnic Relationships
of the USSR Academy of Sciences. The *Large Soviet Encyclopedia* carries his biography.

In one of his books, Dr. Uvachan points out that "The national
minorities of the U.S. — Indians, Blacks, Eskimos, Aleuts and
other tribes — do not have national autonomy and statehood. . . .
The Constitution of the United States totally ignores the country's
multi-national make-up and does not provide for representation of
national minorities . . . "[3] He himself is in the Soviet Congress by
virtue of a specific provision guaranteeing such representation.
Since 1930 there have been seven territorial units, called Nationality
Areas, in the Russian Republic of the USSR. They have governmental autonomy, and one seat each in the Council of Nationalities
of the Supreme Soviet. These territorial units are not reservations.
Although designed to give governmental expression to a particular
people, they are multi-ethnic; in a couple of cases they comprise
two traditionally intertwined peoples. Russians live in them freely,
and their own people live outside them as and if they wish. But it is
an unbroken rule that the governor (Chairperson of the Executive
Committee of the Area (*Okrug*) Soviet) must be of the indigenous
nationality. For example, the Chookchee (or Chukchi) National
Area, which spreads over hundreds of miles of coast on the Arctic
Ocean and Bering Sea facing Alaska, includes only 14,000 Chookchee
in its population of 133,000; the great majority is Russian. This is
similar to the Eskimo-white ratio in Alaska, but there the government
is headed by a Chookchee woman, Lina Tynel. (A U.S. equivalent
would be having an Oglala Sioux as Governor of South Dakota.) These
policies may account for the fact that I have never seen a claim of
unrest among the Indian-type peoples of Siberia, though the U.S.
press reports every instance of dissatisfaction in the Soviet Union.

Tynel's post is not simply window-dressing, nor does she play a
role like those indigenous Bureau of Indian Affairs officials often
rejected as sell-outs by other Native-Americans. She is an educator,
editor, and translator, a graduate of the Leningrad Institute of the
Peoples of the North. In 1977, in an article in the leading Soviet
law journal, she discussed the accomplishments of the divisions of
government already under local control.[4] These were: education
including that of Russians, public health, public services, and
recreational facilities. The Area Soviet also owns all industry and
stores that serve local needs, and she wrote with pride of the

improvements in these businesses, which include dairy, fowl, and fur-fox farms, as well as traditional reindeer-grazing and fur trapping. One remark—"The government farms' cattle needs for coarse feeds are totally met by products of the Chookchee tundra."—represents an agricultural revolution, as farming was unknown only thirty years ago. Discussing traditional reindeer herders, two Western scholars wrote recently that provisions of "the most elementary comforts and services to a population constantly on the move over such inhospitable terrain and under severe natural conditions would in itself be a major undertaking and a very expensive one."[5] But Tynel reports "Sale of goods to the reindeer-breeders and hunters directly in the tundra is widely developed," and have more than doubled over five years to $1,500,000, under conditions of no inflation.

She also reports that—in an area with less population than the Arizona Navajo Reservation—in one five-year period (1970-75) "schools for 4,400 children have been built, pre-school facilities for 2,500, hospitals with 200 beds, an outpatient clinic to handle 300 per day, and community centers with auditorium seating for 1,400. In 1975 97.2 percent of school-age children were in attendance *through high-school, including 99.1 percent of those of the indigenous nationality. More than 65 percent of children of pre-school age attend kindergartens and day nurseries."* [my emphasis-W.M.]

Her article asks for 1) better financing, 2) local control of a broader range of public property, 3) the right to participate in planning operations by major federally-owned industries which work the region's natural resources, and 4) environmental-protection powers over those enterprises. These are essentially new problems that simply didn't exist before tin and coal-mining came in. Her article appeared when a new Constitution was adopted in 1977 and legislation was being drafted to spell out the powers of various levels of government. She lives in a world that is thousands of years more modern than in 1930, and wants the National Areas to have the powers they need in our day.

What happens to the plain citizen in these areas as these changes occur? In the United States, federal practice has often been to push Native-Americans off the reservations. Indians have been sold on the idea of moving to town, and given travel expenses to reach cities, sometimes hundreds of miles away. If things fail to work out there—due to lack of jobs, discrimination, whatever—they are simply told there is no money for return fare. For Native-Americans, life on welfare, high infant mortality, extraordinary

rates of tuberculosis, alcoholism, crime, sharply reduced life expectancy are the fruits of such policies. Other techniques used
recently to control U.S. Indians would be greeted with utter horror
in the Soviet Union: between 1971 and 1975, 42 percent of Indian
women of child-bearing age were sterilized.[6] And in 1977, the
National Catholic Reporter revealed that 25 to 35 percent of Indian
children were being taken from their parents "without warning or
legal notification."[7]

Many of the reservations were created in the 19th century when
the Indians were deported to supposed wastelands. But some 60
percent of the country's coal, uranium, oil, natural gas and lignite
underlie those lands, so today the U.S. Congress faces bills to
abolish reservation and treaty status, which would allow mining
and energy companies to march in and take over. Present policy
toward Indians, in short, is nothing new: if you can't get rid of
them one way, try another. Conditions for Indians have grown even
worse since 1981, under the Reagan Administration.

In the USSR, a Neevkhee scholar went from city to city over
several years and interviewed tribal people who had moved to town.
Old records showed that in 1926, only forty indigenous people in
this region — about one in 300 — were then living in town, doing
temporary work as boatmen and guides. Forty years later, there
were over a thousand in town, or about one in 20, and they work
chiefly in industry — in the manufacture of machinery and ship-
building — or for the government. Nine out of every ten of these
indigenous *industrial workers had SKILLED jobs*: mechanics,
machinists, patternmakers, crane-operator, electrician, steel rolling-
mill operators, welders, boilermakers, riggers, and operating
engineers. He studied a sample of 59; one had a college degree in
engineering, eight had paraprofessional technical training, eleven
more were high-school graduates. (That was in 1967; today high-
school education is compulsory — a Soviet high-school diploma is
about equal to junior college here.) Only three had less than five
years of school, and they were of the older generation. Again,
among oil workers on Sakhalin Island off the Pacific Coast, he
found aborigines in every craft.

Only one indigenous woman in a hundred could read and write
at the 1926 census; by 1967, the survey found a female senior
technologist in charge of an engineering library. In one town there
were twenty-four aborigine women in the clothing industry — one
with a secondary technical education, six high school graduates,
and 13 who had come within a year or two of completing high

school. His most remarkable finding in the field of employment was that, although there are professional and paraprofessional indigenous people living in town *"The majority live and work in their native rural counties."*[8]

In other words, they went back to their own people. Nor do those in urban settings lose their own cultures: He found

> certain traditional elements of clothing worn in the home, ornaments, preferences in foods . . . Often they spend holidays together and visit each other on the occasion of family celebrations. Nanai, Neevkh, Negidal, Ulch, Oodehgay, Oroch, Orok and Evenk families also do not lose contact with their kin in rural localities. Many workers spend their vacations in their native villages or send their children to relatives for their summer vacations.* Often those living in town arrange for vacations during the fall fishing season, when the salmon runs. . . . In turn, rural people, when they visit the city, stay with their acquaintances and kin.
>
> A majority of the indigenous people working at industrial enterprises and living in town have a good knowledge both of their native tongue and of Russian.

In western Siberia where Russians have lived side by side with settled people for 100 to 300 years, there is much intermarriage, but along the Pacific Coast there is little, as people haven't had much time to get used to each other's habits and customs through city life. "The young [indigenous] people prefer to marry spouses from their own districts. . . . They sometimes observe the rules of exogamy† that they know about from their parents or older kinfolk."

What about life in the villages? In 1970, I heard a report on the findings of a group studying the Nanai, who number ten thousand.‡ These people were exclusively hunters and fishermen in 1920; the only occupational division was by sex. The great majority continue to live along the rivers, as always, but only one in five remains a fisherman; nearly as many cultivate the soil. Both fishermen and agriculturalists are organized into collective farms, where each family has a garden and small orchard of its own. They can sell the surpluses, and fish caught outside working hours.

---

*Every employed person in the Soviet Union gets a paid vacation as a matter of law. Three weeks is the minimum.

†Exogamy bars marriage to a person from one's own village or clan, etc.

‡The work was directed by the late Alexi Okladnikov, member of the USSR Academy of Sciences, highly admired in the West for his studies of the East and North. Members of the team spoke to me at his request—this is only the briefest summary of their full-dress joint lecture.

The farms are modern enterprises involving all kinds of other occupations, and providing a variety of services. One-fifth of their people are professionals or paraprofessionals.

This leads to an interesting comparison: In 1978 there were 55 American Indian MDs. Ten years *earlier* there were already 166 physicians from those Soviet peoples whose lives had been entirely traditional. In proportional terms, the figures are even more impressive; among the Soviets there is one indigenous doctor per 1,000 population; among American Indians one per 16,000.

This 16-to-1 advantage is because the Soviet "Indians" are free as a people. This is not merely a matter of having the right to pick yourself up and go — both North American and Soviet aborigenes possess that right. The American Indian has to worry about bigotry because he looks Indian, a problem Soviet aborigines, who also look "different," do not have. In a society that always has unemployment, the real choice for American Indians, is between welfare in town or welfare on the reservation. Statistically, that is the extent of freedom for fully half of that population.

For aboriginal peoples, freedom should mean the right to be traditional or modern — or both. American Indians do not have that choice. They cannot survive by traditional means — most were driven from areas where those means made sense. In other cases their basis for livelihood was destroyed, as in the case of the buffalo, or greatly narrowed, as with salmon fisheries.

No Soviet people wants to be wholly traditional — to hunt without guns or give up radios, education and modern medicine. But most of the Evenki, for example, want to continue living off reindeer and the hunt.[9] (At least they did, before the Northern Trans-Siberian railroad was completed in 1984.) The government pays them excellent prices for sable and other furs, so they pursue their traditional livelihoods. The Nanai, on the other hand, seem attracted by urban life. One-fifth already live in town, and one-half want their children to have what they regard as the advantages of city life.

For all the 160,000 tribal people, there is an affirmative-action program which includes preferential entrance into higher education to overcome the handicap they face as peoples with no tradition of written learning. This is not simply a matter of "fair's fair." Obviously, professionals from indigenous cultures are more apt to stay in their home territories than outsiders, so training indigenous doctors, for example, is one way of assuring that the people will have modern medical care.

This is not to say the Soviet government is neutral as between traditional and modern life. Folk medicine cannot prevent smallpox, diphtheria, and innumerable other conditions. Traditional livelihoods cannot support as many human beings on the same resources as modern agriculture and industry. One Nanai collective farm has three fishing vessels, a sawmill, and dairy cows; it grosses $3,000,000 a year, and provides a better and healthier life for its people than when they fished and hunted by hand — but such an operation needs managers, accountants, veterinarians, animal husbandrymen.

The government pays all costs of child maintenance for aborigenes through the age of 18. For tribes that wander with the reindeer or live in communities too small for a high school, it maintains boarding schools; children spend their summers with their parents. (And the kids are not "hit in the mouth with sticks if they heard us speaking our own language," as American Indians recently complained to an international organization.)

By the early 1960s illiteracy among the *adult* indigenous population had been done away with; among those of school age it had disappeared years earlier.

There are now creative writers of many tribes. Most famous is Chookchee Rytkheu, whose work has been published in English and many Soviet languages.* The Nanai, Khojer; the Nenets, Lapsui; the Neevkhee, Sangi; the Mahnsee, Iuvan; the Evenk, Alitet (he, too, has been published in English); the Even, Tarabukin; the Yukagir, Kurilov; the Koriak, Kekketyn, are all professionals who live by the pen. The Chookchee, Koriaks and Evenki each have full-time professional ethnic dance-and-song companies. Ivory carving of extraordinary skill and beauty flourishes, and workshops making ethnic clothing chiefly of fur, which is eagerly purchased by Russians (parkas, boots) as well as by local people.

At the beginning of this chapter, I mentioned the 10,500,000 Kazakhs, Turkmen and Kirgiz, nomads and sheepherders at the time of the revolution. I have not mentioned them since because there is simply no comparison to the American Indian experience. Their numbers have made it possible for them to develop mass-scale, urban industrial and technological populations. They have full-fledged republics of the Soviet Union.

*He told the Canadian writer, Farley Mowat (*Never Cry Wolf*): "I make more money than the President."[10] Mowat's best-seller, *The Siberians*, grew out of Rytkheu's invitation to visit him.

Kirgizia is on the inner Chinese border, near Afghanistan. The Kirgiz director, Tolomush Okeev (Okay-eff) was born a nomad — he had hardly been off a horse till his teens. We met when one of his feature films was shown in Berkeley, California, so my time in Kirgizia was spent chiefly with his co-workers and friends. They are movie and TV people, although I also met Kirgiz social scientists, a professional painter, and writers — all college graduates. There are now over a thousand Kirgiz with PhDs, and they are to be found in most technological sciences as well as in fields enabling them to study and advance their own ethnic culture.

They *run* those fields. The art museum, a modern block-square building, is the equal of any in any American city of that size. It has a Kirgiz woman director (her assistant was an indigenous Chinese Moslem). The film-makers' organization is headed by a Kirgiz writer, Chingiz (Ghenghis) Aitmatov, who is one of the three or four most popular writers in the USSR today. A play of his has been produced on U.S. public TV, and on stage at the Kennedy Center in Washington, and one of his novels has been published in the United States.[11] Kirgiz had never been written down until Soviet scholars devised an alphabet for it in the 1920s.

Each of these republics, Kirgizia, Kazakhstan, Turkmenia, has a full-fledged, permanent, magnificently housed opera-and-ballet company. The leading coloratura soprano of Kazakhstan, Bibigul Tulegenova, spoke with me about her life and career:

In 1913 there was a terrible famine, and my papa lost both his parents. So he and his brother moved to the city and their life of torment as children began. They would hire themselves out to wealthy people to do whatever they could. Papa got a dombra, [a strummed instrument] and he played. We have a saying that every Kazakh is born either with a dombra or with poetry he brings into the world. He played many instruments — even the piano a little — but since he was from a very poor family, and lost his parents so young, it did not fall to him to develop his talent. After he married, papa became a laborer, loading and unloading things by hand, then he became a fireman. Mama was a housewife. During World War II we lost our father, and mama went to work, because there were seven children to feed. When the war began I was ten. I was the second child, but my older sister was very sickly so whatever could be done in the street — buy bread, other foods, or anything else that had to be done outside the house — that was my job.

During the war my mother worked at a meat-packing plant, as a worker. I was under 13 when I went to work in 1943. That was necessary, to feed the family. There were only women, elderly people of both sexes, and teen-agers. Everyone lived in poverty during the war.

Everything went to the front, everything for victory. We were hungry, barefoot, lacked clothing.

Three of the children died. We were cold. There was a shortage of medicine. Mother worked 18 hours a day, and there was no time to care for the children. [Four daughters survive, including her older sister, now a commodities expert in domestic trade.]

When I was very young, we lived in workers' barracks. Then, before the war, one apartment house was built, and we were allotted an apartment because there were so many children, a two-room apartment. Then, during the War, housing was short, so we lived in one room, another family in the other, and evacuees from the overrun European territories lived in the kitchen.

I sang in school, and I had even sung to my father's accompaniment. When I went to work, I joined the amateur groups of working youth. When I worked in the meat-canning assembly line of the packing plant, I would start singing — I would sing a verse, and the others would join in the chorus.

I would put up a mirror, and posture in front of it to see how I looked. I would sing and dance, and of course that would interrupt the operations — I not only didn't meet the quotas but got in the way of the work. But I learned to do every job on the line, the whole process of meat canning. Finally the department head begged the higher-ups, "get that artist out of here. With her we can't keep the work going."

Finally, I recognized that I was not behaving seriously. Later I was a leading worker — my picture was up on all the honor boards. But no sooner had I adjusted and begun to work for real than the Young Communist League sent me to Alma-Ata to see whether I really had it. But I caught cold on the railroad train and couldn't sing a note. The board looked at me, and shrugged their shoulders; they couldn't understand why I was there. Finally they said: "Little girl, go home and rest up. And come next year and try again."

The boss of my department, Igor Anatolich Lebedev, [a Russian name] was as upset as I was. He very much wanted me to study voice. But mama was very much against it at first. She would say: "What kind of occupation is this, anyhow? You've got to have a job, so you can take care of a family."

When I returned to my home town, we had a city-wide contest of amateur performers. One of the people present was Galina Serebriakova, the writer, who has written novels about Karl Marx.* She heard me sing. She had studied voice in England and Italy when her husband was on diplomatic duty there. She said: "I want to work with that girl."

---

*She had been exiled there as a Trotskyist after her husband had been executed in one of Stalin's purge trials. She was barred from publication for 20 years, and could not leave the town, but otherwise she was allowed to do what she could.

She said to me that the color of my voice was very much like that of Galli-Curci. [The coloratura soprano of 1910-1930, both in Italy and in New York.] Little by little, I began to understand what she was about. Then, in August, 1948, I went back to Alma-Ata for a Kazakhstan-wide contest of amateurs. I sang them Strauss' "The Voice of Spring." They were all amazed. Where did that come from?

People wanted me to study. I said: "No, I am not going to go anywhere to school! I already know how to sing." But they convinced me that talent was like a precious stone that, if it is not polished, will just lie there in the ground and not amount to anything. Because I was not a high-school graduate, they enrolled me in a preparatory grade in the conservatory. In my final year at the conservatory, I went to Leningrad to participate in the First USSR-wide Vocal Conference. Famous people were present as judges, and when I sang Gilda's aria in *Traviata* and Rachmaninoff's "Nightingale," the entire board of judges gave me a standing ovation. I behaved badly. I burst into tears, and couldn't utter a word.

I was immediately accepted into the Kazakh Theater of Opera and Ballet. I made my debut in Verdi's *Rigoletto* in which I sang Gilda. Then I sang Norina in Donizetti's *Don Pasquale*, and the soprano lead in Tschaikovsky's *Queen of Spades*.

Tulegenova's husband, also a Kazakh, is a physicist. Her older daughter — also a physicist — is married to a Russian. Her younger daughter — who sings in the opera company — is married to a man half Kazakh and half Uzbek. "'Altogether, our is an international family."

We talked about her earnings — 500 a month from the theater, plus 300 from the conservatory where she graduated, and now teaches. "And 200 expense money as a member of the parliament of Kazakhstan." (We returned to this later.) This is considerably more than her husband's earnings of 600 rubles. When I remarked on this, she laughed, with a distinct note of satisfaction: "But I have to travel a lot, and he stays home. I spend a lot of money on the road." When I pressed her on the subject, she replied "He is very much in love with me, very proud of me. He's a great defender of my dignity. He helps me in every way, even at home. At home we do everything for ourselves. We do not keep a houseworker — perhaps it's because I came out of such a plain workingclass family — and my children do everything for themselves. We do *not* exploit labor."

If her husband had not helped when the children were young, she pointed out, "I would never have grown to the situation I occupy today. I would never have become a People's Artist of the

Soviet Union, nor could I do all that civic activity." She has been a member of the parliament of the Kazakh Republic for 14 years, and is on the Committee on Protection of Motherhood and Childhood.

When I spoke of the American notion that in the USSR orders come down from on high, she explained her role, "Suppose a woman has many children, and faces some problems. She comes to me as a member of parliament to ask my help. Let's say it's a question of seeing some top-level official, a person it's hard to reach on your own. So she presents her case to me, and that allows me to go and bang on the necessary doors for her."

That's ombudsman work, but not governing, as we understand it, so I asked for another example of the committee's work. "Say there's need for a new school somewhere, or a new children's hospital or pre-school center. Our committee meets, and then submits appropriate proposals to the Supreme Soviet [parliament]. Those things are subsequently carried out by the executive branch. I represent Chimkent Province." Her committee, she told me, includes both men and women, but the chair is a woman.

I commented that she had a pretty full life. It turned out to be still fuller:

We have a USSR-wide central committee of our Union of Performing Artists, and I'm a member of the committee to assist in work in the countryside. If I visit some village on tour, the young people will come and tell me they need such-and-such musical instruments, or sheet music, or their community center lacks this or that. Or they ask me to listen to them perform, and help them — or some boy or girl who has heard me in a small locality will wander into the conservatory and ask to listen to his or her voice. In that way I also scout for talent. That is one of the specific functions of the union's assistance to the country-side.

Our talk took place in San Francisco, where she had performed. I asked where else she had toured. "It would be easier to tell you where I haven't. In the last three or four years I've been in England, Italy, France, Japan, and Austria." Although in her 50s then, and past her prime, she was unquestionably among the dozen greatest sopranos I have ever heard.

My friend, Kirgiz director Tolomush Okeev, and his friends had attended Soviet movie colleges in Moscow and Leningrad but remained completely loyal to their own culture. Their personal values and characters have been shaped in clan-organized societies.

I taped some of our conversations in Kirgizia. A playwright, Bek-Sultan Zhakiev:

During World War II we lost a great many of our dear brothers. Among us, the brothers of our mothers and our fathers are also considered brothers; we don't think of people as cousins or second cousins. . . . Life is my past, which means my ancestors; life is me in the present, my wife, my family; life is my children, my kin. . . .

I received my actual upbringing from my grandfather. He was a man of the very deepest wisdom. That which is good in me I regard as having come from him, while the bad is my own doing. . . .

Art and literature are things of the soul, because what one finds there are both pain and joy, and each of us has both his sufferings and rejoicing. And if the pain and joy of my people reaches the soul of another people, there will be a greater closeness between my people and that other people.

Zhakiev's first play had run 500 performances in the fine, new building of the Kirgiz repertory theater, in a park opposite the capitol building. (It is equipped with earphones providing a Russian translation.) When we went to see a play about ethics and morality at a medical center, the theater was filled with young Kirgiz. A billboard outside announced the next production: *The House of Bernardo Alba,* by Spain's Garcia Lorca—to be performed in Kirgiz, of course. Zhakiev's wife, an accountant, talked with us about her marriage. "Happiness is to find a person who understands you. And I found myself such a person. He is not only an understanding man and husband, but he is also an understanding friend and comrade." She spoke in this way to strangers, foreigners with an openness that I identify with the Kirgiz. Her husband picked up again: "The closest of all friends are one's wife and one's mother. My mother lives far, far away, on the shores of Lake Issyk-Kul,"— eighty-miles-long and high in the mountains—the heartland of the Kirgiz ethnic spirit. "Her mother lives at Talas. There is no present one can give to thank them enough. Our hearts are like mountains. When two hearts live side by side, it is like two mountains. Happiness is when your wife understands you. Happiness is when a friend understands you. Happiness is when *you*, you understood us, and we you."

Another day Aman Alpiev, a TV film-maker, took me for a drive high into their mountains. Their capital city, Frunze, lies at 2,500 feet, buried in greenery, and the mountains outside rise to 16,000 feet. He mused about his life. His father had asked him not to smoke or drink. I said: " 'Well, I do drink, but I promise you, like a man, father.' He said: 'All right, I'll call together all the old men and tell them that my son has given me his word. So if you go

Film director Aman Alpiev and his mother, who still weeps at mention of another son killed in World War II.

back on it, I'll be shamed in their eyes.' I said to Him: 'Father, I can't let you down'."

Although 200,000 of the Kirgiz now live in town, 85 percent are still rural; I asked about that. The TV director said: "Last year I finished a film about a family. A whole dynasty. The father had been grazing sheep since 1928. He had 11 children. Six of them are shepherds. When I spoke to them, I asked: 'How come? You could have become workers or whatever.' One told me: 'I tried it. I went off to town. I didn't like it.' And then the father spoke. 'I feel that if I moved to town there'd be something missing from my life. There's that need that sits inside of me. And my daughter became a shepherd.' One of his sons is a scientist. He said: 'I could have gone to the city, worked in a laboratory at the Kirgiz Academy of Sciences. But I just couldn't make myself. The land calls me back, and that's all there's to it.' He took his PhD, but nonetheless he works at the collective farm. (These farms have testing labs; a few have experiment stations.)

"There are many such among us Kirgiz. It's not only people without schooling — everybody gets an education. People graduate from college and go back to their own land. That man said to me:

American-Russian Institute

Veterinary and shepherd's yurta.

'I can't live without this land here, this hill, that mountain. When I get up in the morning,' he said, 'I have this feeling about my children being right here by me. I can't exist without this. That phrase, native land, that's not just words,' he said. 'I've traveled a lot, including abroad. I get up in the morning and by nightfall I'm unhappy. When I get up, I've got to see my mountains as much as I have to have breakfast'."

The shepherds' incomes are enormous. The best earn more than a high government official or the manager of a big factory, when bonuses for the crop of lambs and for above-average wool yields are added to their base pay. Even though it's their traditional work, the public think they deserve this pay: the temperatures drop to -60 degrees in these mountains, and it's outdoor work in all weather. Indeed, the worse the weather, the more there is to do to protect the stock. This was only October, but at 7,000 feet we saw sleet and fog. "If you look there carefully" (we were passing a hamlet of whitewashed masonry houses: no more yurtas) "every shepherd has two cars." In the Soviet Union, even one car per family is still rare. Shepherds, coal-miners, and top intellectuals are the exceptions to the rule. From the government's point of view, the high cash rewards and access to consumer durables work as incentives to push wool and mutton-and-lamb production as high as possible.

We topped a divide. "Here's Aksa Pass, Arpa Valley. The year before last I did a film here about the shepherds in winter. They spend the year here, but live performances are provided for them, whole parties of entertainers are sent up here. As the saying goes, people need more than meat, they need for the spirit as well. Movies are shown; actors like Chokmorov ride up here."*

The TV film-maker fell silent, and I thought about the Navajo sheep-raisers in the United States. I have before me a New York Times story describing "typical rural Navajos." A couple with ten children, age 2 to 22, live "in a hut, 12 feet in diameter" of cedar logs and mud. The nearest water is ten miles away; there is no mail delivery, no radio, TV, or newspaper. They live 35 miles from town and have 20 to 50 sheep, yielding approximately $1,200 annually.[12] This family, with ten children, would get two hundred dollars per month from the Bureau of Indian Affairs, and some surplus farm products. In 1977, Senator Edward Kennedy reported that tuberculosis on the Navajo Reservation was 13 *times* higher than in the general U.S. population. Rheumatic fever was 80 times higher, hepatitis 56 times. Diphtheria is still epidemic. Children suffer from kwashiorkor, malignant malnutrition common in poor Third World countries, and marasmus, "a gradual wasting of the tissues of the body from insufficient, imperfect food supply."

Hunger diseases haven't existed in the Soviet Union since recovery from World War II. There is still severe crowding, but nowhere in that vast country do twelve people live in a single room — as they do in San Francisco's Chinatown among other places, not just on reservations. Average housing space per family is much less in the USSR than in the U.S. but it is much more fairly divided among the population.

I don't know how that Navajo family is organized, but I did get some idea of a very large family from our guide in Kirgizia. When we returned five years later, she was executive secretary to the two heads of the Kirgiz TV and radio broadcasting system. (Both heads are Kirgiz, one a woman.) Her father was born a shepherd but became a veterinarian. She talked chiefly about her mother, how-

---

*Suimenkul Chokmorov is a truly fine actor and a professional painter. A mountain-born Kirgiz who does his own trick riding scenes, he has been seen in the U.S. in Kurosawa's *Dersu Uzala*, filmed in the USSR.

ever. When Roza said she was one of twelve, and the oldest, she counted for me:

> Let me see now. After me there's a sister who is a dental surgeon. Next comes a sister who graduated from the Department of Agronomy at the Kirgiz College of Agriculture, she works as a field-crop specialist. The fourth is a brother, who is studying at the College of Physical Education. His major is boxing. The fifth, a brother, is doing his compulsory military service. The next, a sister, is studying to be a teacher of German. There are five more, so six of them live at home.
>
> The government gives my mother a large-family grant. She was a Russian-language teacher. [I interrupted, amazed: "a *teacher* and twelve children?" Her reply was matter-of-fact.] I'll explain how mama managed. She would go off to teach school. I was the eldest. I took care of everything. I got up very early, the same time as those who were schoolchildren. I did my gymnastics, fast, made my bed, and all the older children made their own beds. So mother went to work, and when she got home, all of us had our duties. One washed the floors, one cooked dinner, one looked after the littlest ones, and so forth.

My wife asked if the boys also had their duties. "The boys too. In the past, among us boys did nothing. Now we don't accept that anymore. First of all, he's got to do the heavy work." I interviewed her 13-year-old son when we returned in 1982. Summers he helps his father's mother, once a nomad, with her livestock in the mountains. At school as an active member of the Pioneers, Soviet equivalent of the Scouts, he helps people by shopping for them.

For some reason, in the Asian nomad cultures, the women did literally everything except herd the sheep, unlike the settled farmers, where men did the heavy work. But Roza went on:

> Washing the walls, he has to do. Hanging the drapes, he's got to do. In short, whatever is heavy. Of course, now we have washing machines and things. You can sit down in the morning and listen to the radio.
>
> The government was very generous in its help to my mother. It gave her a washing machine. It gave her a dishwasher [still a rare appliance in the Soviet Union]. Mama is a "Mother Heroine."* They have privileges. This is arranged through the city council which issues the financial grant for each child. A certain percentage of the automobiles put on the market is reserved for them too. They get them at a cut price. Then, for each child, she gets two rubles, three rubles per month, until they reach the ages of three to five. The federal government adds more, because she has many children. It begins with seven children.

---

*That title, awarded all women who successfully raise ten or more children, is accompanied by forms of material aid.

The government gave her a house, five rooms with the kitchen. It has a small garden and has all conveniences.

The youngest child still with her mother was in the 5th grade. "This one goes to the school in which instruction is in the English language, so the kids can get a really thorough knowledge of it." (We visited it the next day. Our three 17-year-old guides, two of them Kirgiz, were able to conduct a fluent conversation with us in English about anything and everything, for two hours: environ-

Tom Weber

In rural Kirgizia

mental protection, home-making, art—whatever was being taught in each classroom.)

Roza continued about her mother: "She was given paid leaves, of course." Maternity leave is part of Soviet labor law, for all women with jobs. Sixteen weeks at full pay, now extended to a year, of which the remainder is at part pay.

Mama put us in the nurseries. Nine dollars a month. [This includes food, *five*(!) meals a day.] We were living in a large village and the children of the collective farmers paid nothing at all, because the farm gave the kindergarten the food for the children's meals. In general, kindergartens on farms charge no fees at all, but in the cities one pays a certain percentage of the cost.

Later on they went to the extended-day schools.*

There they did their homework, crafted things, engaged in sports. Then mama would come home. She would help us with our Russian. We regard it as a second native language. It gives us the chance to familiarize ourselves with the literature of the entire world. When we travel around the Soviet Union, we can converse with anyone we meet.†[13]

My mother is 53. And the government has granted her a pension for her 15 years work as a teacher. She is credited with the actual years worked, plus time extra for having so many children—the equivalent of 25 years' seniority.

Every year she gets to travel to the Crimea, [the Soviet Riviera, 2,000 miles away] for vacation. Fare for her is free one way. The pre-revolutionary Kirgiz woman had no such rights. She was totally a thing in the hands of her husband, the master of the house. Our Soviet government has given Soviet women enormous freedoms and opportunities. This means that I can work at the work that I love. I can be fulfilled, and happy to be here because I know that things are serene at home.

Many Central Asian professional women boasted to me about their mothers' large numbers of children. Yet none had more than four themselves. Apparently their other rich life interests have made them decide to limit their families. They certainly have larger homes, incomes, and more child care available than their own mothers had.

The Soviet government grants to large families are intended to stimulate the birthrate in a country with vast unpopulated spaces and undeveloped resources.[14] Yet census figures show that only

---

*Extended-day schools are a development of the past 20 years that provide supervision and a meal for grade-school and junior-high age children until their parents come home. USSR-wide, 11,000,000 are now enrolled.

†The youngest generation speaking: only 30 percent of Kirgiz regard themselves as being fluent in Russian.

Central Asians and Armenians — who traditionally favor large families — continue to have many children, an average of five (more in the country, fewer in town).

TURKMENIA

Turkmenia, west of Kirgizia, is a country of desert sands that makes Navajo country look like grassland. The Turkmen were also yurta-dwellers and nomads who traveled with their herds, but since water is now carried across Turkmenia by a huge canal — only California's Central Valley Project is as long — settled farming has spread across the entire republic from the few oases where it previously existed. A local radio reporter took me to see a collective farm on this irrigated land, outside the capital, Ashkhabad, a few miles from Iran.

An elderly farmer who showed us around explained that the people live not in scattered homes but a village. There was an inside water supply, and they were starting to put in sewer lines. "There's gas and electricity in every home. Except for electric light, all the rest are free. Water is free, gas is free." The farmer went on, "Every bit of what you see here is built by the collective farmers themselves." I found their community center utterly stunning. A gleam of light in the park that stretched beyond the center was the "summer movie theater." I learned there had been no trees before the collective farm, and asked about the homes. "Depends upon the size of the family. They used to be small; now they build them large — there are eight-room houses. They have lots of children. In the past they were of plastered mud over wattles. Now they're of brick, with slate roofs. And they do this out of their personal earnings.

He pointed to an immense area under glass, maybe 15 acres, where vegetables are grown year-round for the nearby capital city. This has made the farm so rich, but that was no stroke of luck. When the city was leveled by a terrible earthquake thirty years earlier, the farmers helped rebuild it — with great assistance in equipment and personnel from the federal government, though this was just after World War II and the entire western part of the USSR had been destroyed. They also helped build the canal, which

Collective-farm greenhouse.

did not reach the village until 1962. This meant that the village I saw — including paved sidewalks — had essentially been completed in 15 years.

The village has 1,500 people, "so when the adult population gathers here to decide matters, there already isn't enough room," the farmer said. We were in the 500 upholstered-seat main auditorium of the glass-and-concrete community center. (In the past, the nomadic Turkmen did not know what a chair was.) I asked what questions are decided collectively? "If we're deciding whether to accept someone's resignation, say to move to town, or somebody from town wants to join us and move here. The biggest issue is, of course, how the income is to be divided at the end of the year. Then, such things as a major construction undertaking. "The board of directors is allowed to decide on small jobs. But on big things, the collective farmers as a whole make up their minds on what they regard as most important at the moment, a large cow-barn or a road or a school."* Though school construction is a government responsibility, collective farms often build them with their own funds to have a new one substantially earlier. "Right now we're building a hospital, seventy beds." The radio reporter put in: "although they already have one," but the farmer explained: "it's a little one."

Our stroll now had reached a smaller hall in the building. "This hall is to help exercise democracy, because the collective farm is built on democratic foundations. There are questions that the body of authorized representatives can decide, without calling together the entire collective farm, and this is the meeting hall for the authorized representatives." The hall held about 150 seats; he confirmed there is one delegate for every ten persons. "When these people go back out into the farm, they explain to those they represent what the discussion was about and report what they had decided. Say I'm a member of that body, and I go to a meeting. You and I work side by side. I know your views. So when I get to the meeting, I know the opinion of my whole brigade, my group of ten. When I express my opinion here in the name of all those, I know my people will support what I say."

A Turkmen Academy of Sciences would have been simply unimaginable in 1930; in 1977 we visited its Institute of History, Archeology, and Anthropology, where we were received by five scholars, all Turkmen, three of them women, including the director. None would look out of place at any gathering of North American Indians, although people might have trouble identifying the tribe.

Rug-making, traditionally a home handicraft, is now centralized in a splendidly light, spacious, and clean factory run by women, as is the factory making the embroidered ethnic gowns women still

---

*This man was not a guide or an official host, but obviously someone who had spent his life working the soil. A boy had called him from his house when we arrived unexpectedly.

Photo by Author

Traditional Turkmen dress. Women no longer wear their wealth sewn to their clothes.

prefer. All its executives are Turkmen college graduates. The director of the art museum is a Russian woman; the Museum of Turkmenian History is directed by a Turkmen woman.

At the University of Kazakhstan, the dean of the Biology Department is a Kazakh woman, resembling an Indian from southern Mexico. She is in charge of 300 instructional staff and researchers, 30 percent of them men. "We have ten male full professors, and I give them orders." She laughed. Kazakhstan now

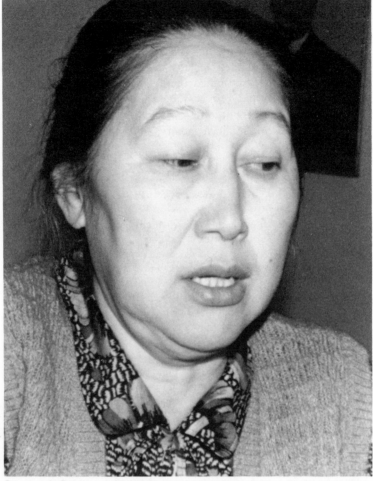

Photo by Author

Dean of Biology, Kazakhstan University. Was exchange professor in United States.

has over 50 higher educational institutions, of which hers is the most important.

No industrial enterprise in *Fortune* magazine's list of the top 500 corporations in the United States is managed by a Black, a Chicano, an American Oriental or an Indian. The Achisai Polymetallic Industries of Kazakhstan, employing 10,000 in mining and refining zinc and lead, are headed by Sakh Moldenkul(ov), a Kazakh. We met in San Francisco, and later spent an evening together in Alma-Ata, capital of Kazakhstan.

"Achisai," he told me, "means 'Bitter Valley.' Prior to the Revolution, lead ore was mined there. And the lives of the local population were bitter." He was born and grew up there. His parents had been rural, but went to work at Achisai when the mine was founded; his mother in a factory, his father as an unskilled construction laborer. He continued:

> At that time—this was about 1932, 1933—the working class was first coming into being in our parts. There were few skilled occupations. My father remained an unskilled worker, because he wasn't able to obtain an education
>
> I finished the 7th grade in 1941, when our country was attacked by Germany, and I went to work in my mother's factory. In 1944 a technical high school was opened in our state capital, Chimkent.* Those were the years when the scale of industry in Kazakhstan was growing by leaps and bounds. I spent four years at that school, graduated as a mining technician, and returned to my own plant. And the, you know, a human being always seeks some direction in which to grow. I entered the College of Mining and Metallurgy here in Alma-Ata. I graduated as a mine-surveyor engineer.
>
> I returned to my own enterprise, and worked over six years as section surveyor in an underground mine, manager of a small open-strip mine, manager of the underground mine. Then I was offered the job as manager of a whole integrated enterprise in another state of Kazakhstan.

He was then 33, and I asked if he was married by that time. "My wife is a physician. We had become acquainted, and got married." Those two simple sentences express two revolutions: first, a Kazakh woman becoming a doctor was then about the equivalent of an American woman becoming an astronaut today; and secondly that they chose each other, instead of being matched by parents.

He has been manager for ten years. I asked how many nationalities were represented at the plant. "Forty-nine." I went further, and asked how he knew this. "That's a social issue," he explained:

> It is the business of the manager to concern himself with all questions of life, conditions off the job, and of work of the people employed. In our country, the manager of an enterprise is required to resolve the entire interrelated set of such questions.

---

*He did not mention that students were provided with housing, food, and a living allowance, plus the free education. Soviet people take that for granted.

A worker takes a job above all at an enterprise that he likes and where working conditions satisfy him — and living conditions, and daily existence: housing, the water supply, electricity, the sewage system, recreational and cultural facilities, schools, child-care centers, swimming pools, outdoor places for relaxation and week-end facilities, and conditions of work.

These are my responsibilities. If we don't handle those problems properly and as an integrated whole, a worker will see that the work is harder than elsewhere — there are fewer mechanical aids, for example; that progress with housing is not being made, child-care centers inadequate, there's no place for him to spend his free time. Our working people today have become very well-informed. They understand these things, they weigh them. They look for a place to work where they can earn more and where life is more comfortable. And so we work on resolving these problems. Our enterprise is out front in terms of industrial equipment: our mines are ultra-modern.

A face of the Mirgalimsia Mine, part of the Achisai Works managed by Mr. Moldenkulov. ". . . our mines are ultra-modern."

Mr. Moldenkul(ov) did not fit one's image of top management. His suit was good, well-fitted, and neat, but it was not in the $500 or $1,000 range. His hotel in San Francisco was modest and he shared a room with another member of his group. His voice was not crisp and commanding, or hail-fellow-well-met, but soft and thoughtful. He was 56.

I asked about relations with the Communist Party. He is a Party member, and said, "The Party is the leading force in our society." I pressed for a concrete reply.

Here's what I'd like to say to you. In life there is truth. One also finds falsehood, deception, stealing, malfeasance, justice. All that complex of realities of life. That is true of every person individually, of every place of employment, of, say, a city; and it is the job of the Party to look after all such things. With us, the Party is the just body to which everyone brings his problems. Do you understand?

For example, sometimes we have arguments. I may have a dispute with a contractor. Say a construction organization has accepted a contract from me to build a hospital, because we have to improve hospital treatment for the workers. Suppose, for one reason or another he does not do the job on time. I go to the city committee of the Party, and say: "Comrade Secretary, the manager of that construction firm is a Communist Party member, and I have a beef with him. He isn't doing what he agreed to, the job he promised is not getting done. He is working on less important jobs instead." The Party Secretary calls him in, and says: "What is this you're doing?"

Vladimir Ilyich Lenin had an expression: "The Party is the mind, the honor, and the conscience of our time." And it is not only when we in leadership positions have disputes, get into fights with each other, but when the individual worker — any citizen whatever — sees anyone at all doing anything at all that is unjust, wrong, he will always go to the city committee of the Party. And he'll say: "So and so is doing this or that, making decisions that are not right, or is engaging in malfeasance," or whatever. And such people are called to account.

What I am saying is this: if the right thing is not brought about, evil is all that would remain. Understand? And in order to see to it that fairness, justice is maintained, to make sure that what is right sinks the firmest roots, that's what we need the Party and its bodies for.

People have to be socialized in the spirit of honesty, conscientiousness, fairness. That's it. And everyone in our country understands this. Everybody. Whether he's a big industrial manager, a big trade union leader, government official, worker, professional: everyone understands this. And in our country the Party enjoys extremely high respect. People love it.

As the head of an enterprise, I cannot permit myself anything illegal, no unjust deed, no bureaucratic act—say stalling on a problem or slighting people's legitimate requests. If I did, they'd call me in and say: "What were you up to there, acting unfairly?" Faith in the Party goes on rising in our country. And the numbers of Communists, members of the Party, grow. Once it consisted of only a few individuals, then some thousands, then tens of thousands, then millions, and now tens of millions in our Party. That's how it is.

I thanked him and he snapped out of the reverie in which those last sentences were spoken, and asked, hopefully: "Did you really understand my meaning?" I told him I thought I did, but he was still locked into his own thoughts. "Sometimes foreigners ask 'What does the Party do? What do the soviets do?' As if they think business managers can handle everything. An executive handles economic questions, of course, he deals with all kinds of questions. "But . . . " I broke in, "There are also moral questions." He nodded, "Moral. Exactly. And that is what our Party concerns itself with. You understand? We have to see to it that life is —right."

NOTES

1. *San Francisco Chronicle*, September 5, 1972.
2. V.N. Uvachan, *The Peoples of the North and Their Road to Socialism* (Moscow: Progress, 1975), p. 72. A superb book, with deepest meaning for Indians, Eskimos, and peoples on all continents existing in tribal societies or with roots therein. Original-source documentation, plus the life experience of the author, born into the Evenk people.
3. V.N. Uvachan, *Put' narodov severa k sotsializmu* (Moscow: Mysl', 1971), p. 351. This is the Russian original of the Uvachan work in English, and is about 50 percent longer.
4. L.G. Tynel' and B.A. Zhuravlev, "Perfecting the Competence of the Soviet of an Autonomous Area," *Soviet Law and Government*, XVII, No. 1 (1978).
5. S.P. and Ethel Dunn, "The Peoples of Siberia and the Far East," in Wayne S. Vucinich (ed.), *Russia and Asia* (Stanford: Hoover Institution, 1972), pp. 244-295.
6. *San Francisco Chronicle*, July 20, 1978.
7. *San Francisco Chronicle*, May 23, 1977.
8. Ch. M. Taksami, "Changes in the Social Makeup of the Minor Peoples of the Far East," *Soviet Sociology*, XIV, No. 3 (1975-76), pp. 26-44, *passim*.
9. Leonid Shinkarev, *Vtoroi Transsib* (Moscow: Politizdat, 1976), pp. 183-190.
10. Farley Mowat, *The Siberians* (Boston: Little, Brown, 1970), p. 50.
11. Chingiz Aitmatov, *The White Ship* (New York: Crown, 1972).
12. Reprinted in *San Francisco Chronicle*, June 23, 1974.
13. "USSR Census Returns," *Soviet Law and Government*, XIX, No. 2 (1980), p. 29.
14. E.B. Gruzdeva and E.S. Chertikhina, *Trud i byt sovetskikh zhenshchin* (Moscow: Politizdat, 1983), Chapter II, Section 1, pp. 74-118.

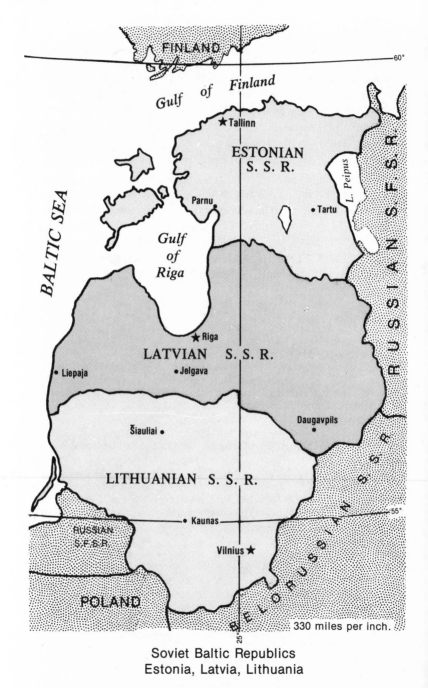

Soviet Baltic Republics
Estonia, Latvia, Lithuania

THUANIA ESTONIA
LATVIA
* Moscow

8

Catholic Lithuania;
Protestant Latvia and Estonia

Lithuania is on the Baltic Sea across from Sweden. Over 800,000 Americans are of Lithuanian birth or descent.[1] When Pope John Paul II was installed in office, he addressed the world in several languages, including Lithuanian — the tongue of the one Soviet nationality that is Roman Catholic. According to Soviet scholars, this is the only nationality there of Christian heritage among whom fully half remain religious.

In pre-Soviet times, too, Lithuania was one of the most religious countries in Europe, For 400 years, an immense Lithuanian-and-Polish state existed, dominated first by Lithuania, then by Poland. It extended clear down to the Black Sea, and ruled the enormous Ukraine as well as Byelorussia and Moldavia. It reached to within 100 miles of Moscow — a Polish king once captured that city.

Moscow today accepts Lithuania's Catholicism as part of that country's cultural tradition in every respect. Pictures of three Catholic churches appear in the official *Large Soviet Encyclopedia* (1970) in the article on Vilnius,[2] formerly called Vilna (Wilno), the Lithuanian capital. There were no churches pictured in the 1951 edition of the same work, published in Stalin's day.

I walked into one of those churches, Sts. Peter and Paul's at twilight on a Saturday. It is a 17th-century baroque structure with an immense chandelier in the form of a sailboat of Murano glass from Venice. Many worshippers were present. I took pictures, but as the lights went on a man grasped my arm, and said severely, "No photography during services." He addressed me in Russian, taking it for granted that a Lithuanian would know better. What struck me was that he obviously felt himself master in his own institution —there was no hesitation in calling to account someone he assumed was Russian. Under the Lithuanian Penal Code "Interference in the performance of religious rites, providing they do not disturb public order or infringe on the rights of citizens, is punishable by imprisonment or corrective labor, for a term of one year or by a fine of up to 100 rubles."

Two scholars from the Lithuanian Academy of Sciences were my hosts — atheists, to judge by their failure to make the signs of reverence all others present did. Nonetheless, they had obvious pride in church art as an expression of their people's genius. They took me to a 16th century shrine of the Madonna in the city's Pointed Gate and persuaded the caretaker to admit us, though it was past closing time. She led us to a jewel-like chamber, where she curtsied to the lovely image and made the sign of the cross. The walls were lined with silver hearts in a great variety of sizes, placed there in gratitude by people who believed their prayers had been answered.

Later, I asked the Foreign Minister of Lithuania his view of the status of the Catholic Church. His reply is more meaningful in light of his own background:

If I lived in India, I could say that I came from the very lowest caste. I was born in 1927. My father had died leaving mother with two children. She worked for landowners. I went to school and worked at the same time, as a shepherd. There were *very* few who were exempted from paying tuition fees, but I did extremely well, and so I got that exemption.

Without a recommendation from the priest, I would not have been accepted into school. In the villages the priest ranked above anyone else, the village headman ranked second and the richest man third. The church exercised total control over the life of the poor peasant. It was a wealthy organization, very much so, it possessed a great deal of land. A Concordat with the Vatican was signed during the capitalist period [1920-1940], and the church intervened very strongly in governmental affairs, and it fought constantly for a dominant position in Lithuania's political life. The prime minister and cabinet members were religious

Catholic church, Vilnius, Lithuania.

Catholics, but even they had various conflicts with the church—the Papal Nuncio was actually expelled for interfering in the country's internal affairs.

In 1940, when we had a People's Government, *not* the Soviet government, we did what the French had done 150 years earlier. We separated the church from the state and from the school, and from its wealth. These three reforms turned the Catholic clergy against us, and that may explain why, during the Nazi occupation, the clergy collaborated *actively* with the occupying forces. The Lithuanian bishops sent Hitler a telegram of congratulations as liberator. Lithuanian Catholicism took a position with respect to the Jewish population that I would call inhuman. There were individual priests who were inclined to help the Jews, but for the most part the Church leadership classed the Jews as Communists automatically, and essentially facilitated the extermination of the Jewish population. This, of course, is something we cannot forgive.

In neighboring Poland the Church took a patriotic position. It participated in the underground struggle against the invaders. In our republic the Catholic Church helped the invaders out of hatred for socialism.

After the war, whether we acted rightly or wrongly, we cited the Bible, saying "Your business is to deal with the life of the soul, and not to build taverns, possess estates, and so forth. Stick to your own affairs. Christ's apostles were all poor." But, of course, who wants to give away their wealth, the millions those selfsame people had put together?

As compared to other countries, our Catholic clergy is very reactionary, very conservative. For example, this is the only Catholic country where the language of the people, Lithuanian, has not yet been introduced into the Mass, into ritual. In some countries there is a movement to modernize the Church; here that does not exist. The Church is flatly against it.

I reminded him of a petition, signed by 17,000 Lithuanians some years earlier, with respect to some kind of suppression, and asked whether the priests and the hierarchy could have done this without broad support. He replied:

The Catholic Church is fighting for repeal of the law separating the Church from the school. Under our laws, the profession of religion and the practice of religion by children is in the hands of their parents until they become adults. The parents may do whatever they wish, as Catholics, but we permit no schools to be established. The Church founded underground schools in violation of our laws.

As to that petition, the very fact that it was possible to do this in our country means there isn't any terror, any force. Imagine having tried to collect signatures on a petition during the German occupation, and how that would have ended!

The hierarchy doesn't like the fact that we have the French system, under which all the affairs of each church are run by a parish committee and the priest is an employee of that committee. In the past the priest was the master: he took in the money, he spent it, and he wasn't accountable to anybody. He paid his tribute to the bishop, and that was it. But now there is a degree of democracy in this matter. He's got to give an accounting to the fifteen or seventeen people on the committee. That's another thing which causes friction.

All sources agree that there are some 700 functioning Catholic churches in Lithuania.[3] As the population is about 3,500,000, that's the equivalent of having 700 in the San Francisco Bay Area.

As we walked away from the Foreign Office, we passed a Russian Orthodox church where services were in progress, with the characteristic polyphonic singing. We soon heard singing of a very different kind: a rock concert in full blast in the late Renaissance commons of the university, lit by a spotlight atop its own church. Students in colorful ethnic dress were selling refreshments from booths as at a country fair.

Vilnius has only half a million people. As in all formerly walled cities, a great deal is packed into its old center: Our walk brought us to a splendid modern high school, named for a woman poet, Salomeja Neris; just around a corner, we found ourselves in the late medieval residential center. As in all the Soviet Baltic cities, this historic core had been lovingly restored and is well kept — a sharp contrast to similar quarters in many French and Italian towns. We dropped, unannounced, into the apartment of a prominent artist — a former student of one of my hosts — in one of the restored buildings. It was two stories high. Officially, he had been assigned one floor as a studio, the other as residence, but he had harmonized them into one with paintings in the living quarters and the studio looking quite homelike.

Painting and language play an exceptional role in Lithuania. Lithuania produced a very important artist, Ciurlionis, (1875-1911),[4] who was a symbolist, and as a consequence Lithuanian art has a noticeably experimental character, far removed from the photographic realism of most publicly-displayed art in the USSR before the 1970s, as volumes of reproductions of Lithuanian art published there in the '60s and even the '50s show. The Ciurlionis Museum, which dates from pre-Soviet times, is in Kaunas (Kovno), Lithuania's second largest city. There is now a special gallery with humidity and temperature controls to preserve his works. He was also a composer, and tapes of his music run constantly in a separate room. Ciurlionis was as far from politics as can be — a few words he wrote give some notion of his insight into the human soul: "Love is the road to the sun, strewn with sharp diamonds, and each has to walk that road barefoot."

Drawers of three-by-five file cards run ceiling high in the Institute of Lithuanian Language and Literature, each card representing one word in that language, with information as to its meaning, where it was reported, and so forth. There are nearly four million cards, I was told, "and we are constantly adding to it." A good working dictionary of even a major language contains about 60,000 words — here were fifty times that many! I asked "Who finds time to collect all these? Where do they come from?" I was told, "Picking words out of books is easy, of course, but this is the living language. We have a staff of over one hundred, including forty-five PhDs. We have gotten words in 700 towns, villages, hamlets." This meant each person on the staff had collected 10,000 unique words — clearly impossible, I objected. "It would be," I was told, "but the schoolteachers everywhere help us. Whenever they encounter an unfamiliar word, they jot it down and send it to us." There are today over 30,000 schoolteachers, and this project has been going on for thirty years. It was begun by a single devoted scholar well over half a century ago, but only two PhDs were trained for this work under the non-Communist government of 1920-40 when the first volume of a complete dictionary was prepared for publication. Today, eleven volumes are in print, and the end is in sight.

Why this enormous interest in the language? Why does the government class this institute as "first-category," meaning it gets budget priority, has first call on equipment, and pays its scholars better than some institutes in the "hard" sciences? An American scholar explains that among Lithuanians there is still a "deeply-felt belief that to become truly important and meaningful, an action must be crystallized into a song or poem."[5] The Institute collects some 20,000 new songs each year.

A second factor is the uniqueness of the language itself, which is more nearly related to ancient Sanskrit than to any other in the Indo-European family. Today, the whole population learns that fact in school, but universal education is fairly recent. But perhaps the major reason for the extreme interest in the language is that it had been suppressed in the past, and a tremendous national pride was built in defending it.

Lithuania was actually the largest and most powerful country in Eastern Europe for centuries. This involved both alliance with Poland and adoption of Catholicism, so the nobility adopted Polish as its tongue — as today, French and English are the official languages of some African countries that had been part of those empires. The Lithuanian peasants, however, continued to adhere to their own unwritten language—a Latin alphabet was devised for Lithuanian in the 16th century.

Most of Lithuania was conquered by the Russian Empire at about the same time as the American Revolution. The tsars tried to Russify—just as German and Polish rulers had earlier tried to impose their cultures—and in the 19th century, publication in the Latin alphabet was forbidden. So books were smuggled in from the Prussian-occupied part of the country, and the "book-carriers" became Robin-Hood heroes to the people. A sculptural monument of one of them from the pre-Soviet period is one of the illustrations to the article on Lithuania in the Russian-language *Large Soviet Encylopedia.*

Finally the tsarist government refused to permit Lithuanian to be taught anywhere. Illegal schools in the native language appeared in the villages, and this was the very period when a literary language appeared: a Catholic bishop, Antanas Baranauskas, wrote poetry that became classic and a self-taught woman, Julia Zemaite, who started to write when nearly fifty, using notebooks made from wrapping paper, has won a permanent place in world literature.

Not until 1904 did the Russian government, fearful of revolution, raise the ban on Lithuanian printing.

During the Russian Revolution of 1917 and the Civil War, a Communist government ruled briefly in Lithuania. It decreed compulsory education in the native language and published some textbooks, but was defeated by a nationalist government favoring capitalism, which had the support of the United States and its allies who permitted the defeated German army to remain in Lithuania to fight communism. The anti-Communist Polish government then seized the capital and held it for twenty years. It sought to Polonize that area. A priest, Rev. Kostas Gajauskas, has written, "St. Nicholas Church was the *only* place where one could hold divine service in the Lithuanian language. Polish chauvinists used to attack Lithuanians after services and beat them for the simple reason that the latter had dared to pray in Lithuanian."[6]

The Lithuanian president,Antanas Smetona, an open admirer of Italy's fascist dictator Benito Mussolini, abolished constitutional government in 1926, and ruled as dictator until the outbreak of World War II in 1939. The Soviet Army moved into Lithuania, and the adjoining Baltic states of Latvia and Estonia, the next year.

It is virtually universally believed in the West that the Soviets moved against the desires of the Lithuanian people. But. Prof.

Jonas Macevicius, head of the Philosophy Institute of the Lithuanian Academy of Sciences, tells a different story. This is the man of desperately poor peasant origin described in the opening chapter. His Communist interpretation is based on his personal experience:

In 1939, 1940, the country was in a state of crisis, a crisis of the political regime. Smetona's fascist government had been discredited among the people — the cracks in the structure were so deep that the fascists had already retreated to coalition with the Christian Democrats and another group. A change in power was already very close. When the measures were taken by the Soviet government for obvious reasons [protection of nearby Leningrad against Hitler's expected attack. W.M.], favorable conditions were created for condemnation of Smetona's government by the entire people. A new system of authority was created by the masses under the leadership of the Communist Party. Not only objective but subjective conditions existed for these changes.

The same kinds of results did not ensue, either in Iran or in Austria when the Red Army was there.*

Neither in Iran nor in Austria did the prerequisites for such changes exist. But here they did, and therefore the events were marked by the triumph of the socialist system. The youth took a very active part in things. I have a very good recollection of that period. [He was 18 in 1940.] The steps taken by the Soviet government, its efforts in the countryside, were implemented by the youth, its strength, its enthusiasm.

There are emigres from our country who had been associated with Hitler who say that the people were compelled by force to obey the Soviet authorities. This is utterly wrong. The Soviet system could not possibly have hung on without popular support.

Another scholar, Prof. Gaidys, picked up the conversation here. Unlike his colleague, he had not been raised in a Communist family but his opinions too are based on his own participation in the events described: "The presence of the Red Army gave the capitalists no opportunity to launch a civil war" he said. "Nor did it permit them to turn for help to Nazi Germany. It was the forces at work within the country itself who made the revolution."

Prof. Maciavicius pointed to "favorable circumstances in our own society. Consider the generals, for example. The head of the army at that time, Lieut. Gen. Vitkauskas, could have moved in either direction, but he did not turn to Germany for help. Lithuania

---

*During World War II, by agreement among the Allies, England occupied the southern half of Iran for five years, 1941-1946, because of the Shah's ties to Nazi Germany.[7] The USSR occupied the northern half, and the United States Army operated the railroads, so as to deliver American Lend-Lease to the Soviet Union. Austria had been part of Hitler's Germany, and Soviet troops occupied Vienna and the eastern part of the country for ten years, 1945-1955.

and Germany had a common frontier in 1939. "He understood the situation, and not a single shot was fired."

Gaidys noted there had been a plan to do this. "Smetona wanted to launch a war, even if only a few symbolic shots were fired, or to take the Lithuanian Army over to Germany. But Gen. Vitkauskas refused, and the capitalist government was deprived of armed force."

Maciavicius picked up the story: "The commanding officer of the military academy, Gen. Karlialis, also showed a grasp of the situation. He took the side of the masses of the people. Demonstrations and parades were occurring, and military units participated in them. When the war broke out [Hitler's attack on the USSR in 1941] the most progressive elements in the officer corps did not turn to the Germans but fought in the ranks of the Soviet Army. Vitkauskas, Karlialis, Gen. Ziburbas, and others organized the 16th Soviet Division, consisting of Lithuanians. I fought in one of the units of that division and I remember those officers. They fought well and created good units. Gen. Vitkauskas subsequently was on the faculty of the Military Academy in Moscow. Clearly if the army had been of a different mind, it might have fought on the other side.

"The people knew what it meant to fall into Germany's hands. There were already the lessons of Czechoslovakia and Austria [in 1938], where national sovereignty was totally destroyed. Here, national sovereignty, in another form, in a different, socialist form, was maintained and continues to this day."

Maciavicius' account is supported by the eyewitness observation of a distinguished American correspondent, Anna Louise Strong, who had covered Russia from 1921 on, the Chinese Revolution, and the Spanish Civil War.

I had the tremendous luck to arrive in Lithuania in July, 1940, just after the Red Army marched in. . . . Nine-tenths of the Lithuanians I talked to thought—and rightly—that they were doing it themselves. Never in any land—in Spain, in Russia, or in China—have I seen a whole people so swiftly come alive. . . . A sovereign state was changing from capitalism to socialism quite constitutionally without destruction of life or property. The thing has never happened before.

"The masses are moving," said one of the Lithuanian progressive intellectuals, "And no one knows how far they will go." The odd thing about it is that that was really the way it felt. . . . A man at the American Legation said to me, . . . "they've started something going among the lower classes that is undermining the whole social structure. You should see my janitor!" . . . I saw tens of thousands like him, workers and peasants who were experiencing the thrill of unwonted power. For a month I lived and moved among the common people of the Baltic, travelling hundreds of miles unhindered and unchaperoned. . . . At the American Legation they told me that "the Russians are starting trade-unions," and seemed surprised when I said that I had been at the meeting and had seen not a single Russian there.

There was tremendous variety in all this organization. Nothing was cut and dried. . . . Some twenty energetic women hiked up to the platform after the meeting, not merely as individuals but as delegates pushed forward by all. "What shall I tell them in America about you?" I asked them. "Tell them," said one, "that we are glad at last to have our word to say." "Tell them that we suffered long but now are happy," said another.

In my talk with the governor of Vilno [Vilnius] . . . he turned to his secretary. "Make a note," he said. "I must announce by radio and send word to the foresters that peasants may have free access to the berries and mushrooms in the woods." Then he turned back to me. "It is a little thing," he said, "but it means much in diet and in human dignity to the peasants. The Polish landlords never allowed it, nor did the Smetona government. I had overlooked it; I have only been three days on this governor's job."

During the election I traveled two hundred miles to visit the rural polling places. . . . When the votes were counted after the election, it was found that 95.5 percent of the total adult electorate had come to the polls. . . . I was not surprised, for I had seen them coming out in the rural districts even in the rain and the mud. At the American Legation they explained that people were afraid not to come to the elections. But Smetona had openly used police terror to make the peasants come to previous elections, yet they had not come. It was not terror that brought them to the places I visited; it was new hope.[8]

The present cabinet is 93 percent Lithuanian, although the population is only 80 percent of that nationality, and even anti-Soviet scholars of that ethnic origin agree that that government upholds Lithuanian interests.[9]

The way the revolution was felt by the ordinary person emerges from Dr. Gaidys' life story: "I still remember how things happened when I was a kid. My parents were peasants with 22 acres of land, 22 acres! In our present Marxist terminology one would say that theirs was a petit-bourgeois mood: to work, to build a good house, get the farm operating properly, and then live a quiet life, those were their ambitions. In striving toward those ends, they willy-nilly found themselves in conflict with the rich. And so my father began to move to the Left on his own, evolved. He was a reader of a paper whose name translates into Russian as *The Lithuanian Peasant*.

"He hadn't been a Communist. Those who aided the fascists during the Nazi occupation, 1941-1944, made him one, so to speak. They said to him: 'You're that kind! You used to say the Soviet government was good.'* Of course, in 1940-1941, my father had said to one person or another: 'What's good is good.' Then, when the Germans came, our kulaks, who helped the fascists, said: 'Hey! You said in those days that Soviet government was good; now we'll show you!' And so they began to persecute him from the very beginning. Once they arrested my father—that time they released him. Then Soviet guerrillas came into being and we established contact. A raid against the partisans, the guerrillas, was organized by the Germans and those who helped them. This time they arrested our whole family. I was in prison [at 16] then for a while. So was my mother. My father returned from a concentration camp only after the war. So he experienced all this on his own neck, so to speak, and it was life itself that brought him to the new viewpoint.

"By telling you this, I want to make a point in terms of my own experience. Those who today support the Soviet government do not consist solely of people from old-time Communist families. They come from the masses of the people, out of the experience of life. Sometimes they agonized over it; sometimes they swayed in one direction and then in another."

Another voice: "Some became Communists during the war, very young, because of the exterminations. In Lithuania the Nazis killed one-quarter of the population, 700,000 people [including 200,000 Jews]. Some were shot here. Some who were taken to Germany. Some died in various situations during the war. There were those who had participated in the partisan movement. As a consequence, it was a long time after the war before our population reached its pre-war numbers."

Prof. Maciavicius went behind the statistics: "The Germans' barbaric measures brought much demoralization and polarization. After the war there were certain difficulties: a portion of the people who had collaborated with the Germans emigrated," many to the United States. "Another portion stayed here and continued their struggle. To save themselves from the Soviet authorities, they established their bandit organizations and armed clashes continued for several years until the last of them was destroyed."

Lithuania's Catholic Archbishop Skvireckas was a principal

---

*In its one year of power, the Soviet government had redistributed land, and instituted free education, giving Gaidys his first chance at schooling.

Photo by Author

Soviet monument to Lithuanian Catholic village burned down, with its inhabitants, for hiding Jewish children from Nazis.

collaborator with the Nazis. He appealed for men to join an S.S. division that exterminated Jews and Communists. And Bishop Vincentas Brizgys' name appeared on a list of war criminals in the U.S. press in 1975. "Many churchmen supported the partisan warfare against the Soviets in the late 1940s," writes an American scholar.[10]

Emigration from Lithuania was not new: 100,000 had left between 1920 and 1940, and 400,000 peasants emigrated in tsarist times and during the turmoil and hardship of the post-World War I civil war. Poverty was the major reason at all times.

After World War II, 96,000 landless and land-poor families were given land taken from those who had more than their own family could operate. The unemployed were given work, and industrial production reached the pre-war level within three years, despite the fact that 80 percent of industry had been destroyed. These measures brought the Soviet government a new source of mass support that rendered the cause of the opposition guerrillas hopeless. From 1959 to 1970, a great many more Lithuanians immigrated to that country than emigrated, including over 20,000 from outside the Soviet Union.

The Soviet years have seen a revolution in the Lithuanian economy. Gross output in agriculture has grown three-fold over the pre-war figure. Traveling between the three historical capitals of Vilnius, Kaunas and Trakai, one sees farm machinery in collective farm centers that resembles, in number and variety, what one would observe in the United States. At the same time, Lithuania has managed to become primarily industrial. There has been a *fifty*-fold rise in that sector, which now accounts for two-thirds of the gross national product. Furthermore, the major types of industry now are those which make a country count in the modern world — computers, TV sets and other electronics, farm equipment, pharmaceuticals, fertilizers, refrigerators, vacuum cleaners, tape recorders. Lacking basic raw materials, Lithuania's economy focuses on skilled labor.

Industry has grown faster in Lithuania than in any other Soviet republic since 1940. Obviously, that would not have been possible without the skill, energy, and efficiency of the Lithuanians themselves. Some nationalist emigres imply that growth was accomplished by the country entirely on its own, but that is rather silly: neither the capital, the natural resources, nor — in view of its war losses — the labor, was available. The equipment, much of the raw materials, the fuel, have been allocated by central planners in Moscow. Lithuania also lacked the educated people to design, engineer, and operate industry. The biggest power plant, for example, was designed in Moscow, Kiev and Riga, and 200 enterprises all over the USSR supplied its components.

Twelve times as many people now hold college and junior college diplomas as in the pre-Soviet period — there are more teachers than there were pupils in 1939. A year more elementary plus high school education is given than in most Soviet republics, and higher education is provided almost exclusively in the Lithuanian language.

Traditional art forms have been lovingly cherished and developed. This is due in part to the special emphasis Moscow places upon ethnic folk dance and song; such world-famous troupes as the Moiseyev Dancers assist both professional and amateur companies. Ballet has existed in Lithuania since the 16th century, when the landed nobility maintained troupes at court. Today there is professional ballet in Kaunas and Vilnius, where I saw *Anna Karenina* danced in 1977, in a performance worthy of any world capital.

The opera house in which it was performed almost demands a superior production. It has a glass facade with luster chandeliers cascading down in tiers from a forty foot high vestibule. Above the orchestra are twenty-two small balconies of varying sizes, and the stage has five movable sections. Its architect, Nijole Buciute, a mother of three, was trained in Soviet times. Another female architect, B. Casperaviciene, has won prominence for designing a large residential district in Vilnius. Women stand out among the designers of Lithuanian furniture, which is popular throughout the USSR.

Despite these accomplishments, I encountered relatively few women in the social science institutes of the Lithuanian Academy of Sciences. There were more even in the Soviet republics of Moslem tradition. Published figures bear out this impression: in 1975, Lithuania ranked lowest of all fifteen Soviet republics in women who have gone beyond elementary school.[11] (As high school education is now compulsory, the figures are doubtless pushed down by data for the older generation. In its youth, the notion that woman's place was in the kitchen, with the children, and in church, prevailed.) The figures are significantly higher for the other Baltic states, which have spent the same amount of time under Soviet rule but where the religious tradition was Protestant. Women are better educated in the republics of Islamic background as well — but they have been Soviet for a quarter century longer. Lithuania is also lowest in terms of the education level of all women who hold jobs.[12] Yet, compared to the West, Lithuanian women are occupationally very far advanced: 45 percent of the judges, for example, are women, incomparably more than in the United States.[13]

And the situation for women is definitely improving. The

Photo by Author

New opera house, Vilnius, Lithuania. Designed by a female architect.

number of female PhDs in Lithuania multiplied six times from 1960 to 1974. In engineering, medicine, teaching, law, accounting, they match women elsewhere in the USSR, and are far ahead of the West.

I have emphasized the prevalence of the Lithuanian language. Yet I have heard school-age children at play speak three languages to each other—Lithuanian, Russian and Polish—switching back and forth with ease. This is what the Soviets call the "convergence" of nationalities. In Belgium, French speakers refuse to use Flemish, though they are required to learn it in school. In the Alto Adige of northernmost Italy, when I asked directions from passers-by in Italian they would respond in German if they happened to be of the German minority —yet they learn Italian in school, and have to know it well. Lithuanian interlingualism shows the decline of ethnic hostility. This is particularly striking when one remembers that Poland was, in the words of a Radio Liberty analyst, "their traditional enemy."[14]

Emigres would have one believe that Russia is regarded as an occupying power. There is certainly a minority in Lithuania whose views crystallized prior to the permanent establishment of Soviet rule, which thinks this way. Some of their children, and a still smaller proportion of their grandchildren, continue to hold such attitudes, as evidenced by occasional demonstrations, petitions and defections. On the other hand, there is the linguistic behavior of children in the streets, the preponderance of Lithuanians in government, and all other spheres of activity, obvious freedom of worship, and positive encouragement of the national culture. Unity in diversity clearly accords with the interests and ethnic dignity of most Lithuanians.

Thus far this chapter—like this book as a whole—has focused on areas of controversy: religion, history, ethnic relations. That is a consequence of the manner in which the USSR is presented to us, which seems to reflect a pervasive fear that we might find something of value in a different social system.

In stable societies, people do not focus on sociopolitical controversy. The USSR is an extraordinarily stable society in comparison with other countries. No government or political official, from the local to the national level, has been assassinated in over 30 years, nor has the government executed anyone on political grounds in that time. In general, people go about their personal lives, and the government bodies engage in constructive endeavor.

That sense of forward motion in an atmosphere of certainty and security came through to me in a long conversation with the vice mayor—and head planner—of Vilnius. There was no "Here's what we'd *like* to do, if we can get the money," or "if the funds aren't cut off." He did not preach or make comparisons to the capitalist world. True, he did say he did not want his city to develop the traffic gridlock suffered by Los Angeles, but to him that was a practical problem, to which he presented practical solutions.

> This year we have 333 structures going up in the city, including 120 apartment houses, about 4,500 apartments. That's an imposing figure. Chiefly we build good, modern apartments, bigger ones all the time. The goal is to have a dwelling room for each member of the family, plus one.
>
> Many people already have apartments meeting that standard, but not everyone does. Why? Because over 40 percent of the housing in Vilnius was destroyed during the war, and we had only 200,000 people before that. The population today is two-and-a-half times that. Then some buildings have simply become obsolete. They don't have the conveniences that are normal in our day so we take them down, replacing them with new housing.
>
> We're putting all our in-patient facilities in a single medical center. An attractive site was allocated, within the city limits but far from its center. There are thick woods all around and bodies of water, there is no noise, the air is good. We've already built a children's hospital with 300 beds, with money earned in Vilnius on a Saturday of free Communist work. This is a Soviet tradition dating back to the first days after the Revolution. Everyone is asked to put in one week-end day of unpaid labor, either at their usual work or something else, and the pay is donated to a specific fund. In recent years that is usually for health care or to benefit children or peace activities.

He went on to talk about a new cancer facility with 450 beds, noting:

> The reason we are stressing construction in medicine now is because we feel that in the field of education, for example, we have no more problems. Virtually all our schools are new. Child-care centers totally satisfy the city's demands, there is no waiting to place your child. Well, if you want to place your child in the center half a block away, it may not have an opening. We may have to offer one five blocks away.

He spoke of three "cities within a city" — the medical center, the university campus (Vilnius University, over 400 years old, is the oldest in the Soviet Union), and a science campus, with a Chemistry Institute already built, an Institute of Biochemistry being built and plans for institutes of zoology and parasitology, semiconductors, mathematics, economics. Finally, there will be a building for the presidium of the Lithuanian Academy of Sciences, which will move there.

> But this does not complete the list of construction jobs. Automotive transport is expanding. If you have your problems in Los Angeles — a large, modern city, consider ours in Vilnius, an old city with narrow and crooked streets. This year we're building our first vehicular tunnel,

to bypass the center of the city underground. That solves many problems — we won't have to destroy any of the built-up part of the city for a freeway and we avoid noise and exhaust-fume pollution.

In the new self-contained housing areas, we'll cut traffic noise by sinking arterial roads and erecting artificial fills. No residential structures will front on through-traffic routes.

Some enterprises will be exiled from the city, so to speak, to reduce air and noise pollution. Our two principal rivers, the Neris and Vilnia, are quite clean — fish flourish, bathing is safe. The principle we adhere to is that all water flowing into the Baltic Sea from Lithuania must be utterly pure, because that's our pearl. Our health resorts are on the seacoast, we take our vacations there and large stretches are rich in fish. All this must be preserved not only for ourselves but for our descendants. Although we are still installing equipment for purification by mechanical means, the second section of the project will be based on biological purification. We calculate that there will be absolutely no pollution of waters by Vilnius at all, and the waters will become cleaner and cleaner.

We are doing a great deal of planting as you've undoubtedly observed — as we say, "greenery is the lungs of the city."

In addition to the opera house, a new major theater for the Lithuanian Theater of Drama was just completed and a new home for the youth theater was just about to open, so the city's cultural institutions are now in totally new facilities, brand new buildings. His very well-organized mind turned next to sports:

In a population of half a million, we have calculated that about 200,000 participate actively. The majority, I suppose, are people like me, whose activity consists of doing setting-up exercises in the morning. Nevertheless, we regard it as necessary to create a modern system of facilities, for we have athletes here of very high international ranking. Our Vilma Bardauskine was the first woman in the world to do a long-jump of more than seven meters. There's a schoolgirl who established a world record in the 200-meter breaststroke. Our men's basketball ranks second in the USSR, and that is tough, probably as tough as in the U.S. This year we're building a city-wide sports center for high-school students.

I told him he had done a convincing job of describing how government works for the people, but asked for a concrete example of how the people are involved in government:

Okay. A number of industrial enterprises had the services of a particular polyclinic, but its quarters were quite small, so the workers sometimes lost a lot of time waiting in line. The workers decided there was a need for a new, modern polyclinic to serve industrial enterprises. At their request, and specifically in response to a mandate from the voters [a formal instruction to a candidate from voters, adopted at a public meeting], we called together the managers of fifteen enterprises and asked them to find the funds to build the polyclinic. We took care of the design work, and it will go up this year.

In the USSR there is no executive branch of government. A mayor or vice-mayor is chosen by the city council ("soviet") from among its members (publicly-elected "deputies"). He told me how citizen initiatives were exercised:

We deputies meet regularly with our constituents, both with the electorate that chose us, and with the entity [usually the work force of an enterprise] that nominated us. I personally was nominated by construction workers. It happens that I reported to them last week. They put forth all the things they would like to see done. For example, they work on jobs far from the center of the city, so they asked for help with transportation. We issued orders for shorter intervals between buses.

We ship hot meals from a special central kitchen to the job sites: soup, a main dish, desert. They complained that sometimes, in winter, the food doesn't stay hot, so we switched to large thermos containers that retain heat a very long time.

Recently, our university president, the distinguuished mathematician Harry Kubelius, met with his constituents. They are in a very distant part of the city, only recently incorporated. It had been a village of about 100 small private homes, with no public telephone, no store, and they wanted those things taken care of. That wasn't simple. It's so far from town that utility lines don't extend out there: no piped heat [from electric power-plant cooling water; a standard Soviet procedure], no water, etc. So it was my job to go out there: this year we'll put in several public phones, the road to town will be improved and we've placed a contract for designing a store.

We have a very sensitive ear for such matters. Any wish of the voters —either mandates or what we call wishes of the electorate—is recorded, checked on regularly, and a decision is taken, with concrete dates of performance: *when* that store has to be built, *when* those public phones have to be operating.

Of course it isn't always *possible* to meet all requests. The people out there had asked for an asphalt-surfaced road. I went out and found that their road was narrow, with gravel surfacing, and the little private homes are virtually flush with the edge of the road. An asphalted road and a highway-type bus requires certain conditions—width, lighting, etc., so we proposed to move those houses. But the people said: "No, let things be as they are. We don't want our houses moved."

If we don't deal with the requests, our constituents won't re-elect us. We'll be unemployed! True, in Vilnius we won't stay out of work, because there's a labor shortage, but others would come to hold our positions, people who will be more sensitive to the matters that concern the electorate.

LATVIA

Lithuania's eastern neighbor, Latvia, with two and a half million people, is a neat little country—not so much in the sense of tidy (it is), but in the youthful slang meaning approval. There is a taken-for granted, not shrill, persistence of ethnic identity, a very civilized air. No bigotry or closed-mindedness about anything. The Letts (Latvians) are just plain sensible.

But as I heard and saw more, my feeling changed from respect to admiration. There is a stark, overwhelming grouping of giant concrete sculptures marking the site of the Nazi death camp at Salaspils. No one who sees it can mistake the Latvians' calm for emotional indifference. The list of nationalities represented among those exterminated specifically names the Jews. (In some other republics, monuments refer only to the mass murder of Soviet citizens, so today's generation gets no notion that the Nazis pursued a policy of total extermination against Jews and Gypsies alone).

The Salaspils monument is perhaps the greatest contemporary sculpture I know—I would rank it with Picasso's *Guernica* in painting. It confronts the most extraordinary complexities in a manner that does not detract from, but increases its emotional impact.

The central cluster is of four men, the bones of their skulls protruding through almost fleshless faces. One can no longer hold himself erect, and has fallen back into the arms of another, who stands as though waiting to be shot, but unyielding. Another has his left fist up in the Communist salute; in front, the fourth figure has his fist high in the air. The title: *Rot Front!*— Red Front, the name of the anti-Nazi movement in Germany before Hitler. I was surprised to see the sign in German—it was Germans who killed the 150,000 victims of Salaspils, and German "Baltic barons" ruled Latvia for centuries. But in Latvia the question is "*Which* Germans?"

The day we were at Salaspils, there happened to be a great many young people there from the German Democratic Republic, part of mass excursions connected with a friendship week. I wondered how the Germans like coming here and was told, "We don't make it a compulsory part of the tour." Salaspils is ten miles outside the capital city, Riga. "But they want to come. They think they should see, and know."

Nazi death-camp-site monument at Salaspils, Latvia.

Photo by Author

I have heard criticism of privilege, of pompous treatment of leaders, and of current policy many times in the USSR. In other republics, it was always in privacy or in the company of close personal friends. Only in Latvia did I hear it in an official party of hosts to a foreigner — it was simply the normal voicing of a personal point of view. There was neither a mental nor real glance over the shoulder.

The director of the History Institute of the Latvian Academy of Sciences, V. Steinbergs, was the very image of a tweedy English professor. When he talked of his work, his words were objective and his voice moderate.[15] But when I asked him to comment on the argument that Latvia is an exploited economic colony of the USSR, he spoke with extraordinary fervor and obvious depth of conviction as he explained that Latvia has virtually no non-agricultural resources and is now the most advanced industrial republic of the Soviet Union due to aid from the Russians and the other peoples.

Steinbergs comes from the very poorest peasantry — his father had two-and-a-half acres, and three boys to leave it to. On the eve of World War I, they migrated eastward in tsarist Russia. Father and mother both toiled as railway construction workers, among many "poor Latvians scattered as far east as Vladivostok on the Pacific Ocean in search of a piece of bread," in his words.

In the Civil War after the Russian Revolution, his father was executed by the Greek forces which were part of the anti-Communist Intervention. His mother, now 86, still lives where she can tend the grave. He himself grew up a railroad worker and was trained as a railway technician. He returned to Latvia as a young man at the end of World War II, went on to teachers' college, and then to graduate study in history.

On his staff is a woman of 36, a PhD, who specializes in the totally new field of relations between the Latvians and non-Soviet socialist peoples. She concentrates on East Germans, Poles, and Bulgarians. She told us her story while showing us the city.

"I was born into a family of fisherfolk — it was very poor, although it worked all the time. They lived on the coast between Ventspils and Cape Kolka. They were pure-blooded Livs, a small remnant, numbering a few hundred, of the Finno-Ugrian Liv people.

"They lived on nothing but potatoes — bread was a luxury eaten from time to time — and on fish. But they all had a great desire for education. They all managed to go to school, except one sister who died, and all got higher education."

This she explained, was in the time of Soviet government,

Latvian professors Steinbergs, Asmane, Cimermanis, and Prikulis.

which was established permanently in 1944. "In the earlier period even high school was a problem. They had to scramble just to exist."

Her parents "also had begun revolutionary activity at a very early age. This was in the 1920s. They organized Young Communist League groups and traveled to other villages and towns, like Ventspils, to set them up."

Latvians had played an extraordinary role in the Russian Revolution in 1917. In the elections for a Constituent Assembly, conducted under the rules set up by Kerensky's anti-Communist Provisional Government, Latvia was the only ethnic area in which the Communists won a majority of the vote — and a very large majority, 72 percent.[16] This victory (and the Latvians' later actions) lends itself to a classical Marxist explanation. It was the most industrial part of Russia, with a large proletariat, working in large factories. Early in this century, when Riga was the third largest city in the Russian Empire, membership in the party supporting Lenin was higher among Letts than among any other nationality in the Empire, higher even than among the Jews, who ranked second.

The Latvian Riflemen regiments organized by the tsar for World War I were solidly Communist by 1917. Lenin chose them, and them alone, to guard the headquarters of the Soviet government in Petrograd. The first commander-in-chief of the newly-organized Russia-wide Red Army was a Latvian. When a populist party, the Social-Revolutionaries, organized a coup against Lenin in the Russian capital in 1918, the only organized armed force available to him was a regiment of the Latvian Riflemen. They faced a somewhat larger force of the opposition and won the day.

The revolution in Latvia was defeated, partly, as the Soviets admit, by the Latvian Communists' ultra-Leftism. In a country still two-thirds rural, they sought immediately to organize large government operated farms. Today, it is believed they should have distributed the great estates among the landless and land-poor as Lenin did.[17] The Latvian (or Lettish) Riflemen retreated into Russia and fought in Lenin's support throughout the country. All Latvians already in high posts were executed in Stalin's purge of 1937. But enough of the Latvian Riflemen survived to organize the core of the two Soviet Latvian army divisions in World War II.[18] And there were enough of their children and others who had fled to Russia so that 100,000 returned to Latvia with the Soviets after the war. The Latvian Riflemen are known throughout the USSR by virtue of a Russian film on that 1918 coup. In Riga there is a monument to them — three stark figures standing back to back with their guns at rest, it towers over the city's central square, backed by a museum in their honor. This is an area with guild halls and medieval churches of typically Scandinavian appearance, interspersed with ancient warehouses of the Hanseatic League. Nearby is the castle of the German Livonian Order that sought to conquer Russia in the 13th century. Buildings rebuilt from the bombed ruins of World War II complete the picture. Across the river one sees the tall building of the Academy of Sciences, a gift from Moscow. The whole history of a people is visible from the monument.

The United States provided the bulk of the arms and uniforms for the anti-Communists within Latvia in 1918. As in Lithuania, the Latvian government thus established was unable to hold power through the ballot, and in 1934 political parties were banned and authoritarian government instituted. The United States still recognizes that government, which has a legation in Washington even though it went out of existence nearly forty years ago!

The scholar from the family of fisherfolk, Dr. Neilande, went on to describe what happened within Latvia. Her own family "took the revolutionary road." One uncle fought in Spain, in the International Brigades, two of her aunts served three-year sentences for their activity in the Young Communist League. "It was illegal in those days. My father, too. He was a Communist Party worker and was in jail for a very long time, eight years. They all came out of jail together, in 1940 — when Soviet government was established, its first decree was to free the prisoners."

"It was a great holiday. Tremendous demonstrations, parades.

American-Russian Institute

Political prisoners of fascist Latvian government freed in 1940.

So my mother came out of the women's prison, and my father from the men's. That was when they first met. They were very active, working on all these things with enthusiasm and had very little time to see each other. And then the war [Hitler's invasion] began. We were evacuated, and I was born there. My father was killed at that time — he was in Moscow, in the Latvian Mission, when a bomb fell on it. My mother went to school during the war, and after the war got a higher education. She's an economist. She was always a very active member of the Party — at one point she worked in the Council of Ministers as an expert in the field of commerce. She's now 65 and still works very actively with her students. She is a very wise person, with very broad vision, wide horizons. She has seen a great deal. She has thought a great deal."

Her father, "a man of peasant birth, enjoyed the very greatest respect. Although he died very young, he was the second-ranking leader of the Communist Party of Latvia. He was also the editor of *Cina*, the Communist Party paper. Latvians are very proud of it because it began publication eight years before the Russians' *Pravda*. Founded in 1904 under the tsar, *Cina* was an underground paper part of the time.

"I didn't know him at all, of course. But I am collecting

American-Russian Institute

Riga, capital of Latvia, on the Baltic Sea.

material on him, and I have never yet met a single person who did not speak of him with love. He was also a man of great modesty, which is not common among people so popular. And he had a tremendous sense of duty, so that he didn't have to have — well, *in those days there was no talk of privilege anyhow.* During the dinner break, he would leave his office and go into a corner somewhere to eat his sandwiches. He didn't want anyone fussing over him. *He had a great distaste for ceremonial occasions, honors, homage.* He believed that all his time had to be given to work for the people. You know, that was also the way people were trained *in those days.* [My emphasis-W.M.]

"A comrade who had been in the same prison cell with my father for years came to see me. He said that when the crisis approached in 1940, the prison warden came to talk with my father. There were underground groups in the prison. The warden, too, was dissatisfied with the political situation, and was conducting some kind of study group of his own. The fact that the warden came to talk politics with my father tells you something about him.

"The people of that time—we have to continue their work. I am very interested in what happened to them, what they fought for, the things that interested them."

The affirmative action program from which Letts benefit today is probably of greater interest to them than a more democratic style. As we discussed the bilingual educational system in Latvia, Dr. Maya Asmane spoke of higher education. "Some republics lack specialized training in certain disciplines — say nuclear physics, molecular chemistry, genetics. Moscow reserved a certain number of admissions in the country's finest universities for people from those republics." I was surprised. I knew this system of preferential admissions existed for the numerically small peoples of the far North, and for Central Asia, but not that it was still necessary for the Baltic republics. She explained, "It's necessary because the number of applicants for leading higher educational institutions is enormous. Therefore a person who does not know Russian well may not make it." The USSR-wide schools obviously are taught in the language serving as common means of communication. So that each republic can train personnel in esoteric fields, she explained, "a stated number of openings is reserved for them in the higher educational institutions of Moscow, Leningrad, and Novosibirsk. This makes it possible for the training of such people to be planned at a policy level."

"This began," she went on, "in 1940." At that time the Baltic states had just become Soviet and higher education lagged far behind the level of even the small countries in the Caucasus, which had been Communist since the Revolution. Moscow made higher education a top priority in all ethnic republics from the very outset. In 1940 Catholic Lithuania had only 30 students per 10,000 population, while Islamic Soviet Azerbaijan had 44, Protestant Estonia 45, and chiefly Protestant Latvia 52. Soviet Georgia and Armenia, with their Eastern Christian traditions, had 77 and 82 respectively.[19]

Another colleague at the History Institute, Dr. Prikulis, put in: "And that also eliminates the need for us to import non-Latvians in these fields."

Consciously or not, he was responding to the complaints of some emigres that Russians are taking over. He continued: "We send our own young graduates for graduate study to a whole lot of places to have them acquire the most advanced knowledge available. Upon their return, they are able to start right out working with maximum effectiveness." Dr. Asmane added, "to develop those lines of inquiry that are promising, new, and haven't yet been pursued here in Latvia."

The Letts are only one percent of the Soviet population. This policy gives them the capacity to grapple with the most complex problems of the late 20th century and helps them develop the self-esteem which flows from that capacity. It is accompanied by measures to cause each people to appreciate other peoples and to understand their interdependence.

Latvia's Open Air Ethnographic Museum furthers this objective. This intriguing and attractive park-like area of 250 acres on the outskirts of Riga contains 80 old-time peasant and fisherfolk cottages, craft workshops, mills and churches moved there from all over Latvia. It was founded under the anti-Communist government of 1920-40, but at that time the museum totally excluded any examples of the material cultures of other peoples, even though they are as much a part of Latvian life, albeit as minorities, as the Letts themselves. In those years, the museum had two distinct political objectives: to win support for a policy of making Latvia an agricultural hinterland for Germany and England, and to persuade people that Latvia could exist in cultural isolation.

Today the museum is still devoted entirely to rural life, but it also contains examples of the life-styles of the Russian, Estonian, as well as Liv peoples, all traditional residents in that country. On our tour we encountered a group of seventeen-year-olds with their teachers. Dr. Asmane explained: "There is a custom in Soviet schools that in September the students visit the neighboring republic. And in May, at the end of the school year, there are special excursion days so the children get to know the physical cultural heritage both of their own republics and adjacent ones." These excursions are free of charge, but this one was special. "These kids won a contest for raising the best school garden and orchard, and a trip was their prize. They themselves decided they wanted to come here." They were urban students from Vilnius in Lithuania. "Our kids from Latvia go to Estonia, to Leningrad, to Kizhi," — a similar Russian north-country outdoor museum, with marvelous multi-domed log churches — "to Moscow, to Belorussia, to the Ukraine. In summer they go to Lake Baikal," — 4,000 miles eastward — "to Novosibirsk," the major city in Siberia. "They also go to Central Asia and the Caucasus."

This summer travel is not limited to high-school students. The authorities promote vacation trips to encourage "internationalist attitudes." I learned that an individual can buy a trip, though travel with a group, through one's trade union, is much cheaper.

The stress on training local people made me wonder whether

that practice was resulting in a tendency toward ethnic "purity" in their own institute's staff. After all, it is concerned with the history of Latvia and related social sciences. Rather than pose the question directly, I asked about the nationalities of their colleagues. They began to think out loud. Dr. Cimermanis, the museum director: "Letts [Latvians] we have, Russians we have, Estonians we have, Belorussians we have . . . " Asmane: "Jews we have; there's even an Armenian." He: "That makes six. Any more?" She: "Poles." He: "Who's Polish?" She mentions a name: "part of my staff." He: "Seven." She: "70 percent, maybe 80 percent Latvians."

All four of my hosts were indigenous, as is the director of their institute.

As we drove back into town from the open-air museum, my hosts' description of the passing scene shed light on Latvian attitudes and realities. They were proud of the good-looking new housing developments—Dr. Cimermanis said, "There are just a few little old houses from before. All the rest was built starting in the 1950s."

Latvia's national hobby is the preservation, writing, and mass performance of songs. On the outskirts of town we detoured to a most unusual kind of amphitheater. Its *stage* was obviously designed to seat what would be an oversize *audience* in the largest of theaters. The previous summer they told me, there had been 15,000 people on stage under a single conductor, while 30,000 in the "audience" joined in those songs everyone knew!

We passed broad meadows. "Here people like to ski in the winter," cross country. Dr. Asmane pointed to "Our new Latvian Film Studios—they even come from Moscow to shoot here. Good indoor studios, fine equipment. We make good documentaries in Latvia, and we've also done a fair number of quite passable feature films. Recently a wide-screen film was done of Janis Rajnis' play, *Blow, Little Breze* based on Latvian folklore."

Rajnis is to Letts what Dante is to Italians, Cervantes to Spaniards—but he lived from 1865 to 1929. That's how recently Latvian literature took shape. He has been translated into over forty languages. The nationalist emigres claim him, and point to the fact that his play about Peter the Great, who conquered Latvia, is not performed, but ignore the fact that he organized a Latvian-Soviet friendship society in 1926, when embittered anti-Communists were in power.

ESTONIA

Pleasure, charm, surprise and puzzlement are an American's reactions
to Soviet Estonia. It is the most Western of Soviet countries, and
we all like as little culture shock as possible. One is pleased by the
attractive cafes and stores, the furnishings, the quality of workman-
ship in all respects. The center of the capital, Tallinn, is an
unspoiled medieval town of pitch-roofed buildings, dominated by a
fairy tale hilltop castle and surrounded by a city wall with twenty-
seven towers. There are extensive neighborhoods of obviously modern
homes — large, with decorative brickwork, a variety of window shapes,
and well-cared-for lawns and gardens. They unmistakeably indicate
a living standard that Americans who can afford to travel regard as
satisfactory. One doesn't associate this with the USSR.

Estonia, with its million and a half very blonde people, is no
isolated island: Tallinn, a city of 400,000 population, is an easy
day's drive west from Leningrad. Located on the Baltic seacoast,
Estonia's language is unintelligible in either Leningrad or Latvia to
the west, but comprehensible in Finland, on the north shore of the
Baltic Sea fifty miles away. Estonia's traditional religion is Lutheranism.

It shares a remarkable distinction with totally different Armenia,
over a thousand miles to the southeast: many Western emigres of
those two nationalities look favorably upon what has happened
there in the Soviet years.

The difference in attitude between Estonian emigres and those
from neighboring Latvia and Lithuania is based on history. Lithuania
was a fundamentally peasant country that had once been a great
European power, and is an island of Catholicism. Latvia had been
the most pro-Communist part of the Russian Empire. Estonia too
had its civil war and German and Anglo-American interference
after the Russian Revolution. It also slid into dictatorship during
the subsequent period of capitalist independence and decline of
industry. Soviet authority was restored during World War II by the
same process as in the other Baltic states. "Western encouragement of
active and even of armed resistance [later was] slowly exposed as a
Cold War instrument serving only Western interests."[20] But all
these phenomena took milder form in Estonia. This makes
one wonder if, within a decade or two, a younger generation of
Western scholars of Latvian and Lithuanian origin may not join

today's of Estonian extraction in drawing conclusions based on reality.

Prof. Tönu Parming of the University of Maryland has written:

If we assess the state of contemporary Estonian culture . . . it must be concluded that it is well and healthy. . . . For the Soviet Union is has become even avant garde. . . . The Soviet Union in many respects is *one of the most culturally pluralistic societies in the world in its institutional structure and momentum*, the result especially of the existence of the republics. . . . We would be hard pressed to find among the "enlightened" Western powers, especially the former colonial ones, examples where written languages for natives were encouraged, where native identities were developed through massive schooling in the native languages, or where a scientific life came to flourish in native languages among national minorities or among colonial subjects. . . . "Folkstudy" is probably more extensive now than it ever has been in Estonian history.[21] [my emphasis — W.M.]

Prof. Rein Taagepera of the University of California provides detail:

Estonia . . . is the world leader in oil shale technology and mining. . . . The elite are predominantly Estonian in the cultural field. . . . Universities are run by Estonians [who] . . . can read everything ranging from Homer and Shakespeare to Segal's *Love Story* and graduate-level physics texts in their own language. . . . Estonian composers like A. Pärt and J. Rääts have been in the forefront of dodecaphonal music in the USSR. The first Soviet jazz festival was held in Estonia. . . . Kafka, Ionesco, and Dostoyevsky were available to Soviet Estonians earlier than to the Russian reading public. . . . In poetry, all modern trends and styles are represented. . . . New word roots and derivatives have been created to keep pace with modern developments; for example, instead of the Russian *lunokhod* [moon vehicle], the Soviet Estonian press uses kuukulgur. . . . Total number of periodicals is higher than in any union republic except Russia and the Ukraine although Estonia has the smallest population of all fifteen.

An 80-page fashion quarterly . . . has a 50,000 circulation in Estonian and 350,000 in Russian, suggesting Union-wide [USSR-wide] prestige. . . . Availability of [TV and radio] sets . . . is highest of all union republics. . . . The first Cybernetics Institute in the Soviet Union was founded in 1960 in Tallinn, Estonia. . . . Other Soviet "firsts" in Estonia include eradication of polio (1958), introduction of money wages for farm workers, and switching to *sovkhoz* [state farm] self-management. . . . The Institute of [Estonian] Language and Literature has a staff of 100.

As a consequence of all this, and the fact that the Estonian living standard is the highest of all Soviet republics, he concludes: "Soviet power is uncontested in Estonia."[22]

Yet the "bourgeois" republic of 1918 — which has existed only as an office in Sweden for the past forty years — is still recognized by the U.S.

The problem of a small nation not wanting to be swamped by a large one does exist, however. I went to an Estonian-language school with an English-language interpreter. Only one-quarter of the Estonians speak Russian fluently [1979 census]. She and the English teacher at that school, best friends, did not hesitate to disagree in my presence over what the teacher called "Russification." She was not referring to culture, but to the influx of Russians to work in Estonia, which has a labor shortage — and a high living standard. Russians are barely over one-quarter of the population, but some worry that if the Estonians ever become a minority in their own republic, it will be abolished. That, they fear, would also affect the ability to preserve and encourage the indigenous culture. But experience elsewhere in the USSR does not support those fears.

The Kirgiz and Kazakhs of those two Central Asian republics have become minorities in their own lands. This is due to immigration of other closely-related Asians* as well as Russians. This has not resulted in a change in their political status. Indeed, the Constitution of 1977 settled the question by freezing all ethnic governmental units at their present status. Where the titular nationality is not a majority, the Communist Party leader and the prime minister are always of that nationality. The development of the language and culture goes full speed ahead, as I describe in other chapters.

My interpreter in Estonia did not regard the influx of Russians as an ethnic danger. She was unhappy, however, that a Russian Orthodox Church was kept open for services in the ancient citadel in this country of Protestant tradition. The citadel was built by German knights to maintain their rule over the Estonians for many centuries. However, the Estonians regard it as the symbol of their own governmental authority, and the major government and Party offices are within its rambling walls.

The atheist government displays sensitivity to the Lutheranism that is the prevalent religious belief. A centuries-old church had

*The combined Turkic-speaking, Islamic-heritage Asians remain majorities in both republics.[23]

lost its steeple during the bombings of World War II. It was rebuilt on the ground as a steel framework, and during my visit a derrick was hauling the steeple back into place. In the USSR, maintenance of church buildings, particularly when of historical value, is a government responsibility. Today churches in use as places of worship are universally well-maintained. Many that were deconsecrated due to negligible attendance have been restored physically as part of the architectural heritage.

I did not find Russians obtrusively present at all. The policeman outside the hotel was Estonian, as were the head of the Intourist travel bureau, the taxi driver, most of the waiters in the hotel, the woman managing a creamery I walked into, the staff of a bookstore, the principals of both the urban and rural schools I visited. Every executive on the collective farm I saw was Estonian. The absence even of adequate knowledge of the Russian language by anyone there made an interpreter essential.

I had visited a prosperous collective farm in the Ukraine and a poor one on the Volga, but the Estonian farm was a different world. The office was not of rambling logs but brick, well-constructed and neatly finished inside and out. The school next door had large windows, complete shop and cafeteria as well as classroom equipment; the homes, all brick, would be absolutely acceptable in any American lower middle-class suburb. Every structure was clearly post-war — actually, as it turned out, built since 1960. The men wore shoes, not boots; suits with sweaters, collar and tie, and they were obviously at ease in such clothing. Not until seven years later did I find farms in other parts of the Soviet Union on a par with this one. There's no reason to think it has stood still in the interval.

This farm made clear how far the authorities have gone in using incentives to make collective farming attractive. The chairman's salary was two-and-a-half times the average income on the farm. He also gets a portion of the profits. His house was not different, except for a room added in the attic, which few others had. The staff accountant, a Mr. Baltsander, said: "In addition, every member of the collective farm, the chairman also, may have his own plot of land. Everyone may grow things there and sell those things. Some people go to the collective farm market themselves, but usually the farm sells for them. The farm also takes the milk from every individual's cow to the dairy every morning."

He explained that the chairman is not the highest-paid person on the farm. "The people who sell the collective farm products on

Photo by Author

Urban private home in Estonia built about 1970. Many are of equal quality.

the market, in town, get *much* more money. And sometimes those people who take care of the pigs get more." I was struck by the difference in these tasks—care of the pigs is what is called productive work, but selling would be called non-productive by Communist standards. Yet this person earns a great deal of money, and a percentage of what he sells.

So the commission merchant and the pig raiser make more than the person who directs their activities. I'd be fascinated to hear Adam Smith, Karl Marx, and the Harvard School of Business Administration discuss that. But it works for everyone on the farm.

Since no one has ownership of the farm's productive property, it is a socialist operation, and there was no evidence whatever of extremes of wealth or poverty.

According to a top Estonian leader writing in a USSR-wide national daily in 1971: "The Estonian peasants, having taken the socialist path, showed themselves to be excellent collectivists. They surpassed in level of production many advanced capitalist countries with the very richest experience in agriculture. This includes their nearest neighbors — Finland, Norway, Sweden . . .

He continued, "We ascribe great importance to cultivating feelings of internationalism among college students and others in school. This goal is furthered by exchange of student construction brigades." These are teams of volunteers, organized each summer at their place of study, which go to the countryside, usually to other parts of the USSR, to build or repair schools, hospitals, farm buildings and homes, install power transmission lines to remote villages, etc.[24]

Foreign journalists feel this apparently works. Charlotte Saikowski of the *Christian Science Monitor* reported: "Among the youth in general . . . there is less concern about the growing proportion of Russians in the republic."[25]

They probably have been too busy taking advantage of the opportunities opened to them. Women have entered many new occupations. For example, in 1959 they headed less than one-third of work teams on Estonian collective farms but by 1970 they were a solid majority: three out of five.[26] Estonia also leads all other Soviet republics in percentage of women holding professional and semi-professional jobs in agriculture — they are veterinarians, crop and animal experts, laboratory technicians, accountants. In Russia women are a third to a half of the persons in such farm posts, but in Estonia well over half.

A survey of the ten occupations Estonian schoolgirls most wished to enter was done under the pre-Soviet regime. When repeated 30 years later, after a generation under socialism, five new choices appeared. Earlier, women could not think seriously of being allowed into them. They were artist-or-musician, language-or-literature scholar, engineer, confectioner-or-cook, and pre-school child-care worker (that "woman's" job simply didn't exist on a significant scale in old Estonia).[27] Today women are at least one-third in each of these fields, and a majority in several. Formerly a female physician was a curiosity in Estonia, but today they are nine doctors out of ten,[28] a higher ratio than in any other Soviet country. Women had also emerged as having a much greater interest in high culture—yet they continue to bear much the larger time burden of maintaining the home. Obviously, time-saving appliances and child-care facilities now make a real difference, and husbands share more.

Generally, the USSR is quite backward in sex education and counseling, but in Estonia, by the early 1970s, courses in "personal hygiene" had been introduced into the general school curriculum and booklets for sex education of youth had been published.

Estonian youth do not wall themselves off culturally. Three-quarters of rural youth speak Russian, as compared with one-quarter of the middle-aged and elderly in the countryside.

The situation in the Soviet Baltic is summed up by Prof. Lynn Turgeon, Hofstra University economist who has taught at Moscow University under the U.S.-USSR official cultural exchange program. Commenting on a speech by Alexander Solzhenitsyn, he wrote: "As a generalization, this area enjoys today by far the highest living standards in the USSR; is a region where the individual non-Russian cultures are flourishing in the arts; and where religious freedom can be witnessed every Sunday in the great cathedrals of Kaunas, Vilnius and Riga. The Baltic Republics in the inter-war years were hardly models of bourgeois democracy and, being capitalist in their orientation, were adversely affected by the Great Depression. It is no exaggeration to say that these talented peoples have never enjoyed a comparable well-being . . . "[29]

NOTES

1. *San Francisco Chronicle*, May 11, 1982, p. 8.

2. *Bol'shaia Sovetskaia Entsiklopediia*, 3rd ed. (Moscow: Sovetskaia Entsiklopediia, 1970), Vol. V, Pl.V, Figs. 1, 2, 3.

3. See J. Rimaitis, *Religion in Lithuania* (Vilnius: Gintaras, 1971), *passim;* J. Ancias, *The Establishment of Socialism in Lithuania and the Catholic Church* (Vilnius: Mintis, 1975), *passim.*

4. Gytis Vaitkunas, *Mikalojus Konstantinas Ciurlonis* (Dresden: Verlag der Kunst, 1975), 201 plates, German translation from Lithuanian.

5. Algirdas Landsbergis, "The Organic and the Synthetic: A Dialectical Dance," in C.W. Simmonds (ed.), *Nationalism in the USSR & Eastern Europe* (Detroit: University of Detroit, 1977), p. 181.

6. Toby Terrar, *Book Review Essay: Lithuanian Catholicism.* Unpublished ms., 1983. In author's possession.

7. "History of Iran," in *Encyclopedia Britannica*, 15th ed. (Chicago: Britannica, 1974), Vol. IX, p. 861.

8. Anna Louise Strong, *The Soviets Expected It* (New York: Dial, 1941), pp. 195-209, *passim*.

9. Thomas Rimeikis, "Political Developments During the Brezhnev Era," in Simmonds, *Nationalism in the USSR*, p. 168.

10. Frederic T. Harned, "Lithuania and the Lithuanians," in Zev Katz (ed.), *Handbook of Major Soviet Nationalities* (New York: Free Press, 1975), p. 125; Jonas Ancias, *The Hatemongers: Anti-Soviet Activity of the Lithuanian Clerical Emigres* (Vilnius: Mintis, 1979), *passim*.

11. TsSU, *Zhenshchiny v SSSR, Statisticheskii sbornik* (Moscow: Statistika, 1975), p. 62.

12. Ibid., p. 63.

13. P. Matveev, "Zhenshchiny-iuristy (statisticheskii material)," *Sotsialisticheskaia zakonnost'*, 1975, No. 9.

14. Dimitry Pospielovsky, *Radio Liberty Dispatch*, June 2, 1972.

15. A. Birons (ed.), *Latvijas PSR Zinatnu Akademijas Vestures Instituts* (Riga: Zinatne, 1976), in Lettish and Russian, 146 pp.

16. A.A. Drizul, *V.I. Lenin i revoliutsionnaia Latviia* (Riga: Zinatne, 1970), p. 112.

17. "Latviiskaia SSR," *Bol'shaia Sovetskaia Entsiklopediia*, 3rd ed. (Moscow: Sovetskaia Entsiklopediia, 1973), Vol. XIV, p. 181, col. 531.

18. V.I. Savchenko, *Latyshskie formirovaniia Sovetskoi Armii na frontakh Velikoi Otechestvennoi Voiny* (Riga: Zinatne, 1975), 577 pp.

19. TsSU SSSR, *Narodnoe obrazovanie, nauka i kul'tura v SSSR* (Moscow: Statistika, 1971), p. 158.

20. Tõnu Parming, "Nationalism in Soviet Estonia Since 1964," in Simmonds, p. 119.

21. Ibid., pp. 121-122.

22. Rein Taagepera, "Estonia and the Estonians," in Katz, *Handbook of Soviet Nationalities*, pp. 75-88, *passim*.

23. "USSR Census Returns," *Soviet Law and Government*, XIX, No. 2 (1980), pp. 36, 38.

24. *Izvestia*, Moscow, September 1, 1971.

25. *Christian Science Monitor*, Sept. 17, 1969.

26. Y.V. Arutyunyan, *A Comparative Study of Rural Youth in the National Regions of the USSR* (Moscow: Soviet Organizing Committee of IV World Congress of Rural Sociology, 1976), p. 6.

27. A. Kelam and H. Mittus, "Izmeneniia v sotsial'nom polozhenii zhenshchiny Estonii," in Soviet Sociological Association Institute of Social Research, *Dinamika izmeneniia polozheniia zhenshchiny i sem'ia* (Moscow: XII International Seminar on Family Research, 1972), pp. 104-110.

28. *Soviet Life*, Washington, D.C., August, 1976, p. 54.

29. Alexander Solzhenitsyn, *Prospects for Democracy and Dictatorship* (New Brunswick, N.J.: Transaction, 1975), p. 80.

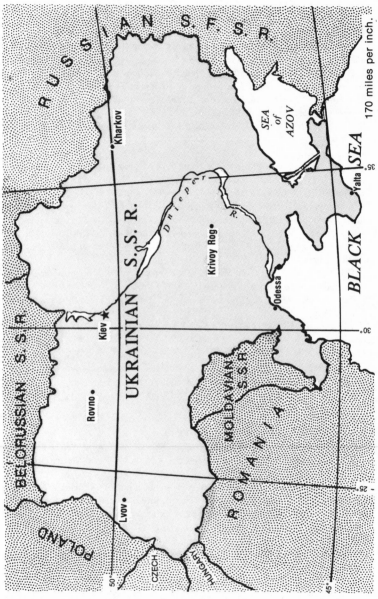

The Ukraine

★Moscow

UKRAINE

The Ukraine:
Power Within a Power

Xenia Masliak is plump, in her early fifties, and unselfconsciously voluptuous in both stance and gesture—a characteristically Ukrainian quality. One hears it in the language, in the repeated exclamation "Oh!" with a rising inflection. One sees it in the best architecture, with its baroque curves and curlicues, lapping over into rococo: the finest mansion in Kiev, the capital, which dates from the beginning of this century, has fantastic huge fishes and sea mammals towering along its roof. The popular Ukrainian film *Shadows of Forgotten Ancestors* portrays this same mood.

I spoke with Xenia on a lazy Sunday at the Masliaks' summer cottage, within walking distance of a pleasant lake in the rolling hills near Lvov, the center of the western Ukraine, where most Ukrainian immigrants to North America came from.

Most of us were sunning ourselves in bathing suits after swimming. Two men, journalists and friends, had the superb bodies of heavyweight weight-lifters, which they had been. One, however, had been temporarily blind from starvation as an infant during World War II; the other, with whom I correspond, has a severe lung condition—traceable to his sufferings in the same period. Another couple present, in their sixties — he Ukrainian, she Jewish — had changed residences over a dozen times during the war to save her life and that of her infant. But the war seemed long ago and far away as I began talking with Xenia, and one of the men strummed his guitar quietly.

She is a professional artist, who works in glass and ceramics, particularly well in the former. A teacher for many years, she is now principal of the art school for children in Lvov. She explained the school's role: "It gives children a chance to develop their talents. In times past, undoubtedly there were children with artistic talent in our towns and villages, but it was very difficult to discover and bring this out. It was very rare for someone to break through and go, say, to Vienna, to study, to Krakow, to Warsaw or Paris. That was an occasion for great joy. But you could count such individuals on the fingers of your hands."

She named Austrian, Polish, and French cities, not Kiev, Moscow, or Leningrad, in the Soviet Union, for a reason. She was born between the World Wars, when the West Ukraine was ruled by capitalist Poland, and any effort to further one's education in the Soviet Union was regarded as treason. The Poles feared anything that might lead to an attempt to unify the western Ukraine with the larger eastern portion which was Soviet and had three-fourths of the Ukrainian people. So Ukrainians were required to look only westward.

At the outbreak of World War II, the USSR regained the West Ukraine, and it became part of the Ukrainian Soviet Socialist Republic.

As Mrs. Masliak explained, "Our leading artists, Kulchitskaia, a woman, Trush, Monastyrskii — they are dead, but have won a firm place in the history of Ukrainian art — got their educations far from our country. There was no opportunity for that here. My school today has 180 children. We accept 50 applicants each year, and graduate 25."

All this is free; her students are mostly from Lvov. "This is because our classes are held after the hours when children attend their regular school or high-school classes. So we can only accept those rural kids who live real close to town. But there is also an art school in the county seat of Chervonograd for the country kids from round about. There are a great many more music schools — virtually every county has one. Right now we're working on expanding the network of art schools, if not yet into every county seat then at least into the larger towns.

Photo by Author

The prerevolutionary owner's child drowned; the parents memorialized it with these aquatic figures. Such is the Ukrainian soul.

She had been teaching twenty-five years and has seen "a really large number of graduates who have gone on to roles of distinction in art."

Her father was a priest. "Initially it was the Greek Catholic (Uniate) Church.* But after the reunification of the western regions with the Ukrainian Soviet Republic, it was the Orthodox Church, and papa went over to it. He died in 1970. He worked till the last day of his life. He is buried in the village where he worked."

I asked if she personally is a religious believer. "After all, I was raised in that spirit by my parents" she replied. But she was more definite about whether her father's vocation affected her career. "Absolutely not. My father did his work, and he was respected, by the officials in the county seat and everywhere. My background had no influence upon my career whatever. Look: I'm a member of the Union of Artists.† My attitudes toward the society

---

*When Poland conquered the Ukraine centuries ago, it forced the Orthodox ("Greek" rite) Church to accept the pope, but was allowed to retain its own liturgy. It was called "Uniate" from this compulsory union with Rome.

†This is not a labor union, but a professional society that one must be admitted to, and membership in which brings many advantages.

in which I live, toward the government that gave me an education, are loyal and sincere. I have been a member of the Union since 1961. My work has been exhibited at many shows under its auspices, and is now constantly on public display."

Because her father was a priest, I asked again about religion. I pointed out that there are more Orthodox churches in the Ukraine than in the rest of the Soviet Union put together — and twice as many in West Ukraine as in the rest of the Ukraine.[1] I asked what percentage of Ukrainians are still religious. "I have no way of knowing, But religious faith is an old, an ancient tradition. One can hardly expect a people to give it up."

I remarked that Central Asian friends in the creative arts have found much of ethical value in the Koran, though they do not practice Islamic ritual, and asked if there was anything like that among people of Christian background who are not churchgoers. She replied: "My father always contended that religion preaches the same ideals as communism. Love your fellow human, and all peoples. My father said all the time that all the finest things taught by religion were to be found in the principles of communism. Religion didn't say: 'Thou shalt kill. Thou shalt steal. Thou shalt be , evil.' It taught children the very best, the very finest. And the Moral Code of Communism is the very finest kind of set of precepts one can instill in a person so as to bring him up right."

The "Moral Code of Communism" was adopted in the Party's Rules as of 1961, and I had always wondered to what degree it had taken root in people's minds. Neither she nor her husband, a nationally known proctologist, were Party members.

There was a young woman of 24 present, Adriana, the fiance of the Masliaks' son. In her swimsuit she appeared extraordinarily muscular, in a way that suggested some sport with which I was not familiar. She spoke perfect English, explaining that she was a conservatory student in musicology and *at the same time* a university student in English — and an equestrienne with 27 wins in flat racing and jumping. Her career plan was to study the influence of Ukrainian music in English-speaking countries. She informed me that Ukrainian songs were particularly popular in Scotland, somewhat less so in Ireland, and also in Canada.

I could not help but think of those who claim that Ukrainian culture is suppressed. Here at this Sunday gathering — a few friends of my host — they included two involved with professional children's theater in Ukrainian (the Ukrainian-Jewish couple), a researcher into recent Ukrainian history (one of the journalists), and now a young women interested in the influence of Ukrainian music in the English-speaking world!

Both of Adriana's parents had been physicians, (her mother was dead), born in the West Ukraine under Polish rule. Their parents were workers she told me. I was surprised to hear they could become doctors in the Western Ukraine under Polish rule, but she said, "It wasn't under Poland. My father started in the '40s after the war, and my mother graduated from medical school in '53." To see if this very early start into a profession in the Soviet period was a reward for special loyalty, I asked: "Were your grandparents Communists?" "No. They were teachers."

In 1980 a group of high-school students from Alberta, Canada, visited the Ukraine. One 11th-grader described his impressions in an Edmonton daily:

> I am of West Ukraine origin, my grandfather coming from there during Polish rule after the First World War.* Then, students were taught only in Polish. The Ukrainians, mainly of Orthodox faith, were not allowed religious freedom and were forced to follow Polish ideals of Catholicism. The Ukrainians now feel they have it better within the Soviet Union than under any foreign, e.g., Polish rule, or trying to go it alone. Things are improving for them and, being the second largest republic in population and importance, they have quite a bit of political clout.[3]

This perceptive capsule conclusion was argued in Kiev in more sophisticated form, by Vitalii Korotych, a poet, novelist, and writer of travel sketches in the Ukrainian language. He said:

> To me the greatest of all terrors is for a people to be driven into isolation. The most difficult periods in the history of the Ukraine were when it stood alone, friendless, or with allies it could not depend upon. This ancient city has been destroyed many times in its history. After the Mongol invasion in the 13th century there was no life here whatever for approximately 300 years. On each such occasion, the resurrection of our civilization began with the emergence of our people from isolation. The entire historical destiny of the Ukraine has been the quest for the life of a normal people, a search for its place in history and of contact with the peoples living around it. In that sense, any nationalism is always a move in the direction of the destruction of one's own people, an attempt to drive it into isolation, to counterpose it to other peoples.

---

*Poverty drove 300,000 to emigrate from the Lvov area alone, 1927-38.[2]

The Ukrainian people has suffered a great deal. The Ukraine has experienced everything having been taken away from it—its land was taken, it lost its cities entirely.

To understand him we need some basic facts. The Ukraine has 50,000,000 people, roughly the population of West Germany, France, England, or Italy. Its history is about as long; the first mention of Kiev appears over 1100 years ago, and its princes adopted Christianity in 988-989 AD, choosing the Orthodox form from the "eastern Rome," Constantinople. Not Moscow but Kiev was the capital of the earliest East Slavic state, which embraced what is now the Ukraine, Belorussia, and the heart of present-day Russia proper. At least four major churches still stand in Kiev from that pre-medieval period, and writings in religion, law, and epic literature have come down from those years.

Fragmented into feudal principalities, the region had little capacity to resist external enemies. In 1239 AD the Mongol-Tatars swept in from Asia, and Kiev fell the next year. Urban populations were exterminated, the seat of Orthodox Christianity was moved to north Russia, and —in the 14th century—western countries began to pick the Ukraine apart, with Lithuania, Poland, Hungary, and what is now Romania each taking a piece, while an Islamic, Turkic-speaking state, the Khanate of the Crimea, came into being along the Black Sea coast.

At about this time, the Ukrainian language and culture began to emerge as distinct from the Russian and Belorussian. This was partly due to the political separation from those eastern Slavic lands, but in the West Ukraine it remained intact across boundaries of its conquerors, perhaps because Lithuanian, Hungarian, and Romanian are non-Slavic languages. Poland constantly sought to force assimilation, above all by compelling the Ukrainian Orthodox Church to accept the dominance of Rome. The cities gradually became non-Ukrainian (Polish plus Jewish plus German, chiefly) over the centuries that followed and in the countryside foreign feudal lords, mainly Polish, divided up the Ukrainian peasants and their lands. Kiev was destroyed again in 1482 by Turks and Tatars from the Crimea. They raided the Ukraine and south Russia for centuries, taking literally millions of male captives who were sold into slavery to Venice, Turkey, and Spain, and worked to death pulling the oars of galleys on the Mediterranean.

Meanwhile Russia had freed itself from the Tatars and pulled together from feudal principalities into a centralized state. There were wars with Polish and Lithuanian lords to its west and the

Crimean Tatars to the south—all oppressors of the Ukrainians. This situation, a shared Orthodox Christian belief, and earlier common history, caused Ukrainian leaders to begin to think of Russia as protector.

Poland was growing stronger. An individual landowner might own hundreds of Ukrainian small towns and villages, and the peasants were reduced to outright serfdom. Huge peasant uprisings occurred, but were suppressed. In 1596, the Orthodox Church was formally absorbed into the Catholic Church as the Uniate Church, over the opposition of most priests and the entire people. Anti-Catholic organizations called the Brotherhoods came into being, and founded schools and printshops.

The Ukraine rebelled in 1648, led by Bohdan Hmelnitsky, who took the portions thus liberated into the Russian Empire in 1654. Further Russo-Polish wars resulted in a treaty whereby the Ukraine from Kiev eastward belonged to Russia, with Poland continuing to hold sway in the west and Hungary ruling the Carpathian mountain country. In 1708-09, even Sweden invaded the Ukraine, but was thrown back by the Russians, aided by Ukrainian Cossacks and the resistance of the peasants. The victor, Peter the Great, suppressed Ukrainian autonomy and began an effort at Russification which continued until the Communist Revolution over 200 years later. He also began exploration for minerals, which brought industry for the first time, but serfdom became even more oppressive under his rule.

Poland was defeated and divided in 1772, and the West Ukraine went to Austria. Now Germanization was superimposed upon Polonization. My own mother, born there at the end of the 19th century, had to study German and Polish, spoke Yiddish at home, and learned Ukrainian to communicate with her father's customers —and taught her son, born in New York, *Viiut vitri* and other Ukrainian folk songs she loved.

When we spoke of the ups and downs of Ukrainian history, the writer Korotych said, "Often its resurrection has begun with a cultural rebirth. The songs remained, the literature remained, and the rebirth of the people began with that. Nationalists claim to find great support in much of the poetry of Shevchenko.* They forget that Shevchenko died in St. Petersburg, and that he found himself most at home among Russian revolutionary democrats, no matter how great a Ukrainian patriot he was." Indeed, cooperation between the Ukraine and Russia today is the logical consequence of the

---

*Taras Shevchenko, 1814-1861, the Cervantes, Dante, or Shakespeare of the Ukraine.

ideals shared by Shevchenko and the Russians Chernyshevsky, Dobroliubov, Nekrasov.* Extremist nationalists would bar the use of the Russian language in the Ukraine, but Shevchenko himself wrote many stories in Russian ("The Musician," "The Painter," and others), and major Russian composers, Mussorgsky, Tchaikovsky, Rachmaninoff, set his verse to music, as did the Ukrainian Lysenko. Shevchenko was stirred to poetry by the oppression of peoples other than his own. Exiled to the Kazakh country near the Caspian Sea, he wrote of them in a feeling of brotherhood. The Russian Nekrasov wrote a poem "On the Death of Shevchenko," and figures of world stature such as Dostoyevsky and Turgenev attended his funeral.[4]

Korotych also said to me: "The penetrating and wise Jew, Sholom Aleichem† was born here in Kiev. Much that is bitter and much that is sweet in his work relates to the Ukraine. Ukrainian intellectuals very often followed the same lines of thought as the Jews, and the tsarist vocabulary even had the phrase: 'Jewified intellectuals' (*zhidovshchvuiushchie intelligenty*), that is, one who acquired the spirit, the outlook of the Jews. In the name of order, the tsarist authorities ran wild against the Jews and the intellectuals, always in association. Likewise, the most intelligent members of the Jewish population were never Jewish chauvinists.

"If I were to start dividing my friends and enemies into those who are Ukrainians and non-Ukrainians, Jews and not Jews, I would be taking a wrong approach from the start. To me, people divide into the honorable and the dishonorable, into the wise and the damn fools. And the question as to whether the person is a Jew, a Ukrainian, or whatever else, is the very last thing that arises in my mind."

These words came in response to my observation that many Jews tend to think of Ukrainians in general as anti-Semites. "Lying in front of me right now are translations of [the Jewish poet] Buchbinder. I am translating his poetry, rendering it into Ukrainian poetry. We have always done this kind of thing." And for him personally, "There is a family tradition. In 1919, when the Petliura nationalists held Kiev, there was a pogrom. My grandfather saw the Jewish tailor who was our next-door neighbor being driven off to be killed. My grandfather was a most typical Ukrainian, with

---

*Liberal revolutionary democratically minded critics and poets active about the time of the freeing of the serfs.

†*Fiddler on the Roof* is an adaptation of his stories.

those sweeping moustaches, Stepan Ivanovich Korotych. He went over to the Petliura crowd, and said, 'This is a living human being just like you; don't beat him,' and so forth. The Petliura man took the glasses the tailor was wearing, gave them to my grandfather, and said: 'Here's a pair of glasses from a Jew for you.' Gramps replied: 'I don't need the glasses. I can see well enough.' The Petliura man smashed the lenses out, and said: 'Here, the frame is of gold. It's for you, because you saved him.' And this Jewish man always refused to take back the glasses frame. Well, we were friends with that family, and so that golden glasses-frame remained in our family as an heirloom."

The Ukraine had participated actively with Russia in the unsuccessful but massive year-long 1905 Revolution against the monarchy. Peasant uprisings encompassed half of the Ukraine: three hundred landlord estates were wrecked; soviets were established in five major cities and industrial towns; thousands were executed, jailed, and exiled, as in Russia. This prompted the first mass-scale emigration to Canada and the U.S. (which produced folk songs like "Oi, Kanado, Kanadochko"). Another million tried to improve their lives by migrating eastward to the virgin soil of Siberia and Kazakhstan, but because government assistance was minimal, fully 70 percent couldn't make it, and returned.

When the great Russian writer, Tolstoy, a pacifist and friend of the peasants, died in 1910, there were demonstrations in Ukrainian cities. When the government massacred striking gold-miners in far-off Siberia in 1912, there were protest strikes in Kiev, and elsewhere in the Ukraine. And when the tsar was overthrown in March, 1917, the Ukraine was active again—indeed, later that spring, the peasant movement against the landlords became virtually a war. When Lenin took power by vote of the Second Congress of Workers' and Soldiers' Soviets in November, the delegates included more than a hundred from the Ukraine. In Kiev itself, the workers' and soldiers' soviets voted to support that revolution only two days later.

At that point a middle-class nationalist Ukrainian government, the Central Rada, was able to take over. Its only hope of survival was to build an alliance with Germany, which then occupied the country and had installed a former tsarist general, Skoropadsky. But when the Germans lost World War I and began to withdraw, a popular uprising forced him out, and former leaders of the Rada, now calling themselves the Directory, took over. However, the Rada had sent punitive expeditions against the peasantry when they sought to divide the landlords' estates, so the Directory's "armies melted away as soon as the Skoropadsky forces had been defeated."[5] The Communists returned to power. All this took place in little over one year, November 1917 to February 1919.

The original head of the Rada government was the distinguished historian Hrushevsky. Although he had played an active part in inviting in the German army, and retreated with it out of the country, when the Civil War was over, he appealed to be allowed to return to the Soviet Ukraine. It was not his native land. He had been born in Poland proper, and began his career in Lvov which was now under anti-Communist Polish rule. But he recognized that a Ukrainian could function as such only in the Soviet Ukraine. He was permitted to return and was elected to both the Ukrainian and USSR academies of science. He wrote a *History of Ukrainian Literature* and a *History of the Ukraine and Rus*, and died of old age in 1934 — a non-Marxist nationalist to the end. The novelist Vinnichenko, who had headed the Directory government, also asked to return. He was allowed to in 1920, and made Vice-Premier in a gesture of reconciliation, but he broke with the Soviets again, and was permitted to emigrate, this time permanently.

All these details are noteworthy because of the continuing activity of Ukrainian nationalists in North American and European universities. They have put out no less than 75 books, have entire journals of their own, and set the tone of Ukrainian-language newspapers. Yet their claim to political legitimacy rests solely upon a single year of rule over sixty years ago.

The struggle in the Ukraine was described with marvelous color by H.M. Odinets, a peasant from the country around Chernigov, who was a member of the Ukrainian delegation to the 1922 convention establishing the Soviet Union.*

Another Ukrainian delegate, then also a peasant, aged 27, reminisced years later about Odinets' speech:

> These words were drowned out in tremendous applause. We all stood up. The excitement of this old man of the poorest peasantry . . . was transmitted to us. Why did we receive Odinets so warmly? Because of his exceptional capacity as an orator? True, he was an attractive speaker. But the main thing lay elsewhere. Odinets was a former member of the secretariat of the Central Rada, a peasant whom Vinnichenko and the other rulers of the bourgeois Rada had seated

---

*Until then there had been four separate Soviet republics: Russia, the Ukraine, Belorussia, and the Transcaucasian Federation, so this gathering was like the U.S. Constitutional Convention of 1787.

alongside themselves as if to say: "see, the peasantry holds power!" What they had later done with that "peasantry in power," Odinets had related in his speech. He personified the path that many of those in the hall had followed. This route had been one of a flare-up of nationalism, wrath against the treason to the nation by the blue-jackets [the nationalist uniform] the fierce terror unleashed by Skoropadsky, Petliura, and Denikin, the return of the gentry landlords and kulaks, followed by a return of sober thinking and a change to the side of the red Soviet banners. . . .

After the speeches and enthusiasm, there was serious work to be done at the convention. He said:

It was decided to gather once again and read and discuss each paragraph of the Declaration and every point of the Treaty [of Union]. That was done at the next gathering of the delegation. . . . We selected a group . . . for the conference of plenipotentiary delegations, at which the documents . . . were to receive preliminary approval of the delegation of the four republics. I, too, was among the group chosen from our Ukrainian delegation. . . . Arguments arose from time to time on interpretation of particular points. . . . For many of us . . . this was a major political schooling. . . . And finally came that long-awaited and solemn day, December 30, 1922. I looked into the faces of the delegates. The Revolution had elevated us to the level of consciously making history.

I recall another December, that of 1917, in our Pesky, deep in the woods. How timid I had been, only five years earlier, at so simple a matter as confiscating the land from the kulaks. And now, all of twenty-seven years old, I was soon to be in charge of Poltava Okrug with a population of three-quarters of a million. Ahead of us were dozens of the most complicated problems: organization of the administration, and furtherance of agriculture and industry. But I thought of this calmly and knew that I would manage.[6]

In a way, these recollections help to answer a very serious question: why was the Ukraine loyal to the USSR in World War II after Stalin massacred its leaders? The reminiscence quoted above cites speeches by two of those later victims, Skrypnik and Zatonsky; the writer honored them in memory. The point is that the new social system growing out of the Revolution developed ten, if not a hundred, new leaders for every one Stalin executed. They came out of the peasantry, the workingclass, and today, their intellectual children. Such leaders could never have developed in the past because the people were locked into illiteracy and hopeless poverty.

First, the majority of Ukrainians could not read or write. Second, all publishing in Ukrainian was prohibited by the tsar in

1876, a ban not lifted until the 1905 Revolution, when he agreed to revoke it in the hope of preserving his rule. When World War I began, there was still no government-run school teaching in the native language, indeed "Ukrainian was not allowed to be used" in public schools.[7] So cultural freedom was a touchstone in determining loyalties in the Civil War of 1918-20.

The beginnings of the cultural revolution are described in the reminiscences of a distinguished Soviet Ukrainian scholar, Prof. V.A. Holobutskii, a specialist in the history of the Cossacks and the Ukrainian War of Liberation of 1648-1654. Though only a boy of 16 in 1919, he had already read not only Shevchenko and Gogol, the classical Ukrainian playwright (*The Inspector-General*) and humorist who wrote in Russian, but all the major Ukrainian-language writers, Franko, Kotliarevskii, and even the several volumes of *Ancient Kiev* (*Kievskaia Starina*). At 21, he took a job as a village librarian:

When I came there in 1924, enormous changes had already occurred. . . . The Committee of Propertyless Villagers was the political center. . . . The propertyless were motivated to engage in collective labor, in a socialized farming operation, and had already undertaken to organize an agricultural cooperative founded on one of the former estates, where equipment, a house, and a large fruit orchard remained. . . . Two cooperative stores and a farm sales co-op were established, a branch of the Workers' International Relief, and a village library. School attendance and the number of teachers were enlarged, a beginning was made toward elimination of illiteracy among adults, and an evening school for youth . . . was founded.

The village library . . . was largely my baby. When I first entered it, this is what I saw. It was all but pitch dark in this little room, with its earth floor and tiny windows. Weak . . . light from a . . . kerosene lamp . . . barely enabled one to see the posters on the walls, the unpainted wooden table with its pile of newspapers and books, and a group of men in homespun *svita* coats and jackets cut down from soldiers' greatcoats. Some . . . were seated on *oslony* [movable benches] and benches fixed to the wall, while others, with cigars clenched in their teeth, sat on their haunches at the enormous stove and emitted their smoke into its sooty black mouth. Everyone was silent and listening to someone who was seated behind the table reading aloud. Behind the voice of the reader one heard the humming of a spinning wheel and the crying of an infant from the other half of the cottage, behind the stove. . . . In those years the village library played an important role in the political and cultural life of the village, and was the carrier of all the progress brought to the people by the Soviet government. It was the political club of the village, a hearth radiating knowledge of politics and science, until then inaccessible to the peasants.

Soon the village library was moved to new quarters. This was a real event in the life of the village. . . . Each room now acquired a special purpose. . . . In the evenings particularly Saturdays and Sundays, our clubhouse was filled to bursting. More and more people of middle age began to come. Oldsters, too. They were all drawn into that whirlpool of ideas and interests by which the country then lived. It is harder to say what we didn't do in the village library than what we did. There were lectures on the origin of the world and of man, on calendar systems. . . . *We organized debates with members of dissident religious groups.* [My emphasis — W.M.] I taught a group of young people . . . the basic principles of surveying . . . I taught them to use the abacus for calculation, to keep elementary ledgers; I gave lectures on history, atheism, Ukrainian literature, etc. . . .

We also had a theater. It was housed in what had been a land-owner's stable. Picture to yourself a narrow, long stone building with a wide door at one end and a stage at the other, with an earthen floor packed hard by the hooves of horses, and crowded with benches. . . . However modest and naive were the notions I and my associates had about the art of the theater or, to be more exact, thanks to this, we felt at home. Nor was there reason not to if, in performing the plays of Karpenko-Kary or Kropivnitskii, we found our audiences responding both with boisterous laughter and sincere tears. . . . We were rewarded with such storms of applause, such unfeigned expressions of satisfaction as a first-rank star of the stage would have envied. As you will have guessed, the theater was packed to the doors.[8]

But this was no idyll. The organization of a socialized farm on a former landlord estate and of cooperative stores by the former landless, once farmhands for the prosperous *kulaks*, deprived the latter of their labor supply and money made by "furnishing" them supplies on credit, as with sharecropping in the American South. Before collectivization in the Ukraine, half of the peasants had no draft animals or implements of their own.[9] Prof. Holobutskii comments "The kulaks fought us stubbornly and blindly, took a revenge constantly and savagely. And I could tell of more than one bloody drama in which our comrades were the victims." Youth were the core of collectivization when it began: 1,364 collective farms [of 27,000] in the Ukraine were headed by people under 30 years old.[10]

Stalin sought to assure victory for collectivization by repressing his opponents — including fellow-Communists who were simply suspected of the slightest disagreement. But the young peasant farm leaders had no way of knowing they were innocent. The youth supported Stalin because, within five years, the collective farms did bring a much better life for the poor.

The Germans and their Romanian allies reoccupied the entire Ukraine during World War II. A writer in Lvov told me his memories of that time.

"The outbreak of war, June 21, 1941, found me 35 miles from here at a place called Sokal; I was nineteen. At noon German land mines were dropped on our artillery battery. When the raid ended, I crawled out of the trench and shook the dirt off me. The first thing I saw was my buddy on his knees in the growing rye, not yet ripe. His guts were spilling out. He cried 'Ivan.' Before I could run to him, he toppled head first into that unripe rye and was dead. He was only 19 years old.

"That was the first day of the war. At the very end, four years later, May 2, 1945, we were in Czechoslovakia. An insurrection against the Germans had begun in Prague, and we were constantly hearing voices in Czech on the radio: '*Ruda Armada na pomot, Ruda Armada na pomot*' — Red Army, help us! I was walking alongside the commander of our unit. Spring had come early. It was real hot, and we had unbuttoned our uniforms. I was thinking that by the time our unit got to Prague the war would be over. Marshal Konev had shifted forces from Berlin to assist the Prague rebellion.

"My commander said to me: 'My mother is a teacher. What a wonderful mother I have! She is so gentle, so kind, so good, so wise.' I remember thinking to myself: 'What a fine guy this is! His father had given his life at Stalingrad, and the son is such a good person. He loves his mother just like a little boy. The war must certainly spare him.' And I looked at him there, next to me. He was so handsome, broad-shouldered, an honest-to-God Russian knight of old, with curly red hair, beautiful light-blue eyes over a broad face. I thought to myself: 'After the war, are the girls ever going to chase you! You are beautiful, and besides, a Hero of the Soviet Union plus twelve other medals.' And I beamed at him. He said: 'What are you smiling about?' I said: 'I won't tell you, so you won't get a swelled head.'

"Suddenly a burst from a machine-gun broke into our conversation. I thought one of our guys was celebrating victory prematurely. But then I saw Alexei grabbing the gun-carriage, then his hands at his chest. There was blood between his fingers. He began to fall. I grabbed his head to cradle and support it. But he slumped, and two minutes later he was dead. Some fascist had concealed himself behind the road embankment.

"No one else in our battery was killed from then until S.S. General Schörner gave up on May 12th, after the official surrender. So that was the very last victim, to me the most precious.

"Every time I recall this, I choke up. It was such an absurd death and so undeserved. He died so young. When I hear people speak of the 20,000,000 Soviet citizens who lost their lives, it is these two who flash before my eyes. Grisha Rymok died on the first day of the war, and Alexei Podosennik died on the last day I saw fighting. All those people were individual human beings who were unable to live out their time, unable to experience their loves, unable to dream their dreams to the end, unable to follow their paths. When we say that we seek to defend peace, we do so in memory of those people who could not live out their lives, could not arrive at the ends of their own roads because of that war. Today the skies are peaceful, our labors are for peaceful purposes. But we paid a very high price for this.

"I recall another incident. In Poland we liberated Oswiecim. The Germans called it Auschwitz. 5,000,000 people died there. Those people who still survived had skins that were earthen, like mummies. All that really remained were their eyes. Immense eyes that were still alive. A buddy and I took one man under the arms so as to help him into a vehicle. He said in Polish: '*Pane towarzysc, jaco nic, nic ne zapomniec, nic ne zapomniec*': mister comrade, *no one, no one* must forget this.

"All people have to be reminded of this, all human beings. Today I just can't understand Israel. The Jewish people suffered so very much, suffered so many victims."*

A woman near by, now a factory worker, said, "I too am a veteran. I served in the Air Force, for four years. I was a volunteer." She was first a gunner but then, because of her skills, was assigned as a ground mechanic. "If someone told me now that another war had begun, I couldn't survive that news. For me that is so terrible that I am ready to give everything I have, and I say this to everybody. I am prepared to live on bread and water, just so there is no war." She was not speaking figuratively, but in the belief that the USSR had to match Reagan's arms build-up to keep him from

---

*The first bombing of Beirut had just occurred when we met in 1979.

pressing the button. "I saw suffering children, who had no roof over their heads, no mama, no papa. I saw what became of old men and women."

The writer summed up: "As the saying goes, our people saw the flaming wolf, the wolf smeared with burning tar. Few Americans have had any such experience. That's why there are many in America who are howling about war. They think they'll survive. They'll hide somewhere. A people as a whole, a country, cannot hide. Reagan doesn't understand this, and there are others who don't. That's what's so horrible." *

These words were recorded at a meeting with the Lvov Peace Committee. By the time everyone there had reminisced, all were crying, including a retired general and a college president.

In 1959, 14 years after the war, I visited a collective farm near Kiev. There were some men, but the war's slaughter of males had not nearly been made up, and there was a general leanness of appearance not natural in so square-built a nationality. The farm chairman, Ivan Kabanets — about 50, beetle-browed and bald, he looked like the film star Wallace Beery minus the fat — spoke about the farm. "The Red Ploughman (*Cheervunnee Hleebahrub* in Ukrainian) was organized in 1928. It was occupied in 1941. *Everything* was destroyed, including the 937 homes. We came back late in 1943. In 1944 we had no tractors, no horses, nothing, only our land."

A journalist in Lvov, Pavel Romaniuk, has his own memories. He was not born until 1940. When the Germans invaded the next year, he and his mother were evacuated by the Soviets on open flat cars. (He learned later that a woman with an infant his age fell asleep, her child fell out of her arms and was killed under the train.) They were finally quartered in a village near the Volga. "You see what I look like now." He is a weightlifter and weighs 220, with no fat. "At that time I became blind from hunger, and had second-degree atrophy of the digestive tract. The first time I saw sugar was in about 1944. I found a piece of it somewhere and brought it home, because it was pretty. I showed it to mama and

---

*Evangelist Billy Graham, preaching in the USSR in September, 1984, found himself on the defensive when clergy and others quoted to him President Reagan's microphone-testing remark, inadvertently recorded: "I have just signed legislation outlawing Russia. The bombs fall in five minutes."

she said: 'That's sugar.' So I took a nibble. Ever since I have been a sugar lover."

I had some understanding of that, I told him; there had been no sugar available in any form for nine months in Moscow when I lived there in 1931-32 while my father held an engineering contract. He said: "But you knew what sugar was. I didn't. I found that in the street. My corneas had become opaque and I was treated by sprinkling sugar in my eyes. I don't know what kind of medical practice that is. They also gave me milk by injection, since I couldn't digest. I still remember that: it was unbelievably painful."

After the war, aid from the United States to its wartime enemy Austria was four times as high, per person, as aid to the Ukraine.[11] Even at that early date, Washington had abandoned humanitarianism for political discrimination, despite the protests of the head of the UN Relief and Rehabilitation Administration (which administered the aid), former New York mayor Fiorello LaGuardia. Italy, also Hitler's ally, got twice as much aid per person as the Ukraine. Yet it was universally recognized that the Ukraine had suffered incomparably more then these Western beneficiaries of assistance. In their desire for peace with the U.S. today, even informed older Ukrainians do not remind one of such things. But it behooves an American to do so.

Ukrainians all know of the aid given to them by Russia and other republics that suffered less in the war. Turkic-speaking Moslem Azerbaijanis helped found the Ukrainian oil and gas industries in 1946-48. Later, the Ukraine was able to aid underdeveloped Soviet Asian peoples or those struck by natural catastrophes. Elsewhere, I describe seeing a figure of Shevchenko in the wall of a school in Tashkent, Central Asia—a school given and built by the Ukraine when that city was levelled by an earthquake in the 1960s. And Ukrainian composers helped write the first Turkmen opera in that desert republic north of Iran in 1941. The first Ukrainian opera had been written in 1863.

The war offered a classical opportunity for opposition to Soviet rule to manifest itself. Famine had occurred during the collectivization period, as even Khrushchev admitted,[12] and Stalin had executed virtually the entire Communist leadership—Ukrainians, Russians, Jews—during his purge in the 1930s.[13] Nevertheless, during the Nazi occupation, the "zone of operation" of "organized Ukrainian nationalism . . . was limited to the former Polish territories"[14] according to the historian, Roman Szporluk.

I heard an echo of this in the 1980s from a college president who is a member of the Lvov Peace Committee. Ukrainian is clearly his habitual language, although he spoke heavily accented Russian for my sake. "I was in the area under German occupation. The situation was such that you could go out into the street, innocent of anything whatever — without even having said a word against the regime that lawlessly occupied our territory — and you could be shot without trial and without warning. They would simply come by, put people up against a wall, and shoot them. Getting from one place in town to another was difficult.

"After the liberation of our area, I reported to the county board of education. They immediately sent me out to be principal of the primary school in my native village. Conditions were such that it was very hard to do one's work, particularly in the villages, especially for a person born in the area where he was assigned a job. I had to sleep in a different house every night, never in my own home."

This, as I guessed, was because of Banderovites.* Teachers were among those at the top of their list to be killed. "Miraculously, they didn't find me. I was young then, and there was a girl who liked me. That's where I ate. And I managed to squirm out of tight situations. Being the principal of a school, I was a target.

"I was one of the first three members of the Young Communist League in our county. My entire life has been associated with that college of which I am now the president. I graduated from it, went to work there, ultimately became a full professor, and then president. Of course, this provides a very interesting story for our students."

In the largest, eastern portion of the Ukraine, which had been Soviet for twenty years, loyalty was overwhelming and active. There were half a million organized Soviet guerrillas, including legendary ethnic Ukrainian heroes such as Kovpak and Popudrenko, and 4,500,000 ethnic Ukrainians fought in the Soviet Army. Clearly, that army would have been fundamentally weakened if there had been basic disaffection among so large a component. The strongly anti-Soviet Alexander Dallin, who devoted an entire book to studying *German Rule in Russia, 1941-1945*, concluded, "The available evidence shows no substantial variation in loyalty among the residents of Slavic areas of the USSR."[15] Two thousand ethnic Ukrainians won the highest Soviet military honor, the title Hero of the Soviet Union.

---

*Bandera was a Ukrainian nationalist, anti-Semitic leader as cruel as Idi Amin and as fascist as Pinochet.

There was an obvious reason for this loyalty. For the bulk of the Ukrainian peasants, workers, and for the professionals newly emerged from those classes, the Soviet system had demonstrated overwhelming economic and cultural advantages. Even the most bitter of all anti-Soviet Ukrainian nationalist scholars grants that, "The current Ukrainian resistance and nationality defense movement . . . has not yet enjoyed the support or active participation of technocrats, government officials, lower and middle echelon Party members, professionals and workers."[16]

The Ukrainian people ignore it; we have given it attention because the mass media in the West seek to create the opposite impression. For example, Jack Anderson, in his nationally-syndicated column of August 17, 1977, wrote of the Ukrainians as "a proud breed of 50 million people who refuse to abandon their ancient culture," as if that were Moscow's goal. Yet all over Kiev, there are movie listings, propaganda billboards, help-wanted posters and store signs in Ukrainian, not Russian. I happened upon a plaque, in Ukrainian, on an apartment house stating that the Yiddish writer Sholem Aleichem once lived there. The USSR-wide circulation of the Ukrainian-language humor magazine *Perets* (Pepper) is far larger than that of its Russian counterpart in proportion to the populations of these two peoples. In proportion to U.S. population, its circulation equals that of *Readers' Digest*, the biggest magazine in the West. A children's weekly, also in Ukrainian, is just as large; no one need worry that the next generation won't know its native language.

In Kiev I interviewed the editor of a women's magazine which is almost as large. Although she resembled the reclusive Greta Garbo in her '50s, this woman was strong and warm. Her manner suggested a life of great responsibilities. Her father had been a coal miner from the age of nine before the Revolution, and had fought in the 1918-20 war against foreign intervention. In World War II when adult men were drafted, her brother had to go to work so young that he needed a box to stand on to reach his machine. She holds a PhD, and has been to the United States. She told me:

Our magazine is called *Radianska Zhinka* (Soviet Woman). It was founded in 1920. The first issue appeared in connection with the first convention of women workers and peasants in our republic. It immediately became the public address system of the women's movement. It became the friend and counsellor of women who were awakening to life outside the home. They found themselves with a great many questions, a great many problems. Their level of education was exceedingly low. Four out of five could not read or write. The women even called it 'the magazine for us girls.' It really spoke to the concerns of the women of that day.

Today the level of education of young women is even higher than among men. But even without statistics, our own experience testifies that women's fervor for knowledge is very intense — all the more so because the opportunities for satisfying this passion are unlimited. Just by nature, women are — it used to be said — of high curiosity. We regard as one of the functions of the magazine transforming curiosity into a new higher quality: the desire for knowledge. That quality gives life richer meaning. We do surveys to identify the interests of our readers, to know their opinions of what we publish. We find women's range of interest today is so broad, so diverse, that it really keeps us on our toes.

I would like to say something about the women who fought in World War II. Their consciences forced them to abandon their own childhoods so as to defend the childhood of all — the children of others, children they did not know — against fascism. They were hardly more than children themselves, but became warriors. Many became what we called "Daughters of the Regiment" when the trains in which they were being evacuated were bombed. They found themselves without parents, without a roof over their heads, and they were saved by soldiers. They sought to help however they could, in partisan detachments or in the front lines. They looked after themselves as best they could, with the soldiers' help.

One such woman I know of now has a PhD, and teaches chemistry in college. Another was so disabled that the doctors predicted a life of immobility. But the fascists had killed her father at the front and her mother had died, so she had to worry about her little sisters. By force of will she regained her strength and went to work rebuilding the coal mines as one of the Young Communist League volunteers.* Today she is a Hero of Socialist Labor [the highest Soviet award]. She is a member of Congress [the Supreme Soviet], and on its Committee on Protection of Motherhood and Childhood, which deals with questions of working conditions for women.

The first woman is Hala Danilko. The second is Halina Nikolaevna Litvinenko, who also has visited the United States. People say of her, she is the essence of motherhood, the very being of motherhood. She does a great deal simply to help bring up other people's children. There are clubs of which she is the sponsor, which compete for the honor of bearing her name. She teaches them what war really means. She teaches them to do everything so that our country and children never experience it again.

---

*Without coal to propel the steam locomotives of that day, nothing could be restarted in the Ukraine.

Culture for the masses, other than folk arts, is entirely a product of the Soviet years. In 1923, ethnic Ukrainians were only one-third of the college students in the Ukraine. Within no more than six years they were a majority, and by 1953, they were 63 percent.[17] By the 1960s a majority of professors in Ukrainian universities were ethnic Ukrainians, and by the 1970s most scientific researchers were Ukrainians as well.[18]

A distinguished female microbiologist, now elderly, brought this history to life. She spoke in Russian for my sake, though her narration was sprinkled with Ukrainian. At the time of the Revolution, she was a half-orphan in a poor urban family, her father was dead, and her mother never re-married. This was in the portion of the Ukraine that has been Soviet since about 1917.

"In 1935 I came to Kiev to do my graduate work, and there were 17 students competing for the one opening." The professor chairing the admissions committee proposed choosing her because she was from the provinces, and did well in the exam. This was strictly affirmative action, because they exempted her from the German-language exam. "I studied there together with my husband. I gave birth to a son at this time. In 1937 I won first prize in a ranking of young scientists. Then came the hard years of the war. We were evacuated to Ufa in the Ural Mountains. I still don't know how it happened that I put a pair of fancy slippers into my suitcase, the first such I had owned. Alongside them I put the manuscript of my dissertation.

"Those were extremely difficult years. We worked on a very serious grain disease caused by poisonous molds. For over a year I knew nothing at all about what had happened to my husband. In 1943 we returned to Kiev. I just don't know where we found the strength to make it. We kept ourselves fed with vegetables we grew ourselves — when we left the Urals we brought back a reserve supply of 1,600 pounds of potatoes that I had raised with my own hands. My mother, my son, my comrades gave me a hand. We had a very close-knit collective. I still have friends in Moscow going back to that time in the Urals; the closeness among us is like that which developed among soldiers at the front.

"Our institute in Kiev had been completely destroyed. The library, the marvelous museum were totally gone. Our soldiers returned with a few sacks of books the Germans had discarded as they fled."

She is one of the Soviet leaders in the field of antibiotics, and, not long ago served in the Ukrainian delegation to the United Nations.*

Although Russians and Jews together outnumbered Ukrainians in their own cities before the Revolution, industrialization brought a great influx of peasants very early, and Ukrainians became a majority of the urban working class by the early 1930s. But they became a majority among students even earlier. This is a striking example of Soviet affirmative action policy and a striking contrast to Western patterns of social mobility: peasant grandfather, worker father, college-educated grandson or daughter. The effort to create an indigenous mass-scale professional stratum (teachers, administrators, doctors) was a top priority.

Farming is overwhelmingly by ethnic Ukrainians. In each of the nine managerial or professional employment categories on collective farms, the Ukraine leads Russia in the percentage with college or technical-agricultural high school education,[19] and nearly half of such posts are held by women.

Extraordinary steps are taken to study Ukrainian history and make it available. For example, a *twenty-six*-volume history of the towns and villages of the Ukraine has been published, a seventeen-volume Ukrainian Soviet Encyclopedia, and a ten-volume dictionary of the Ukrainian language. Over a dozen institutions exist to collect archeological data — they conduct some 100 expeditions in the Ukraine each year, and have first look at all new construction when foundations are dug. They have found the world's oldest musical instruments; a village of 20,000 inhabitants in the 5,000 year old Tripol'e Culture; discovered that the early medieval Slavs (ca 500 AD) had a uniform culture from the Dnieper to the Elbe Rivers and that 11th and 12th century Kiev was built of one- and two-story log houses, like the rest of Old Rus'.[20]

In the Ukraine, the Writers' Union — reserved only to professionals who make their living in that way — has about a thousand members. As everywhere in the Soviet Union today, writing is very far removed from the stereotype of "socialist realism" that Westerners have been led to believe characterizes it. A young poet, Svetlana Iovenko, has recently attracted attention. She writes:

> Were I so beautiful
> as the world has never known,
> I would still stand here before you

---

*For its services in World War II, the Ukraine has a vote of its own in the General Assembly, as does Belorussia, in addition to that of the USSR as a whole.

and not feel the ground beneath me.
   Could I express myself
   not in words but in caressing rays,
   I would still stand here before you,
   my lips sealed dumb.
If one could die of despair,
although supposedly I am alive,
Your word and touch would resurrect me
only to die again from happiness and fear.[21]

Could anything be more universal? This was published in Russian and Ukrainian, in a national magazine, a practice which brings wider renown to Ukrainian poetry than would publication in the Ukraine alone. This technique is used in other arts as well— for example, Ukrainian film festivals in Russian cities mark anniversaries of historical events involving both countries.

No art form lacks development in the Ukraine today: there are permanent opera companies in six cities, musical theater companies in all thirty "state" capitals, and four full-time four-year ballet schools. Affirmative action for children from non-intellectual families is the rule. As Xenia Masliak tells of her art school; "I give children of workers' first priority in admission. Gaining admission is hard, because there are very many talented children, and making choices is very hard. I favor workers' kids because an artist's child will, one way or another, find a means of studying art, and officials will hire private tutors for their children. Such children are prepared for admission; on a purely equal basis of selection, they'd have an advantage. But a worker's kid has nothing but his natural gift. Their entire future depends on us. Further, when such a child has finished his four years with us, I go out of my way to make sure that he gains admission to a high school of the arts." In general, with higher education, she said, "Workers' children and those of peasants get first choice. Young people from the farthest backwoods get preference, because they don't know how to make it on their own, as city kids do."

The history of the Ukraine in this century is summed up, to me, in the background and life of Fyodor Morgun. His grandfather was one of the rebel sailors on the battleship "Potemkin," during the 1905 Revolution, the heroes of Eisenstein's great film. Fyodor grew up on a collective farm in the 1930s, going to school in winter, helping on the farm in summer. His hero grandfather advised him to get a college education in agriculture. "Folks need such people more than any other kind."

He was about to enter college when World War II came. Two years later, he was invalided out with a couple of pieces of shrapnel in him. He got his agriculture degree in the years right after the war, then went off to break the virgin soil in Kazakhstan. At 34, he spoke for his fellow pioneers at a meeting of the Central Committee of the Communist Party, and convinced its members that farm forepersons in such difficult country should receive higher wages.

Because of the very low rainfall in that region, erosion, leading to dust-bowl conditions, was a great problem. He argued for using coulterless ploughs, which loosen the soil without turning it over, to avoid wind erosion. When he returned to the Ukraine, as salaried head of the Communist Party in Poltava, he got one collective farm to till part of its land that way as an example. The crop proved better than any around; the next year the whole farm was ploughed in that manner and the yield was better yet. Today, many farms use this method.

Morgun is the author of several books on farming, and a documentary novel called *Bread and People*, which won him admission to the Writers' Union. He is now a member of the same Central Committee he argued before many years ago, the body that sets policy for the USSR, and elects the Politburo. I find it hard to imagine how anyone could convince him that the Ukraine and Ukrainians are not now equals among equals. The percentage of Ukrainian names in the Soviet cabinet is far higher than their share of the population—and would be higher still if many Ukrainians had not tended to Russify their names in the past.

The children and grandchildren of those who carefully examined every point in the documents of union in 1922 probably have made more use of the rights of self-government than in any other Soviet republic. The USSR takes pride in the fact that its educational system is fairly uniform—children graduating in any republic can go on elsewhere with little disadvantage. But the Ukraine originated the system of an extra year of education for children attending school in languages other than Russian. This also enables them to learn Russian well enough to compete in entrance exams for those colleges where education is in Russian.

The Ukraine pioneered the agricultural reform in which farmers get salaries instead of depending upon co-operative income sharing.

Kiev also led the way by requiring divorcing couples to go through only one court instead of two — it does not require a court hearing at all in uncontested divorces — a procedure since adopted throughout the Soviet Union. The Ukraine also has distinctive laws on the storage and use of arms and ammunition by civilians, the operation of power installations and use of electricity, the protection of major oil and gas pipelines, in matters of inheritance, dwelling leases, notarization, legal age of marriage, guardianship, etc.[22] Clearly, it is no mere clone of Russia.

The day-to-day operation of government at the grassroots level is very much in the spirit of those pioneers of 1922. This conclusion comes not from reading propaganda sources, but professional journals read by Soviet administrators. An article on the functioning of an agricultural county government in the Ukraine describes the operation of its committees: "Things don't happen without reconciliation of differing points of view," and also of conflicting plans. One committee looked into whether the truck-mounted traveling stores were dispatched promptly into the fields and how well sale of goods to sub-units of these large agricultural entities was organized. The Committee on Culture and Education examined how evening entertainments were provided to farm workers during the planting and harvest seasons. There is mention of surprise inspections. All these activities involve unpaid members of elected local government. As in any country, there are foul-ups — for example, two or even three committees may descend on a single local factory at the same time. Sometimes, a county committee isn't large enough to look into readiness of all schools for the school year, so, it asks the committees of village soviets to help, and they do.

Soviet elections don't have the competitive aspect that Americans regard as essential. Under our system, the candidates make promises to the voters. Under theirs, the voters specify platforms, called "mandates", to the candidates which they are obligated to carry out when elected. They in turn will seek the cooperation of citizens. Suppose a road is desired between two villages which the government cannot currently provide equipment and labor for. In that case, it will ask a collective farm to loan equipment, and ask the villagers who will benefit to put in some Sundays of volunteer work.[23]

In the prerevolutionary Ukraine or, virtually anywhere in the old Russian Empire, such services were simply not offered. For example, 80 percent of school-age children in the Ukraine were not in school before the Revolution. Whatever limited beneficial functions government did perform were carried out from the top down, and involved no citizens other than landowners, clergy, and the extremely rare college-educated individual.

The next higher level is that of state (oblast) government. An article in the same professional journal concerns the state of Volhynia, a place-name anyone of Ukrainian descent will find familiar. The governor of Volhynia at the time, Pirozhko by name, wrote: "Deputies [members of the legislature] are very willing to go half-way to meet proposals emerging from the executive committee. But for all this we have a rigid rule: no — to put it in plain language — no pressure on the standing committees [of the legislature]. When their opinion does not accord with our judgments . . . it is the committee, of course, that has the final word."[24]

The governor summed up his evaluation of the legislative committees as follows: "They know how to stand up for themselves and not to be afraid to spoil relationships with somebody or other when that has to be done. When there are grounds for this, they discuss improper behavior by officials at their meetings. . . . Of course we have many unresolved problems. Not all the committees are equally effective in their work."

American-Russian Institute

Extending the Kiev subway system. Public transportation is clean, fast, and frequent; fare — 10 cents.

Material change for the better is occurring so rapidly no one can miss it. In a recent five-year period, the city of Kiev alone gained 39,000 places in child-care centers, 63 libraries, 53 summer camps for high schoolers (financed by enterprises in the city), 13 schools of music and three of art, 18 free health-maintenance clinics, 5,000 hospital beds and housing equivalent to a new city of half a million.[25]

I was in the enormous city park: in one direction, I could see the historic Monastery of the Caves and the Vydubetsky Monastery; in the other, a baroque church and an immense statue of the city's founder, Prince Vladimir, holding a cross high aloft. This is the traditional skyline, and the city planners permit nothing to go up to change it, but beneath it were new elements of the city's thousand-year history. There stands the World War II Memorial, and "Sea Scout" Young Pioneers — girls and boys together — were conducting a parade, a parade so unmilitaristic in dress and marching style that it was more like a stroll. The children were being reviewed by a bemedalled admiral who joined with them in singing a Soviet song: "May There Always Be Mama, may there always be the sun, may always be me."

I struck up a conversation with a man who was directing things through a bull-horn. He was not a volunteer, but a professional. "Our concern is the leisure time of children, youth, older comrades, and retired people. We offer entertainment, games, songs during their free time after work and during lunch hour on the job." The park is immediately adjacent to downtown office buildings and it is equally close to factories and river port facilities.

We passed through a lane devoted to the Moral Code of the Soviet Person. A small billboard shows a white, a Black, and an Asian arm in arm, all working people with strong faces. The legend in Ukrainian, reads "Brotherly solidarity with working people of all countries, and with all peoples." The next billboard shows a family; the legend, from the Moral Code, reads: "Mutual respect in the family, and concern for the upbringing of children."

Good inter-ethnic relations are promoted in the entertainment. "From the Stage of International Friendship, we propagandize friendship among the peoples of the Soviet republics." He had himself participated in the development of a sister republic, which he told me about when I got him to talk of his own life. He was only twenty-nine but, after completing his compulsory military service, he said, "I took part in pioneering the virgin soil country in

Little sister: "We help each other."

Kazakhstan, Soviet Asia. I was there for six and one-half months, but it was the most critical period. The state farms were only just being organized. There was a great deal of grain, and a great shortage of hands, so we had to work very long hours. Ours is a large country, it needs a great deal of grain. We did our best. I sat on that grain, and lay on it, and walked on it. I harvested it with my own hands. I rode to a grain elevator there in Kustanai — when the road was simply jammed with those trucks, truck upon truck, truck upon truck."

The park director's personal feeling toward agriculture, although he was city born and raised, is typical of all Soviet people, regardless of nationality.

He took us next to the amusements section of the park — the "rides," a shooting gallery, and "Our pool parlor — the largest in the city." I said that pool had been regarded as an uncultured game when I was young. He replied: "If you talk about uncultured sports, the very best game may be rendered uncultured, but if people behave themselves as they are doing right here, decently and quietly, why shouldn't they play it?"

One of the pool players gave some insight into why the nationalist dissidents have no support in the Ukrainian working class. Leaning on his cue, he asked what country I was from, about my tape recorder, how I happened to speak Russian. When Mrs. Mandel asked what kind of work he did, he chose to answer more broadly. "I am a native of Kiev, lived here all my life. I work as a trolley-bus driver. Today is my day off — I work two days on and one off." It was a full-time job, he explained, with the hours divided that way. We asked about his schooling. "Last year, I passed my high-school graduation exams as an extern [a system which allows one to take exams without attending classes] and now I have applied for admission to Kiev Polytechnical Institute" where entrance is by competitive examination. He concluded, "Well, and I'm married, have a little boy — he will enter school this year."

Simple. He was socially mobile in accordance with his own ambitions and efforts. He doubtless knew that for his grandparents, mere literacy was an achievement. Our conversation was too brief for him to express any vision beyond himself and his family, but a few days later, as we rode completely across the Ukraine by train, I got to know an 18-year-old senior in a civil engineering junior college. He came from the Ukrainian industrial heartland, the Donbass, and hoped to enter college immediately, in civil engineering. He would prefer, he said, to build residential structures, "because our people need new houses and good apartments." There was no mention of how well it might pay.

In Russia proper, in Volgograd, where the battle of Stalingrad was fought, I ran across a busload of Ukrainian teenagers on a vacation excursion, from "Kiev Region, Vasil'kovskii District,

Plesetskoe Village, the high school." This is an agricultural district. Their month-long tour had already taken them to Moscow and five cities along the Volga. I asked, "Who pays?" A young woman, a high school senior though she was only 16, answered, "We paid ourselves. We earned money in construction — a new school is being built in our village, and we worked on that." I asked her personal plans. "In the past I had many ideas about my future. But now I have one. I would like to be a teacher. So as to educate children — I would like to teach Russian literature and the Russian language." Her enunciation, pronunciation, use of grammar, and self-confidence left me with no doubt that she'd do well.

For her grandmother at that age, travel would have been simply inconceivable. And for a Ukrainian peasant girl to be a teacher in those days was unheard-of. I know a distinguished demographer from Poltava in the Ukraine, now an Academy of Sciences researcher in Moscow. When she was a high-school senior in 1956, her class took a vacation trip to Moscow. Her mother — not a peasant but manager of a small government store in a small city — was shocked when her daughter announced, upon her return that she was determined to attend Moscow University. "What does a girl need to go to college for?" And she told me that her aged grandmother still says "If your husband doesn't beat you, it means he doesn't love you."

In a Canadian feminist magazine, *Upstream*, October 1978, an article entitled "Ukrainian-Canadian Women Have Struggle Inside and Outside Own Community" quoted a speaker at a University of Ottawa conference: "Ukrainian-Canadian women must overcome ethnic discrimination outside the Ukrainian community as well as sex discrimination within it." An accompanying poem on the same theme says: "she will be plump she will multiply she will forgive."

As far as sex discrimination against women in the Ukrainian community is concerned, the Soviet Ukraine would simply be unrecognizeable to people of Ukrainian origin in North America or elsewhere. "The sad songs about women's hard lot have disappeared entirely from the modern wedding ritual."[26] One quarter of the judges in the Ukraine were female by 1975.[27] That was still ten points lower than in Russia, because the Ukrainian figure was pulled down by the data for its western portion where women had had a full generation less to take advantage of the equal opportunities in Soviet society. In the United States the percentage of female judges is only one half as high as in the Ukraine.

Women judges are no longer curiosities in the West, but female managers of large factories certainly are. I recorded one in Kiev. "I was born in 1937 in Luhanka, now called Voroshilovgrad. I am a Ukrainian, so were both of my parents — my father was a teacher, my mother an office worker. The war began, and we were evacuated.

"My father was killed in the war. After that, the family was just my mother and me. She had no trained skill, and she had to support me. I went to school, joined the Young Communist League, was active in it. I graduated from high school and applied for entry into the Academy of Agriculture here in Kiev. I failed to make it by one point, so I entered a junior college. After graduating I worked for a year. Then I returned to Kiev, and entered the College of Consumer-Goods Industries as an evening student. I worked during the day. I got married in my third year, and by the time I graduated I had two children. I managed to hold a job, have two children, and pursue my studies."

She laughed a little, in obvious embarrassment about speaking of her own achievement. I asked: "With whose help?" "The child-care center, and mama also helped when the children were very young. My husband helped a great deal. He also held a job and went to school but helped around the house. He was good in math and the exact sciences — those subjects came harder to me, so he helped with my studies.

"I came to work at this knitgoods mill in my fifth year, the last year in college. I began with a worker's job, inspecting for damages. When I graduated I was given a job as foreperson, then department head, then production manager, and now I'm the head of that mill. So my life story is very simple."

I learned the mill employed 3,800, 85 percent of them women. "Many are studying at the same time: high-school, junior college, college and we have our own evening continuation school. We manufacture knit garments: dresses, suits, for men, women and children. This year our emphasis is particularly on children's wear, because our city is working and struggling to live up to the slogan: 'The Best of Everything for the Children.'

"We put a great deal of time into social concerns, particularly me, because it is the chief's responsibility. At our mill there is no longer any problem of child-care facilities. Every child is provided for in a nursery, a kindergarten and in summer camp."*

I asked about her personal relation with the trade union. "If

---

*The young Ukrainain family of today averages only one and one-half children, but child care facilities are incomparably more numerous than in Canada or the U.S. in proportion to need.

there is some special need, we ask permission from the union to work overtime — the worker gets premium pay, of course, but really extraordinary circumstance must exist before our union will allow a woman worker to work overtime. Our trade unions are extremely protective of the workers. We sign a collective agreement every year: union and management. The workers are naturally very demanding that every point in the agreement be adhered to. It contains provisions on occupational safety and health, working conditions, and vacation and recreation matters. The manager is personally penalized if even a single point in the contract is not lived up to."

A question about ethnic discrimination against Ukrainians would meet with sheer disbelief. Such chauvinism, which can still be encountered among pre-war Russian emigres in the United States, has died out in the USSR. Outside the Ukraine, Ukrainians in the Soviet Union tend to assimilate with the other Slavs — Russians and Belorussians (President Chernenko, born in Siberia to Ukrainian peasants, considers himself Russian), and intermarriage under those circumstances is extremely common. Ukrainians maintain contact with their native culture by subscribing to Ukrainian-language magazines and attending performances by touring theater companies from the Ukraine. I attended one such in Moscow; it was obvious from the laughter at dialogue I missed that the audience was largely Ukrainian. The very theme of the play would have pleased Marusia Petryshyn, the Canadian speaker quoted above. The female lead was a forester who arrests a self-important army major and another male official she caught hunting in a closed season.

The West Ukraine shows its briefer Soviet history in other ways than a lower level of advancement of women: One day in Moscow I ran into a very young man in street clothes with shoulder-length blond hair and a beard. We had met the previous day at the monastery which is the "Vatican" of the Russian Orthodox Church — but there he had been wearing vestments. He was a priest.

We had a long talk, in privacy. I had never conversed with a clergyman in the USSR before. I was surprised to encounter so young a priest (he was 24), and I asked how a person so young had come to be a priest in a country where he would be one of the youngest people in church. He answered, without pridefulness, that profound faith is not given to everyone. But it turned out that he,

Child-care center in Kiev.

and a majority of the students then at the seminary are from the western Ukraine and western Belorussia, which has a similar history. Curious to know if he were from a class in society that had lost by the change to socialism, I asked about his parents.

"Peasants. And it's better for someone like me in the church nowadays—in the past the priesthood almost all came from the prosperous. Today, anyone like me can be a priest." And rise high, he might have added: in 1966, an ethnic Ukrainian was named Metropolitan of Kiev, for the first time in 150 years. By 1975, 13 of 16 bishops in the Ukraine were ethnic Ukrainians, and in the past decade a religious monthly, calendars, and a prayer book have been published in the Ukrainian language.[28]

I asked how he would explain the obvious decline in churchgoing. "In the old days," he answered, "going to church was the thing to do. Today, being a member of the Young Communist League is the thing to do. But we're satisfied. We believe the congregations we have today are the sincerely religious." More than half of all the Orthodox churches now open in the USSR are in the Ukraine.[29] Orthodoxy is the faith of most religious Russians and Belorussians as well as Ukrainians.

I asked him what he thought of the Soviet Government's foreign policy. His answer was most unexpected. "The Church," and it was obvious he included himself, "thinks Nikita Sergeievich [Khrushchev] is doing Christ's work." (This was when Khrushchev was in power.)

"He's an atheist," I replied, "what do you mean?" "Our Lord taught us to turn the other cheek; that is why we clergy will never take up arms, although we have always supported our country when it was attacked. But we believe Khrushchev's foreign policy is turning the other cheek."

He then asked me what I thought of the chances of disarmament. I replied that I thought there were forces opposed to it. He apparently took it for granted that I could not be referring to the Soviet Union. He paused and said, in his mild and thoughtful way, "Then perhaps your working people ought to do what ours did in 1917." Again, we were completely alone, in the open air.

If he is typical of the priesthood, there is obviously nothing in their attitude that could antagonize their flock. For he is, at the same time, a religious man, a patriot, and a believer in his country's present social system.

His attitudes were not purely a product of Soviet times. Xenia Masliuk, the art school principal, told this tale of her priest father: "There is a man still living in a village near the one where my father was stationed. This man was a Communist from long ago. He had been in jail way back under Polish rule—you know, the Communists were persecuted in capitalist times. The police came, they arrested this comrade, they beat up his children. His wife came running to my father, who went to the police and told them to release this man. He gave his own word, 'He is the most decent kind of person, the best person in the whole village. I know him from childhood. I serve that village.' And they let him go. This was in 1939, just before the war."

The attitude of Soviet Ukrainians to Ukrainians abroad was put very neatly by a writer at the Lvov Peace Committee.

"I had a conversation with a visitor from North America who didn't like lots of things here. So I said to him: 'You know what? I

Collective-farm school about 100 miles south of Kiev.

am a Communist, but my mother is religious. She had sons at the front, and she thinks it was God who spared their lives. I don't like this, but can you imagine me cussing out my mother and saying: 'She is a bad person because she is religious'? Wouldn't you call me a skunk?

"You say you love the Ukraine, your motherland. There is just one Ukraine. The Lemkos, the Boikos [ethnic sub-groups] also come from here. But you on the other side of the ocean are cussing us out because we believe in another god; that is, we think as communists. Our people thinks in a different way, has begun to look at life differently. So aren't you being the kind of son I was describing?

"The man was silent, thought a bit, and said: 'Nobody ever put it to me that way before. One must not cuss one's mother. You can't change mothers for a better or a younger or a richer one. She's the only one you have. The same thing is true of the land from which you spring. There's only one'."

Let us close with words from a Ukrainian mother —she who had been in the Air Force, who said she would live on bread and water if that would prevent war:

"I saw so many ruined villages. Children, old people, women came out of caves and ditches, from beneath the earth. God Almighty, how terrible it was to see! The Germans destroyed everything, killed everything, hung people, everyone, everywhere. I will never forget the railroad station at Kalinovka. A beautiful young woman roamed there, insane. Germans had taken her two small children and thrown them under a train.

"I was in Leningrad after the siege had just been lifted. The children couldn't walk any more. They were dying of hunger. People came and asked to take the children and care for them. But the children had to be hospitalized and brought back to health. They had no hair on their heads.

"As a mother, as a grandmother, I wish that all children, all mothers on earth, should never cry, never shed such terrible tears as our women, as our children did during the Great War for the Country. Let there always be peace on earth. Let children always be happy. They are our joy."

NOTES

1. Bohdan R. Bociurkiw, "Religion and Nationalism in the Contemporary Ukraine," in G.W. Simmonds (ed.), in *Nationalism in the USSR & Eastern Europe* (Detroit: University of Detroit, 1977), pp. 82-83.

2. V. Dobrik, "At the Center of Attention Are Questions of Ideological Struggle," *Soviet Law and Government*, XVIII, No. 4 (1980), 6.

3. *Edmonton Journal*, May 29, 1980.

4. E.P. Kiriliuk, "Shevchenko," in *Kratkaia literaturnaia entsiklopediia*, Vol. VIII (Moscow: Sovetskaia Entsiklopediia, 1975), pp. 646-653.

5. Roman Szporluk, "The Ukraine and the Ukrainians," in Zev Katz (ed.), *Handbook of Major Soviet Nationalities* (New York: Free Press, 1975), p. 24.

6. "Recollections of Delegates to the First All-Union Congress of Soviets," *Soviet Studies in History*, III, No. 2, 1974, pp. 82-84.

7. Szporluk, "The Ukraine," p. 23.

8. V.A. Holobutskii, "Pages From My Recollections," *Soviet Studies in History*, V, No. 4, 1967, pp. 15-16.

9. Szporluk, p. 22.

10. "Ukrainskaia SSR," *Bol'shaia Sovetskaia Entsiklopediia*, 3rd ed. (Moscow: Sovetskaia Entsiklopediia, 1976), Vol. XXVI, p. 551, col. 1640.

11. *Chicago Sun*, November 7, 1946.

12. *Khrushchev Remembers*, ed. and trans. Strobe Talbott (Boston: Little, Brown, 1970), p. 74.

13. Roy A. Medvedev, *Let History Judge* (New York: Knopf, 1971), p. 204.

14. Szporluk, p. 25.

15. Alexander Dallin, "German Occupation of the Soviet Union, 1941-1944," in Michael T. Florinsky (ed.), *McGraw-Hill Encyclopedia of Russia and the Soviet Union* (New York: McGraw-Hill, 1961), p. 197.

16. Mykola Stepanenko, "Ukrainian Culture in the Brezhnev-Kosygin Era," in Simmonds, *op. cit. supra* 1, p. 78.

17. R. Sullivant, *Soviet Politics and the Ukraine* (New York: Columbia University, 1962), pp. 110, 392.

18. I.S. Puchkov and G.A. Popov, "Sociodemographic Characteristics of Science Personnel [Part 2]," *Soviet Sociology*, XVI, No. 4 (1978), p. 68.

19. TsSU SSR, *Narodnoe khoziaistvo SSR v 1980 g.* (Moscow: Finansy i Statistika, 1981), p. 288.

20. I.I. Artemenko, "Archeological Research in the Ukrainian SSR," *Soviet Anthropology and Archeology*, XVIII, No. 3 (1979-1980), pp. 37-67, *passim*.

21. *Novy mir*, No. 5 (1978), p. 301.

22. John N. Hazard, "Statutory Recognition of Nationality Differences in the USSR," in Edward Allworth (ed.), *Soviet Nationality Problems* (New York: Columbia University, 1971), pp. 83-116, *passim*.

23. M. Medianets, "The District Executive Committee and the Standing Committees," *Soviet Law and Government*, XVI, No. 2 (1977), pp. 16-28.

24. N. Pirozhko, "The Standing Committees and the Regional Executive Committee," *ibid.*, pp. 3-15.

25. *Pravda*, February 16, 1979, p. 2.

26. V.T. Zinich and V.I. Naulko, "The Convergence of the Peoples of the Ukrainian SSR in Culture and Life-Style," *Soviet Sociology*, XIII, No. 1-2 (1974), p. 18.

27. P. Matveev, "Zhenshchiny-iuristy (statisticheskii material)," *Sotsialisticheskaia zakonnost'*, 1975, No. 9.

28. Bociurkiw, "Religion and Nationalism" pp. 82-83.

29. Ibid.

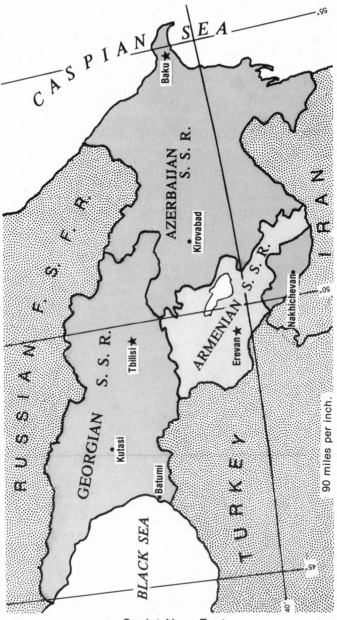

Soviet Near East
Georgia, Armenia, Azerbaijan

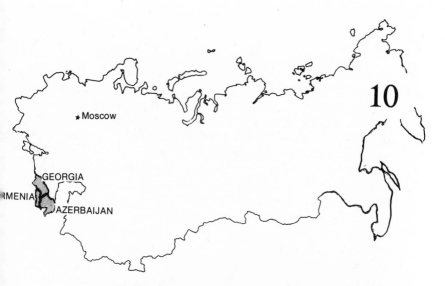

* Moscow

GEORGIA

RMENIA

AZERBAIJAN

10

The Soviet Near East:
Armenia, Azerbaijan, Georgia

There are 5,500,000 Armenians in the world. Three million live in Armenia; another million elsewhere in the USSR, and half a million are in the United States, chiefly in California; the rest are scattered all over the world. Armenia borders Turkey and Iran, Soviet Azerbaijan, which is of Moslem heritage, and Georgia, historically Christian.

Since World War II, 220,000 Armenians have returned to that country from outside the USSR, including even some from the United States.[1] For every 40 who have returned, three have left. As with Jews moving to Israel, "return" is correct only figuratively; hardly any of the immigrant Armenians were born in Soviet Armenia.

Erevan, the capital city, has a million people. My host there, Dr. Emma Karapetian, an anthropologist of the Armenian Academy of Sciences,[2] told an anecdote about a man who toured the world with an Armenian. Wherever they went—China, England, anywhere at all—the Armenian had no trouble communicating. Finally, his companion burst out, "You are so young, and you know so many languages." The Armenian responded, "Nothing of the sort. I just walk into a public place and holler in my own language: 'Hey, any Armenians here'?''

After I stopped laughing I said: "You know, that's also a standard Jewish joke," which brought another burst of sympathetic laughter. I found Armenians in every walk of life totally pro-Israel, including a collective-farm chairman. One scholar told me he knew not one Armenian who favored the Arabs in the last Arab-Israeli war.* One reason for this may be that the Armenians identify the history of the Jews with their own. The 1916 slaughter of 1,500,000 Armenians by the Turks in this century's first genocide left as indelible a memory on them as Hitler's slaughter of millions of Jews did upon that people. Unlike the Jews, who were almost totally out of Palestine for nearly 2,000 years, and had been replaced by another people that had sunk endless generations of roots there, the population of Armenia always remained Armenian in its majority[3] no matter how decimated by massacres and emigration.

The Armenians have existed as a people for 3,500 years, longer than any other ethnic group native to Soviet territory. Erevan, founded in 782 BC, is older than Rome or Athens, and Armenia was the first country to adopt Christianity, in 301 AD. (Ethiopia followed just a generation later.) Armenia's unique alphabet was devised by Bishop Mesrob Mashtotz in 396 AD, a date that marks the beginning of the flourishing of Armenian culture.

Like ancient Palestine, Armenia lay on crossroads for both trade and invasion. Historically, countries so situated have had to conquer or be conquered: Armenia was first divided up by Christian Byzantium and pagan Persia, then taken over by the Arab caliphs. In the 10th century, Armenian cavalry helped the newly-converted princes of ancient Rus hold off invaders; a century later Russians fought alongside Armenians when they sought, unsuccessfully, to hold off the Turks. Prince Vladimir of Kiev married the sister of the emperor of Byzantium, from an Armenian dynasty, and many Armenian craftsmen, artists and doctors moved with her to Russia.

In 1410, when the German Knights of the Teutonic Order sought to conquer Eastern Europe, Armenians joined Poles, Lithuanians and Russians in a great battle to stop them. Russian tsars later granted Armenians the right to free trade with Russia and invited them to participate in the construction of several towns in south Russia. In 1827 Russian forces routed the Persians (Iran)

---

*This was prior to the Israeli invasion of Lebanon, the daily aerial bombing of Beirut, and the Sabra-Shatila refugee-camp massacre.

and liberated Erevan. The tsar annexed Armenia the next year, a move all Armenian scholars since have regarded as beneficial.

The first organization favoring socialism in Armenia was organized in 1902. One of its leaders, Stepan Shahumian, was known (to his enemies) as "the Lenin of the Caucasus." Another, Simon Ter-Petrosyan, known as Kamo, was one of the most extraordinary heroes the modern world has known. For political reasons, the Kaiser's Germany wished to extradite him to tsarist Russia; Kamo feigned insanity to prevent this. To prove him sane, doctors burned him with red-hot rods, put pins under his nails, but he neither trembled nor uttered a sound. He survived to perform feats of daring for the Revolution that put James Bond to shame.

The Turkish genocide upon Armenians came during World War I. No Western country made a serious attempt to come to their assistance; it was again Russia, this time revolutionary Russia, that saved them. The Armenian Soviet Republic was established in late 1920. Textile workers from near Moscow sent looms to establish that industry; equipment for a dairy came from Rostov, the Ukraine supplied grain, Azerbaijan provided oil.

There is a monument in Erevan's main park memorializing the million-and-a-half who died in the 1916 Turkish holocaust (a tree for each!). It is designed with a deep cleft, symbolizing a division that has profound meaning to Armenians. From Erevan, Mt. Ararat—where Noah's Ark is supposed to have touched ground—looms 14,000 feet above the city. On the map it is in Turkey, but to every Armenian anywhere it is Western Armenia. (A Turkish prime minister, worrying about Soviet territorial intentions, complained to then Premier Kosygin about the fact that Ararat is the most prominent feature of the great seal of the Armenian Soviet Republic. Kosygin replied: "You have the moon on your flag. I don't believe you're planning to annex it." I asked Dr. Karapetian about her attitude toward the Turks.

She replied: "We have a history of which you are thoroughly aware. That's not something easy to forget. Understand, that's something personal that happened to so many people." I interjected —she knows I am Jewish—"In my family, fifty people." She continued: "Yes, everyone knows, and not from books. Their mothers and grandmothers told them, from life, how they murdered people, what they did to pregnant women, how they cut off the heads of

Photo by Author

"Armenia Will Rise Again." Holocaust monument in Memorial Park, Erevan.

our finest writers. All that, one cannot forget. But we cannot take an attitude to the Turk of today from that standpoint." She and her colleagues spoke of that time.

"There were Turks . . . " She completed his thought: "who hid Armenians. My mother was saved by a Turk. They wanted to kill her, and he pushed her out of the way. There were a great many such cases. Those stories have been handed down, so that the plain people—the workers, the peasants—make distinctions among them." "They lived among them. They were neighbors. They shared their bread and salt." "No nation can be condemned as such. The people know who it was that massacred the Armenians. It was those in power, the Young Turk Party. As far as the plain people are concerned, the workers and the peasants, I would say that the good relations that existed outweighed the other." "But for us, that period is a stage of history that is behind us. You understand? After that the Soviet socialist system gave us the chance to become what we are today."

That last sentence came up, in one form or another in conversation after conversation. On a bus full of Argentinian tourists, we talked with two men, relatives of a visiting family, who had returned to Armenia thirty years before. They had seen the world — one had served four years in the French Army, had been to Israel, the United States, Argentina. He said: "Thirty years ago there was nothing here. Now look at this place." He spoke with pride of Armenians who had risen to the rank of marshal and admiral in the Soviet forces in World War II, and pointed to the bust of a flyer who had twice won their highest military honor.*

Another returnee, a taxi-driver who had been educated in a German Catholic school in Lebanon and then been a seaman for twelve years told us, "The Soviet Union was nothing fifty years ago, and look at where we are now." In a crowded cafe, a collective-farm chairman and his wife shared our table. They had always lived in Armenia. "We had nothing but villages. Even this city, Erevan, our capital, was only an overgrown village with 30,000 people. Now it has a million, and we have three other cities." Three of their four children were college graduates; the fourth, a daughter, was in medical school. Before the Revolution, Armenia was 90 percent illiterate. A man shining my wife's shoes said he was a returnee. She expressed surprise that he seemed content with a shoe-shine stand; he replied, "But I feel at home here, and both of my children have graduated from college."

With that busload of Argentinian Armenians, we visited Echmiadzin, the Vatican of Armenian Christianity. Soviet Armenians, religious or not, are as proud as those abroad that they were the world's first people to adopt Christianity. Their's is probably the toughest Christian church in the world: it survived when Christianity was very much a minority religion, and it survived the challenge of

---

*Armenia provided virtually an army of volunteers in that war: five divisions organized on an ethnic basis.[4]

Islam in the form of three very different kinds of conquerors—
Persians, Turks, and the Arabs, who destroyed Armenian churches
physically. Armenian monophysite Christianity survived the Russian
Orthodox Church, which is theologically close and tried to dominate
by virtue of being the state church of a great power.

Armenian Christianity also survived the early vigorous atheism
of the Soviet regime. I was present at a service when the Archbishop of
Canterbury, on a state visit, preached to many thousands from all
over Armenia. Congregations in Russian churches, mosques, and
synagogues in the Soviet Union are largely elderly, but here the age
range and styles of dress were typical of street crowds in Erevan.
Religious music is played on the government-administered radio,
and the records of Lucine Zakarian of the Echmiadzin Cathedral
Choir sell out almost overnight.[5]

A Soviet guide said to me that 30 percent of the Armenians are
religious, which makes them third among Soviet nationalities in
retention of religious belief, after Central Asian Moslems and
Lithuanian Catholics. The other 70 percent probably share the
attitudes expressed by the collective farm chairman I sat with in
that cafe. He was a Communist, and strongly sympathetic to the
Jews and Israel, but as to religion, he said, "We're better off
without Christ, Mohammed or Jehovah."

In Erevan, the Soviet government has built, in Armenian style,
a building to house a collection of parchments assembled since the
5th century by the Armenian church. The Matenadaran (Library)
contains some 13,000 ancient Armenian manuscripts, about 2,000
in Arabic, Persian and other languages, and much else. Here a
guide translated a 15th-century document on operations under
anesthesia and suturing with silk thread, writings on music carefully
illustrated with drawings of folksingers and their instruments, and
a manuscript by Aristotle that has not survived in the original
Greek and is known only in retranslation from this Armenian copy.
It is hard not to be overcome with respect for such a people.

One feels Armenia's distinct character not only in the continuity
of its church and cultural traditions, but in the exceptional closeness of
family relations. Dr. Karapetian's colleague, the anthropologist
who had spoken of Armenia's indebtedness to the Soviet system
went on to speak of his own family.

My parents built their house in 1928. My father is no longer alive, but
my mother is. She's 75. Her appearance is still good. In winter she lives
with us. But when summer approaches, in March or April, she travels
to the old home in the country. She says: "I can't live in the city in
summer. There isn't enough air here." [By U.S. standards Erevan is

Gregorian monk at the Geghard Monastery, Echmiadzin, with photo-journalist Tom Weber. This is the oldest Christian church in the world.

extraordinarily green, with very wide streets.]

There's room for all of us, brothers and sisters, to take our vacations there. In summer, my family, that is, my wife, my daughter's family and those of my sisters travel out there, either by turns or at the same time, and that's where I spend my vacation.

I went out there three weeks ago, returned yesterday. Visited my mother there, my wife. Brought back apples.

Among us, the ties between intellectuals and the countryside are very strong. My father was a peasant. I was born in the village in 1923 and went through high school there. I graduated in 1940, and entered the university here in Erevan. I graduated from the university, and have lived here in Erevan since then. My sisters — I have three — also obtained higher educations here, married, have families, live here. All have apartments of their own.*

There is a world in that capsule autobiography. His straightforward advance from farm boy to high school and college student provided a very sharp contrast to the life of the first Armenian I had known in the Soviet Union, a man 15 years older. He had grown up in a totally different time. I was a very young student in Moscow University in 1932 — my father, an engineer, had brought us with him from the United States for a year. The leader of the Young Communist League in my class of biochemistry majors was an Armenian named Poghosian. He was the very picture of the workingman before the age of machinery, with knotted muscles all over — even, it seemed, in his jaw and forehead — and not an ounce of flesh to spare (though that was a hungry time for all). He had been a farm laborer, then an ironworker, and was enthusiastically in favor of the new system. In consequence, he had been sent to a workers' prep school. Now, under the Soviet's affirmative action program, he was studying at the country's finest university. After class each day, his Young Communists would pile into open trucks and ride to construction sites around Moscow, where they taught peasant workers to read and write. Then they'd return to their overcrowded dorms and hit the books till the wee hours — they had little background as students, and studying came hard. By the end of the term he looked like a ghost.

I approached him one day, and said: "At the rate you're going you'll be dead of tuberculosis by the time you're forty. What's the point?" With a look that said I should know what made them tick, he replied in three words I have remembered for over half a century: "We're building socialism!" To him that was no abstraction; it was the opportunity he had been given. He knew a college teaching job awaited him in Armenia upon graduation, that he would be able to train people to overcome the conditions that caused the starvation he had known. Back in Erevan, in 1926

_____
*An unwitting reflection upon the housing situation in Soviet cities until a very few years ago, particularly one that grew as Erevan did.

one-third of the students in city schools had tuberculosis.[6] "Starving Armenians" had become a catch-phrase in the English language. Churches across the United States took up collections for those on the verge of death because of the total ruin resulting from Turkish massacres, followed by World War I that raged across the land, and then the political civil war. Some aid from the United States reached the people, but it was Russia that saved Armenia.

I was reminded of my fellow-student of so long ago as I watched television in my Erevan hotel room — a room overlooking the Soviet-era central square, which is surrounded by buildings of volcanic tufa employing Armenian motifs, and has immense fountains rising and falling in time with recorded music. On the TV was an episode in a serial documentary of Armenia in Soviet times — old newsreels of the first significant industries, built there in the 1930s. Veterans of that effort — now retired working men, engineers, executives — provided a commentary, some in fluent Russian, others in Armenian. Their entire tone and manner, in ad lib recollections, was as I remembered from the '30s. They invariably spoke of "our" cement plant or "our" railroad in both present and past tense. They remembered, without heroics, shortages of supplies and food, "no water," working hard rock with picks and shovels. They reminisced about the satisfaction of getting the job done, whatever overtime it took. Their loyalty was clearly to the system and the USSR as a whole. One got no feeling of conflict between that and their pride in Armenia. Yet in Armenia, more than in any other Soviet republic, one senses a country thinking in its own terms. Perhaps that is because Armenia is the most ethnically pure of all Soviet republics. Some 90 percent of its people are Armenians, and that is the language of everyday life. Park propaganda billboards about the Five-Year Plan were in the local language only, as are inscriptions on some monuments. I have not seen that in any other Soviet republic.

One admires the Armenians for their ability to wrest a living from soil so unbelievably rocky and arid. They say: "stone is our bread" — it makes Maine look like prime farm land. But they do wrest a living; today the Armenians live well, extremely well.

Little more than one-seventh of Armenia is arable land, by far the lowest proportion in any Soviet republic — it is the smallest of them to begin with — little larger than Vermont. What is arable can produce only if irrigated, as Armenia has no rain to speak of. Fortunately, Armenia has an immense mountain lake, Sevan, which irrigates 250,000 acres — an extraordinary engineering feat

New transportation industry headquarters just outside Erevan, Armenia.

for its day. Six dams, each also producing hydropower, one below the other, were built between 1930 and 1962. But before the last went into service, it was realized that the 17 irrigation canals were drawing so much water the lake would be destroyed. So a tunnel was drilled 30 miles through hard rock to bring it the water of a river separated from it by mountains nearly 10,000 feet high. This remarkable effort, one of the world's earliest great environmental-protection projects, took only six years.

I visited a collective farm, close to the city because my time was short. Dr. Karapetian, who does field research there, served as my guide. Its chairman, who missed a meeting at the county offices for my sake — a foreign guest takes precedence over anything — was a graduate veterinarian who had lost an arm in a work accident. He called in the farm's chief engineer, also a middle-aged man, to help answer my questions. The engineer explained his job was to design and build hothouses, and the water, gas and electrical systems that now serve all the homes of the 1,500 inhabitants. (There was no sewage system yet; they apparently use septic tanks.)

The farm is run by an elective board of nine, of whom four are women— an even more revolutionary situation for Armenia than it would be in the United States. One doesn't encounter nearly 50 percent participation by women in the management of our factories in the field — nor in urban businesses for that matter. There were no female operators of field machinery on the collective farm, the chairman told me. Dr. Karapetian said women had done that work during World War II and "proved themselves" in it to their own satisfaction, but, after the war, most decided they preferred jobs more compatible with being near their young children. They also wanted to care for the family's market garden immediately adjoining the house — essentially, to remain housewives. The female board members however have skills requiring higher education: accountancy, veterinary science, etc.

The farm chairman's house had an orchard measuring about 100 by 100 feet, solidly planted with well-tended fruit trees and irrigated. The orchard alone produced an income equal to the average Soviet wage, USSR-wide. All such plots in the village looked to be the same size.

In the Soviet Union, land cannot be bought or sold, leased out or rented. Collective farm management assigns to each member market garden land. Its size is closely limited by law, yet market gardeners on farms close to cities, like the one I visited, benefit greatly by the supply-and-demand price system at the farmers' markets in town. No way has been found to control this unfair advantage over gardeners living farther out without hurting the incentive to produce for the urban population.

The farm chairman's home externally was of the same design and size as the other villagers' — this is a matter of individual choice and pocketbook — though only his slag block walls were painted. Internally, it was as good as any Soviet farm home I've been in: a living room 25 feet by 20, and high ceilings gave it a very spacious feeling. It was very well furnished with a new piano, a large all-wave radio, rugs on floor and wall, a handsome and comfortable long sofa, and an inlaid backgammon set on a side-board.

All told, I had the impression that the five people in the

household lived at a standard that it would take 25,000 1984 dollars per year to maintain in the U.S., and when I was given the actual figures per earner it worked out to that. They insisted that many other families on the farm lived approximately as well or better though the chairman earns the farm's top salary.

We had dinner at the farm chairman's house. Traditionally the Armenian family was patriarchal in the extreme, so it was a pleasant surprise to find a younger male sociologist — a guest — pulling out the extension table and putting on the tablecloth. The hospitality for five unexpected guests was lavish, as among all Soviet peoples. There were distinctly Armenian features such as a large home-made sheep's-milk cheese. This had been the traditional food of the poor, and something any family could bring out for guests, so no table is complete without it. Likewise cognac, Armenia's pride and joy, and a boiled meat. There was also shashlik (bits of meat on a skewer grilled over charcoal) and excellent stewed vegetables common throughout the Caucasus. One Russian contribution was present: vodka.

I made a comment about the wonderful *lavash* bread we were eating. Dr. Karapetian launched into a discussion of Armenian foods — particularly *aris*, a porridge made of wheat and meat — of customs in serving foods, especially at weddings, and of dishes offered primarily to men, and in the morning. I was offered cognac (Winston Churchill called the Armenians' Dvin label the world's best) and, rather than try to match anyone in the Caucasus at offering a toast, I said simply: "To Armenian hospitality." Whereupon they taught me their equivalent of "cheers" which translates as "may things be sweet."

We spoke of the Armenian traditions that remain. I learned that brides still bring dowries — "of course" — and asked whether that didn't prove a disadvantage to families with a preponderance of daughters. "No," came the reply, "because the daughter goes to live with the husband's family, which supports her in many ways." The farm engineer said: "You know our country for many years, you understand what life was like in the '30s. When I got married I had one pair of pants, homespun, and the two legs didn't match. All my wife's belongings fit into a small suitcase. You remember that in those years we young people rejected all tradition. Now we think we can do better by our children."

Dr. Karapetian said the dowry essentially helped young people get started in life. She then raised a toast to the *gerdastan*, the traditional Armenian multi-generation family under a single roof. I

Armenian wedding celebration. The goat is essential to a traditional ritual.

took that as a reaction to my implied criticism of the dowry as no one knows better than she that the *gerdastan* isn't what it used to be — sixty to eighty people under the absolute rule of a patriarch. In her own home it means five: she and her husband, her daughter, a linguist, her sociologist son-in-law, and her grandchild. (She is also her son-in-law's boss on the job. I saw them in both environments, and didn't see any signs that that produced tensions.)

Today only one family in fifty has ten members or more.[7] Dr. Karapetian told me that once, after she presented a paper in Moscow on the modern Armenian family, a female Russian scholar pulled her aside and said, "Is it really true what you said — about even scientists' grandchildren living under the same roof with them? My son is only twenty, and got married, and they insisted on moving out, even though they have no children yet!" Karapetian replied: "Even among intellectuals, in Armenia there would be universal disapproval of such children."

We visited the home of a blue-collar worker. All three grown children were still living at home, one with his wife, a young college graduate. They are all very proud of her as she is unique in that family, in that respect, but she and her husband would have to leave the city — though not Armenia — for her to find work in her specialty. The family objects to this; she is therefore a housewife. Her mother-in-law had gone through her own version of this experience. "My husband didn't let me work when the children were young." She regrets this because the work she found later in life, though it pays well, involves a full day on her feet under considerable tension. The unmarried youngest son wanted to emigrate to the U.S. Political dissent was not involved; I had the impression that the conspicuous consumption and free-wheeling nature of American life, as he pictured it, was what attracted him.

The families we met did not send their pre-school children to child-care centers, though Armenian parents usually send their children to such centers in numbers six times as high as on the eve of World War II,[8] and compared to the United States, in proportion to population, eight times as many Armenian children are in pre-school facilities. The need for such care is about the same: women are 40 percent of those working outside the home in the U.S., and 45 percent in Armenia, and are chiefly in non-farm occupations, urban and rural. That represents a very rapid increase in Armenia in one decade. While it is virtually unheard-of for female college graduates *not* to hold jobs in Soviet countries, somewhat fewer work in Armenia: there women hold 46 percent of all jobs requiring higher education; in the Russian republic of the Soviet Union, women hold 55 percent of such jobs.

Dr. Karapetian's toast was itself the sharpest kind of break with tradition. In the Caucasus the *tamada* (the Georgian word for toastmaster) was an utterly male institution. But no one seemed surprised in the slightest when she rose to speak, glass in hand. True to the duty of the *tamada*, she found something nice to say in sequence about each individual at the table—people she worked with every day, our farmer hosts, and her guest from abroad. She downed a wineglass of cognac for each of us; I sipped, for safety's sake.

On the other hand, Armenia still gives women less power over men than any other Soviet republic, even including those of Moslem tradition. Only 11 percent of Armenia's judges are women, one-third the USSR average.[9] Overall court employment indicates the immense differences among the cultures of Soviet peoples. If a court deprives a citizen of some property in a civil or criminal case, the chance that the officer charged with enforcing that order will be female is only one in 40 in Armenia; in Estonia it is nine out of ten.

Still, in professions based on skill and learning rather than power, the figures are excellent: as everywhere in the USSR, women are a majority of physicians (69 percent in Armenia); among teachers they rose in just nine years, 1966 to 1975, from 51 percent to 62 percent, which puts them well above Soviet countries with Moslem-tradition majorities.

In legislative bodies, too, Armenia shows a constantly rising ratio of women in elective office. This is also true of their degree of activity after election: at this writing the Vice-mayor of Erevan is a woman. She is in charge of education, culture, health, and social services. This participation was made possible by the enormous strides in female education, particularly in the countryside where patriarchalism had its deepest roots.

The Armenian woman used to be much younger than her husband, which reinforced her subordinate status, but this, too, has changed sharply. One study found men over 61 were six to ten years older than their wives, but in the under-30 generation, the age difference fell to between only one and five years.[10] Armenian men live three years longer than the Soviet average, and some observers speculate that this may be related to the fact that Armenian women are somewhat more house-bound than elsewhere.[11]

Today, the ethnic traditional and the universal modern co-exist in all spheres of life. In a variety evening at the Armenian Ballet, we saw classical and modern ballet, a pavanne, and a Ravel's "Bolero" danced in a manner out of a Hollywood spectacular—which won the heaviest applause from the youthful audience.* I asked Dr.

---

*When the State Pop Orchestra of Armenia visited San Francisco in 1975, a respected local critic wrote that it "is truly cross-cultural; employing American jazz techniques and style as the musical medium for Armenian folk and pop traditions.

Karapetian about the attraction to everything Western. She talked of rock music, "The rhythm of the times is more hectic than when we were young. I personally still prefer tangoes and waltzes, but if the kids like it jumpy, so what?" and jeans: "I don't find jeans attractive at all, but if young people do, that's their affair. They're functional, and all taste seems to be running in that direction, doesn't it?"

The mixture of old and new was best expressed, for me, at a performance of the Folk Song and Dance Ensemble, Armenia's version of the Moiseyev Dancers or Mexico's Ballet Folklorica. Armenian folk dances do not have the fire of their Georgian neighbors' or of the Ukrainians, but ballet training has given the peasant dances grace and delicacy without affecting their distinctively Armenian character in the slightest. The house was full, with more young people than older, and they loved it.

The most impressive performance we witnessed was an Armenian opera on a historic theme, in which the head of the church is a major hero — but for this the house was not packed. The language barrier kept me from seeing plays, (a Russian translation was not provided by earphones here) but here, too there is a tradition: Euripides' *Bacchae* was performed in Armenia in 53 BC and Evgenii Vakhtangov, the great associate of Stanislavsky, founder of "Method" acting, was an Armenian.

Armenians share with all the Soviet peoples a tremendous respect for their major cultural figures: in some ways Armenians have perhaps a special love for them. A modern museum of substantial size has been built just for the works of their finest painter, Martiros Saryan, whose life stretched from the time of the Impressionists to his death at 92 in 1972.* Up to the very end, he was still actively at work. An interesting autobiography translated into Russian, with dozens of color reproductions, was published in Moscow. (The second printing alone was 20,000 copies, at under four dollars a copy.) The sophistication of the travelled Armenians tells: I know of no other Soviet work reproducing a painting of lesbian love.[13] The fact that the publishers let that pass, in Moscow in 1971, is itself a sign of changing times. Saryan's

---

... They were indeed impressive: tight, swinging ... contemporary. ... Several of the soloists ... could move immediately into the bands of Don Ellis, Stan Kenton, Woody Herman and the like."[12]

*Another Armenian, Ivan Aivazovsky, was one of the most famous painters in 19th century Russia. Like England's Turner, he focused on seascapes, and was a marvel at picturing sunlight through breaking waves.

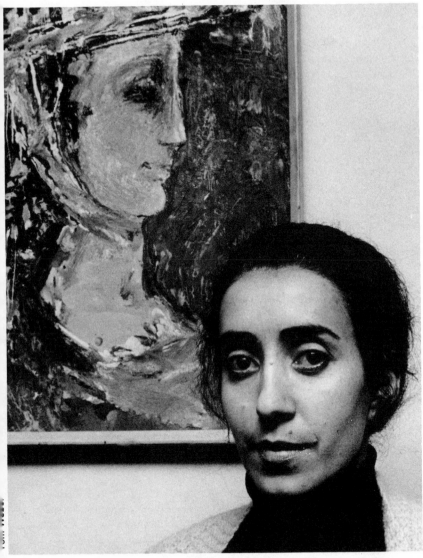

Armenian artist.

published obituary was signed individually by the entire Moscow political leadership, an honor reserved for only the most prominent personalities.

Saryan was born in Russia, not Armenia, lived in Paris and traveled widely in the Near and Middle East. His return is an example of the magnetism Armenia held for Armenians. The Soviets had only to make clear that the Armenians would be able to develop their culture unassimilated. He moved there in 1921. In the same fashion the composer, conductor, and musical organizer Spendarian—also born elsewhere in Russia and educated in Moscow—moved to Armenia permanently in 1924, and worked there the nearly half century of his remaining life. The enormous opera house, with distinctively Armenian exterior, bears his name, as does the opera and ballet company.

The most famous Armenian poet of recent times, Avetik Isahakyan, emigrated in 1911 before the Revolution, but returned permanently from Paris in 1936. The late composer, Aram Khachaturian, is famous throughout the world (everyone has heard at least his "Saber Dance," from the ballet *Gayane*).

However, Armenia is best known in the Soviet Union for its work in natural science. It has more scientists in proportion to population than any other Soviet republic, and ranks ahead of Russia and all other Soviet republics except neighboring Georgia in college students per population. Viktor Ambartsumyan is a world figure in astrophysics, and the school he founded in Armenia is the most important in the USSR in that field.

In order to improve mutual understanding with the other Soviet peoples, Armenia exchanges students with them on a planned basis. One purpose is to make possible direct translation of literature, instead of rendering a text into Russian and from it into the target language. Such exchanges have taken place with Georgia, the Baltic republics, Moldavia, the Ukraine and Belorussia.[14]

The Armenians' attitudes toward their place in the Soviet Union have been very neatly classified by Professor Mary Kilbourne Matossian:

> The Soviet citizen of Armenian birth . . . is satisfied, or unconcerned, with the status of the Armenians. The Armenian Communist . . . believes that the progress of Armenia would have been impossible without sovietization. . . . The fellow-traveling Armenian nationalist . . . believes that Armenia is better off as part of the Soviet Union. . . . He believes that nowhere else can Armenians achieve first-class citizenship without assimilation.[15]

A Stanford student who visited Armenia in 1980, as part of a U.S. debating team confronting Soviet debaters at universities, said students there told him, "Look at all the Near and Middle Eastern countries neighboring ours outside the USSR—wars and civil wars everywhere. We have had internal peace, and no one has touched our soil, for 60 years!"

Armenians defended that internal peace. In World War II, 106 won the Soviet equivalent of the U.S. Congressional Medal of Honor. Sixty Armenians became generals, admirals, even three marshals. Of the 10,000 pre-war inhabitants of the cathedral town of Echmiadzin, 1,100 did not return from the war.

Perhaps the most famous American-born Armenian, writer William Saroyan, willed that half his ashes be sent to Armenia. He had concluded that "socialist Armenia is, to my mind, one of the best practical arguments in favor of the Soviet Union."

Armenia's relations with its Caucasus neighbors, which once presented the same inter-ethnic and inter-religious hostilities that fuel the bloody conflicts now raging to its south — Israeli-Arab, Israeli-Lebanon, Iran-Iraq — is the Soviet model for the Middle East.

AZERBAIJAN

Azerbaijan borders Armenia on the East and Georgia does so on the North. Azerbaijan is Islamic; its people are very closely related to the Turks and speak a language close to Turkish. Indeed, before the Communist Revolution, Azerbaijanis were simply regarded as Turks under Rusian rule. They and Armenians slaughtered each other in what we would call race riots, in Baku, the capital of Azerbaijan, and in Tbilisi, the Georgian capital. All three nationalities were, and are, present in large numbers in both cities. Moreover, in Armenia itself under the tsar, the Armenian peasant's landlord was most often an Azerbaijani.

The prerevolutionary Communists in this region were led by the Armenian Shahumyan, the Georgian Stalin (Jugashvili was his real name), and the Azerbaijani, Meshadi Azim-bek-ogly Azizbek. By preaching that workers had mutual interests against their employers across ethnic lines, they were able to bring an end to these massacres and save a great many lives.

Ever since, the Caucasus nationalities have provided the USSR with major leaders. First there was Stalin, who ruled 1924-53, the longest term in Soviet history. (Azizbek and Shahumyan were shot by the British when they seized Baku in 1918 as part of the anti-

American-Russian Institute

Old shah's palace overlooks Museum of Azerbaijani Literature.

Communist Intervention. To this day, newlyweds in Baku go to the monument to the executed commissars to place part of their wedding bouquets and be photographed.) Then there was the Armenian Anastas Mikoyan, closest collaborator with Nikita Khrushchev, from 1956 on, in undoing the terrorist component of Stalin's rule. Mikoyan also negotiated the end of the Cuban Missile Crisis in 1962 with President Kennedy in Washington and Castro in Havana.

In Baku in the late summer of 1982, I heard extraordinary spontaneous praise for the man who was then simply the head of the Communist Party of Azerbaijan, a small country of 6,000,000. Only in Belorussia had I ever heard that kind of warmth for a local leader. When Brezhnev died suddenly a couple of months later, his successor, Andropov, amazed the West by bringing this Azerbaijani, Geidar Ali Rza ogly Ali(ev), into the Political Bureau where he was named first deputy premier of the Soviet Union. (The amazement stems from the fact that Western scholars, journalists, and politicians had apparently hypnotized themselves into believing that Moslem peoples in the USSR are treated like Blacks in the U.S.)

Aliev is entirely a product of Soviet times. Born in 1923, the son of a worker, he graduated in history from the University of Azerbaijan, itself founded after the Revolution. He is also the product of a subtle aspect of Soviet ethnic policy, for he comes from Nakhichevan, an Azerbaijani enclave surrounded by Iran on one side and once-hostile Armenia on the other. To provide maximum respect for ethnic feelings, this territory, with a population of under a quarter million, was given the status of autonomous republic under the Azerbaijan Soviet Socialist Republic, which it does not directly border.

Aliev's duties have not, however, been associated with ethnic matters. His first job under Andropov was to turn around the lagging Soviet railroad industry. At this writing, he is in charge of consumer-goods industries, which the Chernenko administration has pledged to boost. He has also been sent to Syria to discuss the future of the Near East and Soviet arms aid—definitely a man to watch.

Baku was the first world capital of the oil industry—both before and for years after the Revolution. It is still surrounded by derricks and has many petrochemical plants. It is no longer an oil town, but a cosmopolitan, very 20th century city of over a million. A magnificent waterfront boulevard has been planted along its curving bay on the crazy, wind-whipped Caspian Sea. The downtown traffic hub is at the striking Museum of Azerbaijani *Literature*, with two-story-high statues of its major writers of the past 800 years set into its outside walls, so that even those who never enter it are reminded of this people's cultural tradition on every trip downtown. The Baku museum and its statues date from Soviet times. Such respect for indigenous cultures, particularly of a Moslem people, was unimaginable before the Revolution.

I spoke with the woman director of the museum. She introduced me to my guide, a young woman of less than 30, who spoke Armenian, Russian and Azerbaijani. Her life represented a leap across centuries in the present generation.

She was born in a village in Nakhichevan; "My father and mother are illiterate. I am the eldest daughter. They did everything possible so that I could pursue my education, as with my sister and two brothers. All four of us graduated from a school with Russian as the language of instruction." I asked why her parents sent her to school in Russian rather than Azerbaijani—as illiterate people one would expect them to act on the basis of tradition. She said they knew she would know Azerbaijani in any case—it is a required second language in Russian schools in Azerbaijan—and if she ever chose to live outside Azerbaijan, Russian would naturally give her greater mobility. She uses her perfect Russian professionally to acquaint non-Azerbaijanis with the culture of her own people.

When I graduated I came here to Baku and entered the university, on my own merits: I had been a very good student with straight A's. I entered the Department of Languages and Literature, graduated, and was invited here to work. I have two daughters, one already goes to school—she is also doing very well, in the second grade. My husband is a singer. He earns a great deal more than I do, but as Khanum [her boss] said, this has no significance whatever. [The director's husband earns only half as much as she herself does.] I've chosen a topic and am working on my PhD thesis, and then I'll earn no less than he. [She burst into laughter at this].

And although this is my main work, I have for nearly six years conducted a magazine of the arts on TV. I've met very interesting people: actors, architects, painters. My broadcasts are about their lives, their creative work. My second daughter was born not long ago, and so I had to drop television temporarily, but I'll start it again soon. So that's my life.

She explained that she had stayed home with her baby, at full pay, for six months, then put the baby in a day nursery where she gets four meals and excellent care. "If the baby gets sick, we get sick leave." I asked, "That means you, not the father?" "No, sometimes me, sometimes her father, however it suits us. Not only we, but if a grandmother will care for the child, she will go on receiving pay while she does that."

I am reminded of an eyewitness report of long ago by a writer I knew, Fannina Halle. In her study, *Women in the Soviet East*, based on a visit in 1935, she wrote of Armenians and Azerbaijani:

. . . even among the Armenians . . . there are still cases where the older women—mothers or wives—do not share in the meals, but only wait on their menfolk as they sit at table, and withdraw repeatedly in the pauses to stand silently in a corner, awaiting further orders, with a kerchief held respectfully before their mouths. . . . The daughters-in-law may on no account venture to address their father-in-law. . . . The mother-in-law . . . makes their lives a real hell.

But the position of the women among the Islamic peoples of the Caucasus . . . especially among the Turks of Azerbaijan, was much worse than among the Christian Armenians. . . . They told me their own sad life stores, too, which almost always began with their being sold to an old man at the age of ten or twelve, whom they served as "third" or "fourth" pleasure. . . . One of these women told me how, after the death of her father and elder sister, her only protectors, she was made to marry her brother-in-law of fifty-four, she herself being twelve. She had resolved to drench herself with paraffin and burn herself to death—a form of suicide formerly very common among the women of Azerbaijan, the land of petroleum—but after all she stayed

Tom Weber

Imaddedin Nesimi, founder of philosophical poetry in the Azerbaijani language, with contemporary writer.

with the man and bore him three children. . . . Another woman told how at the age of thirteen she had married a man of fifty-five, and she added: "And if it had been the devil himself who wanted to shut the door behind him in the night, we could have done nothing."

Ms. Halle heard these stories at a center for which there is no longer need: the Cultural Palace of Emancipated Turkish Womanhood. She was most moved by a speech by another who had been married off at thirteen, in 1910. After being widowed with four children this woman became the first female petroleum engineer in Azerbaijan: " 'People used lightly to believe in miracles;' Rahimova almost shouted, 'if I had said in those days that I should become an engineer, they would have dragged me to an asylum. But today—look at me! —the miracle has been performed'."[16]

Azerbaijani culture is preserved and enriched in forms far more popular than a museum of the history of literature. In the city's industrial Shahumyan Borough—named for the Armenian leader —I visited a community center, truly a Palace of Culture, as it is called. Here I saw rehearsals of native drum, dance, and choral groups of children and adults preparing to leave for Moscow to perform at the special session of congress adopting the new Soviet Constitution. The drumming had an intricacy of rhythms and patterns that would win applause anywhere. The center is operated by the Oil, Chemical, and Gas Workers Union; the government-owned oil refining and petrochemical industry pays its bills.

The center has an Azerbaijan theater, an Azerbaijan folk instrument ensemble, and an Azerbaijan dance troupe as well as a Russian theater and folk-dance troupe, and a ballet studio with 250 children. I interviewed the center's director, Tofik, son of Mohammed, grandson of Husein:

> We serve not only the oil workers but the entire population of Shahumy-an Borough regardless of their fields of employment. Here you'll find people who manufacture machinery, construction workers, teachers, shipbuilders and maintenance workers, every stratum of the population.
>
> Our Palace of Culture has over twenty amateur performing groups, a system of extension courses, and the only People's Conservatory of Music in the USSR.* Instruction is free. Faculty and senior students at the Baku Conservatory teach here without pay. We have about 250 instructors in all, providing esthetic education to the workers. There are six departments in the conservatory, teaching composition, choral conducting, vocal, folk instruments, and so forth.
>
> The course is of three years' duration. We accept only manual workers and upon graduation, give them certificates that qualify them for jobs working with amateur arts groups. They have the right to teach in their respective fields.
>
> Further, we provide musical education to the children of petroleum industry workers, both blue-collar and white-collar. The course of instruction is seven years, and follows the curriculum of the music schools in the regular educational system. The teaching is in the

---

*This means it is entitled to grant a professional diploma, although not part of the formal governmental system of musical schooling.

Russian and the Azerbaijan languages. The teachers for Azerbaijan-language groups are Azerbaijanis who have graduated from the conservatory. They also know Russian well, and use that language to instruct those children who don't understand Azerbaijani. [About a quarter of the republic's six million people are not Azerbaijani, including about half a million each of Russians and Armenians.][17]

Again I was reminded of Fannina Halle's half-century old description of Baku. Institutions of this kind, since widely copied in Cuba, China, and all Communist-governed countries, were then in their infancy. An Armenian composer, the musical adviser to that Cultural Palace of Emancipated Turkish Womanhood, rose at the end of its celebration of the fifteenth year of the Azerbaijan Republic and said:

I have lived in Azerbaijan for many years, but formerly I never made the acquaintance of Turks [Azerbaijanis] and took care to avoid them. But what a difference in the last fifteen years! The barrier that separated us all has fallen once and for all. Nowadays the Turkish children smile at me with as much friendliness as the Armenian children, women are sitting here side by side with men, and may this Palace of Culture not only come to be the gateway to culture for the whole East, but attract the attention of Western Europe.[18]

Azerbaijan and Armenia were subsequently able to provide educated personnel, particularly female, to the easterly Turkic-language Islamic-heritage republics before the latter were able to do so themselves. These republics stretch from the opposite, eastern shore of the Caspian Sea to the Chinese border.

At a meeting with leading Azerbaijani writers in 1982, I mentioned Halle's account. A man said: "We have women in the cabinet and as heads of institutes. The Minister of Commerce is a woman; so is the head of the trade unions in this republic and the Minister of Foreign Affairs. The president of the medical school is a woman; the president of the College of Foreign Languages is a woman; the Minister of Education is a woman. The manager of a large clothing factory is a woman. You understand?" The female head of drama and literature broadcasting for the Azerbaijan TV and radio system, Murat-Khan(ova), added: "There are heads of county committees of the Communist Party who are women." Another man: "The chair of the State Planning Commission is a woman." This is the top position in economic planning. "Of 63 members of the Supreme Soviet of Azerbaijan, 22 or 23 are women." There are clearly more women in positions of prominence now than when I wrote my book, *Soviet Women*, in the 1970s.

At the TV-and-radio offices in Baku, I got some idea of the role of the mass media. One regular program deals solely with listener mail, and the broadcasting system sends out reporters to investigate complaints. "Recently the program criticized Khanlar County for its bad roads," one broadcaster told me "The local officials complained about what we had done, but the Central Committee of the Communist Party of Azerbaijan supported us. We've had plenty of cases like that: fierce arguments develop. Nobody likes to be on the receiving end." Murat-Khan interjected: "When such letters of complaint come in, we forward them to the responsible local authorities, and ask them: 'Explain this. What's it all about?' If we get no response, we have a special line of communication through which we can inquire: 'Why are you keeping silent'?" She was referring to the special role of the Communist Party as a way to build a fire beneath those who fail to do what they are supposed to.

"On the other hand, we get mail telling us how we have helped people. And I can tell you that that program of ours is very popular. Sometimes I'll visit places, and the people will tell me: 'Look, a bridge is being built here.' Or in some other place a school or in a third, a road. You know, we sit here in the studios, and to us these are only pieces of paper that pass through our hands, but to the people out there these are the concrete results of the criticisms we have broadcast."

Some of our most instructive experiences in the Soviet Union came because weekends are taken very seriously there. Formal interviews cannot be arranged then, so our local hosts would invite us to take part in their personal plans. In Azerbaijan, Murat-Khan's brother-in-law was being married; would we come to the wedding? Of course.

Each side has its own wedding party, on consecutive days, with both sides invited. The one we attended — with 300 other guests — was held in a restaurant. The restaurant provided the main dish, pilaf, but everything else — of which there was no end — was prepared by family and friends. There was more than enough alcohol, despite the Moslem heritage, though no one got beyond the stage of a happy high. The women were particularly well, and expensively, dressed. As the groom was a musician, the large dance band was made up of his friends. Although the music played was exclusively Azerbaijani, there were many Slavic faces. Everyone was clearly at home with the culture.

The announcement that two American guests were present drew a hearty round of welcoming applause, and another round followed when they discovered I like to dance, and had picked up their hand gestures. There was a ritual aspect to the dancing: tables were arranged to form an aisle leading to the head table, where bride and groom sat, and dancers would move up to the young couple, bow a greeting, and dance back. Custom calls for the pair to remain seated; when they do dance, that is the signal for the party to break up. We were struck by the fact that all the serving and removal of dishes was done by male members of the host clan, including young boys.

Halle had written of how relationships among children of different nationalities had changed; I had the opportunity — years later — to see a classroom-full of ethnically mixed kids who were totally at ease with each other.

On this visit, I was accompanied by Ilya Kamenkovich, a Jewish journalist in Baku. We correspond several times a year (he got my address out of a Soviet paper to which I'd written), so I looked him up. He is semi-retired, and was able to take me to several places I said I'd like to see, including this school. We were able to go without advance notice as he is often asked to speak there (and at a nearby children's "palace" — worthy of the name) on the horrors of the Nazi concentration camps and mass extermination in World War II.

Kamenkovich himself has written two small books on this topic. One is *The Night of the Crying Children*.[19] The front cover photograph shows Nazi soldiers holding their guns on a ghetto child and his mother, both with their hands in the air. The back cover is also a photograph, of Vietnamese children fleeing their homes. One of the stories is taken from a wartime newspaper report, tells of Musia Pinkenson, a child in a Ukrainian city. When the Nazis took him and others out to be shot, he had a violin in his hands; his last act was to play the "Internationale." A monument was erected to him in his home town in the 1980s; in Baku, Kamenkovich organized a candle-light parade.

This first book was published in Baku, in a printing of 40,000 copies. An enlarged edition was published in 1974. This time 100,000 copies were printed, entitled *To Live is Forbidden*.[20] It includes stories of children of all nationalities victimized by the

Photo by Author

Kids built these telescopes in children's recreation center, Baku, Azerbaijan.

Nazis, specifically including Jews like Musia Pinkenson. (During World War II, Azerbaijan provided three ethnic volunteer divisions, over and above its quota of draftees).[21]

I also looked up a botanist, a one-time exchange scholar at the University of California in Berkeley, who lives in Baku. He is Azerbaijani on his father's side, Estonian on his mother's. We spent the evening together with his best friends—one, a school principal, is Jewish; the other, a heart surgeon, is a Russian with a Jewish wife. This information came up only because I asked; they are all simply friends. The school principal's and botanist's wives were both Azerbaijani. Two of the women teach, one of them in medical school.

We went to dinner in what had been a 14th-century caravanserai, a sort of "motel" for camel caravans. Each room is now a private dining room for small parties. The food was Middle Eastern; a band played Azerbaijan music in the central courtyard, and a woman guest did something mildly similar to an Egyptian belly-dance.

Later, we visited two of our hosts' homes. Unlike Moscow's rather cramped housing, both had very large living rooms and a spacious master bedroom—four rooms in all—one more than is usual in Moscow. We thought perhaps these were co-ops, the Soviet equivalent of condominiums, but they were the usual government project housing. The surgeon showed me his rent receipt: *six* rubles a month. The family income, with two incomes and his father-in-law's pension (he lives with them) is 700 rubles. They have a good car, the Volga, fine furniture, a baby grand piano, a Japanese tape deck with stereo speakers, and a collection of antique metal fixtures. The surgeon does most of the work in and for the house, except that his wife cooks. They have two children.

The school principal understands Yiddish, but speaks it poorly. His ethnic origin was, to him, simply a biographical fact, something he neither stressed nor underplayed. (Very like myself, except when I'm writing a book in which this is an issue!) The friends were very proud of each other's achievements. They told me the principal had previously been superintendent of schools for a Baku borough with 18 schools, but quit because he felt he had lost contact with children. As a principal, he continues to teach, though he is responsible for a school of a thousand with a teaching and support staff of a hundred. His father had been killed in World War II, his mother had also served at the front. A grandmother had raised him. He could retire in four more years, at 42, thanks to 20 years of teaching, but plans to continue, and will be able to draw his pension as well. He had converted a small bedroom into a study for himself; their one young child still shares their bedroom. When I took him up on a remark that struck me as male chauvinist, one of the women said: "He does 50 percent of the work in the house." His wife, however, said: "25 percent."

The principal and his wife had just bought a new and better TV. His mother had objected: "Why are you so interested in things?" He replied: "Why not, if I can afford it?" That couple also has a car. Their joint income is only 15 percent above the USSR-wide average.

The three couples spend their vacations, which are long, together. When one said they enjoyed their "personal freedom" I asked what they meant by that phrase. They said they were doing with their lives what they wished, but felt themselves useful citizens.

Our host on that visit to Azerbaijan was Professor Addin Shakir-zadeh. This chunky, gray, and kindly man is a sociologist prominent enough to merit mention in the *Large Soviet Encyclopedia*. He said something I'd heard in every republic: "The intelligentsia are, in their majority, the children of former peasants, former workers." I asked him about his own history.

"I'm also from the village. I am just about as old as the Revolution. I was born in 1920, went to school in my village. Until I was eighteen, I didn't know a single word of Russian. In 1938 I came here and entered the university* as a history major." He was one of four brothers and sisters, all of whom have college educations. "In that international environment, I learned to speak Russian. Here, too, through the Young Communist League, I graduated from a flying school. The war came, and I served in the army, as was our duty to our country. I was in the Tank Army of Marshal Rybalko, which got to Berlin and Prague.

"After the war I entered graduate study. I had graduated in history but now turned to philosophy. My dissertation was on ancient philosophy: Epicurus. I'm sorry I don't have a copy of my book to give you; it sold out. [He smiled with pleasure.] It was published in Moscow, as part of a series, 'Thinkers of the Past'."

His was no ordinary dissertation. On the day he defended it, USSR-wide radio did a nationwide broadcast about it, an exceptional honor. I learned elsewhere that the Institute of Law and Philosophy of the Azerbaijan Academy of Sciences is regarded as the leading center for Greek philosophy in the USSR, ahead of Moscow and Leningrad. "Subsequently," he went on, "I worked in the sphere of philosophy, taught philosophy in the university here. I've been teaching since 1948. I've also worked in the Academy of Sciences of Azerbaijan all this time. But now I've retrained myself for sociology, study our way of life, the mode of life of the workers, the peasants, the professionals: the very things you have seen, how all this came about. We built all this from scratch. These are our achievements, which we are researching, people's moods. Many people don't know what private property *is*." By "private" he meant money-making property: capital in any form. Use-property—a home, car, furnishings—is called "personal," and belongs to its owner essentially as with us.

The creative writer is the person of highest standing among all Soviet peoples, but the Eastern peoples carry this to extraordinary lengths. When the late poet laureate of Armenia would go for a drive, no one would pass him on the road, as that would have been disrespectful. (Everyone knew his license number.) So it seems appropriate to close this section on Azerbaijan with the life and views of a writer:

---

*Founded after the Revolution, as the first higher educational institution in Azerbaijan, it is now one of twelve, in a country of six million people.

I am Jabir Novruz, poet. As you have heard, I am one of the [executive] secretaries of the Writers' Union of Azerbaijan. I was born in 1933 into a very ordinary Azerbaijani family, a peasant family, mountaineers. I come from the same area as Jabarly, our very prominent writer. My family was totally illiterate — my father could not even sign his name. I recall from childhood when a document was brought to us for him to sign, he pressed his finger onto an ink-pad, and signed by fingerprint. I lost my father and a stepfather. My mother raised me; she is now 85.

I graduated from the rural primary school in my village, and came here to Baku to get an education. I first wrote verses back in the village, when I didn't even know what poetry was, what a poet is. But even back in the village they referred to me as the poet. At that time, I had no idea of what horribly hard work writing poetry is, hellish work.

When I came here, I learned that the Writers' Union of Azerbaijan was in this building, and that there was such as thing as Young Poets' Day. So I came here, upstairs, where we have our auditorium. Today I'm in charge of that activity. Those prominent writers invited me in, asked me who I was, from what kind of family, and they recommended me for studies in Moscow. There I studied at the Gorky Institute of Literature.

I graduated in 1957, returned to Baku, to my own homeland, and worked for a long time on the newspaper *Vechernii Baku* (Evening Baku). It appears in both Russian and Azerbaijan editions. Then I headed the Poetry Section of the monthly magazine, *Azerbaijan*, for three or four years. But then a magazine for young writers was founded, in 1967. I was invited to be the editor. So, I'm its founder.

I have also translated many Russian poets into the Azerbaijani language, also Soviet poets who wrote in other languages. My translations of the poetry of Robert Rozhdestvenskii, my friend and a good Russian poet, [and a Jew], have appeared as a book of its own. This year a two-volume collection of my poetry will appear. It is now at the publisher's.

Last September I was in America: Washington, Pittsburgh, Cleveland, Minneapolis, Chicago, New York. We were at colleges and universities. Not only they don't know the writers of the outside world, they don't even know their own. I would pose a question about Shakespeare, and it turned out that they didn't know Shakespeare's works. They were astounded when I told them that we're issuing a 100-volume set of the world's literature here in the USSR in an enormous printing. To us literature is a divine gift to humanity, but there were those who simply didn't know what a book is, for all practical purposes. To tell you the truth, I didn't care for that at all.

I tried to find out which Russian writers they know about: the great ones, the geniuses. Well, they have some knowledge of Dostoyevsky. Their lack of knowledge is simply scandalous. That really amazed me.

Another thing that astounded me is the young people of America. I'm speaking of a large proportion of them, not all. They don't have any ideals. Every time we met with them, they posed the same old question: sex. What kind of sexual freedom do you have, they asked? They said they have sexual freedom, and asked: what's the situation regarding the problem of sexuality in the Soviet Union? I said that no such problem exists. With us, people have a deep respect for each other. Young people fall in love with each other. So what kind of problem is there? When they talk about sexual freedom, they seem to mean freedom from morality. These little girls and boys banging this same question at me all the time. To be honest with you, I found it awful.

I had high expectations: so developed a country. But the moral, the ethical side of things! In that respect, I was very dissatisfied with that country. I really was dismayed by America.

Novruz does not work in an ivory tower. Among other things, he writes song lyrics, which are very popular with radio audiences.

Photo by Author

Home air conditioner plant in Azerbaijan. Men and women do identical jobs on this automated line. Note small plant at the left: it gives early warning of excessive air pollution (like canaries in mines).

SPECTACULAR GEORGIA

The third country of the Caucasus is Georgia. Ethnic Georgians are 3,500,000 of the 5,000,000 living there.

The Georgians are spectacular. They must be the world's only people among whom male toe-dancing is a folk art. It's done in narrow-waisted tunics with cartridge-holders across the chest and a dagger at the waist. George Balanchine, late choreographer and director of the New York City Ballet, was Georgian (real name, Balanchivadze). The men used to regard themselves as God's gift to women — I didn't get that feeling on my 1979 visit, although I had 20 years earlier. Soviet women of other nationalities do seem to find them. attractive, but say they'd "rather die" than marry a Georgian.

Georgia itself is spectacular. The northern border has 16,000-foot mountains and permanent glaciers. Only 85 miles away, there is what was actually the land of the golden fleece, the lush subtropical Black Sea coast. (In the days of Jason's ancient Greek adventurers, placer gold was trapped by the lanolin in sheepskins.) If you crave driving to make your hair stand on end, try the Georgian Military Highway (which is open to foreigners) across the Caucasus. The Georgians have nearly a French interest in food — they are the only Soviet people to have built a movie, a very lively musical comedy, around their cuisine, and hold inter-town contests over whose food is best. Their fine feature film about a 20th century Georgian painter, *Pirosmani*, has become something of a cult film on our college and art film circuit.

Georgian drinking is spectacular. They do it in their own excellent wines. (An empty 20-liter basketry-enclosed jug stands on my patio, once full of Kinzmarauli, Stalin's favorite, given me at the winery and simply the finest I have ever tasted.) Fortunately, they no longer require the guest of honor to down a ram's horn at a time, though that was the practice until very recently. But I have been reduced to a very undesirable state by a lonely Georgian graduate student in Moscow. He had said to me, after 15 minutes acquaintance, "I feel to you as toward my father," then proceeded to order liter after liter. Who could resist such flattery, from a member of a nationality among whom the feeling toward a father is one of reverence? Georgian toasts are spectacular for length, language, and meaning.

Finally, Georgian national pride has been spectacular. When

Khrushchev denounced Stalin's mass murders in 1956, young Georgians paraded in protest and were shot down en masse (at the orders of the local national-police commander, not Khrushchev). In the quarter of a century since—the years of Watts, Detroit, Newark, Miami—nothing of the sort has been reported from the USSR by any sources whatever. Use of guns by Soviet police is regulated as tightly as in England, and is as rare.

A protest parade in Georgia in 1978 not only went physically untouched, with no arrests, but actually won a change in that republic's constitution.[22] The draft of a new constitution specified only "the opportunity to use the native language" as well as "the language of other peoples of the USSR." After a protest parade by several hundred Georgians, the government restored the Georgian language as the sole official one. (The issue was not Georgian versus Russian but another local language, Abkhazian.) Because of unusual economic and political conditions in Georgia, it is difficult to say whether the underlying motivation for the demonstration actually was language.

The Communist Party there is headed by a Georgian, of course, Eduard Shevardnadze. He is greatly admired by my most liberal friends in Moscow. Since 1972, the Party in Georgia has been acting to clean up large-scale corruption. It was the first to reveal to the public that a Minister (of Commerce) had been fired for permitting private capitalism, which is illegal. A Soviet law journal praised this practice of leveling with the people about the reasons for dismissing top officials. In 1976, Georgian TV reported fires and bombings in government buildings. An American correspondent in Tbilisi, the capital, wrote, "the theory that appears most plausible to a cross-section of Georgians—separatists as well as officials—is that these are expressions of protest by private entrepreneurs whose illegal, large-scale profiteering has been squeezed and hurt by government pressure.[23]

Corruption is not uniquely Georgian, but it is more pervasive in the Caucasus and Soviet Asia because of ancient traditions that you got from officials only what you directly paid them for. Russia also had this heritage, but to a lesser degree.

Despite the reference to separatists, Western academic studies find little evidence that they are at all significant, "Samizdat"* documents revealing nationalist tendencies . . . have not surfaced, if they are circulated at all."[24] There is not even a listing for

---

*"Samizdat" is clandestine publishing of materials the government regards as harmful to the society.

Georgia under "nationality dissent" in Rudolf Tokes' *Dissent in the USSR.*[25] The leading authority on Georgia, Professor David Lang of the University of London, explains why:

> If we compare the position of Georgia and adjoining Soviet republics with that of Turkey and Persia, the . . . remarkable improvements in the health and general standard of living . . . look even more striking. . . . Employment of women in qualified work (is) an extremely common phenomenon in Georgia. Industrial workers and peasants are by and large better off than in most places in European Russia. The sharp contrast between the dynamic economic and industrial system and the excellent cultural facilities of Georgia, on the one hand, and, on the other, the chronic instability of some modern countries of the Middle East, or the deplorable backwardness and stagnation of others, leaves little room for denying the positive side of Russia's impact on Georgia. . . . Georgia is at present well insured against drifting back into the vicious circle of ignorance, poverty, and disease, and is able to stand on her own feet economically and industrially in this highly competitive modern age.[26]

That is an understatement. Georgia has produced leading scientists, such as Uznadze, the major Soviet investigator of the unconscious.[27] It is the only Soviet republic with a cabinet department of science, and is looked upon as a model in that respect.[28]

Improvements in inter-ethnic relationships in Georgia have been striking. Twenty-five years ago I found unpleasant attitudes still there. At the Tbilisi farmers' market, in 1959, I got into conversation with a distinguished-looking man who turned out to be a prominent and well-liked surgeon. I told him I had been surprised the previous day, when the middle-aged Armenian driver of the funicular which rises to a spectacular viewpoint above the city pointed out one prominent older building after another—specifying that all had been put up by people whose names ended in "ian,"—prerevolutionary Armenian millionaires. The surgeon snarled: "When the soccer team from Erevan comes here to Tbilisi to play ours, the Armenians come along by the thousands. Know why?" "Why?" "To get a square meal, that's why!"

Today the Armenians are right up there with the Georgians as the best-fed people in the Soviet Union, but in prerevolutionary times Armenian commercial skills had given them dominance in Tbilisi, a dominance the then agricultural Georgians bitterly resented. After the Revolution, hostility between Georgia, Armenia, and Azerbaijan was so extreme that Moscow imposed a Trans-Caucasian Federation so it could mediate among the three.

Rural bookstore in Georgia.

In those years Stalin dictated the destinies of the USSR as a whole. It is universally agreed that he was not a Georgian nationalist. (USSR-wide, Georgians are outnumbered by Russians 50 to one. They had become part of the Russian Empire only a century before the Revolution, and Georgian and Russian are totally unrelated languages.) His executions during the 1930s took a larger percentage of Georgians than perhaps any other nationalilty. That is no proof that his paranoid fears of wide-scale Georgian separatist nationalism were justified. In World War II, the eight volunteer divisions raised in

Georgia were far more, in numbers and proportion to the population, than in any other non-Slavic republic of the USSR.[29] But there were nationalist Georgians among his closest associates, including the murderous head of the secret police, Beria.

Beria objected to the building of a railroad line connecting Armenia directly northward to Azerbaijan, bypassing Georgia, contending that it would harm Georgia's interests.[30] Armenia obtained a direct rail connection eastward to Baku and the Caspian Sea only because USSR defense interests made this necessary. The railroad parallels the Iranian border. The southern half of the north-south line is nearing completion in 1984.

Against this background, it is impressive to read the findings of a very careful study of inter-ethnic relations among workers in a major industrial plant in Tbilisi. Its workers were of eleven nationalities, utterly different as to languages and background. Half were Georgian, a quarter Russian, a tenth Armenian, and so forth. The workers were asked to give the names of their personal friends without being told why. It turned out that seven out of every ten workers had personal friendships outside their own nationality, and over half visit back and forth in the homes of friends of other nationalities — which is especially significant, as in the Caucasus the home is a very private place. (Nationality was determined from the plant's personnel records.)[31]

The situation was equally positive at the management level. There were only two Assyrians working at the enterprise, nevertheless, one headed the largest and most important department. (The Assyrians had been the shoe-shine "boys" of Russia forty years ago.)* His assistants were Georgians, one Russian and a Ukrainian, although Russians were a plurality in that department. The personnel department was headed by a Ukrainian woman, with a staff consisting of Georgians and a Russian; the accounting department was headed by a Georgian, with a Russian woman assistant, and a Russian and Georgian staff. The authors contrasted this with the prerevolutionary situation, when people from outside the Caucasus held 106 of the 123 top jobs in the Trans-Caucasian Railroad. They also cited a standard American work,[32] reporting on a major New England firm where 24 of 26 top management people were WASP, while Irish Catholics were 19 of 22 bottom level managers.

The overall situation in the Caucasus is most neatly summarized by

---

*Numbering 1,000,000 in Iran and the Near East, there are only 25,000 in the USSR, virtually all in Georgia, where they are 1 in 200 of the total population.

a recent American visitor, who wrote: "Georgian and Armenian nationalism . . . is neither anti-Russian nor anti-Soviet. Rather, it is pro-Georgian and pro-Armenian."[33]

In some respects, the uncorrected human eye and ear are entirely too sensitive as instruments, and tend to give exaggerated impressions. The eye-ear impression of the different Soviet countries is one of great diversity. But this is a static view. Looked at historically, asking "how different are they today relative to the past?" one notes a striking trend towards convergence. This is strongly borne out by a study in Georgia directed by Iu V. Arutunian, an ethno-sociologist highly respected in the West.[34] A team of Georgian scholars surveyed ethnic Georgians only, employed at a factory, a collective farm, and two research institutes (one in the social and one in the exact sciences), to get groups with social psychologies as different as possible. They found that loyalty to things distinctly Georgian varied tremendously depending on the aspect of life examined and the group surveyed: No one, not even on the farm, preferred traditional clothing or housing; all wanted the convenient, the modern and the attractive by today's standards. But when it came to food, all preferred Georgian!

The study also found that religious belief declined very sharply with rise in educational level. Very few professionals or para-professionals have their children baptized, and the highly educated rarely celebrate Easter or other holiest days, while at least half the workers and farmers do celebrate them. Yet that itself did not prove to be a measure of whether or not they believe in God. Pleasing the grandparents, or simply the desire for a memorable ceremony, are major factors. Next to food, the desire to retain the ethnic is strongest in music and dance. Among the educated, however, only a bare majority favor the stupendous Georgian folk dances — nearly half are fans of classical ballet. (It has generally been found that assimilation to the arts of other peoples proceeds via professional forms of culture.) Overall, an attractive conclusion emerges from this study: love for one's native culture remains, affection for the most sophisticated forms of other's cultures is super-added.

Anthropologists call all this "culture change," but survey findings don't begin to provide a notion of how people have been transformed. Khevsurs are Georgians in exactly the same sense as dwellers in Appalachia are Americans. They regard themselves as Georgians, and everyone else takes that for granted. But here is Fannina Halle's description of some Khevsurs on the trans-Caucasus road in

Georgian dancers.

1935, well into Soviet times:

"But there are mounted figures, too, that seem to belong to the Middle Ages, in gay robes with embroidered crosses. They wear helmets and chain armor, armplates and breastplates of steel, shield and sword, and lance as well. What people are these? Khevsurs. . . . Nowadays more and more Khevsurs are descending from their hitherto barely accessible *auls* . . . down into the valleys.

The women who used, as I have said, to bring their children into the world in a *samrevlo*, a kind of dog kennel, outside all human habitation, alone, and lying on the icy ground, now go more and more to maternity institutions and hospitals, and learn the use of soap."[35]

In 1979 I interviewed a Khevsur Georgian in Tbilisi who was already ten years old when that was written. (Anthropologists have a bad habit of accepting the idealized recollections of people who adapted themselves to inhuman customs.) This man's parents had been forced to flee their village, penniless, in the mid-1920s. Their crime? They had fallen in love with each other, and wished to marry, but among the Khevsurs it was forbidden to marry a person from one's own village. However, this couple, free-thinking enough to violate iron-clad tradition, both applied for, and were accepted in a Workers' Faculty, an affirmative-action prep-school of those years. (Most of my fellow-students at Moscow University in 1932 came from such schools.) The father went on to become a primary-school teacher, for which one then needed only high-school education plus teacher-training courses. And when his son, Irakli Ochiauri, displayed extraordinary artistic talent, he gained admission to Moscow's Academy of Arts.

When I graduated from the Academy, I set out to conquer the world. With all my naivete and ignorance of life, I thought that in Moscow it would be easy to find my place because I knew of only nine or ten sculptors in Moscow, those of whom one reads in newspapers, magazines, and whose printed reproductions one saw. But I discovered that that wasn't exactly the case — there were dozens. And so I suffered my first disillusionment. In Moscow I was one among many artists just getting started, but I stuck it out there for a year, I did sculpting for the Agricultural Exhibition, but finally left for Tbilisi.

I was virtually penniless, because I spent the travel money given me on a German illustrated volume of Michelangelo which I couldn't resist. So I made it back to Tbilisi with great difficulty. I entered the School of Applied Arts, and also took a job.

I had graduated in Moscow in 1951, and submitted seven works for A Georgian republic-wide exhibition set for 1953. All seven were rejected by the judges out of hand. I didn't understand why — I thought it was simply because they represented the older generation, and refused to recognize the merits of youth. Now, of course, I understand perfectly well that those works were weak, student-type things, and the decision was correct.

I didn't lose heart, of course, but went to a studio some friends of mine had, and began to sculpt a portrait, and at the same time I did a small piece of chasing.* I didn't even know that it was chasing. I thought it was a bas-relief done with a particular technique. Both were accepted — the portrait won me admission to the Union of Artists of the USSR. It also got me a job teaching drawing and sculpture in the Architecture Department of the University of Georgia, which I still do.

I got to know a certain girl there — well, I began to do her portrait, and a year later we were married. But at that time I didn't have anything; I couldn't give her a present. [Teaching was highly honored, but very poorly paid in those years, particularly for a beginning instructor.] My parents had nothing. I had nothing, but I found a way out. In those years the silversmiths used to sit out there in old Tbilisi, near the sulfur baths. I would patronize those baths, early in the morning, and watch them work. So I asked one to sell me a piece of silver, just flat sheet. He was happy to do so, and I went home and began to do a miniature chasing on it — by that time I knew something about that. And I gave that early work of mine as a present to my bride. She wore it.

In 1962 I exhibited a large piece of chasing in a show, which attracted the attention of other sculptors, and from that year on Guruli, Kipshidze, Koiava, Tsomaia, Shavgulidze — these are fine masters — began to take their first steps in chasing, and within three years — that is, in 1965 — we arranged the first exhibition of chasing in Moscow. Again something unexpected happened: by word of mouth, news of chasing, a totally unknown technique there as an art form, spread. It had never been displayed in Georgian exhibits, unless one counts work from olden times, and they organized what amounted to excursions, virtually processions, to see our work.

So chasing became a popular form of Georgian art, not only popular but a legitimized form of Georgian art, and now, it seems to me, one cannot conceive of Georgian art without chasing. I have had one-man shows in Belgium, Austria, West Berlin, Norway. I was present at them. Soon there will be one in Syria. We also showed in Japan, three times, where virtually every piece was sold.

I asked how a Soviet artist makes a living — who buys the work and at what prices? His home has huge rooms and an immense studio, and I asked how this was arranged.

"In the first place," Ochiauri responded, "in order to have a studio and a residence, you need money, and an artist has to earn that by his work. Nothing comes to anyone without work. An artist's work is what he creates; I have to sell what I produce." I pressed, asking "To whom? To the government?" Ochciauri: "To anyone who wants it; I'll explain how that is organized. In the first

---

*Chasing is the art of decorating metal by engraving or embossing.

place, the government, chiefly through the Ministry of Culture, purchases our works — it organizes official exhibitions, and once something is accepted for display, the ministry must buy it.

"One can also participate in USSR-wide exhibitions, but that is much tougher than in one's own republic. Acceptance is a high honor, but again, something accepted for display must be purchased."

He went on: "Work is accepted for display by a jury; once displayed a distinct body, the Appraisal Commission, goes to work. This includes people from the Ministry of Culture, and artists. They fix a price according to certain guidelines." He gave me a concrete example. "A piece of metal chasing up to one square meter [about three feet by three] can be appraised at from 300 to 1,000 rubles." At that time, 300 rubles was two months' average pay in the USSR. "That's a good price, of course. But if you only make it into one exhibition a year, you can't get by on that alone. Many artists therefore also seek other channels. It may be a government commission to decorate, say, a building or hotel or sanatorium or restaurant, a cafe. Many artists also earn money in this way.

"But there are also art-lovers who find themselves with some money, and want to buy — not collectors, but people fond of art. They buy graphic art or paintings or metal chasing to beautify their homes, or friends want to give someone a birthday present, and they come to buy my work. They can do so directly. True, under Soviet law, that isn't entirely proper. We're really supposed to sell through the store of the Artists' Union, but there is indulgence where artists are concerned, and no one stands in the way."

A splendid volume of reproductions of Georgian pottery and chasing, with legends and essays in English and Russian, has been published.[36]

Among the Georgians, as among all non-Russian peoples, women have been prime beneficiaries of Soviet social standards and upbringing. I remember a conversation 25 years ago with a group of Georgians at a lakefront beach. The very few women who gathered around hung back on the edges. When I commented on that, a bantam cock of a man said: "In Georgia we prefer our women in the kitchen." He was not shouted down: indeed, when I expressed disapproval, only one man came to my support; the women said nothing.

But times are apparently changing. In the Arutunian study a

dozen years later, only 17 percent of male workers gave *no* help at home; among the educated, the figure was even smaller: 7 to 10 percent. This does not at all mean that the work is shared equally, of course, but in the past a Georgian man wouldn't have been caught dead doing any "women's work." Asked what they valued in women, men responded that they found qualities as housekeeper less significant than her participation in outside employment. Overall statistics for Georgia bear out such findings: employed women at the professional and paraprofessional levels had doubled in the decade between my conversation and that survey;[37] they held 47 percent of jobs requiring college graduation, vs. 55 percent in Russia.

At Tbilisi's Institute of Audiology, which ranks with Stanford University as a leader in this field, I found young women doing the most sophisticated kind of studies of the electrical potentials generated by hearing. And I talked to the female *doktor* who heads the Institute of Morphology* of Georgia's Academy of Sciences. She told me that factories have women's councils, with a pyramidal structure leading up to one that is Georgia-wide, which sees to it that protective legislation is honored. She regards economic independence as a "very big factor" in women's lives — "The woman can feed herself." Another morphologist, who heads the women's council in their institute, told how it organizes celebrations of "major birthdays": fiftieth or sixtieth, "with humor," and in general gives people a feeling of recognition with "innumerable little things that make the life of the institute more pleasant," like giving presents to newlyweds and birthday celebrants.

At the University of Georgia the faculty of the Foreign Languages Department is 100 percent female, and women were well represented in the law, chemistry, and biology departments.

Unfortunately, the advances in art, in the sciences, in higher education, in the status of women, have been accompanied by an increase in ostentation, often excused as adherence to tradition. This is not at all limited to Georgia, but Georgia has done the most intelligent and vigorous job of studying and seeking to combat this.

In 1975, the Georgian Communist Party set up its own Council on the Study of Public Opinion. An earlier investigation by academics had contentedly noted that educated people and half the working class had discarded "burdensome" ritual practices. But the Party spelled out just what the burden was to the other half of the

---

*The biological study of the form and structure of living organisms.

workers, and to the majority of farm families, who have not only retained traditional practices but made them more elaborate:

"Thus, for example, funerals began to be stretched out to last 7 to 10 days, taking from people a great deal of socially necessary and personal time, money and effort. Weddings and *kelekhi* (Georgian memorial feasts honoring the departed), with many hundreds of persons invited, became obligatory, and often became ordinary drinking bouts with all the consequences that ensue. Sorrow and joys—the deaths of dear ones, and weddings, birthdays or send-offs to army service, more and more often became conditions for collecting money, extorting expensive gifts, and the like."[38]

The Georgian Communists attacked people as moral cowards for going along with this. The opinion poll found 72 percent thought this situation "intolerable"—yet studies showed the same people behaved like conformists in engaging in these practices in their own families or communities. The Georgian Communist Party sociologists sampled a very large population in three cities, 22 rural counties, and three autonomous ethnic entities. They concluded that "private-property tendencies are prevalent and enjoy vitality," i.e., conspicuous consumption and illegal business were rampant.

The steps taken to change this were classically Communist. Communists believe the industrial working class, lacking land or business property, has an inherent stake in socialism, and throughout Soviet history, industrial workers have been sent out to farmlands or ethnic areas to propagandize and organize for Party policies.

In Georgia, the effort to rectify the situation began at the Rustavi steel mill, the base of its heavy industry. Representative groups of workers were called together and shown documents and statistics about the plant. The workers made a series of recommendations, and in response, labor conditions improved, as did the consumer supply situation; favoritism in allocating newly-built apartments was eliminated and a more flexible and equitable system of wages and bonuses introduced.

Other measures, many proposed by workers, were taken to improve production potential. After all these steps, labor productivity increased to the point where the plant, which had been running at a loss, showed a profit. Furthermore, it won the USSR-wide "socialist competition" in the steel industry for 14 consecutive quarters. Three quarters of the workers subsequently polled credited its Communist Party committee for the changes, and for having created "a friendly, close-knit collective." Labor turnover at the plant had been high; now 19 out of 20 expressed satisfaction with their work.

I spent hours speaking to two top executives at that plant, both local peasants who had gained higher engineering educations, including the man in charge of personnel and labor relations. I came away feeling that any worker or union leader who had to deal with him was lucky. Their simple and direct manner of speech made the impression even stronger.

Those workers and other staff members who showed initiative, civic consciousness, and consistency in the four years required to turn that plant around were sent to higher educational institutions. Some have now been placed in strategic posts throughout Georgia to bring about the fundamental changes needed. The late Yuri Andropov won USSR-wide popularity during his one year as leader of the Soviet Union by applying similar principles nationwide to combat corruption, money-grubbing and other faults tackled in Georgia. At this writing, it appears that his successors have continued these policies.

Old Russia's colonial hinterland got low prices for its agricultural products and paid high prices for manufactured goods. Today, Georgian farmers have been able to take advantage of the California-like superiority of their natural conditions with produce from their family garden plots to earn extraordinary prices in farmers' markets elsewhere in the USSR.

As recently as 1940, Georgian population was still rural by two-and-a-half to one. I recall a film set in World War II in which a middle-aged Georgian soldier curses out a Soviet tankman for having unnecessarily run over grape-vines, and then lovingly props them back up. But Georgia is no longer an agricultural hinterland. In 1970 industry accounted for more than half of the national income, and by 1976 the urban population had edged past the rural. Between 1940 and 1970, production of electricity went up twelve fold, steel, mineral fertilizer and truck manufacturing industries had been established, and manufacture of silks, woolens and leather goods had multiplied manyfold.

Agriculture was not neglected over these decades: Georgia is the source of the Soviet Union's tea, and tea production was up six times, canned food eight times. Georgian-owned wineries were producing more in other republics than in Georgia itself. Its agriculture is more mechanized than Russia's and its industrial growth has exceeded Russia's since 1965, which indicates "affirmative action" in industry is being pursued *more* today than before.

American-Russian Institute

Georgian tea has freed USSR of complete dependence on imports of the national beverage.

There are other areas of growth: Georgia now ranks second only to Armenia in persons with more than elementary education. The number of books in the Georgian language has trebled since 1940, and is now over a thousand titles a year.[39] Once the only Georgian art known beyond its borders was the dance, but today its films are well-known around the world, and a mosaic sculptor, Zurab Tsereteli, has decorated a theater in Tokyo and city halls in Canada and Portugal. He also did an outdoor group for a college on Long Island, New York.

NOTES

1. R.P. Jordan, "The Proud Armenians," *National Geographic,* CLIII, No. 6 (1978), pp. 869,872.
2. See E.T. Karapetian, *Rodstvennaia gruppa "Azg u Armian* (Erevan:Akademiia nauk Armianskoi SSR), 1966.
3. M.K. Matossian, *The Impact of Soviet Policies in Armenia* (Leiden: Brill, 1972), p. 12.

4. V.I. Savchenko, *Latyshskie formirovanilia Sovetskoi Armii na frontakh Velikoi Otechestvennoi Voiny* (Riga: Zinatne, 1975), p. 10.

5. *New York Times*, December 18, 1979, p. 6.

6. Matossian, p. 90.

7. TsSU SSSR, *Zhenshchiny v SSSR, Statisticheskii sbornik* (Moscow: Statistika, 1975), p. 91.

8. Ibid., p. 104.

9. P. Matveev, "Zhenshchiny-iuristy (statisticheskii material)," *Sotsialisticheskaia zakonnost'*, 1975, No. 9.

10. A.E. Panian, "The New Life of the Kolkhozniks of the Village of Mrgavan, Artashat Raion, Armenian SSR," *Soviet Anthropology and Archeology*, VIII, No. 2 (1969), pp. 138-139. The entire article is recommended to readers interested in a wide-ranging overall study of Armenian peasant life, and changes in it.

11. V.A. Acharkan, "The Social and Legal Nature of Benefits for Children in Low-Income Families," *Soviet Law and Government*, XV, No. 2 (1976), p. 30.

12. John L. Wasserman, "Jazz with Eastern Flavor," *San Francisco Chronicle*, June 2, 1975.

13. M.S. Sar'ian, *Iz moei zhizni*, 2nd ed. (Moscow: Izobrazitel'noe iskusstvo, 1971), illustration facing p. 86.

14. Nikolai Tikhonov, "Work Worthy of the Highest Respect," *Soviet Studies in Literature*, VII, No. 2 (1971), p. 130.

15. M.K. Matossian, "Communist Rule and the Changing Armenian Cultural Pattern," in E. Goldhagen, ed., *Ethnic Minorities in the Soviet Union* (New York: Praeger, 1968), p. 193.

16. Fannina Halle, *Women in the Soviet East* (New York: Dutton, 1938), pp. 73-4, 288-290.

17. "USSR Census Returns," *Soviet Law and Government*, XIX, No. 2 (1980), p. 36.

18. Halle, pp. 292-293.

19. I. Kamenkovich, *Noch' plachushchikh detei* (Baku: Azerbaidzhanskoe Gosudarstvennoe isdatel'stvo, 1970).

20. Il'ia Kamenkovich, *Zhit' vospreshchaetsia* (Baku: Giandzhlik, 1975).

21. V.I. Savchenko, p. 10.

22. *San Francisco Chronicle*, April 18, 1978.

23. *San Francisco Chronicle*, May 4, 1976.

24. Richard B. Dobson, "Georgia and the Georgians," in Z. Katz, ed., *Handbook of Major Soviet Nationalities* (New York: Free Press, 1975), p. 184.

25. R.L. Tokes, ed., *Dissent in the USSR* (Baltimore: Johns Hopkins, 1975).

26. D.M. Lang, "A Century of Russian Impact on Georgia," in W. Vucinich, ed., *Russia and Asia* (Stanford, Ca.: Hoover Institution, 1972), pp. 240-247, passim.

27. A.S. Prangishvili and E.A. Gersamiya, "Some Interpretations of the 'Uznadze Effect' in Modern Cognitive Psychology." *Soviet Psychology*, XXI, No. 2 (1982-3), pp. 77-103.

28. A.E. Lunev, "Law and the Administration of Scientific Institutions in the USSR," *Soviet Law and Government*, XIII, No. 2 (1974), p. 26.

29. Savchenko, p. 10.

30. Matossian, *Impact of Soviet Policies*, p. 124.

31. A.S. Vacheishvili and E.S. Menabdishvili, "Ethnic Relations in the Social Structure of an Industrial Work Force," *Soviet Sociology*, XI, No. 1, (1972), pp. 3-30.

Port of Baku. Tree-planted parkland extends for a mile on what once was wind-blown sand.

32. D.C. Miller and W.H. Form, *Industrial Sociology* (New York: Harper, 1951).

33. C. Goldberg, "The Not-So-Soviet Republics," *The Nation*, March 19, 1973, p. 357.

34. Iu. V. Arutiunian, "On Certain Tendencies Toward Change in the Cultural Aspect of a Nation," *Soviet Sociology*, XV, No. 1 (1976), pp. 44-62.

35. Halle, pp. 276-277.

36. S. Erlashova, *Georgian Pottery and Chasing on Metal* (Leningrad: Aurora, 1975), 112 plates.

37. TsSU SSSR, p. 76.

38. T.M. Dzhafarli, "The Study of Public Opinion, A Necessary Condition for Adoption of Correct Decisions," *Soviet Law and Government*, XVII, No. 3 (1978-79), pp. 9-21.

39. TsSU SSSR, *Narodnoe Khoziaistvo SSSR v 1980 g.* (Moscow: Finansy i Statistika, 1981), pp. 29, 110, 129, 486-7.

11

The Jews

Many people in the West picture the Soviet Union as consisting chiefly of Russians and Jews. Actually, the 1,800,000 Jews are less than one in fifty of the *non*-Russian "minorities" there; they are outnumbered by fifteen other Soviet nations and peoples.[1]

The interest in Soviet Jews in the United States and Canada is a consequence of their numbers, not in the USSR, but here in the United States. Of all Americans with roots in what is now Soviet territory, Jews are the most numerous, actually outnumbering the Ukrainians, Lithuanians, Armenians and all others *combined*.

There is great disagreement among Jews everywhere as to who should be considered a Jew. They don't even agree on a single definition of anti-Semitism. To non-Jews these questions are even more puzzling.

I therefore turned to the current *Encyclopedia Britannica*, only to find: "There is no agreement on the definition of a Jew."[2]

The Russian-language *Large Soviet Encyclopedia* contains an article titled "Jews," with cross-references to "Judaism," "Kingdom of Israel," "Kingdom of Judea," "Diaspora," "Anti-Semitism," "Zionism," "Jewish Autonomous Region" of the USSR, modern "Israel," "Yiddish" language, "Jewish Literature," "Hebrew," etc. There are also articles such as "Beilis Case," a notorious anti-Semitic frame-up

---

Many of my interviews with Jews are in the chapters on the ethnic areas where they took place (for example, Byelorussia). They are very easily found by referring to the heading in the index, "Jews."

before the Revolution, and *hundreds* of biographies of distinguished Jewish figures of the present and past, in the Soviet Union and worldwide. They are either identified as Jews, i.e.,"Sholom Aleichem, Jewish writer," or as having been born into Jewish families, or have names that only appear among Jews.

That encyclopedia is regarded by Soviet people as *the* authority, and is available everywhere for consultation. Over 600,000 copies were printed, most of which are in libraries. What does a Soviet person who wants to know about Jews find in the article so titled?

"JEWS, the common ethnic name [in Russian *Evrei*]* of the peoples [note the plural] taking their historic origins in the ancient Jews. Live in different countries and pursue the same economic, socio-political, and cultural life as the basic populations of those countries. The overwhelming majority of religious Jews hold to Judaism." So Jews are defined ethnically in the USSR: you can be a Jew and be religious or not.

The historical origins of the dispersion of the Jews are described. The article continues,

In many European countries there were laws that limited their rights and occupations, particularly the right to possess and use land. . . . The Jews were not admitted to guilds. . . . From the middle of the 19th century through the early 20th century the toiling masses of the Jews participated actively in the revolutionary movement in Russia and in Western Europe. [In Soviet eyes that is just about the highest praise one can offer].

The Great October [1917] Socialist Revolution began a new era in the history of all the peoples of Russia, including the Jews. The Soviet government's legislation repealed all limitations upon the rights of Jews and proclaimed a resolute struggle against anti-Semitism. In 1934 the Jewish Autonomous Region was established in Khabarovsk Territory. The Jews participated in the building of the new society jointly with all the peoples of the USSR on the basis of a community of economic, political, and ideological interests and the principles of proletarian internationalism. . . .

Anti-Semitism, which found its extreme expression in fascist Germany, continues to exist in the capitalist countries. The Hitlerites pursued a policy of mass extermination of the Jews (during the 2nd World War, 1939-45, about 6,000,000 were annihilated.)[3]

The matter of language is important in discussing the Soviet Jews. On this we read: "In the majority of cases Jews speak in the language of the country in which they live. A portion of the Jews in countries of Europe and America additionally speak Yiddish, in

---

*Square brackets denote my additions. Material in parentheses is in the original.

which there is a literature (see Jewish Literature); in the USSR, according to the 1970 census, 17.7 percent of the Jews identified Yiddish as their native language.* The official language of the Jews of Israel is Hebrew, which developed on the basis of the literary Old-Jewish language and is used by Jews in other countries only as the language of religious worship. Part of the Jews in Mediterranean countries (called Sephardic) employ the Ladino language, which resembles Spanish.''

Anti-Semitism is defined in another article, actually longer than the one on Jews. Here are its highlights:[5]

"ANTI-SEMITISM, one of the forms of national and religious intolerance, expressed in a hostile attitude toward Jews. In the course of history, anti-Semitism has taken various forms — from religious and psychological prejudices and segregation, manifested chiefly in the relationships of everyday life, to government policies of forcible expulsion of Jews and even their physical extermination (genocide).'' There is a separate article on Genocide.

The article, "Anti-Semitism," describes its history thus:

In Russia anti-Semitism was essentially the accepted doctrine of the government; Jews (unconverted) were limited as to where they could live ("the Pale of Settlement"), they were forbidden to buy land and engage in agriculture, be military officers, be employed in government service, work on the railroads and in the postal service. . . . Anti-Semitism was whipped up by trials accusing Jews of ritual murder (the Velizh Case of the 1820s and 1830s, the Beilis Case of 1913, and others). . . .

The most savage form of anti-Semitism was pogroms, the first wave of which (early 1880s) was launched by reactionary elements after the killing of Alexander II, and the second during the Revolution of 1905-07. The pogromists were led by the Black Hundreds belonging to the "Union of the Russian People," and behind them was the tsarist secret police. Later, during the Civil War the involvement of Jews in the revolutionary movement was the justification offered for the pogroms organized by the followers of Petliura and Denikin, the gangs of Makhno and other "atamany."[†] Russian Social-Democracy, like Marxist parties of other countries, had to wage a struggle both against anti-Semitism and against Jewish nationalism.

---

*The 1979 census showed 14.2 percent did.[4] As in the West, this decline reflects the dying-off of those Jews born in the ghetto, plus linguistic assimilation.

†Petliura and Makhno were anti-Communist leaders in the Ukraine, and "ataman" is the title of Cossack chieftains. In Soviet eyes, a nationality is never guilty, but only the ruling socio-economic classes within it that may succeed in misleading large sections of the people.[6]

The article on anti-Semitism then describes the Nazi death camps of World War II. It continues:

> The smashing of Hitlerite Germany and international condemnation of persecution of the Jews by the Nazi government (which the Nuremberg Trial found to be a crime against humanity) dealt a blow at anti-Semitism. However, it did not disappear in the capitalist countries, although it began to manifest itself in milder form (chiefly in segregation and discrimination against Jews in daily life) and takes on violent forms more rarely (local pogroms such as that in Liverpool in 1947, arson against synagogues, and so forth). Revivals of anti-Semitism usually coincide with intensification of political reaction in various countries.
>
> The socialist system creates the basis for full equality among human beings regardless of racial and national affiliation and, consequently, for the total uprooting of anti-Semitism.

The article does not say that it *has been* uprooted.

If all this had appeared in some single book written by an individual, no matter how widely read, it would not deserve the amount of space given it here. But when published in the one source that has the absolute highest prestige in the public mind in the USSR, the final authority for the mass reader, the high school and college student, it has enormous significance. It says, simply, that Jews have been discriminated against through most of the past two thousand years, that that is wrong, and that anti-Semitism is monstrous.

The leading American academic specialist on the Soviet Jews, Prof. Zvi Gitelman of the University of Michigan, has written that they "play social, political, cultural, and economic roles greater than their numbers would indicate."[7] "Far greater" would have been more accurate. The only "high society" in the psychology of Soviet citizens consists of people associated with science, scholarship, and the arts, particularly literature. There are more Jews with the post-PhD degree *"Doktor"* than members of *any* nationality but the Russians, who outnumber the Jews 100-to-1. Jews have *seventeen times* as many *"Doktors"* as their percentage in the population.[8]

Clearly, Jews are not discriminated against in admission to graduate study or acceptance of theses. Those figures are all the more remarkable in light of anti-Jewish discrimination before the

Revolution. Soviet sources attempt to explain it by saying that Jews are an almost totally urban people, and urban people place a higher value upon education than rural, particularly where farming was a traditional peasant skill involving an implement no more complicated than a plough. Nationalistic Jews explain this disproportion in intellectual achievement as "natural,"* some believe it is because they are "smarter." But the worldwide picture does not support this conclusion; everywhere one finds some peoples who place a higher value on education than others. In the United States, for example, Japanese-Americans rank at the very top, far ahead not only of other Orientals, but of all "whites" — in the proportion of their youngest generation with college diplomas and going on to higher degrees.

Under the Soviets education has become a value in the minds of the Slavic worker and peasant; in earlier times, this was true only of Jews, Armenians and Georgians. Today, even previously pre-literate peoples reach for the maximum possible education.

There is still the question of how the Jews in the USSR achieved their present pre-eminence. Before the Revolution, most Jews were simply legally barred from living in the greatest intellectual centers, Moscow and St. Petersburg. There were some exceptions: occasionally, a young Jewish woman would actually register as a prostitute in order to live in those cities, with higher education as a goal, since prostitutes were not barred. Still, Jews never exceeded 2 percent of the population of St. Petersburg.[9] Half of the Jews lived in smaller cities where high-school education was available to those who could pay for it, the other half lived in the dullest of tiny trading towns of craftsmen and petty merchants, places with virtually no educational facilities. Their own religious schools, for boys only, were taught

---

*A classical example may be seen in the magazine *Jewish Currents*, September, 1984, p. 47. It reports that one or both parents of 50 percent of the 1983 graduates from Moscow's four special mathematics schools were Jewish, in a city where only 3 percent of the population is Jewish. The logical conclusion would be that Jewish children enjoy unhindered, not to say extraordinary, opportunities. Instead, showing that admissions from this group into Moscow's two most prestigious university and college math departments were substantially below the ratio of the non-Jews admitted, the magazine concludes that discrimination against Jews occurred. It pays no attention to the fact that the ratio of Jewish admissions was vastly above the percentage of Jews in Moscow's population. Most important, it assumes Jewish superiority in this field to be a divine or genetic or racial right. It ignores the well-known and admirable Soviet affirmative-action policy of reserving a proportion of admissions for students of nationalities lacking a mathematical tradition, so as to enable them to develop one. The magazine thus embraces the racist Shockley thesis of the genetic superiority and inferiority of various branches of the human family.

chiefly in Hebrew. As they did not use this in daily life, instruction involved rote memorizing. The language of daily existence, Yiddish (based on medieval German), was a further obstacle to social mobility, which required a command of Russian. A religious school might bring in an instructor to teach minimal Russian and basic arithmetic, but most Jews knew just enough Russian or Ukrainian or Polish to engage in transactions with local people, and no more.

Contrary to articles written by anti-Semitic writers in the Soviet Union even today, over a third of the Jews earned their bread by the sweat of their brows, mostly as independent craftsmen—tailors, shoemakers, furriers, even draymen and tar makers. A minority of these physical workers were wage laborers, and, despite all prohibitions, Jewish *peasant* families totalled over 100,000 souls.[10] But nearly two-thirds, the "businesspeople," were often so lacking in capital that they were called, in Yiddish, *luftmenschen*, people who live on air. The men would stand on streetcorners all day trying to swing deals between two others who actually had something to buy or sell. In some cases a man would acquire a single salt herring and cut it into slices and try to earn enough "profit" from their sale to buy bread for his family. At the other extreme, of course, there were wealthy local merchants whose Jewishness was "forgiven" by officials hoping to gain by personal contact. There were also some really rich Jews— they owned a large part of the beet-sugar refining industry, and even financed railroad construction. These few had no difficulty in living in St. Petersburg or Moscow, as the ban did not apply to "merchants of the first guild," whatever their nationality or religion.

Such people were so remote from the general Jewish population that their existence was generally unknown. I myself, with tailors and penniless dealers and rabbis and one innkeeper-and-builder in my ancestry—and even a local landowner before the Jews were driven out of that a century ago—did not know genuine Jewish capitalists existed in old Russia until I began to gather material for this book. In Russian Jewish folklore, the Jewish rich were the Rothschilds of France, not anybody living under the tsar. The children of Russian Jewish *big* businesspeople were allowed to become doctors, lawyers, journalists, but not professors. This resembles the situation facing Atlanta's Black bourgeoisie 50 years ago, though their children could teach in a Negro college.

The Soviet government's policy was to get the majority of non-craftsmen and non-workers into productive labor, which led to a policy we would call "affirmative action." One measure "provided for reserved quotas of vacancies at industrial enterprises for Jewish

American-Russian Institute

Jacob Sverdlov, Jewish president of Soviet Russia when Lenin was prime minister.

young people."[11] This was during the first dozen years after the Revolution, before unemployment was eliminated, so non-Jewish workers sometimes offered the same sort of resistance which has faced affirmative action policies in the United States. In one salt mine east of the Volga, for example, young Jewish workers were chased out with anti-Semitic epithets. But, over time, the policy worked.

Secular schools were established in Yiddish for those who wished to send their children to them, but even in big cities with large Jewish populations, only a minority of parents ever did. In Odessa, only one-quarter of Jewish children were enrolled in Yiddish schools when such schools were at their height, in 1926-27, and in Kharkov only one-sixth.[12] Most parents wanted their children educated in the language that would give them maximum social mobility, usually Russian, sometimes Ukrainian, though in small trading and crafts towns Yiddish was the language of everyday life, and parents sent their children to school in that language.

The government also established trade and technical schools in Yiddish for young *adults* — the direct equivalent of the unemployed hanging around street corners in the U.S. today. Those schools plus the admission quotas put 150,000 Jews into industrial jobs by 1929,[13] but the majority were still small business people, "petty bourgeoisie."

In a country that was then still overwhelmingly rural, though agriculturally backward, offering Jews opportunities on the land was another logical step. This was long before Israel existed, and the kibbutzim in Palestine were few and tiny. The world, and particularly its Jewish communities, was astounded by the Soviet move: Jewish farmers? But by the time of Hitler's invasion, the percentage of Jews working the land had increased from 2 percent at the time of the Revolution to 11 percent, a respectable minority of several hundred thousand souls. The government *gave* them land formerly belonging to great landowners. There were five counties (in the Ukraine and the Crimea) in which Yiddish was the language of government.*[14] Despite Hitler, a few Jewish communities remained there after World War II, or were re-established.

A Soviet journalist who edited the Yiddish paper in one of those counties reminisced forty years later: "For more than 2,000 years the Jews had been divorced from the land — would they cope with the task? I remember as if it were yesterday how much the subject was discussed in the Jewish *shtetlakh* (trading towns). People talked themselves hoarse arguing the matter, meetings went on day and night. . . . "

But the age-old dream of a Jewish country remained. Among the traditionalists and religious, this took the form of Zionism which argued that return to Palestine (now Israel) is the only solution for the Jews, and the only way to end anti-Semitism. Zionism did not deal with the possibility that founding a state in another people's territory would stimulate anti-Semitism there and in neighboring countries.†

The Soviet government sought to compete with Zionism by offering the Jews a large piece of virgin territory. It was forested and well-watered, somewhat larger than present-day Israel, with a climate like that of the Canadian wheat provinces. Located in Siberia, it is called the Jewish Autonomous Region, and popularly known as Birobidjan. The first settlers went there in 1928; six years later the Soviet government decided its worth had been proved, and

---

*Pete Seeger made famous a song originating in them, "Jankoye."

†Since Israel's founding, the World Zionist Organization has demanded unconditional support for Israel from the world's Jews, even if opposed by their own countries.

formally established this entity. A prime consideration was that no pre-existing population had to be displaced, and that the region be open to settlers of all Soviet nationalities, not only Jews. This was only one of many steps taken with respect to the Jews in the first 15 years after the Revolution — we have mentioned abolishing all residence restrictions, education without limit, establishing educational and cultural facilities in Yiddish, retraining for industrial employment and reserving jobs, offering land and government of farm areas. Of all these, the Siberian venture is the only one that did not succeed.* "Failed" would be the wrong term: 10,000 Jews living there today have been described repeatedly as confident, well-established people, by reporters for the major U.S. newspapers.[15] But very few Jews chose that alternative. Most of those who wanted to farm preferred the Ukraine and Crimea, warmer country that they knew well, and the overwhelming majority of Soviet Jews, 90 percent chose city life, but no longer in ghetto neighborhoods and towns. Nor did they remain in what amounted to ghetto occupations.†

All these changes reflected themselves culturally. In the late '20s and early '30s, when Stalin headed the country, there was an unprecedented flourishing of Yiddish culture. Books were published in printing runs never attained elsewhere; a complete Yiddish-language educational system — up to and including universities — was established, a number of professional theater companies came into being and were subsidized by the government. Several newspapers, and magazines, including one in Russian, *Tribuna*, appeared along with a whole new creative literature. The article "Jewish Literature," in the current *Large Soviet Encyclopedia*, which starts with the Bible, describes over sixty professional writers in Yiddish in the USSR, most of whom are also discussed in separate articles.[16]

Assimilation followed the abolition of the ghetto and of the distinctive Jewish economic life, so enrollment in Yiddish-language schools dropped very rapidly before World War II. Exactly as in the U.S., Jews wanted to live in the language of the country and of

---

*Its 50th anniversary in 1984 provided the occasion for a national TV broadcast including 15 minutes of Yiddish music. Tunes of the Hasidic religious sect were performed.

†Much has been made of the identification "Jew" on the internal *pasport*, or I.D. card. All Soviet citizens carry this card (as all French citizens carry "papers") Each *pasport* states the bearer's nationality, not religion, and Jews are a recognized nationality in the USSR. The purpose of the nationality identification was to assist minorities in demonstrating entitlement to affirmative action benefits. The *pasport* is issued at age 16, and a person of mixed parentage may choose the nationality of either parent.

geographic and social mobility. But creative culture, particularly Yiddish literature and theater remained and expanded. As a Moscow- or Leningrad-born generation grew up, a market for Yiddish works translated into Russian appeared, and large numbers of creative people of Jewish ethnic origin began to function in the culture of the country at large, as Russian writers, actors, musicians. One significant and exciting phenomenon was the appearance of a market for Yiddish literature in translation among the non-Jewish population. Sholom Aleichem was universally known in the USSR thirty years before Gentile Americans discovered him through *Fiddler On the Roof.* He and others were translated not only into the languages of the peoples among whom their characters had lived; they also appeared in the languages of the Caucasus and Central Asia. There Jews were of a totally different Oriental type* — and whose very existence was unknown to rank-and-file Russian Jews.

Another aspect of that post-revolutionary period, was the appearance of *positive* Jewish characters in Soviet literature. The major Russian writers — Soviet loyalists, not dissidents — wrote into their works Jews who played prominent parts in the founding and building of the Soviet regime. Everyone in the USSR has read Nobel prize winner Mikhail Sholokhov's *Seeds of Tomorrow* (also called *Virgin Soil Upturned*) in which the hero, Davidov, is sent out to organize a collective farm among Cossacks. This character was based on one of 25,000 ultra-staunch proletarian Communists dispatched by the Party to every corner of the country to do that job. (The real-life Davidov had been a Navy mechanic.) Nearly everyone has read Fadeyev's *The Rout*, a brutally honest story of the Civil War: its hero is a guerrilla leader named Levinson.

There is a very widespread tendency among Jews of Russian-Empire descent in the West to blanket all Ukrainians as anti-Semites. I have found this attitude unwarranted in many conversations with Ukrainians (see Chapter 9 for many interviews). Beyond that, the most prominent Ukrainian writers and poets have played an extraordinary role in discovering and translating Yiddish authors, and in creating the most positive kind of Jewish characters. Actually, this should come as no surprise, because Jews were a very large percentage of the population of Ukrainian cities before Hitler. Again, not only were these Ukrainian writers not dissidents, but, in

---

*They had come from Palestine over the centuries. Those in the Caucasus speak Georgian and a very local tongue, Tat; those in Central Asia speak Farsi, the language of Iran. About half emigrated to Israel in the 1970s.

Matzo factory in Baku. "I have only two interests: go to school and become an engineer and help my people by making the best matzo."

line with well-established European tradition, people with prominent government positions so their proposals in literature carried weight.

For example, Osher Shvartsman, who died fighting in the Civil War, and is regarded as the founder of Soviet Yiddish poetry, was discovered and translated by the Ukrainian poet Pavlo Tychyna, who was Education Minister of the Ukraine 1943-48, its President from 1953 to 1959, and a member of the Central Committee of the Communist Party until his death in 1967. Nor is this an isolated case. In a study published by B'nai B'rith, Prof. Maurice Friedberg of the University of Indiana writes of "the famous Ukrainian Soviet poet Maxim Ryl's'kyj, who had also in his time translated into Ukrainian much Yiddish verse."[17] Ryl's'kyj was chairman of the Ukrainian Writers Association 1943-6, and headed the Institute of Arts Studies of the Ukrainian Academy of Sciences until his death in 1964. Friedberg thinks the "best portrait" of a Jew in the Civil

War is in Oleksandr Kopylenko's Ukrainian novel, and "the strongest affirmation of Jewish ethnic identity, of pride in the Jewish past and readiness to die for a Jewish future" was in a novel by Alexander Ilchenko, a Ukrainian, "known for his preoccupation with Ukrainian history." Being a Ukrainian patriot did not make him anti-Semitic. Aron Burstein, Ilchenko's Soviet Jewish guerrilla, is wounded and captured by the Nazis, and, in Friedberg's summary: "relives his past, his periods of happiness in the Soviet oil fields of Baku and also his moments of anger." He quotes this passage from Ilchenko:

> He recalled feeling outraged by those who did not like his, Aron's, name. But he had despised even more those who wished to change their Jewish names or, even more disgracefully, their patronymics. He, Aron, was proud of his father, a man who smelted tar for a living. He had never concealed that his father was Nathan, he never tried to pass him off as Volodymyr or Mykola. And he himself had always been Aron and Aron he would die. He had once asked his old man — what does his Jewish soul yearn for? "To defeat Fascism. And also, I want," the father continued, "to see my people tilling the earth, mining coal and producing steel — together with all mankind. Equal to all! It's all really very simple," and the wise man grew silent.
>
> Aron, always full of respect for his father, for his ancient name, for the beauty of the sweat of his brow, for his human hopes and aspirations and, yes, for the realization of these hopes — for these he was now dying, bespattered with blood, although, shtetl skeptic that he was, he did not yet believe in his own death.

This aside on Ukrainian writers deliberately brackets the pre-war period discussed above, and the postwar. With respect to the Jews, as with everything else in Soviet life, it is clear today that the horrible events of Stalin's later years were an aberration. All Soviet nationalities have been educated toward internationalism, but — as the passage quoted makes clear — anti-Semitism had never entirely disappeared. Nor has it to this day.

Before discussing the waves of anti-Semitism, it is worth noting that those are fluctuations on a sharply declining curve. *There have been no pogroms or charges of pogroms by anybody, no matter how Zionist or anti-Soviet, since the Soviets gained firm control in 1920,* except where the Nazis ruled in World War II, yet in one two-week period back in 1905, there had been pogroms in 690 communities. A topmost official of the tsar, Pobedonostsev, declared: "We must pursue a policy that will make one-third of the Jews embrace Christianity, *will lead to the extinction of another third of the*

Jewish population, and will compel the last third to emigrate." [my emphasis - W.M.] During the Civil War of 1918-1920, massacres cost the lives of 180,000 Jews; 300,000 children were orphaned. That is utterly gone.

There are no ghettoes, no charges that Jews suffer from the sort of housing discrimination still quite widespread in the United States, where it remains totally legal on the part of small home-owners. (Jews in great cities are surprised to hear this, but my own daughter experienced it in "liberal" Berkeley in the 1960s.)

The very rise of Jews to "social, political, cultural and economic roles (far) greater than their numbers would indicate" is a product of the Revolution. There is also a very great increase in inter-marriage, not only in cities but in formerly medieval places like Daghestan in the Caucasus Mountains. I know American Jews of socially very advanced views who still prefer their children to marry Jews. Many Jews fear intermarriage may mean "ethnic suicide;" others consider such intermarriage as enriching the ethnic cultural mix. In the USSR children of such marriages describe themselves as "Soviet" when census takers ask their nationality. This applies equally to cases in which non-Jewish, but ethnically mixed, parentage is involved. Census takers are specifically instructed not to request documentary identification of nationality.*

In the early Soviet years, there was a temporary rise in anti-Semitism as millions of backward, ignorant people began to move out of their traditional patterns, though it never returned to the level of mass violence. (During World War II, a cousin of my wife's went to visit her husband in a U.S. Army camp in the south. She remembers being told, "You can't be a Jew. Where are your horns?" As that incident illustrates, the most incredible prejudices persist. Why assume that Soviet people were exempt?)

Because of the economic collapse, brought on by the Civil War, Lenin allowed private retail trade and even small manufacturing to resume. Jews, no longer penned into the Pale of Settlement, engaged in these needed occupations in places where they had never previously been seen. Some grew visibly prosperous, and this stimulated anti-Semitism, which their non-Jewish competitors helped along. As late as 1929, a dozen years after the Revolution, one-third of the Jewish population still made its living in private trade.[18] But the rest were convinced that their tribulations as Jews

---

*This invalidates Zionist contentions that there are significantly more Jews than the census figure. Nationalists of any nationality deny the reality of assimilation. Were that true, there would be no such person as a Canadian, American, Argentinian, etc.

were over. In 1931-32 my parents socialized with Jews who were not in trade and they heard, over and over again: "Anti-Semitism is gone." Among my 32 fellow-students in biochemistry at Moscow University, six were Jewish. Had they been limited to their share in the country's population, there would have been only one. Jews and Gentiles alike were of uneducated parentage, except for one Russian and myself. I never got the slightest whiff of anti-Semitism, nor did I ever hear of any from the other Jews; neither did people study (or play) in separate ethnic groups as in "integrated" American institutions today. My father never encountered it at work. My mother once heard such a remark at the opera. Though an extraordinarily proper lady, anti-Semitism was something she could not sit still for, so she turned around and whispered her opinion to the culprit — who shrank into his seat. That was the atmosphere.

World War II added totally new factors to the situation. By the time of Hitler's invasion of the USSR in 1941, all private trade had been forbidden for ten years, the children of its former practitioners had grown up with entirely new occupations and perspectives. The Jewish record in the war was without precedent for a people that had done everything in its power to dodge military service under the tsars (why fight for your oppressors?). Jews rallied to the Soviet colors with greater enthusiasm than *any* other nationality, including the Russians. This is shown by official Soviet statistics on awards of decorations by nationality when calculated in proportion to population. Half a million Jews served in the armed forces; 200,000 died in combat;[19] 121 won the equivalent of the Congressional Medal of Honor. They were not simply fighting Hitler — although, as is said at Passover, "that would have been enough," — they were fighting *for* the government that had most changed the status of the Jews in their entire history, and within a single generation. The army itself typified this: *there were 313 Jewish generals*,[20] probably more than in all other armies combined, in all history. In the United States, the very notion of a Jew being a general would have been snickered at before World War II. When Admiral Hyman Rickover, organizer of the nuclear-submarine fleet, was graduated from Annapolis in 1922, in the class book his "photo, which was among the individual photos of the graduates, was set to one side in a perforated frame for easy removal from the page."[21]

These Soviet Jewish generals were almost exclusively of working-class origin, except those like M.A. Milshtein, a homeless orphan of the previous war, retired, at four-star rank, to direct the Political-Military Department of Moscow's Institute of the U.S.

Tashkent synagogue. Both men are veterans of World War II.

and Canada, the chief extra-governmental body advising on relations with those countries. Ordinary Soviet citizens talk freely with foreigners, as the interviews in this book attest, but people of standing do not speak for quotation without higher permission, as the authorities want the outside world to be perfectly clear about where they stand. Thus Milshtein's words, in an interview with the *N.Y. Times,* are worthy of thought:

"We believe that nuclear war will bring no advantage to anyone and may even lead to the end of civilization. And the end of civilization can hardly be called 'victory.' Our doctrine regards nuclear weapons as something that must never be used. They are not an instrument for waging war in any rational sense. But of course, if we are forced to use them, in reply to their first use by an aggressor, we shall use them."[22]

This was before the election of President Reagan.

One of the generals of Jewish origin to reach five-star rank, Jacob Kreizer, commanded the army at the southern (Black Sea) extreme of the fighting. The Nazis dropped anti-Semitic leaflets among his troops without effect. Another commands the equivalent of the U.S. War College; still another commands the equivalent institution for the engineer corps. Perhaps the most remarkable sign of change was the presence of Lev Dovator, Jewish, as commanding general of a Cossack cavalry corps. Cossack had been a synonym for pogromist.

But the war brought several other phenomena that affects the situation of Soviet Jews today, and U.S.-Soviet relations as well. One was Hitler's policy of extermination of all Jews. Although never mentioned by our mass media, this was accompanied by a policy of limited genocide toward the Slavic peoples with the object of reducing their numbers to a manageable colony incapable of resisting Germany. The gruesome result of these policies was illustrated when, after the war, an enormous mass grave with the remains of 200,000 men, women and children was uncovered at Babi Iar, just outside Kiev.

In response to demands made irresistable by Russian poet Yevtushenko's "Babi Iar," published in the national-circulation *Literary Gazette,* a monument to those victims was finally erected by the Soviets at the site. Controversy over the monument persists to this day because no nationality was mentioned although 70,000 Jews lie buried there. The other side of the controversy was given by Anatoly Kuznetsov in his documentary novel, *Babi Iar*:

"A tattered old man carrying a sack was crossing the ravine.
"Hey, uncle! I shouted. Was it here that they shot the Jews, or farther on?
"The old man stopped, looked me over from head to foot and

'And how many Russians were killed here, and Ukrainians and other nationalities?'

"And he went his way."[23]

This is why there was opposition to a monument that would single out the Jews for mention. On one level, this is understandable: of the 200,000 killed, 70,000 were Jews, 130,000 were not. But it was *all* the Jews who were ordered to Babi Iar, and "only" selected categories of Slavs, and the monument gives no hint of this. Communist Party members and Jews had one thing in common: none were spared.

Yet the quoted passage and the years-long controversy shows that the Nazis' discrimination in degrees of murder served to stir psychological ethnic conflict. Each victim nationality was hurt by the attitude of the others. Frequent stories on Soviet Jews in the Western press never mention Soviet efforts to save them. Prof. Friedberg, in his B'nai B'rith-sponsored study, wrote:

"*The Black Sun*, a Ukrainian novel by Ivan Holovshenko and Oleksa Musiyenko, 1965, states that when Kiev's Jews were ordered to assemble by the Nazis, no Ukrainians thought that they were to be slaughtered, simply because no one thought that tens of thousands of people could all be murdered. Nevertheless, the anti-Nazi underground had warned the Jews against complying with the orders."[24]

In Soviet territory, "anti-Nazi underground" meant Communist, of course.

The Soviets evacuated enormous numbers of Jews from the threatened areas. An Israeli scholar, Prof. Zev Katz, writes: "hundreds of thousands of Jews were evacuated to inner parts of the USSR, saved from extermination by the Nazis."[25]

Immediately after the war, at a press conference in New York, Chief Rabbi Mordecai Nurok of Latvia, a leader of the World Jewish Congress and of the world Mizrachi Organization, said, "It must be emphasized that several hundred thousands of Polish and other Jews found a haven from the Nazis in the USSR."[26] The evacuation was an extraordinary effort. There were no paved roads to speak of, no private vehicles, and the railroads were needed to move troops and munitions in the opposite direction.

Including the refugees from Poland, there were 2,200,000 more Jews within Soviet borders when Hitler attacked the USSR in 1941 than when World War II began in 1939. Those not from Poland were permanent inhabitants of territories added to the

USSR in 1939-40. Some of these lands (Bessarabia, the Baltic) had been detached from Soviet Russia by the anti-Communist foreign intervention of 1918-20. There was also the recovery of the western Ukraine and Belorussia which had been seized by Lithuania-Poland in earlier centuries.

These "Western" Jews added a totally new, and profoundly foreign element to the 3,000,000 "old Soviet" Jews. The latter had shared a process of change — in social system and mentality — with their non-Jewish fellow-citizens. Except for Oriental Jews of the Caucasus, who were only three percent of the pre-war Jewish population, a negligible proportion of the "old Soviet" Jews have been among the 265,000 emigrants since 1965. Professor Katz found that only one percent of the "old Soviet" Jews from Russia, the eastern Ukraine and Belorussia had left by 1974 compared to 47 percent of the Caucasus Jews and 33 percent of the "Western" Baltic Jews.[27] The same pattern held at the end of the decade, according to Prof. Zvi Gitelman of the University of Michigan.[28] By now, about *three* percent of the "old Soviet" have left. But as almost all have come exclusively to the U.S., not Israel, they may be a majority of the recent Soviet immigrants to North America.

Why the immense difference in emigration between the "old" and "new" Soviet Jews? By World War II, anti-Semitism had declined very sharply in long-established Soviet territories; so had Jewish feelings against people of Christian or Islamic background. Maurice Hindus interviewed "in the Ukraine a young Jewish woman, the presiding judge in a Jewish court," in one of the counties where Yiddish was the language of government. In describing the Communists' policies in the 1920s, she said:

"And we don't stop with anti-Semitism, we Jewish revolutionaries don't. Have you ever thought of the Jewish feeling of anti-*Goyism*—anti-Gentilism?" . . . Her own father, a noted Talmudic scholar, had brought her up to believe that in every way the Jew was superior to the *Goy*. She had grown up to esteem the very words *Goy* and *Shaigetz*—young Gentile—as terms of opprobrium. . . . As a judge in court, she went on, she had occasion to observe that now and then there was a Jewish trader who thought lightly of treating a peasant less honorably than a Jew, all because to him the peasant was only a *Goy* anyway! "But we Jewish revolutionaries," she exclaimed with a sense of triumph, "are resolved to smash once for all the fiction of a Jewish superiority, and, when that is achieved, at least one cause of anti-Semitism will have been annihilated."[29]

By 1971, when the Soviet government opened the doors to

Jewish emigration, both anti-Semitism and Jewish feelings of superiority had declined yet further in the areas where the Communists had been in power since 1917.

Jews of the western territories, which came under Soviet rule in 1939-41, had lived with pervasive popular anti-Semitism until that much later date. Governmental anti-Semitism in pre-Communist Poland, Romania and the Baltic was only a touch less crude than in tsarist Russia. The Jews had retained the reciprocal feelings described so vividly by that judge. They were still largely involved in the essentially commerce-focused way of life that was gone in the "core" USSR. Masses were murdered after Hitler's invasion though a tiny minority, mostly Communists, fought as guerrillas and survived. The rest of the Jews were evacuated to the Soviet interior where they were plunged into an utterly strange way of life. Private business was not legal; moreover, the USSR was on the edge of starvation once the Nazis occupied the Ukrainian breadbasket. Workers in war industry got the only relatively tolerable rations — all others got less — and the refugees almost universally lacked industrial skills. For simple survival, they sought additional food and clothing and turned to their one skill: private trade. Joshua Kunitz, authority on the Jew in pre-revolutionary Russian literature and a pre-war traveler in the USSR, wrote in 1953, "They dealt on the black market. . . . They aroused the dislike of many Soviet people" including "many a Soviet Jew."

Most of the "new" Jews, he goes on, "were religious, Orthodox, while a great many were ardent Zionists and nationalists. . . . Their Jewish loyalty was monolithic, undiluted by any other loyalty, whether Polish, Lithuanian, Latvian, Romanian, or Soviet."[30] Menachem Begin was of that background.

In 1945, as soon as Hitler was defeated, a Zionist underground began spiriting these people to Palestine. "This [underground] railroad smuggled several thousand Jews out of the Soviet Union and Soviet-occupied territory so they could go to Palestine." the New York *Times* reported.[31] This, too, created resentment, for the Soviets had lost 20,000,000 people, in the most devastating struggle humanity has yet known; there was a strong feeling that every survivor should help rebuild the country.

The founding of Israel was greeted with feelings ranging from sympathy to wild enthusiasm by Soviet Jews. This was partly a response to Hitler's policy of extermination, partly an echo of the ancient feeling for Israel. Jews living within the pre-war boundaries of the USSR had been shocked to find anti-Semitism when, as soldiers, they encountered peasant masses. As urban people, they had had little such contact.

Even in the war years, Kunitz writes, there were "openly-expressed Zionist sentiments to be found in Soviet-Yiddish literature,"[32] "In the postwar period, . . . the Zionist idea of 'one people,' one culture, one destiny was gaining a firm hold in the [Soviet] Yiddish publications."[33] "The bridges to . . . Jewish life outside the Soviet Union . . . were being rebuilt now with unprecedent fervor. . . . An impressive and articulate minority [of the Soviet Jews] stood exposed as carriers of divided loyalties."[34]

In a world at peace, Soviet authorities might have looked benignly on that enthusiasm for Israel. Certainly, the USSR took a very favorable attitude toward the new state itself: Moscow was actually the first to recognize it diplomatically, and World Zionist leader Nahum Goldman and founding premier David Ben-Gurion repeatedly expressed the view that Israel could not have been established without Soviet support. Unfortunately, the cold war against the USSR broke out immediately.* Stalin, in his paranoia, dismissed the loyalty and bravery with which the Jews had fought for their country and focused instead on their enthusiasm over the founding of Israel and the attempts of some Jews to go there.

In 1948, the entire system of Yiddish-language cultural expression, in all its forms, was shut down. It was not to be restored, in any part, for eleven years, until well after Stalin's death. Twenty-five Jewish leaders, most of them Communists, were secretly arrested, tried and executed. They included many of the country's best-known creative writers, actors, scholars and a famous revolutionary. These Jewish Communists were accused of planning to sever the Crimea from the USSR in time of war. They apparently had proposed creating a Soviet Jewish homeland in that region which had been depopulated by the war, Nazi massacres, and by Stalin's deportation of the indigenous Tatars (a minority of whom had collaborated with the Germans). The sole fact that did link any of these Jews to what had become a foreign state was that some had helped smuggle some people to Palestine.

There were five years of acts that produced real fear in the Jewish population. They culminated in a frame-up of physicians,

*As early as 1951, it was common knowledge that Israel had made itself available as a bombing base for the U.S. in a nuclear war with the USSR. An entire issue of *Colliers*, then one of the most widely circulated magazines, was devoted to a scenario, "confirmed in study and consultation with top political and military thinkers—including high-level Washington officials," for the defeat and occupation of the USSR in World War III by nuclear war. (*Colliers*, Oct 27, 1951, p. 29, p. 6, and whole issue).

chiefly Jewish, accused of planning to kill the Soviet leadership by medical means. This period of intimidation ended only with Stalin's death in 1953. But, as with his general political purges in 1935-37, people at large were not touched. Most of the 431 members of the Jewish cultural intelligentsia arrested during the period lost their lives in concentration camps.[35] But the vast mass of the Jewish population—Jewish generals, factory managers, scientists, Politburo member Kaganovich, USSR-wide police chief Mekhlis, physicians, teachers, collective-farm chairmen, workers—continued at their jobs. Nor was there a clean sweep of the cultural figures. Some, like the writer Emmanuil Kazakevich, turned from writing in Yiddish to Russian, and became famous among the general public for the first time.[36] Synagogues and minyans (small congregations without rabbis) continued to function. However, the baking of matzoh, the unleavened bread required in the Passover service, was restricted or even forbidden, a handicap to religion that persisted until about 1970; today matzoh is produced in adequate quantities.

Maurice Hindus is the Belorussian-Jewish, peasant-born non-Communist American observer of the USSR we have repeatedly quoted. He authored eleven books on that country during Stalin's rule from 1926 on. After Stalin's death, he concluded: "I could never persuade myself that Stalin's post-war anti-Semitism was racial in nature. Rather it was motivated by his disdain of the intellectuality of Jews who were least disposed to swallow his Great-Russian chauvinism, his new and incredible falsifications of history, Russian and foreign, past and present, and by his distrust of their loyalty were the Soviet Union to find itself in a war with the Western world."[37] Stalin's treatment of several other ethnic minorities was even worse. There was deportation accompanied by mass deaths due to deprivation under the conditions of late-war-years devastation. If anti-Semitism means singling out the Jewish people in discriminatory fashion, that term does not apply.

When Hitler invaded the USSR Stalin immediately deported eastward the entire Volga German population of 400,000, just as U.S. President Roosevelt herded the Japanese into concentration camps, also with no more justification than racial bias. Several small nationalities in the Caucasus like the Tatars of the Crimea were also exiled en masse because minorities among them had collaborated with the Nazis during the occupation. This entire policy was repudiated after Stalin's death. First, the facilities for ethnic cultural expression of the exiled peoples were restored, then they were returned to their original territories, except for the

Germans and Tatars, who had already been replaced in their former lands.

The very years of intimidation, 1948-52, saw publication of literature placing Jewish characters in a very favorable light. That occurred under a system in which every single book has to pass a political censor. Joshua Kunitz, whose doctoral work at Columbia had been on *Russian Literature and the Jew*,[38] studied the literature of that period, and in 1953 wrote: "Russian and Ukrainian literature since 1948 has produced not one negative Jewish image." In *Far From Moscow*, by Vasili Azhaev, which won the Stalin Prize for Literature in 1949, the year it was published, "one of the two central heroes is a Jewish Communist leader in the Far East, by the name of Zalkind. He is one of the most appealing Jewish characters in all of literature. . . . A novel that receives the Stalin Award is assured an enormous circulation in the USSR. Why an allegedly anti-Semitic government should publish, honor, and popularize a work of fiction which cannot but dispose the Soviet reader favorably to the Jew is a mystery." The next year, 1950, saw the publication of a novel, *Youth*, by a Ukrainian, Alexander Voichenko, in which "the central character is a most sympathetic and devoted young Communist, a Jew bearing the unmistakeably Jewish name Aaron Itskovich."[39]

The recovery of Yiddish culture began with the founding of the magazine *Sovetish Haimland* in 1961. It was necessary to import type, because even that had been destroyed. Its circulation is larger than that of any other magazine in Yiddish in any country—in fact, it is larger than the combined circulations of the several small Yiddish magazines during the flourishing of that culture in the USSR in the 1930s. It was able to begin because most of the established professional writers in Yiddish had not been killed in the 1948 purge—over 100 survived, and they were its initial contributors. I have interviewed the editor of *Sovetish Haimland*, Aaron Vergelis, who is proud of the fact that he has some extremely young contributors, which he takes as evidence that Yiddish as a language is no mere dying ember. The life of Vergelis, a poet, embodies what might be termed the Communist history of Soviet Jewry. Born in the Ukraine, he grew up in Birobidjan, the Jewish Autonomous Region in Siberia. His first poems were set there. He graduated in literature in Moscow, and is a veteran of World War II. I have mentioned a bust and a bas-relief portrait of two of the writers murdered under Stalin in his office.

His magazine cultivates not only current Yiddish literature, but publishes art, particularly by those who work on Jewish themes.

Photo by Author

Bilingual sign outside Moscow office of literary magazine,
Sovetish Heimland.

The magazine carried Yiddish lessons at first and, starting in 1977,
serialized a new textbook and grammar by Elie Falkovich, a
highly-respected linguist. The alphabet is also readily available in
the *Large Soviet Encyclopedia,* and in the nine-volume *Brief* (!)
Literary Encyclopedia. So that people who understand but do not
read the language can learn to do so on their own. That would
apply to me, for example. A Hebrew-Russian Dictionary, with a
grammar of the Hebrew language, was published in 1963. A
Russian-Yiddish Dictionary was published in 1984. However, it
had been contracted for nearly 20 years earlier, and compiled
before that. Clearly, political attitudes had continued to affect the
authorities' attitude toward Yiddish.

An analysis of the content of *Sovetish Haimland* by the editor of U.S. government magazine, *Problems of Communism*, writing with his father, quite reluctantly grants that: *"Sovetish Haimland* has over the years succeeded in injecting a certain amount of specifically Jewish content in a Yiddish Communist publication. . . . Most of the writing shows no special tendency to glorify Soviet achievements. . . . There has been a marked improvement in its literary quality, a more daring political tone, a growing and frequently quite astonishing attempt at broadening the limits of Jewish national identification. . . . The tendency . . . to increase the latitude of tolerance toward Yiddish literature in all its aspects would not be so noteworthy did it not coincide with an even more unusual demand for a fuller grant of recognition to Hebrew and Hebrew literature. *Sovetish Haimland* fulfills its role as a specifically *Jewish* journal by providing its readers, through its regular section on current events, with some information about Jewish cultural life both inside and outside the Soviet Union."[40]

It has published Israeli Hebrew writers in translation. Collections of Israeli stories and poetry have subsequently been published in book form, in Russian. Publication of new Soviet Yiddish creative literature in book form resumed several years after the magazine appeared and now occurs in a steady and impressive stream. Prof. Gitelman writes that "some of it [is] of very high quality."[41] The printings of individual titles can go as high as 30,000. That is more than at any previous time in Russia, or than in any other country where Yiddish is read. Fluent reading literacy was lower in the past. Interest in literature in the USSR today is the highest, ever, in the world. As of 1984, well over 100 books of new creative literature in Yiddish had been published subsequent to the revival of printing in that language. The Israel-oriented Jewish press in the West keeps this secret by simply not reviewing them in periodicals or newspapers.*

What is most astounding is the translation into other languages of books written in Yiddish. From 1955 to 1970, 466 such titles had been translated into 15 Soviet languages, in an *average* printing of 100,000 copies per book. In the United States, a writer is regarded as having succeeded — this has nothing to do with ethnicity — if his

---

*For example, the monthly *Jewish Currents* presents itself as concerned with the furtherance of Yiddish-language culture. Yet Soviet novels in that language, now published on an average of one per month, are never reviewed, although it carries in literally every issue obscure statistics that it interprets to show alleged restrictions upon Soviet Jews and always finds room for reviews of books on the most esoteric details of Jewish life in the West and in the past.

book sells 15,000. Morris Schappes, the editor of an American Jewish monthly which is unremittingly critical of the USSR with respect to Jews, wrote me expressing his belief that these statistics must pertain to books by authors of Jewish ethnic origin writing in Russian. He is mistaken. Soviet encyclopedias identify writers as Russian if they write in that language, even if their names are unmistakeably Jewish or their biographies read, "born into a Jewish family," or even report that their "first writings" were in Yiddish. For example, Emmanuil Kazakevich is described as a "Russian Soviet writer," who "in the 1930s published verses, song lyrics, and long poems in the Jewish language."[42] But the books that brought him fame were written in Russian, and not on Jewish themes. The term "Jewish writer" is applied to those who write in Yiddish, and it is to them that the statistics I cited apply.

But what of a book on a Jewish theme, written by an ethnically Jewish author, but in Russian, just as American Jews write on Jewish themes in English? For example, there is Anatoly Rybakov's *Heavy Sand*, published in 1978, recently published in the U.S. in English, which tells of the "Rakhlenko family—cobblers, storemen, railroad workers and carters at the start of the story and a far cry from the standard image of Jews in Russia before the 1917 Revolution as downtrodden weaklings living in fear. . . . Told in the first person with a strong Jewish style, [it] demonstrates clearly that the Jews were the primary victims of the German occupying forces in World War II." His characters are "strong personalities proud of their national identity."[43] The Soviet encyclopedia identifies Rybakov as a Russian writer, because of the language in which he works. If this had been Rybakov's only novel, he would have been termed "a Jewish writer expressing himself in Russian."

This is no minor matter of interest only to literary specialists or nationalists. It has to do with the fact that an ethnic culture may develop in an adopted language. The Soviet authorities responsible for the appearance of new periodicals apparently do not recognize this. When they do, it will again be possible for a Jewish magazine to appear in the Russian language, as was the case in the 1930s. Such a publication is all the more needed today, when the great majority of those who identify themselves as Jews by nationality do not know Yiddish, any more than most American Jews do. *Sovetish Haimland* now publishes a Russian-language synopsis section. The present policy on periodicals is also inconsistent, as *books* by Jewish writers on Jewish themes in languages other than Yiddish, including Russian, have been published. Contrary to the opinion of most students of Soviet Jewish affairs, Rybakov's book was not a breakthrough. Itskhokas Meras, a Jew who writes in Lithuanian, has repeatedly published on Jewish themes. Leonid Pervomaisky, a significant novelist writing in Ukrainian, dealt with a Soviet Jewish soldier killed in action in World War II who was posthumously denied credit for heroism due to anti-Semitism. Pervomaisky (1908-1973) was himself Jewish.

Soviet Jews find outlets for creativity and ability in literally every field of endeavor. Yet they continue to find their lives somewhat clouded by remnants of anti-Semitism and the problems arising from Israel's alliance with the United States. Supporters of this alliance have attempted to alienate Jews from their society and to use the Jews to arouse the enmity of the American people against the USSR.

Emigration has been the biggest issue in the past 15 years. It is to be remembered that Soviet education is free, which means that it is a charge on the public purse. When significant emigration began to be permitted about 1970, the Soviets initiated a tax on persons leaving, graduated in terms of their level of educations. Protest abroad caused Moscow to drop that. Now it faces both a brain drain and a loss of the money spent on educating the emigrants. This may have contributed to the reduction in the number of Jews admitted to higher education. It remains about *twice as high as their share in the population*, and *higher than the percentage of Jewish youth in Israel who get into college.* In the 1976-77 school year, there were 48,200 in Israel, and 67,000 Jewish students in the USSR, which has a smaller Jewish population than Israel. The *percentage* of Jews attending college rose during the next two years,* despite the fact that emigration was at its height.[44] Currently, more than one-quarter of all employed Jews in the USSR hold jobs requiring college education. *That is higher than among any ethnic group in the world.* That holds for Russians in the USSR, Jews or white Protestants in the U.S., Jews in Israel, etc. Today, a considerable component of what anti-Semitism one finds in the USSR rests on professional jealousy. This phenomenon is not confined to Jews; Soviet anthropologists have found it as between highly educated Tatars vs. Russians, and the like.

Zionist policy, in disrupting U.S.-Soviet relations, gives ammunition to the anti-Semites. In 1977, in a world plagued with massive human rights violations in Chile, Korea, Ireland, Uganda,

---

*The *number* of Jewish students remains stable: 66,900 in 1979.

and dozens of other countries, U.S. congressmen got up and made speeches for 96 consecutive days on behalf of that many Soviet Jews allegedly denied the right to emigrate or otherwise suffering. The following year a campaign began to "rescue" a sick infant from death at the hands of the Russian monsters. When the child and its parents arrived here, TV camermen zoomed in and the country saw a healthy baby. This was too much even for the *N.Y. Times*, which has not exactly been an innocent bystander in the condemnation of the USSR: "Jessica Katz, the infant daughter of a Russian couple whose efforts to emigrate to the U.S. were aided by widely circulated reports that the child was gravely ill, has apparently been in good health *ever since the campaign in the family's behalf began last spring.* . . . A mistaken impression of the child's condition appears to have been furthered by expressions of humanitarian enthusiasm exaggerated by American Jewish organizations . . ., press reports that repeated and sometimes *amplified those exaggerations*, and a bandwagon of members of Congress and other politicians who signed petitions and even went to Moscow to make appeals"[45] [my emphasis-W.M]. The coordinating organization was the Union of Concern for Soviet Jewry.

In 1979 a campaign began over a man named Anatoly Shcharansky. That year, 2,400 scientists in the U.S. called for curtailing scientific cooperation with the Soviet Union until he is released. Morris Pripstein of the Lawrence Berkeley Laboratory "said American scientists have not taken a group action of this magnitude since they opposed Nazi Germany."[46] That was a sad commentary on their lack of concern for wars and mass-scale injustices in the world — as well as a tribute to the connections and financing of those who organized this action, even if the protestors had an unassailable case. The Shcharansky affair has not yet joined those that preceded it in limbo as this book goes to press. Therefore it is worth citing *Newsweek's* article when he was tried in 1978:

> One U.S. official [in Washington] told *Newsweek*: "What Shcharansky did, in effect, was give [Los Angeles *Times* correspondent] Toth a list of secret defense plants." One State Department official admitted that "in Soviet eyes, Shcharansky is guilty as hell." One of the most damaging bits of evidence . . . was a letter . . . in which a former U.S. military attache in Moscow thanked Toth for his cooperation (and) also passed on praise from Lt. Gen. Samuel Wilson, then head of the Pentagon's Defense Intelligence Agency.[47]

Shcharansky's acts were motivated by refusal to permit him to emigrate on the ground that he had had access to secret data.

These campaigns originate in *"a high-level and semi-secret bureau in the Israeli government which is responsible for Soviet Jewish affairs and reports directly to the prime minister."*[48] *Newsday*, published on Long Island, New York, wrote: "It is not the urging of individual constituents that has created the vast bulk of these letters and protests. What has been stirring the House into activity is a campaign by Jewish groups that work under two umbrella organizations — the National Conference on Soviet Jewry and the Union of Councils on Soviet Jews."[49] Congress has been influenced not only to make speeches and visits to Moscow. It also legislated, in the Jackson-Vanik Amendment of 1973, that the USSR must continue to pay uniquely high tariffs unless and until it amends its emigration practices to meet this congressional ultimatum. And Congress has directly stimulated emigration. In 1972 it appropriated $50,000,000 "to assist in the movement and resettlement of Soviet emigrants." The State Department gave $44,000,000 of that sum to United Israel Appeal, a private organization, for housing *in Israel*, etc.[50] For emigrants coming to the United States, the U.S. spends $1,000 each from the time they step off the train in Vienna.[51] I have yet to read of such assistance to the Mexican immigrants, or the Black Haitians fleeing the murderous Duvalier government.

"When an emigre finally arrives in this country, an apartment, furnished and stocked with food, will be waiting. For the next three months, rent will be paid . . . For as long as they need it, emigres will receive counseling, job assistance, and help in dealing with the American maze of human services."[52] The reference is to Jews alone.

The Washington *Post's* expert on Soviet Affairs, Dusko Doder, did a lengthy survey of the immigrants reasons for coming. He quotes one, now an editor for *Novoye Russkoye Slovo* in New York: "But most of his compatriots, Ostrovsky says, are leaving the Soviet Union for economic reasons. 'They just come and they don't know why'."[53] That corresponded exactly to words I had listened to skeptically from the Jewish sculptor, Zair Azgur, in Belorussia, who compared the emigration to a stampede, mass hysteria. I taped the following comments from a study of the immigrants aired on TV by the Public Broadcast Service in 1983: "Chasing dollars, we have lost our child." "I can think of nothing but my business." "When somebody started a competing business, my first impulse was to go and kill him." A poet: "Here there is endless freedom, and endless indifference to the written word. In Russia the writer is a prophet; here no one will listen." Of the dozens in-

Photo by Author

Zair Azgur, proudly Jewish and Stalinist Communist, with his head of Karl Marx. See interview with him in Chapter 12.

terviewed, two gave anti-Semitism as their reason for leaving the USSR.

Forty percent of those Jews who left the USSR went not to Israel, but to the United States where they have shown little or no interest in Jewish affairs. These 100,000 emigrated not because Jews were being persecuted, but, largely, because private business is prohibited. Many came simply because their skills would command high wages here; a few came to find a wider range of creativity in the arts.

The great majority of those who went to Israel vote for right-wing parties favoring Israeli territorial expansion and maximum squeezing out of Arabs, as do most American Jews who have emigrated to Israel. Such voting patterns suggest their concern in the USSR was not equality but a desire for apartheid.

The overwhelming majority of Soviet Jews, like the overwhelming majority of American Jews, have no desire whatever to leave their native land. Zionism cannot admit that, because it would undermine U.S. government economic and military aid as an ally against the USSR. Therefore it maintains an unending campaign against non-existent persecution of Jews in the Soviet Union.

The Israeli government, the Zionist organizations that accept its policies and promote them abroad, and the U.S. government with its own considerations of oil and anti-Communist policy, have worked for at least thirty years (since the postwar smuggling of Jews from the USSR to Palestine, documented earlier) to wean Soviet Jewish citizens from their society. Clearly, it is preposterous not to expect Moscow to strike back.*

Soviet books, such as one titled *Beware, Zionism!*, therefore become understandable, but the anti-Semitic aspects of some Soviet books on that subject are not.

Such books, and even mass-circulation newspapers, have carried stuff that appears elsewhere in anti-Semitic gutter sheets. For example, they write that the Baptist John D. Rockefeller, Sr., and his descendants are Jews! Editor Vergelis has bitterly attacked such writings in *Sovetish Haimland*, but he said to me only, "Our publishing industry is big, and different things get printed," a vague evasion of a long-standing battle in the Soviet Jewish community.

Marxist Jews, like all Marxists, hold that the worker and the employer (capitalist) are natural enemies. They argue that Zionists would unite all Jews into a nation confronting other nations, as all nations in the capitalist world do, and that such a Jewish nation would increasingly favor capitalism. That is undeniably what has happened in the Israeli economy as well as its foreign policy. Even socialist-minded Zionists in Israel, and their supporters in the West who have no intention of emigrating, back a country founded on taking over a land inhabited by others. The fact that Israel itself, and Zionists everywhere, oppose the establishment of any Palestinian state has brought consistent and near-unanimous United Nations condemnation of Zionism as racist by its own principles.

But this can make the Jewish Marxist a more bitter enemy of the Zionist than non-Jewish Marxists are — it is the Zionist who is directly competing for the mind and emotions of the Jewish worker, employee, intellectual and professional.†

A consequence of this competition for hearts and minds is that

---

*To support Zionist defense of Israel as a beleaguered country is to imagine that the clock stopped prior to 1956, when Israel joined Britain and France in an attempt to take the Suez Canal from Egypt by armed force. Israel, now holding parts of four countries — Jordan's West Bank, Syria's Golan Heights, southern Lebanon and Egypt's Gaza Strip — has thus become an empire.

†More than sixty years ago, an aunt of my wife's committed suicide as a young woman in Vilna (Vilnius) when her traditionalist, business-owning parents would not permit her to marry a Jewish Communist soldier during the Civil War. (The same conflict appears in milder form in *Fiddler on the Roof.*]

many of the books and articles in the Soviet Union that are described (I think correctly) as anti-Semitic in the manner in which they assault Zionism have been written, or passed for publication, or favorably publicized by Jews![54]

As I have noted, *Sovetish Haimland* editor Vergelis has advanced to outright attacks against anti-Semitic books. However, criticisms such as his are published only in the Yiddish language, which is understood by an insignificant fraction of the Soviet population and only a small proportion of Jews themselves!

Were there *no* other attacks on anti-Semitism in the Russian-language press and in literature in various Soviet languages, one might conclude that the Yiddish protests are allowed as a propaganda device to calm Jews abroad. But they do appear, with increasing frequency. I can only guess that in the ongoing struggle, by Vergelis and others, to deal with anti-Semitism ideologically out in the open, in which he has been gaining, thanks in part to protest from abroad by Communist parties among others, the die-hard Jewish anti-Zionists still hold the upper hand and are fighting hard to maintain it.

An encouraging recent development is the appearance in mass-circulation newspapers of articles directly denying canards about the Jews. Others remind people of the special suffering of the Jews in World War II, or forthrightly attack anti-Semitism. As Soviet citizens take literature much more seriously than newspapers, such articles are probably much less important than the rich presence of positive Jewish characters, and the treatment of many problems in creative literature, including false accusations during the 1948-52 "black years," the use of anti-Semitism against a general in the Soviet Army.[55] and of wartime anti-Semitism, in books previously discussed. But because newspapers directly reflect policy, these things are significant.

In the *Literary Gazette*, with 2,500,000 circulation, the highly-respected Lithuanian Jewish Communist hero in the anti-Nazi underground, Henrikas Zimanas, responded to articles that are anti-Semitic under cover of being anti-Zionist. He pointed out, as I have mentioned earlier, that only 200,000 of 6,000,000 American Jews belong to Zionist organizations. He also spelled out the matter of genocide: "The Hitlerites dealt ferociously with Soviet people regardless of nationality, [but] they sought to exterminate the Jews, and the overwhelming majority of them were in fact wiped out."[56] *

---

*Zimanas' wartime headquarters is now a national shrine. See "Overview" chapter for much on him.

Another article, by a non-Jew, dealt with the same issue by bitterly attacking the wide distribution to British schoolchildren of books denying that there had been a holocaust against the Jews. Anti-Semitic novels by a man named Shevtsov were attacked as trash in major publications and withdrawn from circulation although their printings had been quite large. In Chapter 10 I describe the publication in 1975 in a large printing (100,000) of a book on Nazi murder of children, focused on Jews, in Azerbaijan. Since the postwar "black years," many streets and even ships have been named for prominent Jews.

Yet, *Beware, Anti-Semitism!* has *not* been written, although there have been novels, articles and autobiographies making that point; nor are there lectures and courses against anti-Semitism as there were in early Soviet years. There is not much one can do about individuals like the oilworker I heard say: "I've got the money to buy a car, but I can't. It's all the fault of the Jews," or the totally anti-Soviet types who say of Lenin, "Take the Jew out of the Mausoleum," because one of his grandfathers, a Dr. Blank, was a convert from Judaism.

When plain hoodlums burned a synagogue in a Moscow suburb, or when terrorists killed people with a bomb in a subway car and then used their legal right to the last word to say Hitler was right about Jews, all that can be done, and was done, is to punish them for the crimes they did commit. In the latter instance, *Izvestia* carried a lengthy letter by a non-Jewish relative of a victim, denouncing in outrage the anti-Semitic statement by the chief criminal.

In 1982, my wife and I encountered a grossly anti-Semitic Russian collective farm chairman. Our argument was dramatic. The chairman had said that the Fords and Rockefellers were Jews, that Jewish sacred writings call upon Jews to rule the world. I snapped: "That's a Black-Hundred lie," a response more challenging than any words of personal insult as it referred to the home-grown, anti-Communist, anti-Semitic storm troopers of tsarist Russia.

Yet the chairman barged on, and told of being in a military hospital during the war where all the wounded soldiers shared packages from home, except the one Jew, who hogged his. "What do you think of him?" asked the chairman. I answered: "He was a scoundrel." The Party leader of the farm, an ethnic German, said to his chairman: "you can't judge a people by one individual." I realized he must have used that answer often in the years when many Soviet people judged all Germans by Hitler. At this point, a

Kirgiz woman — this farm was in Central Asia; the Kirgiz are of Moslem heritage, and religious belief is widespread — launched into a brilliant attack on racism of any kind. As we left the farm, I said to another Kirgiz woman, representing the county Communist Party: "I imagine there will be some discussion of this incident." She replied, in effect: "You can bet your bottom dollar." By this time, the anti-Semite, a tall and broad man, had shrunk into his shoulders. I pointedly reported the incident to my hosts in the radio systems in both Kirgizia and Moscow.

Perhaps, if their schoolteachers had been vigorously informed about the Jews, even individuals such as this farm chairman would have overcome beliefs usually transmitted in the family. But not only schoolteachers need straightforward, factual answers to stereotypes and slanders.* Once, when I discussed the Jewish issue with a Soviet diplomat who had never showed the slightest traces of anti-Semitism, he commented, "But Jews dominate culture and the arts!" I asked whether Shostakovich or Prokofiev or Khachaturian (the three leading composers of Soviet times) were Jewish. "No." came the reply. I named Sholokhov, Simonov, Shukshin, the three writers most prominent when we were speaking. "No." "Kapitsa, Korolev?": topmost names in science. "No." "So where did you get the idea that Jews 'dominate'?" He shrugged: "That's what people say." Yet this man had been assigned to the country with the largest Jewish population in the world, where no issue was causing his government more difficulty than allegations regarding the Soviet Jews. But Jews are so very large a minority in these fields that to a Russian who comes from a rural area or small city — like this man — where Jews are rare, the contrast is so sharp that they might well seem to be predominant. But he also expressed an anti-Uzbek sentiment, when I said that Soviet consulates need to have "visible minorities" on their staffs.

For people who perpetuate stereotypes not from ill-will, who do not even know they are stereotypes, or what an ethnic stereotype is, popular books — more than one — on the theme *Beware, Anti-Semitism!* are essential. If the topmost Soviet leaders gave this thought, they would realize that hearing such stereotypes repeated can only make people feel insecure.

---

*There are educators who combat this. A child told visiting American relatives that another child in summer camp had taunted her for being Jewish. She complained to the camp's suthorities. They reprimanded the child's counsellor, who had been present, for letting this go by. The guilty child was also reprimanded, and a public discussion held.

Because the Soviet Union is a more centralized country than our own, it is widely believed here, not without deliberate encouragement, that the occasional anti-Semitic publications are proof of governmental anti-Semitism. Today two cabinet members there, Dymshitz and Volodarsky, are Jewish — twice the Jewish ratio in the population. Leonid Zamyatin, head of a department of the Communist Party's Central Committee, who often traveled with Brezhnev, is Jewish. In the Khrushchev period, the N.Y. *Times'* Harrison Salisbury wrote, "The old czarist slogan 'Beat the Jews and save Russia' may be muttered by some hooligans but it gets no official encouragement. . . . The Jews now have powerful and articulate allies within the Soviet intellectual community who are actively seeking to arouse Russians to a feeling of shame and anger at the anti-Semitic stain on the national conscience."[57] Early in the Brezhnev period, Paul Wohl of the *Christian Science Monitor* wrote: "Anti-Semitism still permeates the thinking of many party and state officials *in the provinces up to the middle echelon.* Some of the top leaders have bowed to these prejudices."[58] [my emphasis-W.M.] Brezhnev's wife was Jewish.

Changes required include more than an educational campaign about Jews and anti-Semitism. Jews themselves must be enabled to learn more about their own people through histories. There must also be a new look at the policy which forbids organization on ethnic lines outside the ethnic "states" of the respective nationalities — Birobidjan, in the case of the Jews. It is laughable as well as outrageous that the only Yiddish-language daily is published in that Jewish Autonomous Region near the Pacific Ocean, with only 10,000 Jewish citizens, where virtually no Jewish news is made, though the paper circulates USSR-wide. The same policy means Yiddish can be learned in school only there. However, teachers of Yiddish are being trained there, which indicates their employment elsewhere is envisaged, and there are also courses for creative writers in Yiddish at the Gorky Institute of Literature in Moscow, the top Soviet school in this field.

Similarly, the Jewish Musical Chamber Theater is listed as "of Birobidjan," though its rehearsal hall and offices are in Moscow and it performs virtually everywhere but Birobidjan, for it goes where Jews actually live. (Its work is professionally superb, and includes mime dancing that is totally contemporary in style and unmistakeably Jewish in spirit). Jewish organizations and publications in the West have no sincere interest in Jewish culture in the USSR: they have made no attempt to see this theater's work. Its founding and intentions were accurately described to me by *Sovetish Haimland* editor Vergelis and a poet writing for that magazine, and I described its work on radio broadcasts in California, New York, and Washington, D.C. in 1977 and 1978. Finally, when I interviewed the director of the theater, Yuri Sherling, in 1982, one such publication felt that it had to publish it.

When we spoke, he was 38, "but when I received the opportunity to implement the idea of founding this theater, I was only 32. That made me the very youngest manager, also then the financial manager, as well as artistic director," of a professional theater company in the USSR. He went on: "I was born and raised in a family that had no direct relation to Jewish culture. This is simply my genes calling. My mother, Alexandra Sherling, is an orchestra conductor—she was, in fact, the first female conductor to emerge in the Soviet Union. She graduated from the Leningrad Conservatory as a conductor, conducted a symphony orchestra, and was a very major musical figure in Leningrad."

I asked how he found people to work with him.

I began to study from scratch. I gathered around myself old people who knew the language. I am a musician. I appealed to Choreography School No. 10 for them to demonstrate to me (I should explain that I'm also a choreographer, a graduate of the School of Choreography of the Bolshoi Theater) something Jewish in character. Regrettably, they had by that time totally forgotten, so then I tried an experiment—I danced for them the way I sensed it, and when I saw on their faces tears mixed

Billboard advertising play based on Sholom Aleichem's "Tevye" in Kiev, 1959.

with smiles, I understood that I was on the right track.

Anyhow, that's how our first opera was created. I sat and studied the volumes of the Bible. I studied the history of the Jews of Russia, of Lithuania, of Poland, I studied the Kabbala. . . . We recently did a series of performances in Moscow, true only 10 or 12 days in duration. But it was a big hit — and now we are rehearsing *Fiddler on the Roof*. . . . For the future, it is my intention to put on a folk opera devoted to the legendary Bar-Kochba. . . . I personally have the dream of doing an entire vocal cycle in Hebrew, moreover a cycle of religious songs, inasmuch as this is also a part of our culture — just as Russian choruses perform Orthodox chorales. That's also part of a single culture. I face absolutely no prohibitions on that score, none whatever.

When he did produce *Fiddler on the Roof* the following year, he included a wedding ceremony in Hebrew, the Tevye character also read from the Old Testament in Hebrew, and the entire stage design suggested a synagogue.

His audiences do not fully share his outlook. As he said to me: "Sometimes when we perform in a Jewish small town in Russia, they say to us: 'Why are you singing in Yiddish? Why don't you sing in Russian? We can't understand you.'." He was bitter about the silence about his work in the West:

When the opera [*A Black Bridle for a White Horse*] first saw the light, I received a letter from the U.S. . . . I corresponded for a year or two, and then I arranged for 500 copies of the records of my opera to reach the U.S. Whereupon Sam [his correspondent] wrote to 500 Jewish organizations a letter in which he wrote: "This thing exists." Not one single organization sent a letter in reply. That had a terribly depressing impact on me. I said to Misha [the musical director]: "Why are we busting our guts?"

I deeply regret that our play cannot be seen by your sons. . . . That is an error on the part of your government and of our government, . . . that we cannot touch each other. . . . Ways of doing this have to be sought. Of course, there is one channel for this — that record, even though it is the first."[59]

In New York, I sought to purchase copies, but in that city, with the largest Jewish population in the world, the best of record stores — I went to and phoned many — claimed not to know it existed.

No one in the Soviet Union argues publicly that the policy of the 1930s, in which Jewish magazines in Russian, a Jewish club in Moscow, existed, was wrong. It has not been reinstated today.

Perhaps the authorities ought to give some thought to the meaning of their own figures that the percentage of Jews belonging

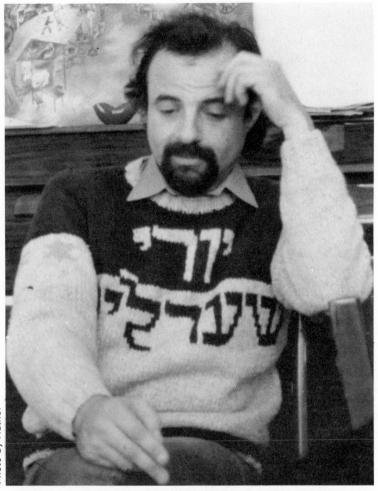

Yuri Sherling, head of Jewish Musical Theater.

to the Communist Party is twice their share in the population, and higher than among any other nationality, including the Russians. [60]

On the other hand, Jews in the West have been so misinformed that as many as 100,000 young people turned out for a demonstration in New York in 1979 which they were told was on behalf of Soviet Jewry. They might give thought to some of my personal encounters in the USSR, which are not at all unique.

I wandered alone into the Kishinev museum devoted to a Moldavian hero of the Revolution, Kotovsky. A group of Soviet people already there was listening to the guide's standard lecture. To emphasize the intelligence of a man from a workingclass family, she pointed out that he was fluent in four languages: Moldavian, Russian, Ukrainian, and Yiddish, though he was not a Jew.

In Berkeley, a dozen years ago I met the chairman of the Department of Foreign Economies of Moscow University. He was traveling alone and meeting with the head of the Federal Reserve Board, the New York Stock Exchange, and others at that level. Samuel Dragilev by name, he was a Jew; when he died in 1975, he received the exceptional honor of an obituary in *Izvestia*, which made the point that he was a veteran of the postrevolutionary Civil War. This kid from the Minsk ghetto had been a cavalryman in the legendary Budenny Army of Red Cossacks. He had also fought in World War II.

In a Kiev streetcar, we once met a sturdy middle-aged Jewish carpenter. He summed up his outlook very simply: "I have six suits. How many do you have?" A materially secure life and a clear track for his children is what he wanted, and believed he had.

Also in Berkeley, and also traveling on his own, I met the most famous documentary film-maker in the Soviet Union, Roman Karmen by name. Jewish, he made the 20-part TV serial, *The Unknown War*, widely shown in the U.S. He had covered the civil war in Spain, Mao's military campaigns in pre-war China, the Soviet fronts of World War II, Ho Chi-minh fighting the French, even President Kennedy during the razor's edge Cuban missile crisis of 1962. He had won the highest Soviet award in the arts three times, and a chestful of war medals.

The head of environmental protection in the Soviet Union, Yuri Israel, whose name is its own ethnic identification, visits the U.S. repeatedly in connection with the cooperative efforts in that field on an official level with American scientists. The Dragilevs, Karmens, Israels, musical soloists like Lazar Berman, Emil Gilels (Hillel), Leonid Kogan (Cohen), the late David Oistrakh, have had dozens of opportunities to defect if they chose. They have not.

When emigration dribbled to nearly a full stop in 1984, it had reached almost exactly the number predicted by Western diplomats at its beginning 13 years earlier. Hedrick Smith had then reported from Moscow: "Western diplomats estimate that as many as 200,000 to 300,000 Soviet Jews would leave, many using Israel as a jumping-off point for Western Europe or North America. That is slightly over 10 percent."[61] Their intelligence sources in the Jewish community were obviously superb.

The late Roman Karmen (left), famed Soviet filmmaker, and Lester Cole, blacklisted American screenwriter who tells of their meeting in his autobiography, *Hollywood Red* (Ramparts, 1982).

It is time for Americans, particularly Jews, to give thought to the fact that nearly 90 percent of Soviet Jews have shown no interest in emigration. That figure rises to 97 percent among those of Yiddish linguistic background whose roots are in the areas that have been Soviet for the full period since the Revolution.

NOTES

1. "USSR Census Returns," *Soviet Law and Government,* XIX, No. 2 (1980), 28-29.

2. "Arts of Jewish Peoples," *Encyclopedia Britannica,* (15th ed.; Chicago: Encyclopaedia Britannica, 1974), Macropaedia X, 196.

3. "Evrei," *Bol'shaia Sovetskaia Entsiklopediia* (3rd ed.; Moscow: "Sovetskaia Entsiklopediia," 1972), IX: 10.

4. "USSR Census Returns," *Soviet Law and Government,* XIX, No. 2, 28-29.

5. "Antisemitizm," in *Entsiklopediia,* II:80.

6. Sub-chapter, "Rasy i rasizm," in S.T. Kaltakhchian, *Marksistsko-Leninskaia teoriia natsii i sovremennost',* (Moscow: Politizdat, 1983), 33-53.

7. Zvi Gitelman, "The Jewish Question in the USSR Since 1964," in George W. Simmonds (ed.), *Nationalism in the USSR & Eastern Europe* (Detroit: University of Detroit, 1977), p. 325.

8. Calculated from Yakov Kapelush, "On Certain Statistics on the 1979 Population," *Sovetish Haimland* No. 12, 1980, translated in *Jewish Affairs,* XI, No. 3 (1981), 8; TsU SSSR, *Narodnoe khoziaistvo SSSR v 1980 g, statisticheskii exhegodnik* (Moscow: "Finansy i Statistika," 1981), p. 95. The former gives 4,400 Jewish *doktora* in 1977; the latter provides 36,000 as the total number of persons in the USSR holding that title that year. Jews are 0.7 percent of the Soviet population.

9. Calculated from N.V. Iukhneva, "Ethnic Aspects of Study of the Population of Prerevolutionary St. Petersburg," in *Soviet Sociology,* XVIII, No. 4 (1980), p. 17.

10. Calculated from I. Zinger, *Jews in the USSR* (in Yiddish), Moscow, 1939, cited in Solomon Rabinovich, *Jews in the Soviet Union,* (Moscow: Novosti, 1967), table, p. 53, and from census data.

11. Ibid., p. 45.

12. Salo W. Baron, *The Russian Jew Under Tsars and Soviets* (New York: Macmillan, 1964), 272.

13. Maurice Hindus, *Humanity Uprooted* (New York: Cape & Smith, 1929), 268.

14. V.I. Naulko, "The Present Ethnic Composition of the Population of the Ukrainian SSR," *Soviet Sociology,* III, No. 1 (1964), 18.

15. Albert Axelbank in *San Francisco Chronicle,* April 19, 1976; Robert C. Toth in *San Francisco Chronicle,* June 15, 1977; also see Samuel Aronoff, *Birobijan and Soviet Jews* (Laguna Hills: author, 1977).

16. "Evreiskaia literatura," in *Entsiklopediia,* pp. 11-13; also "Evreiskaia literatura," in *Kratkaia literaturnaia entsiklopediia* (Moscow: Sovetskaia Entsiklopediia, 1964), 850-861. Here one reads: "A severe blow was dealt to Jewish literature in the period of the cult of Stalin. Many innocent writers and critics were punished and lost their lives," followed by a list of the most prominent (p. 857). Published in 113,000 copies, this encyclopedia is a standard library reference.

17. Maurice Friedberg, *The Jew in Post-Stalin Literature* (Washington: B'nai B'rith, 1970), p. 13.

18. Hindus, 272.

19. *New Statesman,* London, December 15, 1978.

20. Joshua Kunitz, "The Jewish Problem in the USSR," *Monthly Review,* March, 1953, p. 6.

21. *San Francisco Chronicle,* August 7, 1977.

22. *New York Times,* August 25, 1980.

23. Anatoly Kuznetsov, *Babi Yar* (New York: Dial, 1967), xiii.

24. Friedberg, p. 41.

25. Zev Katz, "The Jews in the Soviet Union," in Zev Katz (ed.) *Handbook of Major Soviet Nationalities* (New York: Free Press, 1975), 363.

26. Cited in Henry Frankel, "Review of the Year 5706 — Eastern Europe; Union of Soviet Socialist Republics," in *American Jewish Yearbook* (New York: Jewish Publication Society, 1947), pp. 322-334.

27. Katz, p. 385, Table 15.11.

28. Z. Gitelman, in *Newsletter of the Amer. Assn. for the Advancement of Slavic Studies*, XVIII, No. 3 (1978), pp. 9-12.

29. Hindus, *Humanity Uprooted*, pp. 263-264.

30. Kunitz, "Jewish Problem," p. 9.

31. *New York Times*, January 26, 1953.

32. Kunitz, "Jewish Problem," p. 11.

33. Ibid., p. 20.

34. Ibid., p. 22.

35. William Korey of B'nai B'rith in *New York Times*, August 12, 1972.

36. Margarita Aliger, "A Path in the Rye," *Soviet Studies in Literature*, XVI, No. 4, pp. 30-35.

37. Maurice Hindus, *Crisis in the Kremlin* (Garden City: Doubleday, 1954), p. 11.

38. Joshua Kunitz, *Russian Literature and the Jew* (New York: Columbia University, 1929).

39. Kunitz, "Jewish Problem," p. 25.

40. Joseph Brumberg and Abraham Brumberg, *"Sovyetish Heymland* — An Analysis," in Erich Goldhagen, (ed.), *Ethnic Minorities in the Soviet Union* (New York: Praeger, 1968), 284-300, *passim*.

41. Gitelman, p. 328.

42. "Emmanuil Kazakevich," in *Entsiklopediia*, XI, 134.

43. *San Francisco Chronicle*, October 30, 1978.

44. Kapelush, p. 7.

45. Reprinted in *San Francisco Chronicle*, December 2, 1978.

46. *Berkeley Gazette*, March 1, 1979.

47. *Newsweek*, July 24, 1978, p. 24.

48. *San Francisco Chronicle*, November 9, 1976.

49. Ibid., June 20, 1977.

50. Ibid., October 4, 1973.

51. Ibid., December 3, 1978.

52. *Berkeley Monthly*, January, 1983, p. 14.

53. Reprinted in *San Francisco Chronicle* "Sunday Punch," August 10, 1980, p. 5.

54. Paul Novick, *Jews in the Soviet Union* (New York: Morning Freiheit, 1965), p. 12.

55. Friedberg, p. 55.

56. *Izvestia*, April 21, 1976.

57. Harrison Salisbury, in *New York Times*, February 8, 1962.

58. Paul Wohl in *Christian Science Monitor*, July 12, 1967.

59. William Mandel, "Rebuilding the Moscow Yiddish Musical Theater," *Jewish Currents*, XXXVII, No. 11 (1983), pp. 15-23, *passim*.

60. "KPSS v tsifrakh," *Partiinaia zhizn'*, 1976, No. 10.

61. Hedrick Smith in *New York Times*, December 30, 1971. Knowledge of the intentions of distinctive ethnic components among the Soviet Jews were equally correct. In the same paper, December 1, 1971, Smith reported: "Close students estimate that 40 percent of the Jewish population of Georgia would like to leave." That has proved almost precisely accurate.

Belorussia

BELORUSSIA

★Moscow

12

Belorussia
Vitebsk, Mogilev, Gomel, Minsk . . .

Many people know the name of one Belorussian, Olga Korbut, triple gold-medal winner at the 1972 Olympics, who put gymnastics on the map as a major sport for women. Almost as many will recognize another, Andrei Gromyko, Soviet Foreign Minister for nearly thirty years, and prior to that Ambassador to the United States, born to a peasant family under the tsar.

Relatively few ethnic Belorussians have emigrated to the U.S. or Canada, but a great many Jews will recognize the names of its provincial capitals as the places from which their parents or grandparents came: Vitebsk, Gomel, Mogilev, Grodno, Minsk, the national capital, etc. Before Hitler, Jews were 8 percent of the population, but fully forty percent of the urban population. Today, 1.4 percent of the people of Belorussia are Jewish.

In a way, Belorussia is to Russia as Portugal is to Spain: next door on the West, smaller, with similar but distinct language and people. Both Belorussia and Portugal have a population of about 9,500,000 but Belorussia is about twice as large, roughly the size of Minnesota or Utah. But while Portugal was a great world empire from the 15th century on, Belorussia enjoyed a place in the sun only briefly—when, Belorussians still proudly tell you, their Slavic language was the official tongue of the Grand Duchy of Lithuania, of which Belorussia was a part. But that period ended 300 years ago and from that time until the Russian Revolution of 1917, it was two steps down the ladder of oppression: its people were peasants under Polish landowners, who were themselves under Russian rule. In a sense, the Belorussians were colonials of semi-colonials, perhaps like the Indians and Eskimos of Canada in its early years under Britain. Use of the very word, "Belorussia," was declared illegal in 1840 in an attempt to force assimilation.

Lying between present-day Poland and Russia, Belorussia was on Napoleon's invasion route in 1812, that of the German Kaiser in 1914, and Hitler's in 1941. For twenty years between the World Wars it was divided between the Soviet Union and Poland, but since World War II, it has acquired a single and distinct political identity for the first time in its long history as the Belorussian Soviet Socialist Republic of the USSR. If the Jews were the *people* that lost the greatest proportion of its numbers in World War II, Belorussia was the *country* that did: one person in four — male and female, old and young — was killed or died.

I received unique lessons in Belorussian history via sculpture lessons, during visits with its most important artist, Zair Azgur, a Jew, in Minsk, in 1979 and 1982. He is a portraitist, and I recognized many world figures — Churchill, Stalin, Khrushchev, Ho Chi-minh, Kim Il-Sung, La Pasionaria of the Spanish Republic, the Bulgarian Dimitrov who defied Hitler in his own courtroom, the Chinese writer Lu Hsun, and, in Azgur's words: "the American poet of democratic spirit, one at whose grave I would fall to my knees, Walt Whitman." There was also the greatest Karl Marx I have ever seen, a monumental head that stands in red marble outside the headquarters of the Communist Party of Belorussia. There were Jewish figures: Ibn-Ezra and Judah Ha-Levi, poets in Spain in the 12th century; Jacob Sverdlov, president of Soviet Russia when Lenin was Prime Minister; the writer Boris Polevoi and the contemporary Yiddish-language poet and editor, Aaron Vergelis. There were non-Belorussian and non-Jewish figures as well. But above all, in this assemblage of nine hundred models and casts, the work of a long lifetime — he is nearing 80 — were Belorussians. He would point and explain.

These two princes are Belorussian. This one is Prince Vladimir of Polotsk, who in the 12th century drove out the German crusaders, the "dog-knights," who were constantly attacking eastward into the Slavic lands. He put his mounted troops on boats. And the other one is

Azgur's sculptures of Ibn-Ezra, Jewish poet of Spain, and a Belorussian peasant woman.

Vasilyek of Minsk. Generally speaking, I have no love for princes, but a prince who defended his native land is as dear to me as any other person, and so I did them with pleasure.

That's Harkusha, leader of a peasant rebellion of the 17th century. The early period of feudalism in Belorussia was extremely cruel. They had become slaves for all practical purposes, as Lenin said. But here and there, there were dreamers who thought that they had to free themselves.

Belorussia had a splendid history: there were peasant uprisings and rising of the craftsmen. That one over there is Stakhov Mitkovich, one of the leaders of the 17th century struggle for free city status and freedom for the craftsmen. So he was the first proletarian leader in Belorussia—he held the town of Mogilev for three years. He had an arsenal of his own — that's how the working class came into being there — and the Polish troops were unable to enter the city. But then some traitor betrayed him, and the troops, of course [and Azgur drew his finger across his throat.].

At the time of the Russian Revolution the life of the Belorussian peasantry was not fundamentally different than it had been in the 17th century, except that serfdom no longer existed.

This shows in the writings of a truly great observer of the Soviet Union, Maurice Hindus. Born about 1890 on a Belorussian peasant farm and raised there into his teens, he emigrated to the U.S., and returned to his native village in 1923, producing a marvelous book, *Broken Earth*.

He describes a "rich" house — it boasted "the only shingled roof in the village."

At last we stopped at the old home, a log hovel with a big mud-puddle before it . . . the living-room with its huge brick oven and dirt-crusted floor, serving as of old the manifold purposes of kitchen, dining-room, parlor, bedroom, nursery and hen-coop. . . . Not a chair, not a mirror, not a washstand, not a dresser. Not a picture . . . flies as thick, as vicious as ever. The floor damp, slippery, littered; the air hot, smoky, smelly. . . . My young cousin . . . seemed gloriously unconscious of the noxious dross and the blighting barrenness about him.

The town itself has no sidewalks; scarcely a shade-tree; not a patch of lawn; not a flower bush; the little heaps of manure lying as of old at every house right by the open well. And the fields were cut as of yore into narrow strips, narrower than in my boyhood days, which spoke of increased population, of further subdivisions [among sons] and of consequent decreased land-holdings and enhanced want. Some of the strips by actual measuring were no more than three paces in width . . . too preposterously small to grow enough bread even for mere man and wife. Yet there were families in the village that had to live off such puny holdings.

He witnessed a peasant woman beating a neighbor girl to within an inch of her life for stealing radishes from her garden. When men tried to pull her away, she yelled: "I should kill her!" This was not a famine year; just an ordinary one.

After a lapse of nineteen years Hindus visited the annual county fair and saw "Beggars, blind and lame, eternal reminders of misfortune and misery, leaning on stout crutches and led by children, were droning ancient chants to the accompaniment of ancient instruments. . . . Tons of conversation must precede every transaction, however small. . . . "

But he also saw the first changes: "There were no gamblers about as in the old days, no card and watch-chain tricksters and no fortunetellers with all manner of alluring schemes to coax copecks out of the pockets of credulous muzhiks. And though the peasants are addicted to the use of home-brew, there was not a single drunkard in sight. Nor were there any bloody brawls as in the old days."

In Hindus' village a mob of peasants complained to him about everything and anything:

"They've promised us a school-house, and where is it? Our children run about the streets all winter and are growing wild." The chairman of the village Soviet pushed forward and shouted: "Have not the Soviets offered you the private residence of the [Polish] landlord? It's only fifteen versts from here, and if you'd all get together you could move that magnificent home . . . in less than a week, and then you'd have one of the finest school-houses in Russia. . . .

But when it came to taking something for themselves, the peasants seized what they could get. The chairman went on: "Each of you wanted to grab all he could at once, and you fell on the forests like pigs on a potato field, and you hewed down every stick in sight. And what's been the result? Don't you see what you've done? Our river is drying up, and soon we won't even have a place to soak our flax and do our washing." [Ecological consciousness, 1923!]

But a dozen youth were ready to move the landlord's house if their elders wouldn't. They took Hindus out to a meadow one evening, and presented their point of view:

"And who ever saw a newspaper in this village in the old days?" continued Vassil. . . . "But now the Soviet is sending one over quite often, and pamphlets and books, too, so that the people here have a chance to know what is going on in the outside world where there are railroads, factories, and machines. And think of the change in the army! A miracle that is! In former times what was a soldier? A slave, a dog, to be kicked by drunken officers. . . . Now, when a muzhik boy goes to the army, nobody weeps. He goes away for only a short time, and during his service his family enjoy certain privileges, get a reduction in the amount of their taxes for one thing, and when he comes back he is a cultured man. He can read and write. He knows who Marx was and what he taught. . . . He believes in the Revolution . . . he knows that workmen or peasants, be they Russians or Americans or Chinamen, are brothers and should never go to war and shoot one another."

Hindus met separately with the women. They "laughed boisterously when I passed around a handful of candy, a luxury of luxuries to the muzhik." Here, too, the generation gap was sharp.

A toothless old woman asked him: "Tell me, do they allow a daughter-in-law in America to drive her husband's old mother from the house?" . . . . *"Babushka* (little grandmother)," said one of the girls, "why don't you go to town and complain to the Soviets?" "How can I go empty-handed? I haven't even an egg or a piece of pork to give the Soviet man."* "The devil only knows why they won't let us drink homebrew'" a middle-aged woman asked. "Because," the girl who had a Communist brother hastened to reply, "they don't want the men to get drunk and beat up their wives."

Hindus pondered what he had seen: "Unlike the men, these women grieved over things other than of the flesh. . . . It was a crime to beat a child. It was a crime to take a sip of home-brew. It was a crime to give an official a gift. . . . Never before had I fully realized the immensity of the task they [the Soviets] had under-taken—to build a new society in a land where not only the flail and the sickle were in universal use, but where the mass of the people were so elemental, so unenlightened, so woefully unmoral, that innocently enough their very age-old vices and perversities they had exalted into rights and virtues as indispensable to their being as the bread they ate. Here was a people sodden in medieval dross; who, confronted with the colossal task of retrieving them from it, would not commmit ugly and cruel blunders? Perhaps the Soviets have committed more than their share. Who shall say?"

Candidly, I love that sentence about vices and perversities. I've had my bellyfull in recent years of the *kind* of non-judgmental cultural relativism which says that whatever a people does is part of its culture and therefore all right. Deep down, this "liberalism" is a subtle excuse for doing nothing about the hunger, disease, and ignorance that afflict all "traditional societies" and for leaving them in a situation that permits easy, minimal-cost exploitation.[1] Hindus wrote, of his year-long 1923-24 visit:

> Again and again while visiting village Soviets I was under the illusion that I was in some school where grown men and women were taught the rudiments of civilized living—the proper way to cultivate this or that crop; decent care of human and animal health; the effective method to combat epidemics, fires, droughts; and above all respectable personal behavior. . . . Whenever in a moment of forgetfulness a peasant ad-dressed an official as "master" or "your honor" or removed his hat and sought to kiss the official's hand and in other ways to make obeisance

---

*The bribery that still exists is rooted in those deep folk attitudes.

to him, he was severely upbraided and reminded that the days of fawning and cringing before so-called superiors was past and that a muzhik was the equal of any man and must never demean himself before anyone.

Each time I encounter, in the Soviet Union, evidences of a consciousness of rank and status that offend me as an American, I remind myself that the feudal attitudes Hindus described still existed there in the 1920s.

Throughout Hindus' visit, his fellow-villagers complained that the government had refused to break up a Polish landowner's estate, but instead had converted it into an experimental farm. Finally, he went to see the man the peasants angrily called the Red Landlord. He was 29, but his hair and stubble beard had turned gray. He complained of the peasants stealing from the public farm, but added; "Wasn't I taught to steal when I was a boy? Hardly an evening but I'd row over in a canoe to the landlord's meadow, cut a heaping basketful of grass for our calf, and sneak back home. . . . Without that stolen grass we couldn't raise our calf."

He told Hindus of an anti-Semitic pogrom incited by a tsarist general turned guerrilla, showed him a lovely chapel on the estate that the peasants had stripped for its bricks, iron, tin, wood, despite the fact that they regarded themselves as religious, and then took him to a beautiful grove of birch, elm, oak, and fir, once the landlord's private picnic and driving ground. He said:

> Do you realize that if we had not kept guards out there day and night, nothing would have been left of it by this time, not a stick of wood, not a spear of grass? . . . Why, think! we could turn this grove into a public park and in summer children could come here with competent instructors and play and study and hear stories.
> . . . Here our children could learn to understand nature, flowers, trees, birds; the sky, the stars, the seas, the mountains. Here they could be taught to love all the poor peoples in the world, all of them, white and black and red and the others, and all living things, too, and then they wouldn't be stealing birds' nests and killing birds with stones as peasant boys used to in my boyhood days. And Sundays we could all come here, with our families, have picnics, lectures, dances, theatrical performances, concerts. And then we'd all be happy and learn to know each other and the world, and strive for the peace and the happiness of all poor mankind. We shall come to that yet. We shall, only give us time, give us time. [2]

Thirty-five years later, and on many subsequent visits, I saw such parks, doing precisely what he had predicted, on each of the Soviet collective farms I visited in the European West, in the Caucasus South, and in the sandy one-time deserts of Central Asia.

Belorussian peasant life was very similar to that of the Russians; as a matter of fact, Hindus, knowing that Belorussia meant nothing to his American readers, said he was writing of the Russian peasant. Only forty years later, in the last of his dozen books on the Soviet Union, did he identify "my native village" as being Belorussian. The only concrete difference was that the landlord was Polish, rather than Russian, that there were Jews in the countryside — they were essentially forbidden to live in Russia proper — and that swamp meadows played an important role in farming. Today there are collective farms in Belorussia headed by Jews. Prerevolutionary illiteracy was actually worse in Russia than Belorussia. This must be understood if one is to form some judgment of the amount of assistance the Russians were able to give other Soviet peoples in the early years of what was essentially a bootstrap operation.

Belorussian folk and urban culture became differentiated from Russian partly because Russia was overrun by, and paid tribute to, Tatars for several centuries, while Belorussia was not. Indeed, this seems to be the origin of the name: "belyi" (pronounced *byeh*lee) means "white," which signified freedom. Belorussia was ruled by Lithuania, then Poland; the Lithuanian kings originally permitted religious tolerance but Poland enforced Catholicism, using the device of a Uniate Church of the Eastern Rite.

Belorussian folk dance is particularly rich — about a hundred different patterns are known, many of them still performed in a synthesis with games and song, as in ancient times. Wood-carving and reed inlay, pottery, decorative sewing and jewelry had distinctive Belorussian characteristics. But above the folk peasant level cultural life was so underdeveloped at the time of the Revolution that some, even among the Communists, argued that Belorussia as a distinct nation was a figment of the imagination. Yet in 1921 Joseph Stalin accurately forecast how that people's potential would develop and manifest its ethnic distinctness. Speaking at a Communist Party Congress, he said, in reply to the debate on his report on nationality policy:

> I have here a note alleging that we Communists are cultivating the White-Russian nationality artificially. This is not true, because there is a White-Russian nation, which has its own language distinct from Russian, and it is therefore possible to raise the cultural level of the White-Russian people only in its native language. . . . About forty

years ago Riga [capital of Latvia] was a German town; but since towns grow by influx from the countryside . . . , Riga is now a purely Lettish [Latvian] town. About fifty years ago all the towns of Hungary bore a German character; now they are Magyarised. The same will be true of White Russia, in the towns of which non-White-Russians still predominate.[3]

The use of the Belorussian language in schools, particularly in literacy courses for adults, brought the literacy rate up to ninety percent within ten years after Hindus' 1923 visit. Industrialization, bringing urbanization, changed the ethnic character of the cities: in 1929-30, Belorussian workers edged past Jewish workers to a ratio of 5 to 4 in urban employment for wages.[4] Today's total employment in industry is 25 times greater, and added employees consists essentially of Belorussians who have come from the farms, particularly since World War II, when industry was wiped out, and everything had to be rebuilt from scratch. As Stalin predicted, the cities and towns are now overwhelmingly Belorussian.

In government, an affirmative-action program was pursued from the outset, limited only by the requirement of literacy and the need for at least some people with organizational experience and a clear notion of the new system. As a consequence, Belorussians were already sixty-one percent of the office-holders by 1930[5] and as much as seventy-two percent in the countryside.

While Belorussians were a geographic nationality, they had never constituted a country until the Revolution, so boundaries were difficult to draw, especially as there is no natural physical border in the flat East European plain, nor any abrupt change from majority Belorussian to majority Russian areas. Initially the Belorussian Soviet Socialist Republic was fairly small, but as the ethnic composition of the countryside became clear, the Russian Republic ceded large territories to Belorussia in the 1920s. As late as the 1960s, part of a county was transferred "at the request of the local population," according to an emigre scholar.[6] With territories regained from Poland in 1939, Belorussia is now six times as large as at its founding in 1919. The Soviet explanation for these shifts is interesting in terms of problems presently facing countries in Africa and elsewhere:

The Soviet republics were born as republics of population mixed by nationality. Considerable areas in which populations of some other nationality predominated were often included within their boundaries. Such incorporation was dictated primarily by economic and administrative desirability. Otherwise the borders of many nationality entities would have taken on very freakish shapes and would have violated established economic ties. *In "disputed" cases preference usually was given to the peoples less developed in the socio-economic and cultural respect,* incorporating economically more developed areas into those republics, even if people of a different nationality (usually Russian) predominated in them, the purpose being to further the more rapid and harmonious development of these republics.[7] [my emphasis — W.M.]

The increased visibility of Belorussians in government, plus the addition of substantial territories, increased the people's confidence in Soviet government. By 1927, forty-eight percent of those eligible voted in the elections — about the level as in the U.S. today — and by 1929, it had risen to sixty percent.[8] By 1934, that is, before the terror of Stalin's late period made the meaning of such figures questionable, USSR-wide election turnout was eighty-five percent, with little difference among the Slavic republics.[9]

Sculptor Azgur's portraits show us the kind of Belorussians who have emerged and developed since the Revolution. "That's Vera Khoruzhaia. She was a very great hero, a partisan, a leader of the underground, a Communist, a Marxist." She had fought in the 1918-1920 Civil War starting at age 15, became a village schoolteacher, was assigned to work underground in the then Polish-occupied western portion of Belorussia, served eight years in prison, then returned to the Soviet portion. When the Nazis invaded, she again went underground to head a group of Soviet guerillas, was caught, tortured mercilessly, and executed — at age 38. He also pointed to "the first chairman of the Belorussian Central Executive Committee, Cherviakov," executed by Stalin during the 1937 purge on false charges of being a Polish spy.

But more than politics was happening in those years. The Belorussian Opera and Ballet Theater was founded in 1933, and one bust portrays "Rita Mlodek, People's Artist of Belorussia, a dramatic soprano with timbre of rarest beauty, remarkable cantilena, an extraordinarily musical person," in Azgur's opinion, and one of the original members of the company. Another portrait was of the composer Bogatyrev, a graduate of the Byelorussian Conservatory, founded in 1932, writer of symphonies that have had international performance, and operas on Belorussian historical themes.

There was a portrait of his own wife, a landscape painter; another of the poet Luzhanin, first published in 1925, a founder of post-revolutionary Belorussian literature; and of the short-story writer and novelist Yanka Bryl.

Now that woman over there: I captured only a tenth of the beauty she possessed when she posed for me. It was 1942, during the war. The enemy had penetrated terribly deeply into our territory and exterminated an enormous number of people. I had just learned that the Nazis had buried my mother alive in the city of Vitebsk, and that she lay in the common grave of living people who died thus. You can imagine how distraught I was. This woman was one of our intelligence agents, from Vitebsk, my home town. She was the first to receive the Order of the Red Star. When she walked into the studio, I simply stood there stunned. I saw her green military uniform. She had a sack over her shoulder, and the long neck of a swan, a face of amazing harmony and attractiveness.

I began to model her. My legs shook, my knees shook; I didn't know what to do with myself. I was simply overwhelmed. The phrase, "fell in love," just doesn't apply, because it was simply impossible not to love her. I didn't know which way to turn, and maybe the work suffered as a consequence. She gave me four hours of her time. Immediately afterward she was taken by plane and dropped by parachute in the wild Vitebsk country, those woods that our partisans controlled.

German officers had fallen to their knees before her. They thought she was of the Potocki family, of the highest Polish nobility. She probably played upon that belief of their's. She was beautiful in life, and beautiful in history.

I asked about a figure of a workingman done in black?

That's Bat'ka Minai—Old Man Minai—who was a terror to the German fascists in the Vitebsk country. He always had shelter for the partisans and for our intelligence agents. The Germans offered stupendous sums for his capture. A book-length poem has been written on him, in ballad form, by our major Belorussian poet, Arkaii Kuleshov, called *The Ballad of the Three Hostages*. His children were taken as hostages, and they were killed.

The ordinary Belorussian is also very much present in Azgur's studio:

That one is titled, "Cradle Song." Look at her, that madonna. But she is no madonna. As you see from her dress and all, she is a woman of our times, the wife of a young blacksmith in the village of Korolev Stan. We went there just after the war ended — saw little diapers hanging, just rags actually, I heard a song of trepidation and happiness. She sang "And maybe you will be a bad one, and maybe you will be such a kind father, and maybe, my little son, you will be a partisan," improvising the words as she went, to the tune of an ancient lullaby. And then she came out to treat us to *kvass* as a chaser for all that *syromuch* we had drunk, and I saw her face. Don't you see trepidation and happiness in that face? I wanted her to show both a mother's alarm over the uncertainty of her baby's future—and be singing!

His portraits of postwar Belorussians are a remarkable survey of characters and occupations. There is a youngish philosopher, a woman pharmacist, and "The one with his head held proudly high is a policeman who writes remarkable verse and songs, and performs them. That kind of cop interests me, and I'm waiting for the time when all police in all countries will be of poetic nature."

Other than Soviet foreign policy, no question about the USSR interests foreigners as much as that people's attitude toward its leaders. When I pointed to a male bust and asked: "who is that intellectual?" Azgur replied, with a note of real pride "That the leader of the Communist Party of Belorussia, Petr Masherov, who is also a member of the Political Bureau of the Central Committee of the Communist Party of the whole USSR. We're all in love with him. He is a wonderful Party Secretary, a wonderful friend, a man who has given himself wholly to the people, who doesn't care whether it is day or night or whether he has a moment of rest. He's just wearing himself out, and we're so concerned about him"*

Throughout the interview, I was struck by this aged sculptor's remarkable combination of pride in his Belorussian people, his own Jewish heritage, and his total respect for other peoples and their personalities: he is a true internationalist. (His autobiography reflects all this even more fully.)10

At the time of the Revolution, Belorussia was as backward as any underdeveloped country in the world today, although it was not far from the heart of Europe. The life span was 32 years. Village names like "Moss-eaters" and the custom of carefully splitting an ordinary wooden match in four speak for themselves. One reason for this extreme situation involved physical geography: fully one-third of Belorussia consists of swamps. People lived in forest clearings on slight rises above water level. As late as 1944, a full generation after the Revolution, Anna Louise Strong, whose eye-witness knowledge of the USSR equalled Hindus', could say in the present tense:

Each tiny hamlet is shut off from its neighbors for most of the year. During spring floods they go from island to island in canoes driven by

*Since I saw Azgur, Masherov has died, in his early sixties.

sail or paddle or pulled across shallows by long-horned oxen. In summer they cannot travel at all. Only when winter freezes the marshes is there firm travel over the snow. Then peasants venture out to trade their scanty harvest for salt, matches, and a bit of cotton goods. . . . Salt is so precious that the salt water in which potatoes have been boiled is kept for many boilings for weeks.[11]

Some of the customs preserved into the '50s under the guise of adherence to Christianity were grossly barbaric, in consequence of this isolation.[12] Even in the '60s, one could find "healers" whose diagnostic techniques had absolutely nothing to do with the patient to be treated.[13]

An anti-Soviet scholar writes of the Belorussian language and culture that they were subject to "*official* vilification and *derision* [my emphasis — W.M.] . . . in western Belorussia, under Poland, before 1939 [as] in pre-1917 tsarist Belorussia" and adds that that has "never" been the case under the Soviets.[14] Under Poland, the Belorussian peasant averaged seventeen and one-half acres of land, not much of it tillable, while the Polish landowner averaged two thousand five hundred.[15]

As late as 1979, I was the first American ever to visit the town of Molodechno, just a few miles east of the Polish border. Before World War II, it had been a Polish and Jewish *shtetl* (small rural town) of 6,500 people. Today it is a "Silicon-valley" electronics town ten times as large, and overwhelmingly Belorussian, as virtually all the newcomers have moved in from the surrounding countryside.

Three city officials, including the mayor, showed me around, with Chamber-of-Commerce boosterism, but at dinner the mood was different. The vice-mayor had joined the Soviet Army at age 16, as soon as the Nazis invaded; he had been permanently and visibly disabled. His father and three uncles — four brothers — had all been killed. We had just heard the news that presidents Carter and Brezhnev had signed the SALT II Treaty, and he began to think out loud:

"But the Cold War is apparently being heated up by those who have a stake in it. How can anyone say that our country has designs upon the territory of others? We have so much land, we have things to do that we have barely begun. I read recently that our small planet can feed not 6 billion people, as now, but 45 billion people, if people work on that instead of for war. But what's happening today? This year my wife and I had a new baby, and you look at the papers and see how many children in the world are dying of starvation, of malnutrition, of disease." He paused for a moment, and the mayor took over:

Clearly, you've been wondering all day, just who are these people who run Molodechno? Well, take me. My father and mother worked for a Polish landowner as farm laborers. In 1939, when the Red Army liberated us from Poland, my father knew happiness for the first time: he was given 12 acres of land, making him a prosperous peasant. But that happiness didn't last long. In 1941 we came under Nazi occupation. I remember that time very well because I was already nine years old. True, we were saved by the fact that within six months this became a guerrilla-governed zone. The Belsky Guerrilla Detachment was quartered in our village, a Jewish force of 200. Three of them, three brothers, were quartered in our cottage. They would wash up there. My mother would do their laundry. This lasted two years, until liberation.

The third city official joined in:

I was only six, but I remember well two German punitive expeditions. In 1942 the Germans drove out everybody in our village; some were put into a *shtetl*, Rakov, and they set it afire—along with the Jews who lived there. There were over 1,500 people altogether. I was in a hamlet four miles away, and one couldn't breathe because of the smoke and the odor of burning human flesh. In 1945, notice came that my father had been killed, in April—only one month before Hitler was defeated.

My parents were also farm laborers, and now my mother had the three of us to take care of. Well, all of us got educations, in the Soviet years: the others went through high school. I received a college education. I came to this town in 1959—I worked in construction, first as a foreman, then as a superintendant, then as chief of construction on a project, then as chief engineer and finally as manager of a construction enterprise. Then they elected me to the city council.

He smiled with pride and sighed with embarrassment at the same time.

I asked why all the city officials I had met were men. He replied: "That's simply because we happen to be here. More than half the department heads are women: the Social Welfare Department is headed by a woman, the Department of Culture is headed by a woman, the head of the Finance Department is a woman, and we could extend that list."

This would have been utterly impossible in western Belorussia under Polish rule.

The story of change for women emerges very poignantly from a survey of marital and family relations conducted by anthropologists

Mayor and war-veteran vice-mayor of a "Silicon-Valley" town.

in 1972-73 among peasants over 60 years of age in western Belorussia. Less than one-sixth had been able to marry for love; the rest were wed because of their parents' desires, or because they needed a female hand, or because the dowry would provide land and livestock. One man of 76 had told how as a young man he had married a woman 20 years his senior who was an invalid from birth. But as he was one of five sons in a family with five acres, his choice was to be a landless farm laborer or, by marriage, to inherit his father-in-law's land. When he became the son-in-law, he began to beat his wife which, in his own words, "hastened her death."*

After World War II, when Belorussia was united, the great landed estates in the west were taken from their owners and given to the landless and land-poor who were subsequently organized into collective farms. Here income was based not on how much land one had, but simply on how much work one did and how well. This brought a fundamental change in family relationships and,

---

*Dozens of novels from as many different cultures all over the world tell us that such behavior was not limited to Belorussia or the Russian Empire, but has been one consequence of that kind of property relationship.

above all, in the status of women, as the 1972-73 survey found when it talked to young couples who had grown up without any consciousness of the factors that had governed marriage in the past.

One in twenty had married simply because they were lonely, another one in twenty because the woman had become pregnant or given birth out of wedlock. *Only one in sixty* reported marrying to improve economic status. All the rest had married out of love or affection. While parents objected to the marriage partner in one case out of five, this did not stop the marriage in one single instance.

There are more divorces today. The prerevolutionary family was stable, the anthropologists concluded, after interviewing 180 elderly couples or widowed individuals, because "the peasant woman regarded marriage as the sole possible means of existing." Also, divorce as a mortal sin, and "Infinite forbearance and submissiveness was instilled in women by the entire tenor of peasant life." Not one of the elderly could remember a single pre-Soviet case of a woman with children leaving a drunkard husband. By the time of the survey three-quarters of the women who initiated divorces bcause their husbands were alcoholic were women with children. As members of the collective farms in their own right, or with other jobs, and with child-care facilities available, they had nothing to fear. In the words of the study:

> Today, under conditions in which equality between men and women has been attained, when the collective farm woman has become economically independent of her husband and has come to regard herself as a person, she will not tolerate infringement of her human dignity, whether due to her husband's drunkenness or grossness, cruelty, or whatever.[16]

This is a form of human right in the USSR that critics have managed not to notice. Comparisons might be embarrassing.[17]

Another reflection of changing attitudes is that three-fifths of the men surveyed participate in housework to some degree. The other two-fifths still don't, but women balance this out somewhat by putting in fewer hours than men on the collective farm, and half said they do not even feel obliged to work daily on the garden each family retains. Most important, they have real leisure. When we picked up a woman hitch-hiker on her way home from market, we passed some children from a child-care center out walking with their teachers. Our passenger said, "Yes, now I can sit and watch television in the evening with my husband." Perhaps the revolution in mentality is best illustrated by the following totally civilized, rational, calm and thoroughly literate joint petition for divorce filed by a collective-farm couple in a rural court. (Lawyers are never involved in uncontested cases.)

> After discussing our relationship, we decided that there is no reason to remain married. . . . Although we are married nine years and have two children, we have no feeling for and attachment to each other. With such indifference to each other, it will be better for us if we dissolve the marriage. This will also be better for our children. We will make a voluntary division of our property.
>
> In court, the wife declared that by mutual agreement she would remain in the house. Her earnings working with dairy cattle were quite good, the researcher observes: It is noteworthy that the wife asked the court not to exact support payments from him, because they had come to agreement themselves on everything pertaining to material assistance to the children.[18]

Not surprisingly, people capable of dealing with their personal affairs on such a level show substantial interest and participation in public affairs. The Soviet system of government provides for very much larger legislative bodies at all levels, from village councils up, than we are accustomed to. The idea is to encourage more rank-and-file citizens to take part. A study of village soviets in Belorussia showed that ordinary members made half to three-quarters of the speeches discussing the reports of the executive branch.[19]

In the forlorn Belorussian swamps, one may ask, what is there to talk about? One thing they talk about is getting rid of the swamps. Over three million acres have been drained and put to agricultural use. The quality of farming has improved tremendously: although much grain land has been shifted to purposes for which the soil is better suited, the grain crop is eighty percent higher than before the Revolution. There is now eight times as much land under fruits and berries, in a country where people used to live chiefly on potatoes, as in Ireland, supplemented by rye bread. Much of the drained land is used for feed crops; meat production is up over three-fold and milk four-fold. The country has become a major producer of sugar beets and of flax, supplying a large linen industry. However, dust-bowl problems have begun to appear in some drained former wetlands.

But Belorussia has long since ceased to be characterized by agriculture. Half its people live in town. Where there was only one city of more than 100,000 before the Revolution, now there are ten, including a genuine metropolis, the capital, Minsk, with a million

Photo by Author

Woolen mill "Palace of Culture."

and a quarter people and a subway. We visited a huge, modern woolens mill, employing 6,000, which included two impressive facilities across a square from its main structure. One was an overnight sanatorium, where workers who are run down but not sick can stay for 24 days free of the stresses and responsibilities of a possibly crowded home life. As they do their regular jobs during the day, this does not cut into their vacation time. It consists of two buildings with a park-like garden between. The public rooms have truly fine decorations to provide an atmosphere of relaxation.

The other facility across from the mill is its recreation center, the "Palace of Culture." Its paid staff of 60 helps lead twenty creative arts amateur groups for adults and twenty-four for children — including not only music, dance, and acting, but model-aircraft building, radio construction, etc. involving some 1,200 people in all. There are four or five entertainment events each week, and dances Saturdays and Sundays. The workers are surveyed to determine what kind of activities they want. Altogether, over one thousand events are staged each year in this attractive building and in the plant, during rest periods, in the dormitory recreation rooms, on the square in front of the building, etc. Everything is free, except movies.

Walking through the building, I saw volleyball, fencing, exhibition ballroom dancing practice, a children's theater group, and the headquarters of the city's International Friendship Club. Students from 76 foreign countries are to be found in higher educational institutions in Minsk. The center was placed here because the mill's workers and management had rich experience gained when young Vietnamese people came to study in the local textiles high schools. The mill's personnel also maintain a direct link with Potsdam County in East Germany, which the workers' dance ensemble had visited three times.

The mill also has an athletic club, which fields crews and teams in rowing, gymnastics, volleyball, basketball, bicycling, cross-country skiing, canoeing, hockey, and ice-skating. It is proud of having produced an Olympic champion.

The recreation center was so superb that I asked how typical it is, and learned there are five others like it in Minsk, of which one, that of the railroad workers, was described as even better. The centers also help keep up the Soviet tradition of maintaining contact between the urban workingclass and the countryside as the performing groups tour throughout Belorussia. "In the evenings we gave our performances, and daytime we helped them with their work in the fields."

We arrived at the spinning and weaving floors of the woolens mill an hour behind schedule and found the machinery shut down for the lunch break. Hearing a voice over a loudspeaker, I hastened toward a crowd of women in a cleared loading area, where one, middle-aged, was speaking.

I was orphaned when I was five years old. People say that children forget. No, I haven't forgotten a single thing. I haven't forgotten how, for years on end, I picked up rotten potatoes in the fields to have something to eat in the early spring. I haven't forgotten how, hunting for mushrooms after the war ended, we found the arm of one soldier and the leg of another. I haven't forgotten one thing of all that, and no mother should forget any of that. Defend peace on earth, treasure it. May peace last forever.

A young weaver was given the floor next, and proposed a resolution addressed to the UN General Assembly, "No differences between social systems or ideologies should be allowed to cloud over the goal common to all peoples of preserving the peace. The idea of mutual freezing of the nuclear arsenals of the United States and the Soviet Union is understood by and dear to Soviet people."

As soon as I realized the subject of the meeting, I suggested to our guides that they ask Mrs. Mandel to speak, as she is active in

Women for Peace. The women on the shop floor, obviously un-
prepared for visitors, whispered among themselves for a moment,
then agreed, and she spoke to them in Russian.

Mention has been made of the foreign students in the colleges and
University of Belorussia in Minsk. Belorussia had no higher educational institutions before the Revolution. Today it has thirteen, with
a total enrollment approaching 100,000, a figure that indicates the
civilized flavor of the city. And the change in property relationships
is again reflected by the fact that half the students in a crowd I
photographed outside the Minsk Institute of Technology were
women. Nor are they isolated from their rural roots. They were
standing outside because it was potato harvest time, and as the
USSR has no surplus labor force to channel into seasonal farm
labor, students and others are trucked out for a few weeks for such
work. They are paid, get some fresh air and use their muscles, and
bring the peasants contact with broad horizons. (Soviet sources
recognize that this is extremely inefficient. It takes three students
to do as much as one experienced rural person).

I wondered whether those students, some of whom don't like
this, had any idea of what life was like for their grandparents, even
after the Revolution, when Hindus described Belorussia.

Perhaps the meaning of what has happened in this formerly
illiterate peasant land emerges most strikingly when one cites the
achievements of Belorussia in fields whose existence its people did
not dream of, or which in fact did not exist.

The Institute of Technical Cybernetics, founded in 1965, works
on computer automation of engineering, particularly the design of
new machinery; it is officially recognized as the center guiding all
such research throughout the Soviet Union.[20] A Belorussian scientist
developed the methods and apparatus for diagnostics of low-tem-
perature plasmas. Advanced work is done in quantum electronics.
Another Belorussian founded soil enzymology, a new field of
research. On the eve of World War I, there were a dozen researchers
in Belorussia;[21] on the eve of World War II 4,400; in 1970 61,400,
of whom 68 percent were ethnic Belorussians.

Moscow, in its current drive to improve quality of output,
awards the right to affix an emblem of quality to industrial
products very sparingly. USSR-wide, only 7 percent of Soviet
products are entitled to bear it, but in Belorussia the figure is 13

Woolen mill workers listening to Mrs. Mandel at noon-hour peace rally.

percent, ahead of Estonia and Latvia, which are considered equivalent to Western Europe in their standards.[22] Of Belorussia's exports, 88 percent are industrial, only 5 percent agricultural,[23] the rest are crafts. In no less than twenty industries, Belorussia's share of USSR output exceeds its share of population. Belarus tractors made in Minsk are used in our southern states, in Canada, and in sixty other countries. And life in the countryside has so improved that population now flows in both directions: in 1968 and 1969, 177,000 people moved to town, but 53,000 moved from town to take jobs in industry and offices in rural areas.[24]

Nor has culture been lost sight of in the rush to science. There are nine permanent professional theater companies, and three puppet theaters. The government college of theater arts was founded in 1945, although 3,000,000 people — much more than a third of the population who survived the war — were without roofs over their heads in Belorussia.

High culture is not reserved for the intelligentsia. There are some thirty thousand amateur groups in the performing arts, one

Photo by Author

Head of children's naturalist and environmental-protection station.

hundred fifty-six in painting, drawing, and sculpture, enrolling half a million people, all told.

As everywhere in the Soviet Union, literature remains the art of highest status. Among contemporary Belorussian writers, Vasil Bykov is popular USSR-wide in Russian translation. His novel, *Sotnikov*, was made into an internationally acclaimed film, *The Ascent*, by the leading female Soviet director. (But, while his Sotnikov has been hailed in the West as a Christ-like figure, in a long conversation I found Bykov to be stubbornly male-chauvinist.)

Because Belorussian resembles Russian more closely than any other language in the USSR, the pattern of its use may suggest the future of languages less closely related. That pattern is not a simple one: On the one hand, between 1964-1973, the total single-issue circulation of *magazines* published in Belorussian increased fifty percent, to 1,800,000 copies. On the other hand, circulation of *newspapers* in Russian has pulled ahead of that in Belorussian. In their cities, Belorussians almost universally assimilate to the Russian language, while those in the countryside retain their own language. However, fully half the rural parents now want their children to go to schools taught in Russian though the educational authorities have not caught up with this change in orientation. All this has led an emigre scholar to conclude that "one should keep in mind a more flexible concept of bilingualism, multiculturalism, and bi-nationalism."[25]

As a Soviet exchange student of Belorussian nationality in the United States told Prof. Nicholas Vakar:

> For us, he said, Russian is the Soviet language, not just the language of the Russians. It is a world language like English or French. Through it, we are participants in world history and culture. Russian is not a mark of social distinction as French was in prerevolutionary Russia. . . . It is a matter of practical necessity . . . skilled labor has been coming to Belorussia from all parts of the Soviet Union. . . . Belorussian is no longer needed to remind us that we are a people. He pointed out that this was a general trend in his generation, not only in Belorussia but throughout the Soviet Union. . . . My young man . . . declared that it was . . . the Belorussian *political state* that made him feel Belorussian.[26]

The mood of Belorussia comes through best in the life story of one of the two paid workers in its national Peace Fund:

> When the war started, I was 13 years old. The first thing the women, including young girls, did was to take care of our wounded soldiers. They would find themselves in occupied territory, and make contact with the peasants. We would get hold of a set of the flowing garments that old men used to wear and dress a wounded soldier in this. A girl would walk each of them to the outskirts of town, and then hide them with the people of some village. Ultimately these stranded soldiers became the core of a band of guerrillas.
>
> When we had established a guerrilla brigade I was assigned to reconnaissance work. My job was to find out what German units were arriving, where their punitive expeditions were headed and to transmit this information to our guerrillas. We were girls of 15, 16, 18, who, at the risk of our lives, would get jobs as kitchen workers, potato peelers, with German units. We studied German intensively in order to understand what we heard, but made believe we couldn't understand.
>
> The fascists committed terrible atrocities in our land. In our small town they had a gallows standing permanently in the town square, and there was always someone's body hanging from it. Yet the guerrilla movement developed to such a degree that the Germans were besieged

in the small towns they held — they would build bunkers, fortifications, but could no longer emerge from those towns.

We had entire counties that were Soviet country even though Belorussia as such was behind the German lines, and people would find their way to those counties to join the guerrillas. To counter the guerrilla movement, the fascists had to pull back entire military units from the front, complete with tanks and artillery. They would comb the woods, and burn alive all life they encountered — an entire hamlet would be packed into some large structure, and it would be set afire.

One such, we both knew, was Khatyn. It has been converted into an extraordinary monument. There is a giant Rodin-like statue of a peasant grandfather holding the body of his dead grandson. Around this are the rebuilt chimneys of each of the burnt homes, with a bell permanently tolling, very slowly, in each. Then there is a graveyard in Khatyn in which each headstone bears the name of a village forever wiped off the face of the earth, and the number of people who died in its flames. It is immense.

Finally, there is a wall that goes on and on, with small and large barred niches, each representing a named Nazi death camp in Belorussia, with the number of people killed in each. Visiting children customarily take off their red Young Pioneer bandannas and leave them wrapped around the bars as a remembrance. The ensemble fits into no existing canon of architecture or sculpture. But it stirs one to the depths.

She continued:

Those who attempted to run out were chased, caught, and thrown back into the fire. Then the newspapers would report that such and such a guerrilla troop had been wiped out by a punitive expedition. But those "partisans" were aged men, women, and young children, from infants at the breast to those 12 and 13 years old.

Finally, I was about to be arrested, but I was warned in time, so I left and joined a guerrilla force. I was assigned to the "war of the rails." Before our army launched its offensive westward through Belorussia, the central staff of the guerrilla movement ordered all brigades to blow up all railway lines, so the fascists would be unable to move reinforcements to the front. Aircraft dropped us these little plastic explosives. We attached them to the rails in front of and behind every single train. So we blew up the whole railway system in one night. We also mined all the paved roads, and set up ambushes. So that's what my participation consisted of.

She smiled, as though relieved that her recital had come to an end. Her male co-workers added: "The partisans of Belorussia dealt Hitler's army greater losses than the entire Second Front

Each headstone memorializes a village destroyed forever when Belorussia lost one-fourth of its people in World War II.

established in Western Europe by the British and American forces during all of World War II.*

I asked the first speaker to continue her narration. At the end of the war she was 17.

I had finished the sixth grade before the war. In July, 1944, I was discharged and went to work and simultaneously to night school. During vacations, I crammed to catch up to my age group, and was promoted three grades by exams without having to attend. I became a journalist, graduated the university by correspondence, then went to work for a publishing house, and for the past eleven or twelve years have been working for our Committee to Safeguard Peace.

This work is so near and dear to me because the war stole my childhood. Do you understand what it meant for me, at age 13, to see those gallows, those firing-squad executions, those bonfires of books? I was in love with books. During the war I wasn't able to get books in Russian; I studied Polish simply so I would be able to read books. And today I look at my children, at all our children. They don't know what war is. They don't know what hunger is.

---

*Having been the United Press (now UPI) expert on Russia during that war, I know this to be true, and documented it in a book of those years, *A Guide to the Soviet Union* (New York: Dial, 1946).

She was a guerrilla as a young girl, now a full-time peace worker. "The atom bomb is not going to distinguish whether you are a communist, a socialist, or a capitalist."

Her male co-worker broke in: "And may they never know." Her voice now showed excitement for the first time:

And may they never know the alarm of looking at the sky in fear and trembling, waiting for bombs to fall. Here in Belorussia the women participate *very* actively in the struggle for peace. Our people suffers deeply whenever they learn of others' suffering. If blood flows anywhere, if people are dying anywhere, particularly women, children, old people, the pain tears at our hearts. It is because the people here *know* what war is, they *know* what a misfortune it is to humanity.

Nobody compels them to work on their day off and have the earnings credited to the Peace Fund. It's because they all want to find a way to feel they are *part* of this cause. Not everybody is capable of speaking at a rally or of talking on the radio, but when they make a financial contribution they feel as though they are becoming part of this effort.

I was in England as one of six women from the Soviet Union, with nine American women. There's such propaganda being conducted there — the questions people ask seemed savage, wild. We are willing to cooperate with any organization that favors peace. In our work we do not focus on the things that separate us — we consider what we have in common. The atom bomb is not going to distinguish whether you are a communist, a socialist, or a capitalist. People have to understand that nuclear bombs are no toys. And that any kind of limited nuclear war is simply out of the question.

Woman is mother — she brings life. And it is up to her to socialize her children. People are not born soldiers, not born as killers. People are born for happiness. And the duty of a woman is to make sure that her son does not become a killer. The women of the United States can make a very big contribtion. It is necessary to compel the government to understand that in such a war there will be no victory. No one will remain alive if all the weapons now existing are exploded.

Spend a few days in Belorussia, speak to people in any walk of life. It is hard to avoid the conclusion that for this nation that lost one-fourth its people, keeping the peace may now well be the single most important component of its national psychology.

When one considers what Belorussia emerged from in the three generations since the Revolution, this ethic can re-inspire the faith of the most jaded in the humanist potential of the race.

NOTES

1. Eric R. Wolf, *Anthropology* (Englewood Cliffs: Prentice-Hall, 1964), pp. 21-23; M.C. Howard and P.C. McKim (Boston: Little, Brown, 1983), *Contemporary Cultural Anthropology* (Boston: Little, Brown, 1983), pp. 12-13; Gerald Berreman, "Is Anthropology Alive? Social Responsibility in Social Anthropology," *Current Anthropology*, IX, December, 1968, pp. 391-96.

2. Maurice Hindus, *Broken Earth* (New York: International Publishers, 1926), pp. 68-9, 86, 90, 133-134, 153-155 passim, 191-203 passim, 216, 283-284.

3. Joseph Stalin, *Works* (Moscow: Foreign Languages Publishing House, 1953), V, pp. 48-49.

4. A. Rysakoff, *The National Policy of the Soviet Union* (New York: International Publishers, 1931), p. 27.

5. Ibid., p. 62.

6. Jan Zaprudnik, "Belorussia and the Belorussians," in Zev Katz (ed.), *Handbook of Major Soviet Nationalities* (New York: Free Press, 1975), p. 49.

7. V.I. Kozlov, *Natsional'nosti SSR* (Moscow: Statistika, 1975), p. 51.

8. Rysakoff, *The National Policy*, p. 63.

9. William Mandel, "Democratic Aspects of Soviet Government Today," *American Sociological Review*, IX (1944), pp. 257-266.

10. Zair Azgur, *To, chto pomnitsia* (Minsk; Belarus', 1977), 416 pp.; 32 plates.

11. Anna Louise Strong, *Peoples of the USSR* (New York: Macmillan, 1944), pp. 90-91.

12. V.Iu. Leshchenko, "The Position of Women in the Light of Religious-Domestic Taboos among the East Slavic Peoples in the Nineteenth and Early Twentieth Centuries," *Soviet Anthropology and Archeology*, XVII, No. 3 (1978-79), pp. 22-40.

13. L.I. Min'ko, "Magical Curing," *Soviet Anthropology and Archeology*, XII, No. 1, pp. 3-33; No. 2, pp. 34-60; No. 3, pp. 3-27 (1973).

14. Zaprudnik, "Belorussia," p. 64.

15. *Revoliutsionnyi put' kompartii Zapadnoi Belorussii (1921-1939 gg.)*, (Minsk: Belarus', 1966), p. 24.

16. V.T. Kolokol'nikov, "Marital and Family Relations among the Collective Farm Peasantry," *Soviet Sociology*, XVI, No. 3 (1977), pp. 18-34, *passim*.

17. William Mandel, *Soviet Women* (Garden City: Doubleday Anchor, 1975), pp. 248-249.

18. Kolokol'nikov, "Marital and Family Relations," p. 26.

19. A.T. Leizerov, "A Study of the Effectiveness of Village and District Soviets in Belorussia," *Soviet Law and Government*, XIV, No. 1 (1975), pp. 84-97.

20. *Bol'shaia Sovetskaia Entsiklopediia* (3rd ed.; Moscow: Sovetskaia Entsiklopediia, 1970), Vol. III, col. 424.

21. Ibid., col. 420.

22. M.I. Kulichenko, "The Socioeconomic Foundations for the Mutual Influence and Enrichment of National Cultures under Conditions of Developed Socialism" *Soviet Law and Government*, XVII, No. 1 (1978), p. 64.

23. Vitaut Kipel, "Some Demographic and Industrial Aspects of Soviet Belorussia During 1965-1975," in George W. Simmonds (ed.), *Nationalism in the USSR and Eastern Europe* (Detroit: University of Detroit Press, 1977), p. 98.

24. Z.I. Monich, V.G. Izokh, and I.V. Prudnik, "The Working Class in the Structure of the Rural Population [Part II]," *Soviet Sociology*, XV, No. 3 (1976-77), p. 19.

25. Jan Zaprudnik, "Developments in Belorussia Since 1964," in Simmonds, ibid, p. 111.

26. Nicholas P. Vakar, "The Belorussian People Between Nationhood and Extinction," in Erich Goldhagen (ed.), *Ethnic Minorities in the Soviet Union* (New York: Praeger, 1968), pp. 224-226, *passim*.

INDEX

William Mandel's writing is grounded on ten visits to the USSR, beginning with a year of residence when he attended Moscow University in 1931-32. He has traveled in all 15 ethnic republics, many more than once, and recorded on tape first-hand accounts of Soviet peoples from all walks of life.

Mr. Mandel was the United Press (UPI) Expert on Russia during World War II. He was a Hoover Institution Fellow at Stanford University and has taught at the University of California at Berkeley, San Francisco and San Jose State Universities, and the Golden Gate University Law School.

He has broadcast a weekly radio program on the Soviet Union and its peoples over the Pacifica Radio Network for 27 years. He lives with his wife in Berkeley, California.

Many photographs in this book were taken by Tom Weber, author, foreign correspondent, and veteran photojournalist. Weber spent several months in the Soviet Union, covered seven thousand miles, and brought back 3500 photographs, from which these were selected. Other photographs, some of unique historical value, were generously contributed by the American-Russian Institute of San Francisco, California.